WAY OF THE PEACEFUL WARRIOR

AND

SACRED JOURNEY OF THE PEACEFUL WARRIOR

DAN MILLMAN

BARNES & NOBLE BOOKS
NEW YORK

Published by MJF Books
Fine Communications
322 Eighth Avenue
New York, NY 10001

Way of the Peaceful Warrior and Sacred Journey of the Peaceful Warrior
Library of Congress Catalog Card Number 03-111614
ISBN 1-56731-638-7

Published by arrangement with HJ Kramer
in a joint venture with New World Library.

Cover painting by Terry Lamb

Manufactured in the United States of America on acid-free paper

MJF Books and the MJF colophon are trademarks of Fine Creative Media, Inc.

QM 10 9 8 7 6 5 4 3 2 1

WAY OF THE PEACEFUL WARRIOR

Contents

Acknowledgments

An ancient saying goes, "We have no friends; we have no enemies; we only have teachers." My life has been blessed with many teachers and guiding influences who, in their own ways, have contributed to the writing of this book.

The love and faith of my parents, Herman and Vivian Millman, gave me a foundation of courage to begin the Way.

My first editor, Janice Gallagher, asked the questions and made the suggestions that helped to shape this book.

A special acknowledgment to Hal Kramer, whose keen publishing instincts led him to take a chance on the book.

Finally, my heartfelt gratitude to Joy, my wife, companion, friend, and teacher, who has energized my spirit all along.

And, of course, there's Soc.

To the Ultimate Warrior of Peace, of whom Socrates is but a twinkling reflection—Who has no name yet many, and Who is the Source of us all.

Warriors, warriors we call ourselves.
We fight for splendid virtue, for
high endeavor, for sublime wisdom,
therefore we call ourselves warriors.

—AUNGUTTARA NIKAYA

Preface

An extraordinary series of events took place in my life, beginning in December 1966, during my junior year at the University of California at Berkeley. It all began at 3:20 A.M., when I first stumbled upon Socrates in an all-night gas station. (He didn't volunteer his real name, but after spending time with him that first night, I named him on impulse after the ancient Greek sage; he liked the name, so it stuck.) That chance encounter and the adventures that followed were to transform my life.

The years prior to 1966 had smiled upon me. Raised by loving parents in a secure environment, I was later to win the World Trampoline Championship in London, travel through Europe, and receive many honors. Life brought rewards, but no lasting peace or satisfaction.

Now I realize that I had, in a sense, been sleeping all those years and just dreaming I was awake—until I met Socrates, who came to be my mentor and friend. Before that time, I'd always believed that a life of quality, enjoyment, and wisdom were my human birthright and would be automatically bestowed upon me as time passed. I never suspected that I would have to learn *how* to live—that there were specific disciplines and ways of seeing the world I had to master before I could awaken to a simple happy, uncomplicated life.

Socrates showed me the error of my ways by contrasting them with *his* way, the Way of the Peaceful Warrior. He constantly poked fun at my own serious, concerned, problematic life, until I came to see through his eyes of wisdom, compassion, and humor. And he never let up until I discovered what it means to live as a warrior.

Often I sat with him far into the early morning hours— listening to him, arguing with him, and, in spite of myself, laughing with him. This story is based on my adventure, but it *is* a novel. The man I called Socrates did, in fact, exist. Yet he had a way of blending into the world, so it's been difficult at times to tell where he left off and other teachers and life experiences began. I have taken liberties with the dialogue and with some time sequences and have sprinkled anecdotes and metaphors into the story to highlight the lessons Socrates would want me to convey.

Life is not a private affair. A story and its lessons are only made useful if shared. So I've chosen to honor my teacher by sharing his piercing wisdom and humor with you.

The Gas Station at Rainbow's End

Life begins," I thought, as I waved goodbye to mom and dad and pulled away from the curb in my reliable old Valiant, its faded white body stuffed with the belongings I'd packed for my first year at college. I felt strong, independent, ready for anything.

Singing to myself above the radio's music, I sped North across the freeways of Los Angeles, then up and over the Grapevine, connecting with Route 99, which carried me through the green agricultural flatlands stretching to the foot of the San Gabriel Mountains.

Just before dusk, my winding descent through the Oakland hills brought me a shimmering view of San Francisco Bay. My excitement grew as I neared the Berkeley campus.

After finding my dormitory, I unpacked and gazed out the window at the Golden Gate Bridge and the lights of San Francisco sparkling in the darkness.

Five minutes later I was walking along Telegraph Avenue, looking in shop windows, breathing the fresh Northern California air, savoring the smells drifting out of tiny cafés. Overwhelmed by it all, I walked the beautifully landscaped paths of the campus until after midnight.

The next morning, immediately after breakfast, I walked down to Harmon Gymnasium, where I'd be training six days a week, four muscle-straining, somersaulting, sweaty hours each day, pursuing my dreams of becoming a champion.

Two days passed, and I was already drowning in a sea of people, papers, and class schedules. Soon the months blended together, passing and changing softly, like the mild California seasons. In my classes I survived; in the gym, I thrived. A friend once told me I was born to be an acrobat. I certainly looked the part: clean cut, short brown hair, a lean, wiry body. I'd always had a penchant for daredevil stunts; even as a child I enjoyed playing on the edge of fear. The gymnastics room had become my sanctuary, where I found excitement, challenge, and a measure of satisfaction.

By the end of my first two years I had flown to Germany, France, and England, representing the United States Gymnastics Federation. I won the World Trampoline Championship; my gymnastics trophies were piling up in the corner of my room; my picture appeared in the *Daily Californian* with such regularity that people began to recognize me, and my reputation grew. Women smiled at me. Susie, a savory, unfailingly sweet friend with short blond hair and a toothpaste smile, paid me amorous visits more and more often. Even my studies were going well! I felt on top of the world.

However, in the early autumn of 1966, my junior year, something dark and intangible began to take shape. By then I'd moved out of the dorm and was living alone in a small studio behind my landlord's house. During this time I felt a growing melancholy, even in the midst of all my achievements. Shortly thereafter, the nightmares started. Nearly every night I jerked awake, sweating. Almost always, the dream was the same:

I walk along a dark city street; tall buildings without doors or windows loom at me through a dark swirling mist.

A towering shape cloaked in black strides toward me. I feel rather than see a chilling specter, a gleaming white skull with black eye sockets that stare at me in deathly silence. A finger of white bone points at me; the white knucklebones curl into a beckoning claw. I freeze.

A white-haired man appears from behind the hooded terror; his face is calm and unlined. His footsteps make no sound. I sense somehow, that he is my only hope of escape; he has the power to save me, but he doesn't see me and I can't call to him.

Mocking my fear, the black-hooded Death whirls around to face the white-haired man, who laughs in his face. Stunned, I watch. Death furiously makes a grab for him. The next moment the specter is hurtling toward me, as the old man seizes him by his cloak and tosses him into the air.

Suddenly the Grim Reaper vanishes. The man with the shining

white hair looks at me and holds out his hands in a gesture of welcome. I walk toward him, then directly *into* him, dissolving into his body. When I look down at myself, I see that I'm wearing a black robe. I raise my hands and see bleached white, gnarled bones, come together in prayer.

I'd wake up screaming softly.

One night, early in December, I lay in bed listening to the howling wind driving through a small crack in the window of my apartment. Sleepless, I got up and threw on my faded Levis, a T-shirt, sneakers, and down jacket, and walked out into the night. It was 3:05 A.M.

I walked aimlessly, inhaling deeply the moist, chilly air, looking up into the star-lit sky, listening for a rare sound in the silent streets. The cold made me hungry, so I headed for an all-night gas station to buy some cookies and a soft drink. Hands in my pockets, I hurried across campus, past sleeping houses, before I came to the lights of the service station. It was a bright fluorescent oasis in a darkened wilderness of closed food joints, shops, and movie theaters.

I rounded the corner of the garage adjoining the station and nearly fell over a man sitting in the shadows, leaning his chair back against the red tile station wall. Startled, I retreated. He was wearing a red wool cap, grey corduroy pants, white socks, and Japanese sandals. He seemed comfortable enough in a light windbreaker though the wall thermometer by his head registered 38 degrees.

Without looking up, he said in a strong, almost musical voice, "Sorry if I frightened you."

"Oh, uh, that's okay. Do you have any soda pop?"

"Only have fruit juice here. And don't call me 'Pop'!" He turned toward me and with a half smile removed his cap, revealing shining white hair. Then he laughed.

That laugh! I stared blankly at him for one more moment. He was the old man in my dream! The white hair, the clear, unlined face, a tall slim man of fifty or sixty years old. He laughed again. In my confusion I somehow found my way to the door marked "Office" and pushed it open. Along with the office door, I had felt another door opening to another dimension. I collapsed onto an old couch, and shivered, wondering what might come screaming through that door into my orderly world. My dread was mixed with a strange fascination that I couldn't fathom. I sat, breathing shallowly, trying to regain my previous hold on the ordinary world.

I looked around the office. It was so different from the sterility and disarray of the usual gas station. The couch I was sitting on was covered by a faded but colorful Mexican blanket. To my left, near the entryway, stood a case of neatly organized traveler's aids: maps, fuses, sun glasses, and so on. Behind a small, dark brown walnut desk was an earth-colored, corduroy-upholstered chair. A spring water dispenser guarded a door marked "Private." Near me was a second door that led to the garage.

What struck me most of all was the homelike atmosphere of the room. A bright yellow shag rug ran its length, stopping just short of the welcome mat at the entry. The walls had recently been painted white, and a few landscape paintings lent them color. The soft incandescent glow of the lights calmed me. It was a relaxing contrast to the fluorescent glare outside. Overall, the room felt warm, orderly, and secure.

How could I have known that it was to be a place of unpredictable adventure, magic, terror, and romance? I only thought then, "A fireplace would fit in nicely here."

Soon my breathing had relaxed, and my mind, if not content, had at least stopped whirling. This white-haired man's resemblance to the man in my dream was surely a coincidence. With a sigh, I stood, zipped up my jacket, and sallied forth into the chill air.

He was still sitting there. As I walked past and stole a last quick look at his face, a glimmer in his eyes caught mine. His eyes were like none I'd seen before. At first they seemed to have tears in them, ready to spill over; then the tears turned to a twinkle, like a reflection of the starlight. I was drawn deeper into his gaze until the stars themselves became only a reflection of his eyes. I was lost for a time, seeing nothing but those eyes, the unyielding and curious eyes of an infant.

I don't know how long I stood there; it could have been seconds or minutes—maybe longer. With a start, I became aware of where I was. Mumbling a goodnight, feeling off balance, I hurried toward the corner.

When I reached the curb, I stopped. My neck tingled; I felt that he was watching me. I glanced back. No more than fifteen seconds had passed. But there he was, *standing on the roof,* his arms crossed, looking up at the starry sky! I gaped at the empty chair still leaning back against the wall, then up again. It was impossible! If he had been changing a wheel on a carriage made from a giant pumpkin drawn by huge mice, the effect couldn't have been any more startling.

In the stillness of the night, I stared up at his lean shape, an imposing presence, even at a distance. I heard the stars chime like bells singing in the wind. Suddenly, he snapped his head around and stared directly into my eyes. He was about sixty feet away, but I could almost feel his breath on my face. I shivered, but not from the cold. That doorway, where reality dissolved into dreams, cracked open again.

I looked up at him. "Yes?" he said. "Can I help you?" Prophetic words!

"Excuse me, but . . ."

"You are excused," he smiled. I felt my face flush; this was starting to irritate me. He was playing a game with me but I didn't know the rules.

"All right, how did you get up on the roof?"

"Get up on the roof?" he queried, looking innocent and puzzled.

"Yes. How did you get from that chair," I pointed, "up to that roof, in less than twenty seconds? You were leaning back against the wall, right there. I turned, walked over to the corner, and you . . ."

"I know exactly what *I* was doing," his voice boomed. "There is no need to describe it to me. The question is, do you know what *you* were doing?"

"Of course I know what I was doing!" I was getting angry now; I wasn't some child to be lectured to! But I desperately wanted to find out the old man's gimmick, so I held my temper and requested politely, "Please, sir, tell me how you got up on the roof."

He just stared down at me in silence until the back of my neck began to get prickly. Finally he replied, "Used a ladder. It's around back." Then, ignoring me, he looked upward again.

I walked quickly around back. Sure enough, there was an old ladder, leaning crookedly against the back wall. But the ladder's top was at least five feet short of the roof's edge; even if he could have used it—which was highly doubtful—that wouldn't explain how he got up there in a few seconds.

Something landed on my shoulder in the darkness. I gasped, and whirled around to see his hand. Somehow, he'd gotten *off* the roof and crept up on me. Then I guessed the only possible answer. He had a twin! They obviously got their kicks scaring the wits out of innocent visitors. I accused him immediately.

"All right, Mister, where's your twin? I'm nobody's fool."

He frowned slightly, then started to roar with laughter. Hah! That clinched it. I was right; I'd found him out. But his answer made me less sure of myself.

"If I had a twin, do you think I'd be wasting my time standing here, talking with 'nobody's fool'?" He laughed again and strode back towards the garage, leaving me standing open-mouthed. I couldn't believe the nerve of this guy.

I hurried to catch up with him. He walked into the garage and started to tinker with a carburetor under the hood of an old green Ford pickup. "So I'm a fool, huh?" I said, sounding even more belligerent than I'd intended.

"We're all fools together," he replied. "It's just that a few people know it; others don't. You seem to be one of the latter types. Hand me that small wrench, will you?"

I handed him his damn wrench and started to leave. Before I left, though, I had to know. "Please, tell me, how did you get up to the roof so fast? I'm really puzzled."

He handed me back the wrench, saying, "The world's a puzzle; no need to make sense out of it." He pointed to the shelf behind me. "I'll need the hammer and the screwdriver now, over there."

Frustrated, I watched him for another minute, trying to figure out how to get him to tell me what I wanted to know, but he seemed oblivious to my presence. I gave up and started toward the door when I heard him say, "Don't go." He wasn't pleading; he wasn't commanding. It was a matter-of-fact statement. I looked at him; his eyes were soft.

"Why shouldn't I go?"

"I may be useful to you," he said, deftly removing the carburetor like a surgeon in the middle of a heart transplant. He set it down carefully, and turned to face me.

I was gaping at him.

"Here," he said, handing me the carburetor. "Take this apart and put the pieces in that can to soak. It will take your mind off your questions."

My frustration dissolved into laughter. This old man could be offensive, but he was interesting, too. I decided to be sociable.

"My name's Dan," I said, reaching out to shake his hand, smiling insincerely. "What's yours?"

He placed a screwdriver in my outstretched hand. "My name doesn't matter; neither does yours. What *is* important is what lies beyond names and beyond questions. Now, you will need this screwdriver to take apart that carburetor," he pointed.

"Nothing lies beyond questions," I retorted. "Like how did you fly up on that rooftop?"

"I didn't fly—I jumped," was his poker-faced reply. It's not magic, so don't get your hopes up. In your case, however, I may have to perform some very difficult magic. It looks as if I'm going to have to transform a jackass into a human being."

"Who the hell do you think you are, anyway, to be saying these things to me?"

"I am a warrior!" he snapped. "Beyond that, who I am depends on who you *want* me to be."

"Can't you just answer a straight question?" I attacked the carburetor with a vengeance.

"Ask me one and I'll try," he said, smiling innocently. The screwdriver slipped and I skinned my finger. "Damn!" I yelled, going to the sink to wash the cut. Socrates handed me a Band-Aid.

"All right then. Here is a straight question." I determined to keep my voice patient. "How can you be useful to me?"

"I have already been useful to you," he replied, pointing to the bandage on my finger.

That did it. "Look, I can't waste my time here any longer. I need to get some sleep." I put the carburetor down and got ready to leave.

"How do you know you haven't been asleep your whole life? How do you know you're not asleep right now?" he intoned, a twinkle in his eye.

"Whatever you say." I was too tired to argue anymore. "One

thing, though. Before I leave, will you tell me how you pulled off that stunt earlier?"

He walked up to me, reached out, and grasped my hand. "Tomorrow, Dan, tomorrow." He smiled warmly, and all my earlier fear and frustration were washed away. My hand, my arm, then my whole body started to tingle. He added, "It's been pleasant seeing you again."

"What do you mean 'again'?" I began, then caught myself; "I know, tomorrow, tomorrow." We both laughed. I walked to the door, stopped, turned, stared at him, then said, "Good-bye—*Socrates*."

He looked bewildered, then shrugged good-naturedly. I think he liked the name. I left without another word.

I slept through my eight o'clock class the next morning. By the time my afternoon gymnastic workout started, I was awake and ready to go.

After running up and down the bleacher stairs, Rick, Sid, and I, along with our teammates, lay on the floor, sweating and panting, stretching our legs, shoulders, and backs. Usually I was silent during this ritual, but today I felt like telling them about last night. All I could say was, "I met this unusual guy at a gas station last night."

My friends were more involved with the stretching pain in their legs than in my little stories.

We warmed up easily, doing a few handstand push-ups, some sit-ups, and leg raises, and then began our tumbling series. As I flew through the air again and again—as I swung around the high bar, did scissors on the pommel horse, and struggled through a new muscle-straining ring routine—I wondered about the mysterious feats of the man I'd named "Socrates." My ruffled feelings urged me to avoid him, but I had to make sense out of this enigmatic character.

After dinner, I quickly read through my history and psychology assignments, wrote a rough draft of an English paper, and raced out of the apartment. It was 11:00 P.M. Doubts began to plague me as I neared the station. Did he really want to see me again? What could I say to impress upon him the fact that I was a highly intelligent person?

He was there, standing in the doorway. He bowed, and with a

wave of his arm welcomed me into his office. "Please, remove your shoes—a custom of mine."

I sat down on the couch and put my shoes nearby, in case I wanted to make a hasty exit. I still didn't trust this mysterious stranger.

It was starting to rain outside. The color and warmth of the office was a comfortable contrast to the dark night and ominous clouds outside. I started to feel at ease. Leaning back, I said, "You know, Socrates, I feel as though I've met you before."

"You have," he answered, again opening the doorway in my mind where dreams and reality became one. I paused.

"Uh, Socrates, I've been having this dream—you're in it." I watched him carefully, but his face revealed nothing.

"I've been in many people's dreams; so have you. Tell me about your dream," he smiled.

I told him, in as much detail as I could remember. The room seemed to darken as the terrible scenes became vivid in my mind, and my familiar world began to recede.

After I finished, he said, "Yes, a very good dream." Before I could ask him what he meant by that, the station bell clanged, and clanged again. He put on a poncho and went outside into the wet night. I stared out the window, watching him.

It was a busy time of evening: the Friday-night rush. Things got pretty hectic, with one customer driving in after another. I felt silly just sitting there so I went out to help him, but he didn't seem to notice me.

An endless line of cars greeted me: two-tones, reds, greens, blacks, hard-tops, pickups, and foreign sports cars. The moods of the customers varied as much as their cars. Only one or two people seemed to know Socrates, but many people looked twice at him, as if noticing something odd but indefinable.

Some of the people were in a party mood, laughing loudly and blaring their radios while we waited on them. Socrates laughed right along with them. One or two customers were sullen, putting forth a special effort to be unpleasant, but Socrates treated one and all with the same courtesy—as if each person were his personal guest.

After midnight, the cars and customers became more scarce. The cool air seemed unnaturally still after having been filled with raucous noise and activity. As we entered the office, Socrates thanked me for my assistance. I shrugged it off but was pleased that he'd noticed. It had been a long time since I'd helped anyone with anything.

Once inside the warm office, I remembered our unfinished business. I started talking as soon as I flopped onto the couch. "Socrates, I have a couple of questions."

He held his hands in a gesture of prayer, looking upwards to the office ceiling as if asking for divine guidance—or divine patience.

"What," he sighed, "are your questions?"

"Well, I still want to know about the roof, and why you said, 'I'm pleased to see you *again,*' and I want to know what I can do for you and how you can be useful to me. *And,* I want to know how old you are."

"Let's take the easiest one, for now. I'm ninety-six years old, by your time." He was not ninety-six. Fifty-six, maybe; sixty-six at the outside; seventy-six, possible but amazing. But *ninety-six?* He was lying—but why would he lie? And I had to find about the other thing he had let slip, too.

"Socrates, what do you mean 'by your time'? Are you on Eastern Standard Time or are you," I joked feebly, "from outer space?"

"Isn't everyone?" he replied. By then, I had already considered that as a distinct possibility.

"I still want to know what we can do for each other."

"Just this: I wouldn't mind having one last student, and you obviously need a teacher."

"I have enough teachers," I said too quickly.

"Oh, do you?" He paused. "Whether you have a proper teacher or not depends upon what you want to learn." He rose lightly from his chair and walked to the door. "Come with me. I want to show you something."

We walked to the corner, from where we could see down the avenue to the lights of the business district and beyond them to the lights of San Francisco.

"The world out there," he said, waving his arm across the horizon, "is a school, Dan. Life is the only real teacher. It offers many experiences, and if experience alone brought wisdom and fulfillment, then elderly people would all be happy, enlightened masters.

But the lessons of experience are hidden. I can help you learn from experience to see the world clearly, and clarity is something you desperately need right now. Your intuition knows this is true, but your mind rebels; you've experienced much, but you've learned little."

"I don't know about that, Socrates. I mean, I wouldn't go that far."

"No, Dan, you don't know about it yet, but you will. And you will go that far and beyond; I can assure you."

We headed back for the office just as a shiny red Toyota pulled in. Socrates continued talking as he opened the gas tank. "Like most people, you've been taught to gather information from outside yourself; from books, magazines, experts." He stuck the gas nozzle into the tank. "Like this car, you open up and let the facts pour in. Sometimes the information is premium and sometimes it's low octane. You buy your knowledge at the current market rates, much like you buy gasoline."

"Hey, thanks for reminding me. My tuition check for next quarter is due in two days!"

Socrates just nodded and continued to fill the customer's tank. When the tank was full, Socrates kept pumping gas, until fuel started overflowing the tank and pouring down onto the ground. A flood of gasoline ran across the pavement.

"Socrates! The tank is full—watch what you're doing!"

Ignoring me, he let the flood continue—saying, "Dan, like this gas tank, you are overflowing with preconceptions; full of useless knowledge. You hold many facts and opinions, yet know little of yourself. Before you can learn, you'll have to first empty your tank." He grinned at me, winked, and turning the pump off with a click, added, "Clean up the mess, will you?"

I got the feeling he was referring to more than the spilled gas. I hurriedly watered down the pavement. Soc took the driver's money and gave him back some change and a smile. We walked back to the office and settled in.

"What are you going to do, fill me full of *your* facts?" I bristled.

"No, I'm not going to burden you with more facts; I'm going to show you 'body wisdom'. Everything you'll ever need to know is within you; the secrets of the universe are imprinted on the cells of your body. But you haven't learned inner vision; you don't know how to read the body. Your only recourse has been to read books and listen to experts and hope they are right. When you learn body wisdom, you'll be a Teacher among teachers."

I made an effort not to smirk. This gas station attendant was accusing my professors of ignorance and implying that my college education was pointless! "Oh, sure Socrates, I understand what you mean by this 'body wisdom' idea, but I don't buy it."

He shook his head slowly. "You understand many things but have realized practically nothing."

"What is that supposed to mean?"

"Understanding is one dimensional. It is the comprehension of the intellect. It leads to knowledge, which you have. Realization, on the other hand, is three dimensional. It is the simultaneous comprehension of the 'whole-body'—the head, heart, and physical instincts. It comes only from clear experience."

"I'm still not with you."

"Do you remember when you first learned to drive? Prior to that time, you'd been a passenger; you only understood what it was. But you *realized* what it was like when you did it for the first time."

"That's right!" I said. "I remember feeling, "So that's what it's like!"

"Exactly! That phrase describes the experience of realization perfectly. One day, you'll say the same thing about life."

I sat quietly for a moment, then piped up. "You still haven't explained 'body wisdom.' "

"Come with me," Socrates beckoned, leading me toward the door marked "Private." Once inside, we were in total darkness. I started to tense, but then the fear gave way to keen anticipation. I was about to learn my first real secret: body wisdom.

The lights flashed on. We were in a bathroom and Socrates was peeing loudly into the toilet bowl. "This," he said proudly, "is body wisdom." His laughter echoed off the tile walls as I walked out and sat down on the couch and glared at the rug.

When he came out, I said, "Socrates, I still want to know . . ."

"If you are going to call me 'Socrates'," he interrupted, "you might at least do the name honor by allowing me to ask the questions, on occasion, and you can answer them. How does that sound?"

"Fine!" I responded. "You just asked your question, and I answered it. Now it's my turn. About that flying stunt you pulled the other night . . ."

"You are a persistent young man, aren't you?"

"Yes, I am. I didn't get where I am today without persistence. And that's another question you got a straight answer for. Now, can we deal with some of mine?"

Ignoring me, he asked, "Where are you today, right now?"

Eagerly, I started talking about myself. However, I noticed that I was being sidetracked from getting answers to my questions. Still, I told him about my distant and recent past and about my inexplicable depressions. He listened patiently and intently, as if he had all the time in the world, until I finished several hours later.

"Very well," he said. "But you have still not answered my question about where you are."

"Yes I did, remember? I told you how I got to where I am today: by hard work."

"Where are you?"

"What do you mean, where am I?"

"Where *are* you?" he repeated softly.

"I'm here."

"Where is here?"

"In this office, in this gas station!" I was getting impatient with this game.

"Where is this gas station?"

"In Berkeley."

"Where is Berkeley?"

"In California."

"Where is California?"

"In the United States."

"Where is the United States?"

"On a land mass, one of the continents in the Western Hemisphere. Socrates, I . . ."

"Where are the continents?"

I sighed. "On the earth. Are we done yet?"

"Where is the earth?"

"In the solar system, third planet from the sun. The sun is a small star in the Milky Way galaxy, all right?"

"Where is the Milky Way?"

"Oh, brother," I sighed impatiently, rolling my eyes. "In the Universe." I sat back and crossed my arms with finality

"And where," Socrates smiled, "is the Universe?"

"The Universe is, well, there are theories about how it's shaped . . ."

"That's not what I asked. Where is it?"

"I don't know—how can I answer that?"

"That is the point. You cannot answer it, and you never will. There is no knowing about it. You are ignorant of where the Universe is, and thus, where you are. In fact, you have no knowledge of where anything is; nor do you know what anything is or how it came to be. It's a mystery.

"My ignorance, Dan, is based on this understanding. Your understanding is based on ignorance. I am a humorous fool; you are a serious jackass."

"Listen," I said, "there are things you should know about me. For one thing, I'm already a warrior of sorts. I'm a damn good gymnast." To punctuate what I'd said and to show him *I* could be spontaneous, I stood up from the couch and did a standing backward somersault, landing gracefully on the carpet.

"Hey," he said, "that's great. Do it again!"

"Well, it isn't really that terrific, Soc. It's pretty easy for me, in fact." I did my best to keep the condescension out of my voice but was unable to hold back a proud smile. I was used to showing this sort of thing to kids at the beach or the park. They always wanted to see it again, too.

"All right now, Soc, watch closely." I leaped upward and was just turning over when someone or something tossed me through the air. I landed in a heap on the couch. The Mexican blanket from the back of the couch wrapped itself around me, covering me. I poked my head out from the covers quickly, looking for Socrates. He was still sitting across the room, twelve feet away, curled in his chair and smiling mischievously.

"How did you do that?" My confusion was as total as his look of innocence.

"Did you like the ride?" he asked. "Do you want to see it

again?" adding, "Don't feel badly about your little slip, Dan; even a great warrior like you can make a boo-boo now and then."

I stood numbly and straightened the couch, tucking the blanket back in. I had to do something with my hands; I needed time to think. How had he done it? Another question that would go unanswered.

Socrates padded softly out of the office to fill the tank of a pickup truck full of household belongings. "Off to cheer up another traveller on his journey," I thought. Then I closed my eyes and pondered Soc's apparent defiance of natural laws, or at least, common sense.

"Would you like to learn some secrets?" I hadn't even heard him come in. He was seated in his chair, his legs crossed.

I crossed my legs, too, and leaned forward eagerly. Misjudging the softness of the couch, I leaned a little bit too far and tipped over. Before I could untangle my legs, I found myself sprawled face down on the rug.

Socrates was beside himself with laughter. I sat up quickly, ramrod straight. One look at my stolid expression almost made Soc completely helpless with mirth. More accustomed to applause than to ridicule, I leaped to my feet in shame and anger. Soc cut himself short; his face and voice were charged with authority.

"Sit down!" he commanded, pointing to the couch. I sat. "I asked you if you wanted to hear a secret."

"I do—about rooftops."

"*You* get to choose whether or not you want to hear a secret. *I* choose what it is about."

"Why do we always have to play by your rules?"

"Because it's my station, that's why." Soc spoke with exaggerated petulance, possibly mocking me further. "Now pay close attention. By the way, are you comfortable and, uh, stable?" he winked. I just clenched my teeth.

"Dan, I have places to show you and tales to tell. I have secrets to unfold. But before we begin this journey together, you must appreciate that a secret's value is not in what you know, but what you *do*."

Soc took an old dictionary from his drawer and held it in the air. "Use whatever knowledge you have but see its limitations. Knowledge alone does not suffice; it has no heart. No amount of knowledge will nourish or sustain your spirit; it can never bring you ultimate happiness or peace. Life requires more than knowledge; it requires intense feeling and constant energy. Life demands *right action* if knowledge is to come alive."

"I know that, Soc."

"That's your problem—you know but you don't *act*. You're not a warrior."

"Socrates, I just can't believe that. I know at times I've acted like a warrior, when the pressure was really on—you should see me in the gym!"

"Granted that you may, in fact, experience the mind of a warrior on occasion; resolute, flexible, clear, and free of doubt. You can develop the body of a warrior, lithe, supple, sensitive, and filled with energy. In rare moments, you may even feel the heart of a warrior, loving everything and everyone who appears before you. But these qualities are fragmented in you. You lack integration. My task is to put you back together again, Humpty."

"Wait a damn minute, Socrates. Though I don't doubt you have some unusual talents and like to surround yourself with an air of mystery, I don't see how you can presume to put *me* back together. Let's look at the situation: I'm a college student; you service cars. I'm a world champion; you tinker in the garage, make tea, and wait for some poor fool to walk in so you can frighten the wits out of him. Maybe I can help put *you* back together." I didn't quite know what I was saying, but it felt good.

Socrates just laughed, shaking his head as if he couldn't quite believe what I'd said. Then he came over to me and knelt down at my side, saying, "You, put me back together? Maybe you will have that chance someday. But for now, you should understand the difference between us." He poked me in the ribs, then poked me again and again, saying, "The warrior acts . . ."

"Damn it, stop that!" I yelled. "You're getting on my nerves!"

". . . and the fool only reacts."

"Well what do you expect?"

"I poke you and you get irritable; I insult you and you react with pride and anger; I slip on a banana peel and . . ." He took two steps away from me and slipped, landing with a thud on the carpet. I couldn't hold it in. I bellowed.

He sat up on the floor and turned to face me, making a final point. "Your feelings and reactions, Dan, are automatic and predictable; mine are not. I create my life spontaneously; yours is determined by your past."

"How can you assume all this about me, about my past?"

"Because, I've been watching you for years."

"Sure you have," I said, waiting for the joke. None came.

It was getting late, and I had a lot to think about. I felt burdened by a new obligation, one I wasn't sure I could fulfill. Socrates came in, wiped his hands, and filled his mug with spring water. As he sipped slowly, I said, "I've got to go now, Soc. It's late and I have a lot of important schoolwork to do."

Socrates remained quietly seated as I stood and put on my jacket. Then, as I was about to go out the door, he spoke slowly and carefully. Each word had the effect of a gentle slap on my cheek.

"You had better reconsider your 'importances' if you are to have even a chance of becoming a warrior. Right now, you have the intelligence of a jackass; your spirit is mush. You do have a great deal of important work to do but in a different classroom than you now imagine."

I had been staring at the floor. I snapped my head up to face him, but I couldn't look him in the eye. I turned away.

"To survive the lessons ahead," he continued, "you're going to need far more energy than ever before. You must cleanse your body of tension, free your mind of stagnant knowledge, and open your heart to the energies of true emotion."

"Soc, I'd better explain my time schedule. I want you to understand how busy I am. I'd like to visit with you often, but I have so little time."

He looked at me with somber eyes. "You have even less time than you might imagine."

"What do you mean?" I gasped.

"Never mind that now," he said. "Go on."

"Well, I have these goals. I want to be a champion gymnast. I want our team to win the national championships. I want to graduate in good standing, and that means books to read and papers to write. What you seem to be offering me instead is staying up half the night in a gas station, listening to—I hope you won't take this as an insult—a very strange man who wants to draw me into his fantasy world. It's crazy!"

"Yes," he smiled sadly, "It is crazy." Socrates sat back in his chair and looked down at the floor. My mind rebelled at his helpless-old-man ploy, but my heart was drawn to this robust old eccentric who claimed to be some kind of "warrior." I took my jacket off, removed my shoes, and sat back down. Then a story that my grandfather had told me came to mind:

There was once a beloved king whose castle was on a high hill, overlooking his shire. He was so popular that the nearby townspeople sent him gifts daily, and his birthday celebration was enjoyed throughout the kingdom. The people loved him for his renowned wisdom and fair judgments.

One day, tragedy struck the town. The water supply was polluted, and every man, woman, and child went insane. Only the king, who had a private spring, was spared.

Soon after the tragedy, the mad townspeople began speaking of how the king was acting "strangely" and how his judgments were poor and his wisdom a sham. Many even went so far as to say that the king had gone crazy. His popularity soon vanished. No longer did the people bring him gifts or celebrate his birthday.

The lonely king, high on the hill, had no company at all. One day he decided to leave the hill and pay a visit to the town. It was a warm day, and so he drank from the village fountain.

That night there was a great celebration. The people all rejoiced, for their beloved king had "regained his sanity."

I realized then that the crazy world that Socrates had referred to was not his world at all, but mine.

I stood, ready to leave. "Socrates, you've told me to listen to my own body intuition and not depend upon what I read or what people tell me. Why, then, should I sit quietly and listen to what you tell me?"

"A very good question," he answered. "There is an equally good answer. First of all, I speak to you from my own experience; I am not relating abstract theories I read in a book or heard second-hand from an expert. I am one who truly knows his own body and mind, and therefore, knows others' as well. Besides," he smiled, "how do you know that I'm not your body intuition, speaking to you now?" He turned to his desk and picked up some paperwork. I had been dismissed for the evening. My whirling thoughts carried me into the night.

I was upset for days afterwards. I felt weak and inadequate around this man, and I was angry about the way he treated me. He constantly seemed to underestimate me; I wasn't a child! "Why should I choose to play a jackass sitting in a gas station," I thought, "when here, in my domain, I'm admired and respected?"

I trained harder than ever in gymnastics—my body burned with fever as I flew and fought my way through routine after routine. Yet it was somehow less satisfying than before. Every time I learned a new move or received a compliment, I remembered being tossed through the air onto the couch by that old man.

Hal, my coach, became concerned about me and wanted to know if anything was wrong. I reassured him that everything was fine. But it wasn't. I didn't feel like joking around with the guys on the team anymore. I was just confused.

That night I had my Grim Reaper dream again, with a difference. A chortling Socrates, decked out in the Grim Reaper's gloomy get-up, pointed a gun at me that went off, shooting out a flag that said, "Bang!" I woke up giggling instead of groaning, for a change.

The next day I found a note in my mailbox. All it said was, "Rooftop secrets." When Socrates arrived that night, I was already sitting on the station steps, waiting for him. I'd come early to question the day attendants about Socrates—to find out his real name, maybe even where he lived—but they didn't know anything about him. "Who cares anyway?" one yawned. "He's just some old geezer who likes the night shift."

Soc removed his windbreaker, "Well?" I pounced. "Are you finally going to tell me how you got up on the roof?"

"Yes, I am; I think you're ready to hear it," he said seriously. "In ancient Japan, there existed an elite group of warrior assassins."

He said the last word with a hissing sound, making me acutely aware of the dark silence lurking outside. My neck started to get that prickly feeling again.

"These warriors," he continued, "were named *ninja*. The

legends and reputation surrounding them were fearful. It was said that they could change themselves into animals; it was even said that they could fly—for short distances only, of course."

"Of course," I agreed, feeling the door to the dream world blow open with a chill gust. I wondered what he was leading up to, when he beckoned me into the garage where he was working on a Japanese sports car.

"Got to change the plugs," Socrates said, ducking his head under the sleek hood.

"Yes, but what about the rooftop?" I urged.

"I'll get to it in a moment, as soon as I change these plugs. Be patient. What I'm about to tell you is worth waiting for, believe me."

I sat toying with a mallet lying on the work table.

From Socrates' corner I heard, "You know, this is very amusing work, if you really pay attention to it." For him it was, perhaps.

Suddenly he put down the plugs, ran over to the light switch, and flicked it. In a darkness so total that I couldn't even see my hands in front of me, I began to get nervous. I never knew what Socrates would do, and after that talk about *ninja*. . . .

"Soc? Soc?"

"Where are you?" he yelled from directly behind me.

I spun around fell onto the hood of a Chevy. "I—I don't know!" I stammered.

"Absolutely right," he said, turning on the lights. "I guess you are getting smarter," he said, with a Cheshire cat grin.

I shook my head at his lunacy and perched myself on the Chevy's fender, glancing under the open hood to find its innards missing. "Socrates, will you quit clowning and get *on* with it?"

As he deftly screwed in the new plugs, unsnapped the distributor cap, and examined the rotors, he continued.

"These *ninja* were not practitioners of magic. Their secret was the most intense physical and mental training known to man."

"Socrates, where is this all leading?"

"To see where something leads, it's best to wait until you reach the end," he replied and continued with the story.

"The *ninja* could swim wearing heavy armor; they could climb sheer walls like lizards, using only fingers and toes in tiny cracks. They designed imaginative scaling ropes, dark and nearly invisible, and used clever means of hiding; tricks of distraction, illusion, and escape. The *ninja,*" he finally added, "were great jumpers."

"Now we're getting somewhere!" I almost rubbed my hands in anticipation.

"The young warrior, when still a child, would be trained in jumping in the following manner: He was given a corn seed and told to plant it. Just as the stalk was beginning to grow, the young warrior would jump over the small stalk many, many times. Each day the stalk would grow; each day the child would jump. Soon the stalk was higher than the child's head, but that wouldn't stop him. Finally, if he failed to clear the stalk, he would be given a new seed and would begin over. Eventually, there was no stalk that the young *ninja* could not leap over."

"Well, then what? What is the secret?" I asked, waiting for the final revelation.

Socrates paused and took a deep breath. "So you see, the young *ninja* practiced with cornstalks. *I* practice with gas stations."

Silence filled the room. Then, suddenly, Soc's musical laughter pealed through the station; he was laughing so hard he had to lean against the Datsun he'd been working on.

"So that's it, huh? That's what you were going to tell me about rooftops?"

"Dan, that is all you can know until you can *do,*" he answered.

"You mean you're going to teach me how to jump up on the roof?" I asked, my demeanor suddenly brightening.

"Perhaps so, perhaps not. Each of us has our own unique talents. You *may* learn to jump up on rooftops," he grinned. "For now, toss me that screwdriver, will you?"

I threw it to him. I swear he grabbed it out of the air while looking in the other direction! He finished with it quickly and tossed it back to me, yelling, "Heads up!" I dropped it and it fell to the floor with a loud clatter. This was exasperating; I didn't know how much more ridicule I could take.

The weeks passed quickly, and my sleepless nights became commonplace. Somehow, I adjusted. And there was another change: I found that my visits with Socrates were becoming even more interesting to me than gymnastics practice.

Each night while we serviced cars—he put the gas in, I did windows, and both of us joked with customers—he would encourage me to talk about my life. He was strangely silent about his own, meeting my questions with a terse, "Later," or answering in complete non sequiturs.

When I asked him why he was so interested in the details of my life, he said, "I need to understand your personal illusions to grasp the scope of your illness. We are going to have to clean your mind before the door to the warrior's way can open."

"Don't you touch my mind. I like it just the way it is."

"If you really liked it the way it is, you wouldn't be here now. You've changed your mind many times in the past. Soon, you're going to do it in a more profound way." After that, I decided I was going to have to be very careful with this man. I didn't know him all that well, and I still wasn't sure how crazy he was.

As it was, Soc's style was constantly changing, unorthodox, humorous, and even bizarre. Once he ran screaming after a little white dog that had just peed on the station steps—right in the middle of a lecture he was giving me on the "supreme benefits of an unshakably serene composure."

Another time, about a week later, after we'd stayed up all night, we walked to Strawberry Creek and stood on a bridge, looking down at the stream overflowing with the winter rains.

"I wonder how deep the stream is today?" I casually remarked, gazing absent-mindedly down into the rushing waters. The next thing I knew, I'd splashed into the churning, muddy brown water.

He had tossed me off the bridge!

"Well, how deep is it?"

"Deep enough," I sputtered, dragging myself and my waterlogged clothes to shore. So much for idle speculation. I made a mental note to keep my mouth shut.

As the days passed I started to notice more and more differences between us. In the office, I'd devour candy bars when I got hungry; Soc munched on a fresh apple or pear or made himself herb tea. I fidgeted around on the couch while he sat serenely still on his chair, like a Buddha. My movements were awkward and noisy compared to the way he softly glided across the floor. And he was an old man, mind you.

There were many small lessons that awaited me each night, even in the early days. One night I made the mistake of complaining about how people at school just didn't seem to act very friendly toward me.

Softly, he said, "It is better for you to take responsibility for your life as it is, instead of blaming others, or circumstances, for your predicament. As your eyes open, you'll see that your state of health, happiness, and every circumstance of your life has been, in large part, arranged by you—consciously or unconsciously."

"I don't know what you mean, but I don't think I agree with it."

"Well, here's a story about a guy like you, Dan:

On a construction site in the Midwest, when the lunch whistle blew, all the workers would sit down together to eat. And with singular regularity Sam would open his lunch pail and start to complain.

"Son of a gun!" he'd cry, "not peanut butter and jelly sandwiches again. I hate peanut butter and jelly!"

Sam moaned about his peanut butter and jelly sandwiches day after day after day. Weeks passed, and the other workers were getting irritated by his behavior. Finally, another man on the work crew said, "Fer crissakes, Sam, if you hate peanut butter and jelly so much, why don't you just tell yer ol' lady to make you something different?"

"What do you mean, my ol' lady?" Sam replied. "I'm not married. I make my own sandwiches."

Socrates paused, then added, "So you see, we all make our own sandwiches in this life." He handed me a brown bag with two sandwiches in it. "Do you want cheese and tomato or tomato and cheese?" he asked, grinning.

"Oh, just give me either," I jested back.

As we munched, Socrates said, "When you become fully responsible for your life, you can become fully human; once you become human, you may discover what it means to be a warrior."

"Thanks, Soc, for the food for thought, and for belly." I bowed grandly. Then I put on my jacket and got ready to leave. "I won't be by for a couple of weeks. Finals are coming up. And I also have some hard thinking to do." Before he could comment I waved goodbye and left for home.

I lost myself in the semester's last classes. My hours in the gym were spent in the hardest training I'd ever done. Whenever I stopped pushing myself, my thoughts and feelings began to stir uneasily. I felt the first signs of what was to become a growing sense of alienation from my everyday world. For the first time in my life, I had a choice between two distinct realities. One was crazy and one was sane—but I just didn't know which was which, so I committed myself to neither.

I couldn't shake a growing sense that maybe, just maybe, Socrates was not so eccentric after all. Perhaps his descriptions of my life had been more accurate than I'd imagined. I began to really see how I acted with people, and what I saw began to disturb me. I was sociable enough on the outside, but I was really only concerned about myself.

Bill, one of my best friends, fell from the horse and broke his wrist; Rick learned a full twisting back somersault that he'd been working on for a year. I felt the same emotional response in both cases; nothing.

Under the weight of my growing self-knowledge, my self-esteem was sinking fast.

One night, just before finals, I heard a knock at my door. I was surprised and happy to find toothpaste Susie, the blond cheerleader I hadn't seen in weeks. I realized how lonely I'd been.

"Aren't you going to invite me in, Danny?"

"Oh! Yes. I'm really glad to see you. Uh, sit down, let me take your coat, would you like something to eat? Something to drink?" She just gazed at me.

"What is it, Susie?"

"You look tired, Danny, but . . ." she reached out and touched my face. "There's something . . . your eyes look different, somehow. What is it?"

I touched her cheek. "Stay with me tonight, Susie."

"I thought you'd never ask. I brought my toothbrush!"

The next morning I turned over to smell Sue's tousled hair, sweet like summer straw, and to feel her soft breath on my pillow. "I should feel good," I thought, but my mood was grey like the fog outside.

For the next few days, Sue and I spent a lot of time together. I don't think I was very good company, but Sue's spirits were enough for both of us.

Something kept me from telling her about Socrates. He was of another world, a world in which she had no part. How could she understand when I couldn't even fathom what was happening to me?

Finals came and went. I did well, but I didn't care. Susie went home for spring vacation, and I was glad to be alone.

Spring vacation was soon over, and warm winds blew through the littered streets of Berkeley. I knew that it was time to return to that warrior's world, to that strange little gas station—this time perhaps more open and more humble than before. But now I was more sure of one thing. If Socrates cut at me with his sharp wit again, I was going to slash right back!

BOOK ONE

THE WINDS OF CHANGE

1

Gusts of Magic

It was late evening. After my workout and dinner, I took a nap. When I awoke it was nearly midnight. I walked slowly through the crisp night air of early spring toward the station. A strong breeze blew from behind me, as if impelling me forward along the campus paths.

As I neared the familiar intersection, I slowed down. A light drizzle had begun, chilling the night. In the glow from the warmly lit office I could see Soc's shape through the misted window, drinking from his mug, and a mixture of anticipation and dread squeezed my lungs and accelerated my heart beat.

I looked down at the pavement as I crossed the street and neared the office door. The wind gusted against the back of my neck. Suddenly chilled, I snapped my head up to see Socrates standing in the doorway, staring at me and sniffing the air like a wolf. He seemed to be looking right through me. Memories of the Grim Reaper returned. I knew this man had within him great warmth and compassion, but I sensed that behind his dark eyes lay a great unknown danger.

My fear dissipated when he gently said, "It's good that you've returned." He welcomed me into the office with a wave of his arm. Just as I took off my shoes and sat down, the station bell clanged. I wiped the mist off the window and looked out to see an old Plymouth limp in with a flat tire. Socrates was already headed out the door wearing his army surplus rain poncho. Watching him, I wondered momentarily how he could possibly have frightened me.

Then rain clouds darkened the night, bringing back fleeting images of the black-hooded death of my dream, changing the pattering of the soft rain into bony fingers drumming madly on the roof. I moved restlessly on the couch, tired from my intense workouts in the gym. The Conference Championships were coming up next week, and today had been the last hard workout before the meet.

Socrates opened the door to the office. He stood with the door open and said, "Come outside—now," then left me. As I rose and put on my shoes, I looked through the mist. Socrates was standing out beyond the pumps, just outside the aura of the station lights. Half-shrouded in darkness, he appeared to be wearing a black hood.

I was *not* going out there. The office was like a fortress against the night—and against a world outside that was beginning to grate on my nerves like noisy downtown traffic. Nope. I wasn't going out. Socrates beckoned me again, then again, from out in the darkness. Surrendering to fate, I went outside.

As I approached him cautiously, he said, "Listen, can you feel it?"

"What?"

"Feel!"

Just then the rain stopped and the wind seemed to change directions. Strange—a warm wind. "The wind, Soc?"

"Yes, the winds. They're changing. It means a turning point for you—now. You may not have realized it; neither did I, in fact—but tonight is a critical moment in time for you. You left, but you returned. And now the winds are changing." He looked at me for a moment, then strode back inside.

I followed him in and sat down on the familiar couch. Socrates was very still in his soft brown chair, his eyes riveted upon me. In a voice strong enough to pierce walls but light enough to be carried by the March winds, he announced, "There is something I must do now. Don't be afraid."

He stood. "Socrates, you're scaring the hell out of me!" I stammered angrily, sliding back in the couch as he slowly came toward me, stalking, like a tiger on the prowl.

He glanced out the window for a moment checking for possible interruptions, then knelt in front of me, saying softly, "Dan, do you recall that I told you we must work on changing your mind before you can see the warrior's way?"

"Yes, but I really don't think . . ."

"Don't be afraid," he repeated. "Comfort yourself with a saying of Confucius," he smiled. " 'Only the supremely wise and the ignorant do not alter.' " Saying that, he reached out and placed his hands gently but firmly on my temples.

Nothing happened for a moment—then suddenly, I felt a growing pressure in the middle of my head. There was a loud buzzing, then a sound like waves rushing up on the beach. I heard bells ringing, and my head felt as if it was going to burst. That's when I saw the light, and my mind exploded with its brightness. Something in me was dying—I knew this for a certainty—and something else was being born! Then the light engulfed everything.

I found myself lying back on the couch. Socrates was offering me a cup of tea, shaking me gently.

"What happened to me?"

"Let's just say I manipulated your energies and opened a few new circuits. The fireworks were just your brain's delight in the energy bath. The result is that you are relieved of your lifelong illusion of knowledge. From now on, ordinary knowledge is no longer going to satisfy you, I'm afraid."

"I don't get it."

"You will," he said, without smiling.

I was very tired. We sipped our tea in silence. Then, excusing myself, I rose, put on my sweater, and walked home as if in a dream.

The next day was full of classes and full of professors babbling words that had no meaning or relevance for me. In History 101, Watson lectured on how Churchill's political instincts had affected the war. I stopped taking notes. I was too busy taking in the colors and textures of the room, feeling the energies of the people around me. The sounds of my professors' voices were far more interesting than the concepts they conveyed. Socrates, what did you do to me? I'll never make it through finals.

I was walking out of class, fascinated by the knobby texture of the carpet, when I heard a familiar voice.

"Hi, Danny! I haven't seen you for days. I've called every night, but you're never home. Where have you been hiding?"

"Oh, hi Susie. It's good to see you again. I've been . . . studying." Her words had danced through the air. I could hardly understand them but I could feel what she was feeling—hurt and a little jealous. Yet her face was beaming as usual.

"I'd like to talk more, Susie, but I'm on my way to the gym."

"Oh, I forgot." I felt her disappointment. "Well," she said, "I'll see you soon, huh?"

"Sure."

"Hey," she said. "Wasn't Watson's lecture great? I just love hearing about Churchill's life. Isn't it interesting?"

"Uh, yeah—great lecture."

"Well, bye for now, Danny."

"Bye." Turning away, I recalled what Soc had said about my "patterns of shyness and fear." Maybe he was right. I wasn't really that comfortable with people; I was never sure of what to say.

In the gym that afternoon, however, I certainly knew what to *do*. I came alive, turning on the faucet of my energy full blast. I played, swung, leaped; I was a clown, a magician, a chimpanzee. It was one of my best days ever. My mind was so clear that I felt exactly how to do anything I tried. My body was relaxed, supple, quick, and light. In tumbling, I invented a one and one-half backward somersault with a late half twist to a roll; from the high bar, I swung into a full twisting double flyaway—both moves, the first ever done in the United States.

A few days later, the team flew up to Oregon for the Conference Championships. We won the meet and flew home. It was like a dream of fanfare, action, and glory—but I couldn't escape the concerns that plagued me.

I considered the events that had occurred since the other night's experience of the bursting light. Something had certainly happened, as Soc had predicted, but it was frightening and I didn't think I liked it at all. Perhaps Socrates was not what he seemed; perhaps he was something more clever, or more evil than I'd suspected.

These thoughts vanished as I stepped through the doorway of the lighted office and saw his eager smile. As soon as I'd sat down, Socrates said, "Are you ready to go on a journey?"

"A journey?" I echoed.

"Yes—a trip, travel, sojourn, vacation—an adventure."

"No, thanks, I'm not dressed for it."

"Nonsense!" he bellowed, so loudly that we both looked around to see if any passersby had heard. "Shhh!" he whispered loudly. "Not so loud, you'll wake everyone."

Taking advantage of his affability, I blurted out, "Socrates, my life no longer makes sense. Nothing works, except when I'm in the gym. Aren't you supposed to make things better for me? I thought that's what a teacher did."

He started to speak, but I interrupted.

"And another thing. I've always believed that we have to find our own paths in life. No one can tell another how to live."

Socrates slapped his forehead with his palm, then looked upward in resignation. "I am part of your path, baboon. And I didn't exactly rob you from the cradle and lock you up here, you know. You can take off whenever you like." He walked to the door and held it open.

Just then, a black limousine pulled into the station, and Soc affected a British accent: "Your car is ready, sir." Disoriented, I actually thought we were going on a trip in the limousine. I mean, why not? So, befuddled, I walked straight out to the limo and started to climb into the back seat. I found myself staring into the wrinkled old face of a little man, sitting with his arm around a girl of about sixteen, probably off the streets of Berkeley. He stared at me like a hostile lizard.

Soc's hand grabbed me by the back of my sweater and dragged me out of the car. Closing the door, he apologized: "Excuse my young friend. He's never been in a beautiful car like this and just got carried away—didn't you, Jack?"

I nodded dumbly. "What's going on?" I whispered fiercely out of the side of my mouth. But he was already washing the windows. When the car pulled away, I flushed with embarrassment. "Why didn't you stop me, Socrates?"

"Frankly, it was pretty funny. I hadn't realized you could be so gullible."

We stood there, in the middle of the night, staring each other down. Socrates grinned as I clenched my teeth, I was getting angry. "I'm really tired of playing the fool around you!" I yelled.

"Well, you have to admit that you've been practicing the role so diligently, you've got it nearly perfect." I wheeled around, kicked the trash can, and stomped back toward the office. Then it occurred to me. "Why did you call me Jack, awhile ago?"

"Short for jackass," he said, passing me.

"All right, god damn it," I said as I ran by him to enter the office. "Let's go on your journey. Whatever you want to give, I can take!"

"Well, now. This is a new side of you—spunky Danny."

"Spunky or not, I'm no flunky. Now tell me, where are we headed? Where am I headed? I should be in control, not you!"

Socrates took a deep breath. "Dan, I can't tell you anything. Much of a warrior's path is subtle, invisible to the uninitiated. For now, I have been showing you what a warrior is *not* by showing you your own mind. You can come to understand that soon enough—and so I must take you on a journey. Come with me."

He led me to a cubbyhole I hadn't noticed before, hidden behind the racks of tools in the garage and furnished with a small rug and a heavy straight-backed chair. The predominant color of the nook was grey. My stomach felt queasy.

"Sit down," he said gently.

"Not until you explain what this is all about." I crossed my arms over my chest.

Now it was his turn to explode. "*I* am a warrior; *you* are a baboon. I will not explain a damn thing. Now shut up and sit down or go back to your gymnastics spotlight and forget you ever knew me!"

"You're not kidding, are you?"

"No, I am not kidding." I hesitated a second, then sat.

Socrates reached into a drawer, took out some long pieces of cotton cloth, and began to tie me to the chair.

"What are you going to do, torture me?" I half-joked.

"No, now please be silent," he said, tying the last strip around my waist and behind the chair, like an airline seat-belt.

"Are we going flying, Soc?" I asked nervously.

"In a manner of speaking, yes," he said, kneeling in front of me, taking my head in his hands and placing his thumbs against the upper ridges of my eye sockets. My teeth chattered; I had an excruciating urge to urinate. But in another second, I had forgotten all. Colored lights flashed. I thought I heard his voice but couldn't quite make it out; it was too far away.

We were walking down a corridor swathed in a blue fog. My feet moved but I couldn't feel ground. Gigantic trees surrounded us; they became buildings; the buildings became boulders, and we ascended a steep canyon that became the edge of a sheer cliff.

The fog had cleared; the air was freezing. Green clouds stretched below us for miles, meeting an orange sky on the horizon.

I was shaking. I tried to say something to Socrates, but my voice came out muffled. My shaking grew uncontrollable. Soc put his hand on my belly. It was very warm and had a wondrously calming effect. I relaxed and he took my arm firmly, tightening his grip, and hurtled forward, off the edge of the world, pulling me with him.

Without warning the clouds disappeared and we were hanging from the rafters of an indoor stadium, swinging precariously like two drunken spiders high above the floor.

"Ooops," said Soc. "Slight miscalculation."

"What the hell!" I yelled, struggling for a better handhold. I swung myself up and over and lay panting on a beam, twining my arms and legs around it. Socrates had already perched himself lightly on the beam in front of me. I noticed that he handled himself well for an old man.

"Hey, look," I pointed. "It's a gymnastics meet! Socrates, you're nuts."

"*I'm* nuts?" he laughed quietly. "Look who's sitting on the beam next to me."

"How are we going to get down?"

"Same way we got up, of course."

"How *did* we get up here?"

He scratched his head. "I'm not precisely sure; I had hoped for a front-row seat. I guess they were sold out."

I began to laugh shrilly. This whole thing was too ridiculous. Soc clapped a hand over my mouth. "Shhhh!" He removed his hand. That was a mistake.

"HaHaHaHaHa!" I laughed loudly before he muffled me again. I calmed down but felt giddy and started giggling.

He whispered at me harshly. "This journey is real—more real than the waking dreams of your usual life. Pay attention!"

By this time the scene below had indeed caught my attention. The audience, from this height, coalesced into a multicolored array of dots, a shimmering, rippling, pointillist painting. I caught sight of a raised platform in the middle of the arena with a familiar bright blue square of floor-exercise mat, surrounded by various gymnastic apparatus. My stomach rumbled in response; I experienced my usual precompetition nervousness.

Socrates reached into a small knapsack (where had that come from?) and handed me a pair of binoculars, just as a female performer walked out onto the floor.

I focused my binoculars on the lone gymnast and saw she was from the Soviet Union. So, we were attending an international exhibition somewhere. As she walked over to the uneven bars, I realized that I could hear her talking to herself! "The acoustics in here," I thought, "must be fantastic." But then I saw that her lips weren't moving.

I moved the lenses quickly to the audience and heard the roar of many voices; yet they were just sitting quietly. Then it came to me. Somehow, I was reading their minds!

I turned the glasses back to the woman gymnast. In spite of the language barrier, I could understand her thoughts: "Be strong . . . ready. . . ." I saw a preview of her routine as she ran through it mentally.

Then I focused on a man in the audience, a guy in a white sports shirt in the midst of a sexual fantasy about one of the East German contestants. Another man, apparently a coach, was engrossed with the woman about to perform. A woman in the audience watched her too, thinking, "Beautiful girl . . . had a bad fall last year . . . hope she does a good job."

I noticed that I was not receiving words, but feeling-concepts—sometimes quiet or muffled, sometimes loud and clear. That was how I could "understand" Russian, German, or whatever.

I noticed something else. When the Soviet gymnast was doing her routine, her mind was quiet. When she finished and returned to her chair, her mind started up again. It was the same for the East German gymnast on the rings and the American on the horizontal bar. Furthermore, the best performers had the quietest minds during their moment of truth.

One East German fellow was distracted by a noise while he swung through handstand after handstand on the parallel bars. I sensed his mind drawn to the noise; he thought, "What? . . ." as he muffed his final somersault to handstand.

A telepathic voyeur, I peeked into the minds of the audience. "I'm hungry. . . . Got to catch an eleven o'clock plane or the Dusseldorf plans are shot. . . . I'm hungry!" But as soon as a performer was in midflight, the minds of the audience calmed too.

For the first time, I realized why I loved gymnastics so. It gave me a blessed respite from my noisy mind. When I was swinging and somersaulting, nothing else mattered. When my body was active, my mind rested in the moments of silence.

The mental noise from the audience was getting annoying, like a stereo playing too loud. I lowered my glasses and let them hang. But I had neglected to fasten the strap around my neck, and I almost fell off the rafter trying to grab them as they plummeted straight for the floor exercise mat and a woman performer directly below!

"Soc!" I whispered in alarm. He sat placidly. I looked down to see the damage, but the binoculars had disappeared.

Socrates grinned. "Things work under a slightly different set of laws when you travel with me."

He disappeared and I was tumbling through space, not downward but upward. I had a vague sense of walking backwards from the edge of a cliff, down a canyon, then into a mist, like a character in a crazy movie in reverse.

Socrates was wiping my face with a wet cloth. Still strapped to the chair, I slumped.

"Well," he said. "Isn't travel broadening?"

"You can say that again. Uh, how about unstrapping me?"

"Not just yet," he replied, reaching again for my head.

I mouthed, "No, wait!" just before the lights went out and a howling wind arose, carrying me off into space and time.

I became the wind, yet with eyes and ears. And I saw and heard far and wide. I blew past the east coast of India near the Bay of Bengal, past a scrubwoman busy with her tasks. In Hong Kong, I whirled around a seller of fine fabric bargaining loudly with a shop per. I raced through the streets of São Paulo, drying the sweat of German tourists playing volleyball in the hot tropical sun.

I left no country untouched. I thundered through China and Mongolia and across the vast, rich land of the Soviet Union. I gusted through valleys and alpine meadows of Austria, sliced cold through the fjords of Norway. I tossed up litter on the Rue Pigalle in Paris. One moment I was a twister, ripping across Texas; the next, I was a gentle breeze, caressing the hair of a young girl contemplating suicide in Canton, Ohio.

I experienced every emotion, heard every cry of anguish and every peal of laughter. Every human circumstance was opened to me. I felt it all, and I understood.

The world was peopled with minds, whirling faster than any wind, in search of distraction and escape from the predicament of change, the dilemma of life and death—seeking purpose, security, enjoyment; trying to make sense of the mystery. Everyone everywhere lived a confused, bitter search. Reality never matched their dreams; happiness was just around the corner—a corner they never turned.

And the source of it all was the human mind.

Socrates was removing the clothstrips which had bound me. Sunlight streaked through the windows of the garage into my eyes—eyes that had seen so much—filling them with tears.

Socrates helped me into the office. As I lay trembling on the couch, I realized that I was no longer the naive and self-important youth who had sat quaking in the grey chair a few minutes or hours or days ago. I felt very old. I had seen the suffering of the world, the condition of the human mind, and I almost wept with an inconsolable sadness. There was no escape.

Socrates, on the other hand, was jovial. "Well, no more time to play games right now. My shift is almost up. Why don't you shuffle on home and get some sleep, kiddo?"

I creaked to my feet and put my arm in the wrong sleeve of my jacket. Extricating myself, I asked weakly, "Socrates, why'd you tie me down?"

"Never too weak for questions, I see. I tied you down so you wouldn't fall off the chair while you were thrashing around playing Peter Pan."

"Did I really fly? It felt like it." I sat down again, heavily.

"Let's say for now that it was a flight of the imagination."

"Did you hypnotize me or what?"

"Not in the way you mean—certainly not to the same degree you've been hypnotized by your own confused mental processes." He laughed, picked up his knapsack (where had I seen it before?), and prepared to leave. "What I did was draw you into one of many parallel realities—for your amusement and instruction."

"How?"

"It's a bit complicated. Why don't we leave it for another time." Socrates yawned and stretched like a cat. As I stumbled out the door I heard Soc's voice behind me. "Sleep well. You can expect a little surprise when you awake."

"Please, no more surprises," I mumbled, heading for home in a daze. I vaguely remember falling onto my bed. Then blackness.

I awoke to the sound of the wind-up clock ticking loudly on the blue chest of drawers. But I owned no wind-up clock; I had no blue chest of drawers. Neither did I possess this thick quilt, now in disarray at my feet. Then I noticed that the feet weren't mine either. "Much too small," I thought. The sun poured through the unfamiliar picture window.

Who and where was I? I held onto a quickly fading memory, then it was gone.

My small feet kicked off the remaining covers, and I leaped out of bed, just as Mom yelled, "Danneeeey—time to get up, sweetheart." It was February 22, 1952—my sixth birthday. I let my pajamas fall to the floor and kicked them under the bed, then ran downstairs in my Lone Ranger underwear. In a few hours my friends would be arriving with presents, and we'd have cake and ice cream and lots of fun!

After all the party decorations were thrown out and everyone had gone, I played listlessly with my new toys. I was bored, I was tired, and my stomach hurt. I closed my eyes and floated off to sleep.

I saw each day pass like the next: school for a week, then the weekend, school, weekend, summer, fall, winter and spring.

The years passed, and before long, I was one of the top high school gymnasts in Los Angeles. In the gym, life was exciting; outside the gym, it was a general disappointment. My few moments of fun consisted of bouncing on the trampoline or cuddling in the back seat of my Valiant with Phyllis, my first curvy girlfriend.

One day coach Harold Frey called me from Berkeley, California, and offered me a scholarship to the University! I couldn't wait to head up the coast to a new life. Phyllis, however, didn't share my enthusiasm. We began arguing about my going away, and we finally broke up. I felt bad but was consoled by my college plans. Soon, I was sure, life was really going to begin!

The college years raced by, filled with gymnastics victories, but very few other high points. In my senior year, just before the Olympic gymnastics trials, I married Susie. We stayed in Berkeley so I could train with the team; I was so busy I didn't have much time or energy for my new wife.

The final trials were held at UCLA. When the scores were tallied, I was ecstatic—I'd made the team! But my performances at the Olympiad didn't live up to my expectations. I returned home and slipped into relative anonymity.

My newborn son arrived, and I began to feel a growing responsibility and pressure. I found a job selling life insurance, which took up most of my days and nights. I never seemed to have time for my family. Within a year Susie and I were separated; eventually she got a divorce. A fresh start, I reflected sadly.

One day I looked in the mirror and realized that forty years had passed; I was old. Where had my life gone? With the help of my psychiatrist I had overcome my drinking problem; and I'd had money, houses, and women. But I had no one now. I was lonely.

I lay in bed late at night and wondered where my son was—it had been years since I'd seen him. I wondered about Susie and about my friends from the good old days.

I now passed the days in my favorite rocking chair, sipping wine, watching TV, and thinking about old times. I watched children play in front of the house. It had been a good life, I supposed. I'd gotten everything I'd gone after, so why wasn't I happy?

One day, one of the children playing on the lawn came up to the porch. A friendly little boy, smiling, he asked me how old I was.

"I'm two hundred years old," I said.

He giggled, said, "No you're not," and put his hands on his

hips. I laughed, too, which touched off one of my coughing spells, and Mary, my pretty, capable young nurse, had to ask him to go.

After she had helped me regain my breath, I gasped, "Mary, will you let me be alone for a while?"

"Of course, Mr. Millman." I didn't watch her walk away—that was one of life's pleasures that had died long ago.

I sat alone. I had been alone my whole life, it seemed. I lay back on my rocker and breathed. My last pleasure. And soon that, too, would be gone. I cried soundlessly and bitterly. "God damn it!" I thought. "Why did my marriage have to fail? How could I have done things differently? How could I really have lived?"

Suddenly I felt a terrible, nagging fear, the worst of my life. Was it possible that I had missed something very important—something that would have made a real difference? "No, impossible," I assured myself. I cited all my achievements aloud. The fear persisted.

I stood up slowly, looked down at the town from the porch of my hilltop house, and wondered: Where had life gone? What was it for? Was everyone . . . "Oh, my heart, it's—ahh, my arm, the pain!" I tried to call out, but couldn't breathe.

My knuckles grew white as I clutched the railing, trembling. Then my body turned to ice, and my heart to stone. I fell back into the chair; my head dropped forward.

The pain left abruptly, and there were lights I'd never seen before and sounds I'd never heard. Visions floated by.

"Is that you, Susie?" said a distant voice in my mind. Finally, all sight and sound became a point of light, then vanished.

I had found the only peace I'd ever known.

I heard a warrior's laugh. I sat up with a shock, the years pouring back into me. I was in my own bed, in my apartment, in Berkeley, California. I was still in college, and my digital clock showed 6:25 P.M. I'd slept through classes and workout!

I leaped out of bed and looked in the mirror, touching my still-youthful face, shivering with relief. It had all been a dream—a lifetime in a single dream, Soc's "little surprise."

I sat in my apartment and stared out the window, troubled. My dream had been exceptionally vivid. In fact, the past had been entirely accurate, even down to details I'd long forgotten. Socrates had told me that these journeys were real. Had this one predicted my future, too?

I hurried to the station at 9:50 P.M. and met Socrates as he arrived. As soon as he stepped inside and the day-shift attendant left, I asked, "All right, Soc. What happened?"

"You know better than I. It was your life, not mine, thank God."

"Socrates, I'm pleading with you"—I held out my hands to him. "Is that what my life is going to be like? Because if it is, I see no point in living it."

He spoke very slowly and softly, as he did when he had something he wanted me to pay particular attention to. "Just as there are different interpretations of the past and many ways to change the present, there are any number of possible futures. What you dreamed was a highly probable future—the one you were heading for had you not met me."

"You mean that if I had decided to pass by the gas station that night, that dream would have been my future?"

"Very possibly. And it still may be. But you can make choices and change your present circumstances. You can alter your future."

Socrates made us some tea, and set my mug down softly next to me. His movements were graceful, deliberate.

"Soc," I said, "I don't know what to make of it. My life these past months has been like an improbable novel, you know what I mean? Sometimes I wish I could go back to a normal life. This secret life here with you, these dreams and journeys; it's been hard on me."

Socrates took a deep breath; something of great import was coming. "Dan, I'm going to increase my demands on you as you become ready. I guarantee that you'll want to leave the life you know and choose alternatives that seem more attractive, more pleasant, more 'normal.' Right now, however, that would be a greater mistake than you can imagine."

"But I *do* see the value in what you're showing me."

"That may be so, but you still have an astonishing capacity to fool yourself. That is why you needed to dream your life. Remember it when you're tempted to run off and pursue your illusions."

"Don't worry about me, Socrates. I can handle it."

If I had known what was ahead, I would have kept my mouth shut.

2

The Web of Illusion

The March winds were calming. Colorful spring blossoms spread their fragrance through the air—even into the shower room, where I washed the sweat and soreness from my body after an energy-filled workout.

I dressed quickly and skipped down the rear steps of Harmon Gym to watch the sky over Edwards Field turn orange with the sun's final glow. The cool air refreshed me. Relaxed and at peace with the world, I ambled downtown to get a cheeseburger on the way to the U.C. Theater. Tonight, they were showing *The Great Escape,* an exciting film about a daring escape of British and American prisoners of war.

When the film was over I jogged up University Avenue toward campus, heading left up Shattuck, and arrived at the station soon after Socrates came on duty. It was a busy night, so I helped him until just after midnight. We went into the office and washed our hands, after which he surprised me by starting to fix a Chinese dinner—and beginning a new phase of his teaching.

It started when I told him about *The Great Escape.*

"Sounds like an exciting film," he said, unpacking the bag of fresh vegetables he'd brought in, "and an appropriate one, too."

"Oh? How's that?"

"You, too, Dan, need to escape. You're a prisoner of your own illusions—about yourself and about the world. To cut yourself free, you're going to need more courage and strength than any movie hero."

I felt so good that night I just couldn't take Soc seriously at all. "I don't feel like I'm in prison—except when you have me strapped to a chair."

He began washing vegetables. Over the sound of running water, he commented, "You don't see your prison because its bars are invisible. Part of my task is to point out your predicament, and I hope it is the most disillusioning experience of your life."

"Well thanks a lot, friend," I said, shocked at his ill-will.

"I don't believe you have understood me." He pointed a turnip at me, then sliced it into a bowl. "Disillusion is the greatest gift I can give you. However, because of your fondness for illusion, you consider the term negative. You commiserate with a friend by saying, 'Oh, what a disillusioning experience that must have been,' when you ought to be celebrating with him. The word dis-illusion is literally a 'freeing from illusion'. But you cling to your illusions."

"Facts," I challenged him.

"Facts," he said, tossing aside the tofu he'd been dicing. "Dan, you are suffering; you do not fundamentally enjoy your life. Your entertainments, your playful affairs, and even your gymnastics are temporary ways to distract you from your underlying sense of fear."

"Wait a minute, Soc." I was irritated. "Are you saying that gymnastics and sex and movies are bad?"

"Not inherently. But for you they're addictions, not enjoyments. You use them to distract you from what you know you should do: break free."

"Wait, Socrates. Those aren't facts."

"Yes, they are, and they are entirely verifiable, even though you don't see it yet. You Dan, in your conditioned quest for achievement and entertainment, avoid the fundamental source of your suffering."

"So that's what you think, huh?" I retorted sharply, unable to keep the antagonism out of my voice.

"That was not something you really wanted to hear, was it?"

"No, not particularly. It's an interesting theory, but I don't think it applies to me, that's all. How about giving me something a little more up beat?"

"Sure," he said, picking up his vegetables and resuming his chopping. "The truth is, Dan, that life is going wonderfully for you and that you're not really suffering at all. You don't need me and you're already a warrior. How does that sound?"

"Better!" I laughed, my mood instantly brightened. But I knew it wasn't true. "The truth probably lies somewhere in between, don't you think?"

Without taking his eyes off the vegetables, Socrates said, "I think that your 'in between' is hell, from my perspective."

Defensively I asked, "Is it just me who's the moron, or do you specialize in working with the spiritually handicapped?"

"You might say that," he smiled, pouring sesame oil into a wok and setting it on the hot plate to warm. "But nearly all of humanity shares your predicament."

"And what predicament is that?"

"I thought I had already explained that," he said patiently. "If you don't get what you want, you suffer; if you get what you don't want, you suffer; even when you get exactly what you want, you still suffer because you can't hold onto it forever. Your *mind* is your predicament. It wants to be free of change, free of pain, free of the obligations of life and death. But change is a law, and no amount of pretending will alter that reality."

"Socrates, you can really be depressing, you know that? I don't even think I'm hungry anymore. If life is nothing but suffering, then why bother at all?"

"Life is not suffering; it's just that you will suffer it, rather than enjoy it, until you let go of your mind's attachments and just go for the ride freely, no matter what happens."

Socrates dropped the vegetables into the sizzling wok, stirring. A delicious aroma filled the office. I relinquished all resentment. "I think I just got my appetite back." Socrates laughed as he divided the crisp vegetables onto two plates and set them on his old desk, which served as our dining table.

He ate in silence, taking small morsels with his chopsticks. I gobbled the vegetables in about thirty seconds; I guess I really was hungry. While Socrates finished his meal, I asked him, "So what are the positive uses of the mind?"

He looked up from his plate. "There aren't any." With that, he calmly returned to his meal.

"Aren't any! Socrates, that's really crazy. What about the creations of the mind? The books, libraries, arts? What about all the advances of our society that were generated by brilliant minds?"

He grinned, put down his chopsticks, and said, "There aren't any brilliant minds." Then he carried the plates to the sink.

"Socrates, stop making these irresponsible statements and explain yourself!"

He emerged from the bathroom, bearing aloft two shining plates. "I'd better redefine some terms for you. 'Mind' is one of those slippery terms like 'love'. The proper definition depends on your state of consciousness. Look at it this way: you have a brain that directs the body, stores information, and plays with that information. We refer to the brain's abstract processes as 'the intellect'. Nowhere have I mentioned mind. The brain and the mind are not the same. The brain is real; the mind isn't.

" 'Mind' is an illusory outgrowth of basic cerebral processes. It is like a tumor. It comprises all the random, uncontrolled thoughts that bubble into awareness from the subconscious. Consciousness is not mind; awareness is not mind; attention is not mind. Mind is an obstruction, an aggravation. It is a kind of evolutionary mistake in the human being, a primal weakness in the human experiment. I have no use for the mind."

I sat in silence, breathing slowly. I didn't exactly know what to say. Soon enough, though, words came.

"You certainly have a unique perspective, Soc. I'm not sure what you're talking about, but you sound really sincere."

He just smiled and shrugged.

"Soc," I continued, "Do I cut off my head to get rid of my mind?"

Smiling, he said, "That's one cure, but it has undesirable side effects. The brain can be a tool. It can recall phone numbers, solve math puzzles, or create poetry. In this way, it works for the rest of the body, like a tractor. But when you can't stop thinking of that math problem or phone number, or when troubling thoughts and memories arise without your intent, it's not your brain working, but your mind wandering. Then the mind controls you; then the tractor has run wild."

"I get it."

"To really get it, you must observe yourself to see what I mean. You have an angry thought bubble up and you *become* angry. It is the same with all your emotions. They're your knee-jerk responses to thoughts you can't control. Your thoughts are like wild monkeys stung by a scorpion."

"Socrates, I think . . ."

"You think too much!"

"I was just going to tell you that I'm really willing to change. That's one thing about me; I've always been open to change."

"That," said Socrates, "is one of your biggest illusions. You've been willing to change clothes, hairstyles, women, apartments, and jobs. You are all too willing to change anything except yourself, but change you will. Either I help you open your eyes or time will, but time is not always gentle," he said ominously. "Take your choice. But first realize that you're in prison—then we can plot your escape."

With that, he pulled up to his desk, picked up a pencil, and began checking off receipts, looking like a busy executive. I got the distinct feeling I'd been dismissed for the evening. I was glad class was out.

For the next couple of days which soon stretched to weeks, I was too busy, I told myself, to drop in and visit with Socrates. But his words rattled around in my mind; I became preoccupied with its contents.

I started keeping a small notebook in which I wrote down my thoughts during the day—except for workouts, when my thoughts gave way to action. In two days I had to buy a bigger notebook; in a week, that was full. I was astounded to see the bulk and general negativity of my thought processes.

This practice increased my awareness of my mental noise; I'd turned up the volume on my thoughts that had only been subconscious background Muzak before. I stopped writing, but still the thoughts blared. Maybe Soc could help me with the volume control. I decided to visit him that night.

I found him in the garage, steam-cleaning the engine of an old Chevrolet. I was just about to speak when the small, dark-haired figure of a young woman appeared in the doorway. Not even Soc had heard her enter, which was very unusual. He saw her just before I did and glided toward her with open arms. She danced toward him and they hugged, whirling around the room. For the next few minutes, they just looked into each other's eyes. Socrates would ask, "Yes?" and she'd answer, "Yes." It was pretty bizarre.

With nothing else to do, I stared at her each time she whirled by. She was a little over five feet tall, sturdy looking, yet with an aura of delicate fragility. Her long black hair was tied in a bun, pulled back from a clear, shining complexion. The most noticeable feature on her face was her eyes—large, dark eyes.

My gaping must have finally caught their attention.

Socrates said, "Dan, this is Joy."

Right away, I was attracted to her. Her eyes sparkled over a sweet, slightly mischievous smile.

"Is Joy your name or a description of your mood?" I asked, trying to be clever.

"Both," she replied. She looked at Socrates; he nodded. Then she embraced me. Her arms wrapped softly around my waist in a very tender hug. All at once I felt ten times more energized than ever before; I felt comforted, healed, rested, and totally lovestruck.

Joy looked at me with her large, luminescent eyes, and my own eyes glazed over. "The old Buddha's been putting you through the wringer, has he?" she said softly.

"Uh, I guess so." Wake up, Dan!

"Well, the squeeze is worth it. I know, he got to me first."

My mouth was too weak to ask for the details. Besides, she turned to Socrates and said, "I'm going now. Why don't we all meet here Saturday morning at ten and go up to Tilden Park for a picnic? I'll make lunch. It looks like good weather. OK?" She looked at Soc, then at me. I nodded dumbly as she soundlessly floated out the door.

I was no help to Socrates for the rest of the evening. In fact, the rest of the week was a total loss. Finally, when Saturday came, I walked shirtless to the bus station. I was looking forward to getting some spring tan, and also hoped to impress Joy with my muscular torso.

We took the bus up to the park and walked cross-country over crackling leaves scattered in thick piles among the pine, birch, and elm trees surrounding us. We unpacked the food on a grassy knoll in full view of the warm sun. I flopped down on the blanket, anxious to roast in the sun, and hoped Joy would join me.

Without warning, the wind picked up and clouds gathered. I couldn't believe it. It had begun to rain—first a drizzle, then a sudden downpour. I grabbed my shirt and put it on, cursing. Socrates only laughed.

"How can you think this is funny!" I chided him. "We're getting soaked, there's no bus for an hour, and the food's ruined. Joy made the food; I'm sure she doesn't think its so . . ." Joy was laughing too.

"I'm not laughing at the rain," Soc said. "I'm laughing at *you*." He roared, and rolled in the wet leaves. Joy started doing a dance routine to "Singin' in the Rain." Ginger Rogers and the Buddha—it was too much.

The rain ended as suddenly as it had begun. The sun broke through and soon our food and clothes were dry.

"I guess my rain dance worked." Joy took a bow.

As Joy sat behind my slumped form and gave my shoulders a rub, Socrates spoke. "It's time you began learning from your life experiences instead of complaining about them, or basking in them, Dan. Two very important lessons just offered themselves to you; they fell out of the sky, so to speak." I dug into the food, trying not to listen.

"First," he said, munching on some lettuce, "neither your disappointment nor your anger was caused by the rain."

My mouth was too full of potato salad for me to protest. Socrates continued, regally waving a carrot slice at me.

"The rain was a perfectly lawful display of nature. Your 'upset' at the ruined picnic and your 'happiness' when the sun reappeared were the product of your thoughts. They had nothing to do with the actual events. Haven't you been 'unhappy' at celebrations for example? It is obvious then, that your mind, not other people or your surroundings, is the source of your moods. That is the first lesson."

Swallowing his potato salad, Soc said, "The second lesson comes from observing how you became even more angry when you noticed that I wasn't upset in the least. You began to see yourself compared to a warrior—two warriors, if you please." He grinned at Joy. "You didn't like that, did you, Dan? It might have implied a change was necessary."

I sat morosely, absorbing what he'd said. I was hardly aware that he and Joy had darted off. Soon it was drizzling again.

Socrates and Joy came back to the blanket. Socrates started jumping up and down, mimicking my earlier behavior. "God damn rain!" he yelled. "There goes our picnic!" He stomped back and forth, then stopped in mid-stomp, and winked at me, grinning mischievously. Then he dove onto his belly in a puddle of wet leaves and pretended to be swimming. Joy started singing, or laughing—I couldn't tell which.

I just let go then and started rolling around with them in the wet leaves, wrestling with Joy. I particularly enjoyed that part, and I think she did too. We ran and danced wildly until it was time to leave. Joy was a playful puppy—yet with all the qualities of a proud, strong woman. I was sinking fast.

As the bus rocked and rolled its way down the curving hills overlooking the Bay, the sky turned pink and gold in the sunset. Socrates made a feeble attempt to summarize my lessons while I did my best to ignore him and snuggle with Joy in the back seat.

"Ahem—if I may have your attention," he said. He reached over, took my nose between two of his fingers, and turned my face toward him.

"Wad to you wad?" I asked. Joy was whispering in my ear as Socrates held onto my nose. "I'd rather listed to her thad to you," I said.

"She'll only lead you down the primrose path," he grinned, releasing my nose. "Even a young fool in the throes of love cannot fail to see how his mind creates both his disappointments and his—joys."

"An excellent choice of words," I said, losing myself in Joy's eyes.

As the bus rounded the bend we all sat quietly, watching San Francisco turn on her lights. The bus stopped at the bottom of the hill. Joy rose quickly and got off the bus, followed by Socrates. I started to follow, but he glanced back and said, "No." That was all. Joy looked at me through the open window.

"Joy, when will I see you again?"

"Perhaps soon. It depends," she said.

"Depends on what?" I said. "Joy, wait, don't go. Driver, let me off!" But the bus was pulling away from them. Joy and Soc had already disappeared into the darkness.

Sunday I sank into a deep depression over which I had no control. Monday in class I hardly heard a word my professor said. I was preoccupied during the workout, and my energy was drained. I'd not eaten since the picnic. I prepared myself for my Monday night gas station visit. If I found Joy there I'd make her leave with me—or I'd leave with her.

She was there, all right, laughing with Socrates when I entered the office. Feeling like a stranger, I wondered if they were laughing at me. I went in, took off my shoes, and sat.

"Well, Dan, are you any smarter than you were on Saturday?" Socrates said. Joy just smiled, but her smile hurt. "I wasn't sure you'd show up tonight, Dan, for fear I might say something you didn't want to hear." His words were like small hammers. I clenched my teeth.

"Try to relax, Dan," Joy said. I know she was trying to help, but I felt overwhelmed, criticized by both of them.

"Dan," Socrates continued, "If you remain blind to your weaknesses, you can't correct them—nor can you play up your strengths. It's just like gymnastics. Look at yourself!"

I could hardly speak. When I did, my voice quavered with tension, anger, and self-pity. "I *am* l—looking. . . ." I didn't want to act like this in front of her!

Blithely, Socrates went on. "I've already told you that your compulsive attention to the mind's moods and impulses is a basic error. If you persist, you'll remain yourself—and I can't imagine a worse fate!" Socrates laughed heartily at this, and Joy nodded approvingly.

"He can be stuffy, can't he?" she grinned at Socrates.

I sat very still and clenched my fists. Finally I could speak. "I don't think either of you is very funny." I kept my voice tightly controlled.

Socrates leaned back in his chair and, with cold-blooded cruelty, said, "You're angry, but doing a mediocre job of hiding it, jackass." ("Not in front of Joy!" I thought.) "Your anger," he continued, "is proof of your stubborn illusions. Why defend a self you don't even believe in? When are you going to grow up?"

"Listen, you crazy old bastard!" I screeched. "I'm fine! I've been coming here just for kicks. And I've seen what I needed to see. *Your* world seems full of suffering, not mine. I'm depressed all right, but only when I'm here with you!"

Neither Joy nor Socrates said a word. They just nodded their heads, looking sympathetic and compassionate. God damn their compassion! "You both think everything is so clear and so simple and so funny. I don't understand either one of you and I'm not sure I want to."

Blind with embarrassment, confusion, and pain, I lurched out the door, swearing to myself that I would forget him, forget her, and forget I had ever walked into that station late one starry night.

My indignation was a sham, and I knew it. What was worse, I knew they knew it. I'd blown it. I felt weak and foolish, like a small boy. I could bear losing face in front of Socrates, but not in front of her. And now I felt sure I'd lost her forever.

Running through the streets, I found myself going in the opposite direction from home. I ended up in a bar on University Avenue, near Grove Street. I got as drunk as I could, and when I finally made it to my apartment, I was grateful for unconsciousness.

I could never go back. I decided to try and take up the normal life I'd tossed aside months ago. The first thing was to catch up in my studies if I was to graduate. Susie loaned me her history notes, and I got psychology notes from one of my teammates. I stayed up late writing papers; I drowned myself in books. I had a lot to remember—and a lot to forget.

At the gym, I trained to exhaustion. At first, my coach and teammates were delighted to see this new energy. Rick and Sid, my two closest workout buddies, were amazed at my daring and joked about "Dan's death wish"; I threw any move, ready or not. They thought I was bursting with courage. I knew I wanted to get hurt—I wanted a physical reason for the ache inside.

After a while, Rick and Sid's jokes turned to concern. "Dan, did you notice you're getting circles under your eyes? When's the last time you shaved?" Rick asked.

Sid thought I was getting too lean. "Is something wrong, Dan?"

"That's my business," I snapped. "No, I mean, thanks, Sid, but I'm fine. Lean and mean, y'know?"

"Well, get some sleep now and then, anyway, or there'll be nothing left of you by summer."

"Yeah, sure thing." I didn't tell him that I wouldn't mind disappearing.

I turned what few ounces of fat I had left into gristle and muscle. I looked hard, like one of Michelangelo's statues. My skin shone pale, translucent, like marble.

I went to movies almost every night but couldn't get the image of Socrates sitting in the station, maybe with Joy, out of my mind. Sometimes I had a dark vision of them both sitting there, laughing at me; maybe I was their warrior's quarry.

I didn't spend time with Susie or any of the other women I knew. What sexual urges I had were spent in training, washed away by sweat. Besides, how could I bear staring into other eyes, now that I had looked into Joy's? One night, awakened by a knock, I heard Susie's timid voice outside. "Danny, are you in? Dan?" She slid a note under the door. I didn't even get up to look at the note.

My life became an ordeal. Other people's laughter hurt my ears. I imagined Socrates and Joy, cackling like warlock and witch, plotting against me. The movies I sat through had lost their colors; the food I ate tasted like paste. And one day in class, as Watkins was analyzing social influences of something or other, I stood up and heard myself yell, "Bullshit!" at the top of my lungs. Watkins tried to ignore me, but all eyes, about 500 pairs, were on me. An audience. I'd show them! "Bullshit!" I yelled. A few anonymous hands clapped, and there was a smattering of laughter and whispering.

Watkins, never one to lose his tweed-suited cool, suggested, "Would you care to explain that?"

I pushed my way out of my seat to the aisle and walked up to the stage, suddenly wishing I'd shaved or worn a clean shirt. I stood facing him. "What has any of this stuff got to do with happiness, with life?" More applause from the audience. I could tell he was sizing me up to see if I was dangerous—and decided I might be. Damn straight! I was getting more confident.

"Perhaps you have a point," he acquiesced softly. My God, I was being humored in front of 500 people! I wanted to explain to them how it was—I would teach them, make them all see. I turned to the class and started to tell them about my meeting a man in a gas station who had shown me that life was not what it seemed. I started on the tale of the king on the mountain, lonely amidst a town gone mad. At first, there was dead silence; then, a few people began laughing. What was wrong? I hadn't said anything funny. I went on with the story, but soon a wave of laughter spread through the auditorium. Were they all crazy, or was I?

Watkins whispered something to me, but I didn't hear. I went on pointlessly. He whispered again. "Son, I think they're laughing because your fly is open." Mortified, I glanced down and then out at the crowd. No! No, not again, not the fool again! not the jackass again! I began to cry, and the laughter died.

I ran out of the hall and through the campus until I could run no more. Two women walked by me—plastic robots, social drones. As they passed, they stared at me with distaste, then turned away.

I looked down at my dirty clothes which probably smelled. My hair was matted and uncombed; I hadn't shaved in days. I found myself in the student union without remembering how I got there, and slumped into a sticky, plastic-covered chair and fell asleep. I dreamt I was impaled on a wooden horse by a gleaming sword. The horse, affixed to a tilting carousel, whirled round and round while I desperately reached out for the ring. Melancholy music played off-key, and behind the music I heard a terrible laugh. I awoke, dizzy, and stumbled home.

I'd begun to drift through the routine of school like a phantom. My world was turning inside out and upside down. I had tried to rejoin the old ways I knew, to motivate myself in my studies and training, but nothing made sense anymore.

Meanwhile, professors rattled on and on about the Renaissance, the instincts of the rat, and Milton's middle years. I walked through Sproul Plaza each day amid campus demonstrations and walked through sit-ins as if in a dream; none of it meant anything to me. Student power gave me no comfort; drugs could give me no solace. So I drifted, a stranger in a strange land, caught between two worlds without a handhold on either.

Late one afternoon I sat in a redwood grove near the bottom of campus, waiting for the darkness, thinking about the best way to kill myself. I no longer belonged on this earth. Somehow I'd lost my shoes; I had on one sock, and my feet were brown with dried blood. I felt no pain, nothing.

I decided to see Socrates one last time. I shuffled toward the station and stopped across the street. He was finishing with a car as a lady and a little girl, about four years old, walked into the station. I don't think the woman knew Socrates; she could have been asking directions. Suddenly the little girl reached up to him. He lifted her and she threw her arms around his neck. The woman tried to pull the little girl away from Socrates, but she wouldn't let go. Socrates laughed and talked to her, setting her down gently. He knelt down and they hugged each other.

I became unaccountably sad then, and started to cry. My body shook with anguish. I turned, ran a few hundred yards and collapsed on the path. I was too weary to go home, to do anything; maybe that's what saved me.

I awoke in the infirmary. There was an I.V. needle in my arm. Someone had shaved me and cleaned me up. I felt rested, at least. I was released the next afternoon and called Cowell Health Center. "Dr. Baker, please." His secretary answered.

"My name is Dan Millman. I'd like to make an appointment with Dr. Baker as soon as possible."

"Yes, Mr. Millman," she said in the bright, professionally friendly voice of a psychiatrist's secretary. "The doctor has an opening a week from this Tuesday at 1 P.M.; would that be all right?"

"Isn't there anything sooner?"

"I'm afraid not. . . ."

"I'm going to kill myself before a week from this Tuesday, lady."

"Can you come in this afternoon?" Her voice was soothing. "Will 2 P.M. be all right?"

"Yes."

"Fine, see you then, Mr. Millman."

Doctor Baker was a tall, corpulent man with a slight nervous tic around his left eye. Suddenly, I didn't feel like talking to him at all. How would I begin? "Well, Herr Doktor. I have a teacher named Socrates who jumps up on rooftops—no, not off of them, that's what I'm planning to do. And, oh yes—he takes me on journeys to other places and times and I become the wind and I'm a little depressed and, yes school's fine and I'm a gymnastics star and I want to kill myself."

I stood. "Thank you for your time, doctor. I'm suddenly feeling great. I just wanted to see how the better half lived. It's been swell."

He started to speak, searching for the "right" thing to say, but I walked out, went home, and slept. For the time being, sleep seemed the easiest alternative.

That night, I dragged myself to the station. Joy was not there. Part of me suffered exquisite disappointment—I wanted so much to look into her eyes again, to hold her and be held—but part of me was relieved. It was one-on-one again—Soc and me.

When I sat down he said nothing of my absence, only, "You look tired and depressed." He said it without a trace of pity. My eyes filled with tears.

"Yes, I'm depressed. I came to say good-bye. I owe you that. I'm stuck halfway, and I can't stand it anymore. I don't want to live."

"You're wrong about two things, Dan." He came over and sat beside me on the couch. "First, you're not halfway yet, not by a long shot. But you are very close to the end of the tunnel. And the second thing," he said, reaching for my temple, "is that you're not going to kill yourself."

I glared at him. "Says who?" Then I realized we were no longer in the office, we were sitting in a cheap hotel room. There was no mistaking the musty smell, the thin, grey carpets, the two tiny beds, and the small, cracked, second-hand mirror.

"What's going on?" For the moment, the life was back in my voice. These journeys were always a shock to my system; I felt a rush of energy.

"A suicide attempt is in progress. Only you can stop it."

"I'm not trying to kill myself just yet," I said.

"Not you, fool. The young man outside the window, on the ledge. He's attending the University of Southern California. His name is Donald; he plays soccer and he's a philosophy major. He's in his senior year and he doesn't want to live. Go to it." Socrates gestured toward the window.

"Socrates, I can't."

"Then he'll die."

I looked out the window and saw, about fifteen stories below, groups of tiny people looking up from the streets of downtown Los Angeles. Peeking around the side of the window, I saw a light-haired young man in brown Levis and a T-shirt standing ten feet away on the narrow ledge, looking down. He was getting ready to jump.

Not wanting to startle him, I called his name softly. He didn't hear me; I called again. "Donald."

He jerked his head up and almost fell. "Don't come near me!" he warned. Then, "How do you know my name?"

"A friend of mine knows you, Donald. May I sit on the ledge here and talk to you? I won't come any closer."

"No, no more words." His face was lax, his monotone voice had already lost its life.

"Don—do people call you Don?"

"Yeah," he answered automatically.

"OK, Don, I guess it's your life. Anyway, 99 percent of the people in the world kill themselves."

"What the hell is that supposed to mean?" he said, an edge of life coming back into his voice. He started gripping the wall more tightly.

"Well, I'll tell you. The way most people *live* kills them—you know what I mean, Don? They may take thirty or forty years to kill themselves by smoking or drinking or stress or overeating, but they kill themselves just the same."

I edged a few feet closer. I had to choose my words carefully. "Don, my name is Dan. I wish we could spend more time talking; we might have some things in common. I'm an athlete too, up at U.C. Berkeley."

"Well . . ." he stopped and started to shake.

"Listen, Don, it's getting a little scary for me to sit here on this ledge. I'm going to stand up so I can hold on to something." I stood slowly. I was shaking a little myself. "Jesus," I thought. "What am I doing out on this ledge?"

I spoke softly, trying to find a bridge to him. "Don, I hear there's going to be a beautiful sunset tonight; the Santa Ana winds are blowing some storm clouds in. Are you sure you never want to see another sunset, or sunrise? Are you sure you never want to go hiking in the mountains again?"

"I've never been up to the mountains."

"You wouldn't believe it, Don. Everything is pure up there—the water, the air. You can smell pine needles everywhere. Maybe we could go hiking together. What do you think? Hell, if you want to kill yourself, you can always do it after you've at least seen the mountains."

There—I'd said all I could say. Now it was up to him. As I talked, I'd wanted more and more for him to live. I was only a few feet from him now.

"Stop!" he said. "I want to die . . . now."

I gave up. "All right," I said. "Then I'm going with you. I've already seen the goddamn mountains anyway."

He looked at me for the first time. "You're serious, aren't you?"

"Yeah, I'm serious. Are you going first, or am I?"

"But," he said, "Why do you want to die? It's crazy. You look so healthy—you must have a lot to live for."

"Look," I said. "I don't know what your troubles are, but my problems dwarf yours; you couldn't even begin to grasp them. I'm through talking."

I looked down. It would be so easy: just lean out and let gravity do the rest. And for once, I'd prove smug old Socrates wrong. I could exit laughing, yelling, "You were wrong, you old bastard!" all the way down, until I smashed my bones and crushed my organs and cut myself off from the coming sunsets forever.

"Wait!" It was Don, reaching out for me. I hesitated, then grasped his hand. As I looked into his eyes, Don's face began to change. It narrowed. His hair grew darker, his body grew smaller. I was standing there, looking at myself. Then the mirror image disappeared, and I was alone.

Startled, I took a step backward, and slipped. I fell, tumbling over and over. In my mind's eye, I saw the terrible hooded spectre waiting expectantly below. I heard Soc's voice, yelling from somewhere above, "Tenth floor, lingerie, bedspreads—eighth floor, housewares, cameras."

I was lying on the office couch, looking into Soc's gentle smile.

"Well?" he said. "Are you going to kill yourself?"

"No." But with that decision, the weight and responsibility of my life once again fell upon me. I told him how I felt. Socrates grasped my shoulders, and only said, "Stay with it, Dan."

Before I left that night, I asked him, "Where is Joy? I want to see her again."

"In good time. She'll come to you, later perhaps."

"But if I could only talk to her it would make things so much easier."

"Who ever told you it would be easy?"

"Socrates," I said, "I have to see her!"

"You don't have to do *anything* except to stop seeing the world from the viewpoint of your own personal cravings. Loosen up! When you lose your mind, you'll come to your senses. Until then, however, I want you to continue to observe, as much as possible, the debris of your mind."

"If I could just call her . . ."

"Get to it!" he said.

In the following weeks, the noise in my mind reigned supreme. Wild, random, stupid thoughts; guilts, anxieties, cravings—noise. Even in sleep, the deafening soundtrack of my dreams assaulted my ears. Socrates had been right all along. I *was* in prison.

It was a Tuesday night when I ran to the station at ten o'clock. Bursting into the office, I moaned, "Socrates! I'm going to go mad if I can't turn down the noise! My mind is wild—it's everything you told me!"

"Very good!" he said. "The first realization of a warrior."

"If this is progress, I want to regress."

"Dan, when you get on a wild horse that you believe is tame, what happens?"

"It throws you—or kicks your teeth in."

"Life has, in its own amusing way, kicked your teeth in many times."

I couldn't deny it.

"But when you *know* the horse is wild, you can deal with it appropriately."

"I think I understand, Socrates."

"Don't you mean you understand you think?" he smiled.

I left with instructions to let my "realization stabilize" for a few more days. I did my best. My awareness had grown these past few months, but I entered the office with the same questions: "Socrates, I've finally realized the extent of my mental noise; my horse is wild—how do I tame it? How do I turn down the noise? What can I do?"

He scratched his head. "Well, I guess you're just going to have to develop a very good sense of humor." He bellowed with laughter, then yawned and stretched—not the way most people usually do, with arms extended out to the side, but just like a cat. He rounded his back, and I heard his spine go crack-crack-crack-crack.

"Socrates, did you know that you looked just like a cat when you stretched?"

"I suppose I do," he replied nonchalantly. "It's a good practice to copy the positive traits of various animals, just as we might imitate positive qualities of some humans. I happen to admire the cat; it moves like a warrior.

"And as it happens, you have modelled yourself after the jackass. It's time you started to expand your repertoire, don't you think?"

"Yes, I suppose it is," I answered calmly. But I was angry. I excused myself and went home early, just after midnight, and slept for five hours before my alarm woke me and I doubled back toward the station.

At that moment, I made a secret resolution. No more playing victim, someone he could feel superior to. I was going to be the hunter; I was going to stalk him.

It was still an hour until dawn, when his shift would end. I hid in the bushes that lined the bottom edge of campus, near the station. I would follow him and somehow find Joy.

Peering through the foliage, I watched his every move. My thoughts quieted in the intensity of my vigil. My sole desire was to find out about his life away from the station—a subject about which he'd always been silent. Now I'd track down the answers myself.

Like an owl I stared at him. I saw as never before how smooth, how graceful he was. He washed windows without a wasted movement, slipped the nozzle into the gas tank like an artist.

Socrates went into the garage, probably to work on a car. I grew weary. The sky was already light when I roused myself from what must have been a few minutes of shut-eye. Oh, no—I'd missed him!

Then I saw him, busy with his last-minute duties. My heart constricted as he walked out of the station, crossed the street, and headed directly to where I sat—stiff, shivering, and achy, but well hidden. I just hoped he didn't feel like "beating around the bush" this morning.

I faded back into the foliage and calmed my breathing. A pair of sandals glided past, no more than four feet from my temporary lair. I could barely hear his soft footsteps. He followed a path that forked right.

Quickly but cautiously I scampered along the path like a squirrel. Socrates walked at a surprising clip. I barely kept up with his long strides and nearly lost him, when, far ahead, I saw a head of white hair entering Doe Library. "What," I thought, "could he be doing there of all places?" Tingling with excitement, I closed in.

Once past the large oak door, I cut past a group of earlybird students who turned and laughed, watching me. I ignored them as I tracked my prey down a long corridor. I saw him turn right and disappear. I sprinted over to where he had disappeared. There could be no mistake. He had entered this door. It was the men's room, and there was no other exit.

I didn't dare go in. I stationed myself in a nearby phone booth. Ten minutes passed; twenty minutes. Could I have missed him? My bladder was sending out emergency signals. I had to go in—not only find Socrates, but to make use of the facilities. And why not? This was my domain after all, not his. I would make him explain. Still, it would be awkward.

Entering the tiled bathroom, I saw no one at first. After finishing my own business, I started to search more carefully. There was no other door, so he still had to be there. One guy came out of a stall and saw me hunched over, looking under the stalls. He hurried out the door with wrinkled brow, shaking his head.

Back to the business at hand. I ducked my head for a quick look under the last stall. First I saw the backs of a pair of sandaled feet, then suddenly Soc's face dropped into view, upside down with a lopsided grin. He obviously had his back to the door and was bending forward, his head down between his knees.

I stumbled backwards in shock, completely disoriented. I had no good reason for my bizarre bathroom behavior.

Socrates swung the stall door open and flushed with a flourish, "Whoooeee, a man can get constipated when he's being stalked by a junior warrior!" As his laughter thundered through the tiled room, I reddened. He'd done it again! I could almost feel my ears lengthen as I was once again transformed into a jackass. My body churned with a mixture of shame and anger.

I could feel my face turn red. I glanced at the mirror, and there, tied neatly in my hair, was a perky yellow ribbon. Things began to make sense: the people's smiles and laughter as I'd walked through campus, the strange look I'd gotten from my fellow bathroom occupant. Socrates must have pinned it to my head while I dozed off in the bushes. Suddenly very tired, I turned and walked out the door.

Just before it swung shut, I heard Socrates say, not without a tone of sympathy in his voice, "That was just to remind you who is the teacher and who is the student."

That afternoon, I trained like the unleashed furies of hell. I talked to no one, and wisely, no one said a word to me. I quietly raged and swore I'd do whatever was necessary to make Socrates acknowledge me as a warrior.

One of my teammates stopped me on my way out and handed me an envelope. "Someone left this in the coach's office. It's addressed to you, Dan. A fan of yours?"

"I don't know. Thanks, Herb."

I stepped outside the door and ripped open the envelope. On an unlined piece of paper was written: "Anger is stronger than fear, stronger than sorrow. Your spirit is growing. You are ready for the sword—Socrates."

3

Cutting Free

The next morning, fog had rolled in off the Bay, covering the summer sun, chilling the air I awoke late, made some tea, and ate an apple.

I decided to relax before tackling my daily activities, so I pulled out my small TV and dumped some cookies into a bowl. Switching on a soap opera, I immersed myself in someone else's problems. As I watched, mesmerized by the drama, I reached for another cookie and discovered that the bowl was empty. Could I have eaten all those cookies?

Later that morning, I went running around Edwards Field. There I met Dwight, who worked up at the Lawrence Hall of Science in the Berkeley Hills. I had to ask his name a second time, because I "didn't catch it" the first time; another reminder of my feeble attention and wandering mind. After a few laps, Dwight remarked about the cloudless blue sky. I had been so lost in thought, I hadn't even noticed the sky. Then he headed for the hills—he was a marathon runner—and I returned home, thinking about my mind—a self-defeating activity if ever there was one.

I observed that in the gym I kept my attention focused precisely on every action, but when I stopped soaring, my thoughts would again obscure my perception.

That night I walked to the station early, hoping to greet Socrates at the beginning of his shift. By now I'd done my best to forget about yesterday's incident in the library and was ready to hear any antidote to my hyperactive mind that Soc cared to suggest.

I waited. Midnight arrived. Soon after, so did Socrates.

We had just settled into the office when I started to sneeze and had to blow my nose. I had a slight cold. Soc put the tea kettle on, and I began, as was my custom, with a question.

"Socrates, how do I stop my thoughts, my mind—other than by developing a sense of humor?"

"First you need to understand where your thoughts come from, how they arise in the first place. For example, you have a cold now; its physical symptoms tell you that your body needs to rebalance itself, to restore its proper relationship with sunlight, fresh air, simple food; to relax into its environment."

"What does all this have to do with my mind?"

"Everything. Random thoughts that disturb and distract you are symptoms, too, of 'dis-ease' with your environment. When the mind resists life, thoughts arise. When something happens to conflict with a belief, turmoil is set up. Thought is an unconscious reaction to life."

A car rolled into the station bearing a formally dressed older couple who sat like two ramrods in the front seat. "Come with me," Soc ordered. He removed his windbreaker and his cotton sportshirt, revealing a bare chest and shoulders with lean, well-defined muscles under smooth, translucent skin.

He walked up to the driver's side of the car and smiled at the shocked pair. "What can I do for you folks? Gasoline to fuel your spirits? Perhaps oil to smooth out the rough spots in your day? How about a new battery to put a little charge in your life?" He winked at them openly and stood his ground, smiling, as the car lurched forward and sped away from the station. He scratched his head. "Maybe they just remembered that they left the water running at home."

While we relaxed in the office, sipping our tea, Socrates explained his lesson. "You saw that man and woman resist what to them represented an abnormal situation. Conditioned by their values and fears, they haven't learned to cope with spontaneity. I could have been the highlight of their day!

"You see, Dan, when you resist what happens, your mind begins to race; the same thoughts that impinge upon you are actually created by you."

"And your mind works differently?"

"My mind is like a pond without ripples. Your mind, on the other hand, is full of waves because you feel separated from, and often threatened by, an unplanned, unwelcome occurence. Your mind is like a pond into which someone has just dropped a boulder!"

As I listened, I gazed into the depths of my tea cup, when I felt a touch just behind the ears. Suddenly my attention intensified; I stared deeper and deeper into the cup, down, down . . .

I was underwater, looking up. This was ridiculous! Had I fallen into my tea cup? I had fins and gills; very fishy. I whipped my tail and darted to the bottom, where it was silent and peaceful.

Suddenly, a huge rock crashed into the water's surface. Shock waves slapped me backwards. My fins whipped the water again and I took off, seeking shelter. I hid until everything quieted down again. As time passed, I became accustomed to the little stones that sometimes fell into the water, making ripples. The large plunks, however, still startled me.

In a world filled with sound and dryness again, I lay on the couch, looking up, wide-eyed, at Soc's smile.

"Socrates, that was incredible!"

"Please, not another fish story. I'm glad you had a nice swim. Now, may I continue?" He didn't wait for an answer.

"You were a very nervous fish, fleeing every large ripple. Later, you became used to the ripples but still had no insight into their cause. You can see," he continued, "that a magnificent leap of awareness is required for the fish to extend its vision beyond the water in which it is immersed to the source of the ripples.

"A similar leap of awareness will be required of you. When you understand the source clearly, you'll see that the ripples of your mind have nothing to do with you; you'll just watch them, without attachment, no longer compelled to overreact every time a pebble drops. You will be free of the world's turbulence as soon as you calm your thoughts. Remember—when you are troubled, let go of your thoughts and deal with your mind!"

"Socrates, how?"

"A not-so-bad question!" he exclaimed. "As you've learned from your physical training, leaps of gymnastics—or of awareness—don't happen all at once; they require time and practice. And the practice of insight into the source of your own ripples is meditation."

With that grand announcement, he excused himself and went to the bathroom. Now it was time to spring my surprise on him. I yelled from the couch, so he could hear me through the bathroom door. "I'm one step ahead of you, Socrates. I joined a meditation group a week ago. I thought I'd do something myself about this old mind of mine," I explained. "We sit together for half an hour each evening. I'm already starting to relax more and get some control over my thoughts. Have you noticed I've been calmer? Say, Soc, do you practice meditation? If not, I can show you what I've learn—"

The bathroom door blasted open and Socrates came straight at me, screaming a blood-curdling shriek, holding a gleaming samurai sword over his head! Before I could move, the sword slashed at me, cutting silently through the air, and stopped inches over my head. I looked up at the hovering sword, then at Socrates. He grinned at me.

"You sure know how to make an entrance. You scared the shit out of me!" I gasped.

The blade ascended slowly. Poised over my head, it seemed to capture and intensify all the light in the room. It shone in my eyes and made me squint. I decided to shut up.

But Socrates only knelt on the floor in front of me, gently placed the sword between us, closed his eyes, took a deep breath, and sat perfectly still. I watched him for a while, wondering if this "sleeping tiger" would waken and leap at me if I moved. Ten minutes passed, then twenty. I figured maybe he wanted me to meditate, too, so I closed my eyes and sat for half an hour. Opening my eyes, I watched him still sitting there like a Buddha. I started to fidget and got up quietly to get a drink of water. I was filling my mug when he put his hand on my shoulder. Water sloshed over my shoes as my hand jerked.

"Socrates, I wish you wouldn't sneak up on me like that. Couldn't you make some noise?"

He smiled, and spoke. "Silence is the warrior's art—and meditation is his sword. It is the central weapon you'll use to cut through your illusions. But understand this: the sword's usefulness depends upon the swordsman. You don't yet know how to use the weapon, so it can become a dangerous, deluding, or useless tool in your hands.

"Meditation may initially help you to relax. You put your 'sword' on display; you proudly show it to friends. The gleam of this sword distracts many meditators into further illusion until they ultimately abandon it to seek yet another 'inner alternative'.

"The warrior, on the other hand, uses the sword with skill and deep understanding. With it, he cuts the mind to ribbons, slashing through thoughts to reveal their lack of substance. Listen and learn:

Alexander the Great, marching with his armies through the desert, came upon two thick ropes tied in the massive, convoluted Gordian knot. No one had been able to untie it until the challenge was given to Alexander. Without a moment's hesitation he drew his sword and in one powerful blow he cut the knot in two. He was a warrior!

"That is how you must learn to attack the knots of your mind—with the sword of meditation. Until one day you transcend your need for any weapon at all."

Just then an old VW bus with a new coat of white paint and a rainbow painted on its side, chugged into the station. Inside sat six people, hard to tell apart. As we approached them, we could see that there were two women and four men, all dressed from head to toe in the same blue outfits. I recognized them as members of one of the many new spiritual groups in the Bay area. These particular people self-righteously avoided acknowledging our presence, as if our worldliness might contaminate them.

Socrates, of course, rose to the challenge, immediately affecting a combination limp and lisp persona. Scratching himself profusely, he was the perfect Quasimodo. "Hey, Jack," he said to the driver, who had the longest beard I'd ever seen, "Ya want gas, or what?"

"Yes, we want gas," the man said, his voice as smooth as salad oil.

Socrates leered at the two women in the back and, sticking his head in the window, he whispered loudly, "Hey do you *meditate?*" He said it as if he were referring to a solitary form of sexual release.

"Yes, we do," said the driver, cosmic superiority oozing from his voice. "Now, will you put gas in our vehicle?"

Soc waved at me to fill the tank, while he proceeded to push every button the driver had. "Hey, ya know, you look kinda like a girl in that dress, guy—don't get me wrong, it's real pretty. And why don't you shave; what are ya hiding under that fuzz?"

While I cringed, he went from bad to even worse. "Hey," he said to one of the women, "Is this guy your boyfriend? Tell me," he said to the other man in the front seat, "Do you ever do it, or do you save it up like I read in the *National Enquirer?"*

That about did it. By the time Socrates counted out their change—with agonizing slowness (he kept losing count and starting over)—I was ready to burst out laughing and the people in the van were trembling with anger. The driver grabbed his change and drove out of the station in a very unsaintly way. As their van pulled out, Socrates yelled, "Meditation is good for you. Keep practicing!"

We'd no sooner returned to the office when a big Chevy pulled into the station. The clang of the business bell was followed by an impatient "ooga-ooga" from a musical horn. I went out with Socrates to help.

Behind the wheel sat a forty-year-old "teenager" dressed in flashy satin clothes, topped with a large feathered safari hat. He was extremely jittery and kept tapping the steering wheel. Next to him, batting false eyelashes in the rearview mirror as she powdered her nose, sat a woman of indeterminate age.

For some reason, they offended me. They looked asinine. I wanted to say, "Why don't you act your age?" but I watched and waited.

"Hey man, ya got a cigarette machine here?" the hyperactive driver said.

Socrates stopped what he had been doing and with a warm smile said, "No sir, but there's an all-night market down the road." Then he returned to checking the oil, giving it his full attention. He returned the change as if he were serving tea to the emperor.

After the car sped away we remained at the pump, smelling the night air. "You treated these people so courteously but were positively obnoxious to our blue-robed seekers, who were obviously on a higher evolutionary level. What's the story?"

For once, he gave me a simple, direct answer. "The only levels that should concern you are mine—and yours," he said with a grin. "These people needed kindness. The spiritual seekers needed something else to reflect upon."

"What do I need?" I blurted.

"More practice," he answered quickly. "Your week-long meditation practice alone didn't help you stay calm when I ran at you with the sword, nor did it help our blue-robed friends when I poked a little fun at them.

"Let me put it this way: A forward roll is not the whole of gymnastics. A meditation technique is not the whole of the warrior's way. If you fail to understand the complete picture, you might be deluded, practicing only forward rolls—or only meditation—your whole life, thus reaping only fragmented benefits of training.

"What you need to stay on the right track then, is a special map that covers the entire terrain you will explore. Then you'll realize the uses—and limits—of meditation. And I ask you, where can you get a good map?"

"At a service station, of course!"

"Well then, sir, step into the office and I'll give you just the map you need." We entered laughing, through the garage door. I plopped onto the couch; Socrates settled without a sound between the massive arm rests of his plush chair.

He stared at me for a full minute. "Uh-oh," I said nervously under my breath. "Something's up."

"The problem is," he sighed at last, "that I can't describe the terrain for you, at least not in so many . . . words." He rose and walked towards me with that shine in his eye that told me to pack my suitcases—I was going on a trip.

For an instant, from a vantage point somewhere in space, I felt myself expanding at the speed of light, ballooning, exploding to the outermost limits of existence until I *was* the universe. Nothing separate remained. I had become everything. I was Consciousness, recognizing itself; I was the pure light that physicists equate with all matter, and poets define as love. I was one, and I was all, outshining all the worlds. In that moment, the eternal, the unknowable had been revealed to me as an indescribable certainty.

In a flash, I was back in my mortal form, floating among the stars. I saw a prism shaped like a human heart, which dwarfed every galaxy. It diffracted the light of consciousness into an explosion of radiant colors, sparkling splinters of every rainbow hue, spreading throughout the cosmos.

My own body became a radiant prism, throwing splinters of multi-colored light everywhere. And it came to me that the highest purpose of the human body is to become a clear channel for this light—so that its brightness can dissolve all obstructions, all knots, all resistance.

I felt the light diffracted across the systems of my own body. Then I knew that awareness is how the human being experiences the light of consciousness.

I learned the meaning of attention—it is the intentional channeling of awareness. I felt my body again, as a hollow vessel. I looked at my legs; they filled with warm, radiant light, disappearing into brightness. I looked at my arms, with the same result. I focused attention on every part of the body, until I became wholly light once again. Finally, I realized the process of real meditation—to expand awareness, to direct attention, to ultimately surrender to the Light of Consciousness.

A light flickered in darkness. I awoke to Socrates shining a flashlight back and forth across my eyes. "Power failure," he said, baring his teeth like a Halloween pumpkin as he held the light up to his face. "Well, is it all a bit clearer now?" he asked, as if I had just learned how a light bulb worked, rather than seen the soul of the universe. I could hardly speak.

"Socrates, I owe you a debt that I can never repay. I understand everything now, and I know what I must do. I don't suppose I'll be needing to see you again." I was sad that I had graduated. I would miss him.

He looked at me, a startled expression on his face, then started to laugh more uproariously than I'd ever seen before. He shook all over; tears ran down his cheeks. Finally he calmed and explained his laughter. "You haven't quite graduated yet, junior; your work is hardly started. Look at yourself. You are fundamentally the same as when you stumbled in here months ago. What you saw was only a vision, not a conclusive experience. It will fade into memory, but even so, it will serve as a basis for your practice. Now relax and stop acting so serious!"

He sat back, as mischievous and wise as ever. "You see," he said lightly, "these little journeys do save me some difficult explanations I must go through to enlighten you." Just then, the lights flashed on, and we laughed.

He reached into his small refrigerator next to the water cooler and brought out some oranges, which he started to squeeze into orange juice as he continued. "If you must know, you're doing me a service, too. I'm also 'stuck' in a place in time and space, and owe a kind of debt myself. A lot of me is tied up with your progress. In order to teach you," he said, tossing the orange rinds back over his shoulder into the wastebasket (making a perfect shot every time), "I literally had to put a part of me in you. Quite an investment, I assure you. So it's a team effort all the way."

He finished the juice and handed me a small glassful. "A toast then," I said, "to a successful partnership."

"Done," he smiled.

"Tell me more about this debt. To whom do you owe it?"

"Let's say that it's part of the House Rules."

"That's silly, that's no answer at all."

"Silly it may be, but still I must abide by a particular set of rules in my business." He took out a small card. It looked normal enough, until I noticed a faint glow. In embossed letters, it said,

Warrior, Inc.
Socrates, Prop.
Specializing in:
Paradox, Humor,
and Change

"Keep it safe. It may come in handy. When you need me—when you really need me—just hold the card in both hands and call. I'll be there, one way or the other."

I put the card carefully in my wallet. "I'll keep it safe, Socrates. You can count on it. Uh, by the way, you wouldn't have one of those cards with Joy's address on it, would you?"

He ignored me.

We were silent then, as Socrates began to prepare one of his crisp salads. Then I thought of a question.

"Socrates, how do I do it? How do I open myself to this light of awareness?"

"Well," he asked, answering a question with a question, "what do you do when you want to see?"

I laughed. "I look! Oh, you mean meditation, don't you?"

"Yep!" he answered. "And here's the core of it," he said as he finished cutting the vegetables. "There are two simultaneous processes: One is *insight*—the willing of attention, the channeling of awareness to focus precisely on what you want to see. The other process is *surrender*—letting go of all arising thoughts. That is real meditation; that is how you cut free of the mind."

"And, I just happen to have a story along these lines:

A student of meditation was sitting in deep silence with a small group of practitioners. Terrified by a vision of blood, death, and demons, he got up, walked to the teacher, and whispered, '*Roshi,* I've just had horrible visions!'

'Let it go,' said his teacher.

A few days later, he was enjoying some fantastic erotic fantasies, insights into the meaning of life, with angels and cosmic decoration—the works.

'Let it go,' said his teacher, coming up behind him with a stick and giving him a whack."

I laughed at the story and said, You know Soc, I've been thinking . . ." Socrates gave me a whack on the head with a carrot, saying, "Let it go!"

We ate. I stabbed at my vegetables with a fork; he picked up each small bite with wooden chopsticks, breathing quietly as he chewed. He never picked up another bite until he was completely done with the first, as if each bite was a small meal in itself. I kind of admired the way he ate as I chomped merrily away. I finished first, sat back, and announced, "I guess I'm ready to have a go at real meditation."

"Ah, yes." He put down his chopsticks. " 'Conquering the mind.' If only you were interested."

"I am interested! I want self-awareness. That's why I'm here."

"You want self-image, not self-awareness. You're here because you have no better alternatives."

"But I do want to get rid of my noisy mind," I protested.

"That is your greatest illusion of all, Dan. You're like the man who refuses to wear glasses, insisting 'they aren't printing the newspapers clearly anymore.' "

"Wrong," I said, shaking my head back and forth.

"I don't really expect you to see the truth of it yet, but you need to hear it."

"What are you getting at?" I asked impatiently, my attention drifting outside.

"Here is the bottom line," Socrates said, in a voice that firmly held my attention. "You identify with your petty, annoying, basically troubling beliefs and thoughts; you believe that you are your thoughts."

"Nonsense!"

"Your stubborn illusions are a sinking ship, junior. I recommend that you let them go while there's still time."

I stifled my rising temper. "How can *you* know how I 'identify' with my mind?"

"OK," he sighed. "I'll prove it to you: what do you mean when you make the statement, 'I'm going to my house'? Don't you naturally assume that you are separate from the house that you are going to?"

"Well of course! This is stupid."

Ignoring me, he asked, "What do you mean when you say, 'My body is sore today'? Who is the 'I' who is separate from the body and speaks of it as a possession?"

I had to laugh. "Semantics, Socrates. You have to say something."

"True enough, but the conventions of language reveal the ways we see the world. You do in fact, act as if you were a 'mind' or a subtle something inside the body."

"Why would I possibly want to do that?"

"Because your greatest fear is death and your deepest craving is survival. You want Forever, you desire Eternity. In your deluded belief that you are this 'mind' or 'spirit' or 'soul', you find the escape clause in your contract with mortality. Perhaps as 'mind' you can wing free of the body when it dies, hmm?"

"It's a thought," I grinned.

"That's exactly what it is, Dan, a thought, no more real than the shadow of a shadow. Here is the truth: consciousness is not *in* the body; rather, the body is *in* consciousness. And you *are* that consciousness; not the phantom mind which troubles you so. You are the body, but you are everything else too. That is what your vision revealed to you. Only the mind is deluded, threatened by change. So if you will just relax mindless into the body, you'll be happy and content and free, sensing no separation. Immortality is already yours, but not in the way you imagine or hope for. You have been immortal since before you were born and will be long after the body dissolves. The body is consciousness; it is immortal. It only changes. The mind—your own personal beliefs and history and identity—is the only mortal; so who needs it?"

Socrates signed off by relaxing into his chair.

"Socrates," I said, "I'm not sure all of that sank in."

"Of course not!" he laughed. "In any case, the words mean little unless you realize the truth of it yourself. Then you'll be free at last and will fall helplessly into eternity."

"That sounds pretty good."

He laughed. "Yes, I'd say it is 'pretty good'. But right now, I'm only laying the groundwork for what comes next."

"Socrates, if I'm not my thoughts, what am I?"

He looked at me as if he'd just finished explaining that one and one are two and I'd then asked, "Yes, but what are one and one?" He reached over to the refrigerator, grasped an onion, and shoved it into my hand. "Peel it, layer by layer," he demanded. I started peeling. "What do you find?"

"Another layer."

"Continue."

I peeled off a few more layers. "Just more layers, Soc."

"Continue peeling until there are no more layers. What do you find?"

"There's nothing left."

"There's something left, all right."

"What's that?"

"The universe. Consider that as you walk home."

I looked out the window; it was almost dawn.

I came in the next night after a mediocre meditation session, still brimming with thoughts. There wasn't much early evening business, so we sat back, sipping peppermint tea, and I told him about my lackluster meditation practice.

"Yes, your attention is still diffused. Let me tell you a story:

A Zen student asked his roshi the most important element of Zen.

The roshi replied, "Attention."

"Yes, thank you," the student replied. "But can you tell me the second most important element?" And the roshi replied, "Attention."

Puzzled, I looked up at Soc, waiting for more. "That's all, folks," he said.

I stood up to get some water, and Socrates asked, "Are you paying close attention to your standing?"

"Uh, yes," I answered, not at all sure that I was. I walked over to the dispenser.

"Are you paying close attention to your walking?" he asked.

"Yes, I am," I answered, starting to catch onto the game.

"Are you paying close attention to how you talk?"

"Well, I guess so," I said, listening to my voice. I was getting flustered.

"Are you paying attention to how you think?" he asked.

"Socrates, give me a break—I'm doing the best I can!"

He leaned toward me. "Your best is not good enough! The intensity of your attention must *burn*. Aimlessly rolling around a gym mat doesn't develop a champion; sitting with your eyes closed and letting your attention roam doesn't train your awareness. The intensity of your practice brings proportionate benefits. Here is a story:

In a monastery, I sat day after day, struggling with a *koan*, a riddle my teacher had given me in order to spur the mind to see its true nature. I couldn't solve it. Each time I went to the roshi, I had nothing to offer him. I was a slow student and was becoming discouraged. He told me to continue working on my koan for one more month. "Surely then," he encouraged me, "you will solve it."

A month passed, and I tried my best. The koan remained a mystery.

"Stay with it one more week, with fire in your heart!" he told me. Day and night the koan burned, but still I could not see through it.

My roshi told me, "One more day, with all your spirit." At the end of the day I was exhausted. I told him, "Master, it's no use—a month, a week, a day—I cannot pierce the riddle." My master looked at me a long time. "Meditate for one more hour," he said. "If you have not solved the koan by then, you will have to kill yourself."

"Why should a warrior sit around meditating? I thought this was a way of action."

"Meditation is the action of inaction; yet you are quite correct that the warrior's way is more dynamic. Ultimately, you will learn to meditate your every action. Yet at the beginning, sitting meditation serves as a ceremony, a special time set aside to increase the intensity of practice. You must master the ritual before you can expand it properly into daily life.

"As a teacher I will use every method and artifice at my command to get you interested and to help you persevere with the work ahead. If I had just walked up to you and told you the secret of happiness, you would not have even heard me. You needed a guy to fascinate you, do a soft shoe, or jump up on rooftops before you could get a little interested.

"Well, I'm willing to play games, for a little while at least, but there comes a time when every warrior must walk the path alone. For now, I'll do what is necessary to keep you here, learning this way."

I felt manipulated and angry. "So I can grow old sitting in this gas station like you, waiting to pounce on innocent students?" I regretted my remark as soon as it slipped out.

Socrates, unfazed, smiled and spoke softly. "Don't mistake this place, or your teacher, Dan. Things and people are not always as they seem. I am defined by the universe, not by this station. As to why you should stay, what you can gain, isn't it obvious? I am completely happy, you see. Are you?"

A car pulled in, clouds of steam surrounding its radiator. "Come," Soc said. "This car is suffering and we may have to shoot it and put it out of its misery." We both went out to the stricken car, whose radiator was boiling and whose owner was in a foul mood, fuming.

"What took you so long? I can't wait around here all night, damn it!"

Socrates looked at him with nothing less than loving compassion. "Let's see if we can't help you, sir, and make this only a minor inconvenience." He had the man drive into the garage where he put a pressure cap on the radiator and found the leak. Within a few minutes he'd welded the hole shut but told the man that he would still need a new radiator in the near future. "Everything dies and changes, even radiators," he winked at me.

As the man drove away, the truth of Soc's words sank in. He really was completely happy! Nothing seemed to affect his happy mood. In all the time I'd known him, he had acted angry, sad, gentle, tough, humorous, and even concerned. But always, happiness had twinkled in his eyes, even when tears welled up in them.

I thought of Socrates as I walked home, my shadow growing and shrinking as I passed under each street light. I kicked a stone into the darkness as I neared my apartment, walking softly down the driveway to the back, where my little converted garage waited under the branches of a walnut tree. It was only a few hours away from dawn.

I lay in bed but couldn't sleep. I wondered whether I could discover his secret of happiness. It seemed even more important right now than jumping up onto rooftops.

Then I remembered the card he had given me. Quickly, I got out of bed and turned on the light. Reaching into my wallet, I extracted the card. My heart started to beat rapidly. Socrates had said that if I ever really needed him to hold the card in both hands and just call. Well, I was going to test him.

I stood for a moment, trembling; my knees were starting to shake. I took the softly glowing card in both hands and called, "Socrates, come in Socrates. Dan calling." I felt like a complete fool, standing there at 4:55 A.M., holding a glowing card, talking to the air. Nothing happened. I tossed it carelessly onto the dresser in disgust. That's when the light went out.

"What!" I yelled as I spun around trying to sense if he was there. In classic movie style, I took a step backward, tripped over my chair, bounced off the edge of the bed, and sprawled to the floor.

The light went back on. If someone had been within earshot, that person might have assumed I was a student having trouble with ancient Greek studies. Why else would I be yelling at 5:02 in the morning, "Goddamn it, Socrates!"

I'd never know whether the blackout had been a coincidence or not. Socrates had only said he'd come; he hadn't said how. I sheepishly picked up the card to put it back into my wallet, when I noticed it had changed. Underneath the last lines, "Paradox, Humor, and Change," appeared two words in bold print: "Emergencies Only!"

Laughing, I fell asleep in no time at all.

Summer workouts had begun. It was good to see old familiar faces. Herb was growing a beard; Rick and Sid were cultivating their dark summer tans and looked slimmer and stronger than ever.

I wanted so much to share my life and the lessons I'd been learning with my teammates, but I still didn't know where to begin. Then I remembered Soc's business card. Before warm-up began, I called Rick over.

"Hey, I want to show you something." Once he saw that glowing card and Soc's "specialties," I knew he'd want to know more about it; maybe they all would.

After a dramatic pause, I pulled the card and flipped it over to him. "Take a look at that; pretty strange, huh? That guy is a teacher of mine."

Rick looked down at the card, turned it over, then looked back up at me, his face as blank as the card. "Is this a joke? I don't get it, Dan."

I looked at the card, then turned it over. "Uh," I grunted, stuffing the piece of paper back into my wallet, "just a mistake, Rick. Let's warm up." I sighed inwardly. This was bound to strengthen my reputation as the team eccentric.

Socrates, I thought, what a cheap trick—disappearing ink!

That night, I had the card in my hand when I walked into the office. I threw it down on the desk. "I wish you'd quit playing practical jokes, Socrates. I'm tired of looking like an idiot."

He looked at me sympathetically. "Oh? Have you been looking like an idiot again?"

"Socrates, come on. I'm asking you—will you please quit it?"

"Quit what?"

"The gag with the disappear—" Out of the corner of my eye I caught a soft glow from the vicinity of the desk:

Warrior, Inc.
Socrates, Prop.
Specializing in:
Paradox, Humor,
and Change.
Emergencies Only!

"I don't get it," I murmured. "Does this card change?"

"Everything changes," he replied.

"Yes, I know, but does it disappear and appear again?"

"Everything disappears and appears again."

"Socrates, when I showed it to Rick, there was nothing there."

"It's the House Rules," he shrugged, smiling.

"You're not being particularly helpful; I want to know how . . ."

"Let it go," he said. "Let it go."

Summer passed quickly, with intensive workouts and late nights with Socrates. We spent half the time practicing meditation and the other half working in the garage or just relaxing over tea. At times like these I would ask about Joy; I longed to see her again. Socrates would tell me nothing.

With vacation's end imminent, my mind drifted back to the coming classes. I had decided to fly down to L.A. for a week's visit with my parents. I would put my Valiant in garage storage here, and buy a motorcycle while down in L.A., then drive it up the coast.

I was walking down Telegraph Avenue to do some shopping and had just come out of the pharmacy with toothpaste when a scrawny teenager came up to me, so close I could smell stale alcohol and sweat. "Spare some change, can't you?" he asked, not looking at me.

"No, sorry," I said, not feeling sorry at all. As I walked away, I thought "Get a job." Then vague guilts came into my mind; I'd said no to a penniless beggar. Angry thoughts arose. "He shouldn't walk up to people like that!"

I was halfway down the block before I realized all the mental noise I had tuned into, and the tension it was causing—just because some guy had asked me for money and I'd said no. In that instant I let it go. Feeling lighter, I took a deep breath, shook off the tension, and turned my attention to the beautiful day.

That night at the station I told Socrates my news.

"Soc, I'm flying down to L.A. in a few days to visit my folks. I'm going to buy a motorcycle while I'm down there. And I just learned this afternoon that the United States Gymnastics Federation is flying Sid and me to Lubiana, Yugoslavia, to watch the World Gymnastics Championships. They think we're both potential Olympians and want to give us some exposure. How abut that?"

To my surprise, Socrates just frowned, saying, "What will be, will be."

I chose to ignore this and started out the door. "Well, bye for now, Soc. See you in a few weeks."

"I'll see you in a few hours," he responded. "Meet me at Ludwig's fountain, at noon."

"OK!" I answered, wondering what was up. Then I said good night.

I got six hours' sleep and ran to the fountain just outside the Student Union. Ludwig's fountain was named after a dog who used to frequent the spot. Several other dogs were romping and splashing there, cooling off from the August heat; a few little kids were wading in the shallow water.

Just as the Campanile, Berkeley's famous bell tower, began to chime the noon hour, I saw Soc's shadow at my feet.

I was still a little sleepy.

"Let's walk," he said. We strolled up through campus, past Sproul Hall, beyond the Optometry School and Cowell Hospital, up beyond the football stadium, into the hills of Strawberry Canyon.

Finally, he spoke.

"For you, Dan, a conscious process of transformation has begun. It cannot be reversed; there's no going back. To try and do so would end in madness. You can only go forward now; you're committed."

"You mean like in an institution?" I tried to joke.

He grinned. "Perhaps there are similarities."

We walked silently then, in the shade of the overgrown bushes along the running trail.

"No one can help you beyond a certain point, Dan. I'll be guiding you for a while, but then even I must stand back, and you will be alone. You'll be tested severely before you're done. You'll have to develop great inner strength. I only hope it comes in time."

The mild Bay breeze had stopped and the air was hot; still, I felt a chill. Shivering in the heat, I watched a lizard scurrying through the underbrush. Soc's last few words had just registered. I glanced over at him.

He was gone.

Frightened, not knowing why, I hurried down the path. I didn't know it then, but my preparations had ended. My training was about to begin. And it was to begin with an ordeal I almost didn't survive.

BOOK TWO

THE WARRIOR'S TRAINING

4

The Sword is Sharpened

After storing the Valiant in a rented garage, I boarded the "F" bus to San Francisco, connecting with Airport Transit, which got caught in a traffic jam; it looked as if I'd be late for my flight. Anxious thoughts began to arise; I felt my belly tense—then, as soon as I noticed it, I let it all go as I'd been trained. I relaxed and enjoyed the scenery along Bayshore Freeway, reflecting on my growing mastery over stressful thoughts which had habitually plagued me in the past. And as it turned out, I caught my plane with seconds to spare.

Dad, an older version of me with thinning hair, wearing a bright blue sport shirt over his muscular chest, met me at the airport with a strong handshake and warm smile. Mom's face crinkled sweetly as she greeted me at the door of their apartment with hugs and kisses and news about my sister and nieces and nephews.

That evening I was treated to one of Mom's latest piano pieces—Bach, I think it was. The next morning at dawn, Dad and I were out on the golf course. All the while, I'd been tempted to tell them about my adventures with Socrates, but thought better of silence. Perhaps I'd explain it all in writing someday. It was good to visit home, but home seemed so long ago and far away.

When Dad and I were sitting in the sauna at Jack LaLanne's Health Spa after our golf game, he said, "Danny, college life must agree with you. You're different—more relaxed, nicer to be around—not that you weren't nice to be around before . . ." He was searching for the right words, but I understood.

I smiled. If he only knew.

I spent most of my time in L.A. looking for a motorcycle and finally found a 500 cc Triumph. It took me a few days to get comfortable with it and I almost fell twice, each time thinking I'd seen Joy coming out of a store or disappearing around a corner.

My final day in L.A. soon arrived. Early the next morning I'd zoom up the coast to Berkeley, meet Sid that evening, and we'd take off for Yugoslavia and the World Gymnastics Championships. I relaxed around the house during the day. After dinner, I took crash helmet in hand and left the house to shop for a travelling bag. As I walked out the door, I heard Dad say, "Be careful, Dan, motorcycles are hard to see at night." His usual caution.

"Yeah, Dad, I'll be careful," I yelled back. Then I gunned the bike and pulled out into the traffic feeling very macho in my gymnastics T-shirt, faded Levis, and work boots. Invigorated by the cool evening air, I headed south toward Wilshire. My future was about to change, because at that moment, three blocks ahead, George Wilson was preparing to make a left turn on Western Avenue.

I roared through the dusk; the street lights flashed by as I approached Seventh and Western. I was about to cut through the intersection when I noticed a red and white Buick facing me, signaling for a left turn. I slowed down—a small precaution which probably saved my life.

Just as my bike entered the intersection the Buick suddenly accelerated, turning directly in front of me. For a few more precious seconds, the body I was born with was still in one piece.

There was time enough to think, but not to act. "Cut left!" my mind screamed. But there was oncoming traffic. "Swerve right!" I'd never clear the fender. "Lay it down!" I'd slide under the wheels. My options were gone. I slammed on the brakes and waited. It was unreal, like a dream, until I saw a flashing image of the driver's horrified face. With a terrible thud and the musical sound of tinkling glass, my bike smashed into the car's front fender—and my right leg shattered. Then everything sped up horribly as the world turned black.

I must have lost and regained consciousness just after my body somersaulted over the car and crashed onto the concrete. A moment of blessed numbness, then the pain began, like a searing, red-hot vise, squeezing and crushing my leg tighter and tighter until it became more than I could bear and I started to scream. I wanted it to stop; I prayed for unconsciousness. Faraway voices: ". . . just didn't see him . . ." ". . . parents' phone number . . ." ". . . take it easy, they'll be here soon."

Then I heard a faraway siren, and hands were removing my helmet, lifting me onto a stretcher. I looked down and saw a white bone sticking out through the torn leather of my boot. With the slam of the ambulance door, I suddenly recalled Soc's words, ". . . and you'll be tested severely before you're done."

Seconds later, it seemed, I was lying on the X-ray table in the emergency room of L.A. Orthopedic Hospital. The doctor complained of fatigue. My parents rushed into the room, looking very old and very pale. That's when reality caught up with me. Numb and in shock, I began to cry.

The doctor worked efficiently, anesthetizing me, snapping my dislocated toes back into place, and sewing up my right foot. Later, in the operating room, his scalpel sliced a long red line deep into my skin, cutting through the muscles that had worked for me so well. He removed bone from my pelvis and grafted it to the fragments of my right thigh bone. Finally, he hammered a narrow metal rod down the center of my bone, from the hip; a kind of internal cast.

I was semiconscious for three days, in a drugged sleep that barely separated me from the agonizing, unrelenting pain. Sometime in the evening of the third day I awoke in darkness when I sensed someone quiet as a shadow, sitting nearby.

Joy got up and knelt by my bedside, stroking my forehead as I turned away in shame. She whispered to me, "I came as soon as I heard." I wished her to share my victories; she always saw me in defeat. I bit my lip and tasted tears. Joy gently turned my face to hers and looked into my eyes. "Socrates has a message for you, Danny; he asked me to tell you this story:"

I closed my eyes and listened intently.

An old man and his son worked a small farm, with only one horse to pull the plow. One day, the horse ran away.

"How terrible," sympathized the neighbors. "What bad luck."

"Who knows whether it is bad luck or good luck," the farmer replied.

A week later, the horse returned from the mountains, leading five wild mares into the barn.

"What wonderful luck!" said the neighbors.

"Good luck? Bad luck? Who knows?" answered the old man.

The next day, the son, trying to tame one of the horses, fell and broke his leg.

"How terrible. What bad luck!"

"Bad luck? Good luck?"

The army came to all the farms to take the young men for war. The farmer's son was of no use to them, so he was spared.

"Good? Bad?"

I smiled sadly, then bit my lip again as I was assaulted by a wave of pain.

Joy soothed me with her voice. "Everything has a purpose, Danny; it's for you to make the best use of it."

"How will I ever make use of this accident?"

"There are no accidents, Danny. Everything is a lesson. Everything has a purpose, a purpose, a *purpose,*" she repeated, whispering in my ear.

"But my gymnastics, my training—it's over."

"This is your training. The pain can purify the mind and body; it burns out many obstructions." She saw the questioning look in my eyes, and added, "a warrior doesn't seek pain, but if pain comes, he uses it. Now rest, Danny, rest." She slipped out behind the entering nurse.

"Don't go, Joy," I muttered and fell into a deep sleep, remembering nothing more.

Friends visited and my parents came every day; but for most of twenty-one endless days I lay alone, flat on my back. I watched the white ceiling and meditated for hours, battered by thoughts of melancholy, self-pity, and futile hope.

On a Tuesday morning, leaning on new crutches, I stepped out into the bright September sunlight and hobbled slowly to my parents' car. I'd lost almost thirty pounds, and my pants hung loosely on protruding hip bones; my right leg looked like a stick with a long purple scar down the side.

A fresh breeze caressed my face on this rare, smogless day. The wind carried flowered scents I'd forgotten; the chirping of birds in a nearby tree mixed with the sounds of traffic created a symphony for my newly awakened senses.

I stayed with my parents for a few days, resting in the hot sun and swimming slowly through the shallow end of the swimming pool, painfully forcing my sutured leg muscles to work. I ate sparingly—yogurt, nuts, cheese, and fresh vegetables. I was beginning to regain my vitality.

Friends invited me to stay with them for a few weeks at their home in Santa Monica, five blocks from the beach. I accepted, welcoming the chance to spend more time in the open air.

Each morning I walked slowly to the warm sand, and, laying my crutches down, sat by the waves. I listened to the gulls and the surf, then closed my eyes and meditated for hours, oblivious to the world around me. Berkeley, Socrates, and my past seemed lost, in another dimension.

Soon I began to exercise, slowly at first, then more intensely, until I was spending hours each day sweating in the hot sun, doing push-ups, sit-ups, curls. I carefully pressed up to hand-stands, then pumped up and down, again and again, puffing with exertion until every muscle had worked to its limit and my body glistened. Then I would hop one-legged into the shallow surf and sit dreaming of lofty somersaults until the salt water washed my shining sweat and soaring dreams into the sea.

I trained fiercely until my muscles were as hard and defined as a marble statue. I became one of the beach "regulars" who made the sea and sand their way of life. Malcolm the masseur would sit down on my blanket and tell jokes; Doc, the Rand Corporation think-tank whiz, would drop by my blanket every day and talk with me about politics and women; mostly women.

I had time—time to consider all that had happened to me since I'd met Socrates. I thought about life and its purposes, death and its mystery. And I remembered my mysterious teacher—his words, his animated expressions—mostly though, I remembered his laughter.

The warmth of the October sun faded into the November clouds. Fewer people came to the beach, and during this time of solitude, I enjoyed a peace I'd not felt for many years. I imagined staying on the beach my whole life, but I knew I'd be going back to school after Christmas.

My doctor gave me the results of my X-rays. "Your leg is healing well, Mr. Millman—unusually well, I should say. But I caution you; don't get your hopes up. The nature of your accident doesn't make it likely that you'll be able to do gymnastics again." I said nothing.

Soon I waved good-bye to my parents and boarded a jet; it was time to return to Berkeley.

Rick picked me up at the airport; I stayed with him and Sid for a few days until I found a studio in an old apartment house near campus.

Each morning, gripping my crutches tightly, I'd make my way to the gym and train on the weight machines, then fall exhausted into the swimming pool. There, assisted by the water's buoyancy, I'd force my leg to the point of pain, trying to walk—always, always to the point of pain.

Afterwards, I would lie on the lawn behind the gym, stretching my muscles to retain the suppleness I'd need for future training. Finally, I rested, reading in the library until I fell into a light sleep.

I had called Socrates to tell him I was back. He wasn't much for talking on the phone and told me to visit him when I could walk without crutches. That was fine with me; I wasn't ready to see him yet.

It was a lonely Christmas that year until Pat and Dennis, two of my teammates, knocked on my apartment door, grabbed me, grabbed my jacket, and practically carried me down to the car. We drove toward Reno, up into the snow, and stopped at Donner Summit. While Pat and Dennis ran through the snow, wrestling, throwing snowballs, and sledding down the hill, I hobbled carefully through the snow and ice and sat on a log.

My thoughts floated back to the coming semester, and to the gymnastics room. I wondered if my leg would ever heal straight and strong. Snow dropped from a branch, thudding with a slushy sound to the frozen ground, waking me from my reverie.

Soon, we were driving home. Pat and Dennis were singing bawdy songs; I watched white crystals float down around us, glittering in our car's lights as the sun began to set. I thought about my derailed future and wished that I could leave my whirling mind behind me, buried in a white grave beside the road in the snowy mountains.

Just after Christmas I made a brief visit to L.A. to see my doctor, who let me trade in my crutches for a shiny black cane. Then I headed back to school and to Socrates.

It was Wednesday night at 11:40 P.M. when I limped through the doorway of the office and saw Soc's radiant face. I was home again. I'd almost forgotten what it was like to sit and sip tea with Socrates in the quiet of the night. It was a more subtle, and in many ways greater, pleasure than all my athletic victories. I looked at this man who had become my teacher and saw things I'd never seen before.

In the past I had noticed a light that seemed to encircle him, but I'd assumed it was only my tired eyes. I wasn't tired now, and there was no doubt about it—it was a barely perceptible aura. "Socrates," I said "There's a light shining around your body. Where does it come from?"

"Clean living," he grinned. Then the bell clanged and he went out to make someone laugh, under the pretext of servicing a car. Socrates dispensed more than gasoline. Maybe it was that aura, that energy or emotion. Anyway, people nearly always left happier than when they had arrived.

It wasn't the glowing, however, that impressed me most about him; it was his simplicity, his economy of motion and of action. I hadn't truly appreciated any of this before. It was as if I saw more deeply into Socrates with every new lesson I learned. As I came to see the complexities of my mind, I realized how he had already transcended his.

When he returned to the office I asked, "Socrates, where is Joy now? Will I see her again soon?"

He smiled as if glad to hear my questions again. "Dan, I don't know where she is; that girl is a mystery to me—always was."

I then told Socrates about the accident and its aftermath. He listened quietly and intently, nodding his head.

"Dan, you're no longer the young fool who walked into this office over a year ago."

"Has it been a year? It seems like ten," I joked. "Are you saying I'm no longer a fool?"

"No, only that you're no longer young."

"Hey, that's real heartwarming, Soc."

"But now you're a fool with spirit, Dan. And that's a very big difference. You still have a faint chance of finding the gate and passing through.

"Gate?"

"The realm of the warrior, Dan, is guarded by a gate. It is well hidden, like a monastery in the mountains. Many knock, but few enter."

"Well, show me the gate, Socrates. I'm ready, I'll figure a way to get in."

"It's not so simple, bumpkin. The gate exists inside you, and you alone must find it; I can only guide you. But you're not ready yet, not nearly ready. If you attempted to pass the gate now, it would mean your almost certain death. There's much work to be done before you're prepared to knock at the gate."

When Socrates talked, it sounded like a pronouncement. "Dan, we've talked much; you've seen visions and learned lessons. I teach a way of life, a way of action. It's time you became fully responsible for your own behavior. To find the gate, you must first learn to follow . . ."

"The House Rules?" I volunteered.

He laughed, then the bell clanged as a car rolled smoothly through a rain puddle into the station. I watched through the misty window as Socrates walked quickly out into the drizzle, wearing his poncho. I could see him put the gas nozzle in, go around to the driver's side, and say something to a bearded, blond-haired man in the car.

The window misted over again, so I wiped it clean with my sleeve in time to see them laughing. Then Socrates opened the door to the office, and a draft of cold air slapped me harshly, bringing with it my first awareness that I didn't feel well at all.

Socrates was about to make some tea, when I said, "Please, sit down, Soc. I'll make tea." He sat, nodding his head in approval. I leaned against the desk, feeling dizzy. My throat was sore; perhaps the tea would help.

As I filled the kettle and placed it on the hot plate, I asked, "Do I have to build some kind of road to this gate, then?"

"Yes—in a sense, everyone must. You pave the way with your own work."

Anticipating my next question, he said, "Anyone—any human being,.male or female, has within, the capacity to find the gate and pass through, but very few are *moved* to do so; few are interested. This is very important. I didn't decide to teach you because of any inherent capacity you possessed—as a matter of fact, you have glaring weaknesses along with your strong points—but you have the *will* to make this journey."

That stuck a resonant chord. "I guess you could compare it to gymnastics, Soc. Even someone who is overweight, weak, or inflexible can become a fine gymnast, but the preparation is longer, more difficult."

"Yes, that's exactly what it's like. And I can tell you this: your path is going to be very steep."

My head felt feverish, and I started to ache all over. I leaned against the desk again and out of the corner of my eye saw Socrates come toward me, reaching out for my head. "Oh no, not now; I'm not up to it," I thought. But he was only feeling my feverish forehead. Then he checked the glands in my neck, looked at my face and eyes, and felt my pulse for a long time.

"Dan, your energies are way out of balance; your spleen is probably swollen. I suggest you visit a physician, tonight—now."

I was feeling really miserable by the time I limped to Cowell Hospital. My throat was burning, my body aching. The doctor confirmed Soc's diagnosis; my spleen was badly swollen. I had a severe case of mononucleosis and was admitted to the infirmary.

During that first fitful, feverish night, I dreamed that I had one huge leg and one shrivelled one. When I tried to swing on the bars or tumble, everything was crooked, and I fell, fell, fell into the late afternoon of the next day, when Socrates walked in with a bouquet of dried flowers.

"Socrates," I said weakly, delighted by his unexpected visit, "you shouldn't have."

"Yes I should have," he replied.

"I'll have the nurse put them in a vase; I'll think of you when I look at them," I grinned weakly.

"They're not to look at—they're to eat," he said, leaving the room. A few minutes later, he returned with a glass of hot water. Crushing some of the flowers, he wrapped them in a piece of cheesecloth he'd brought and dipped the tea bag into the water. "This tea will strengthen you, and help cleanse the blood. Here, drink." It tasted bitter—strong medicine.

Then he took a small bottle of yellow liquid in which were floating more crushed herbs, and massaged the liquid deep into my right leg, directly over the scar. I wondered what the nurse, a very pretty, businesslike young woman, would say if she came in.

"What is that yellow stuff in the bottle, Soc?"

"Urine, with a few herbs."

"Urine!" I said, pulling my leg away from him with disgust.

"Don't be silly," he said, grabbing my leg and pulling it back. "Urine is a very respected elixir in the ancient healing traditions."

I closed my tired, aching eyes; my head was throbbing like jungle drums. I felt the fever starting to rise again. Socrates put his hand against my head, then felt the pulse in my wrist.

"Good, the herbs are taking effect. Tonight should be the crisis; tomorrow, you'll feel better."

I managed a barely audible, "Thank you, Doc Soc."

He reached over and put his hand on my solar plexus. Almost immediately, everything in my body intensified. I thought my head would explode. The fever started to burn me up; my glands pulsated. Worst of all was a terrible burning pain in my right leg at the site of the injury.

"Stop it Socrates, stop it!" I yelled.

He took his hand away and I collapsed into the bed. "I've just introduced a little more energy into your body than you're used to," he explained. It will accelerate the healing processes. It burns only where you have knots. If you were free of obstructions—if your mind was clear, your heart open, and your body free of tension, you'd experience the energy as an indescribable pleasure—better than sex. You'd think you were in heaven, and in a way, you'd be right.

"Sometimes you scare me, Socrates."

"Superior people are always held in fear and awe," he grinned. "In some ways you are superior, too, Dan, at least on the outside. You look like a warrior; slim, supple, and strong from your rudimentary preparation in gymnastics. But you have a lot of work to do before you earn the kind of health *I* enjoy." I was too weak to argue.

The nurse walked in. "Time to take your temperature, Mr. Millman." Socrates had risen politely when she entered. I lay in bed looking pale and miserable. The contrast between the two of us had never felt greater than at that moment. The nurse smiled at Socrates, who grinned back. "I think your son is going to be just fine with a little rest," she said.

"Just what I was telling him," Soc said, his eyes twinkling. She smiled at him again—was that a flirtatious look she gave him? With a rustle of white, she walked out of the room, looking blatantly appealing.

Socrates sighed. "There's something about a woman in uniform." Then he put his hand on my forehead. I fell into a deep sleep.

The next morning, I felt like a new man. The doctor's eyebrows rose as he checked my spleen, felt for my swollen glands, and rechecked my chart. He was dumbfounded. "I can't find anything wrong with you, Mr. Millman." He sounded almost apologetic. "You can go home after lunch—uh, get plenty of rest." He walked out, staring at my chart.

The nurse rustled by again. "Help!" I yelled.

"Yes?" she said, stepping inside.

"I can't understand it, nurse. I think I'm having heart trouble. Every time you go by, my pulse gets erotic."

"Don't you mean erratic?" she said.

"Oh, whatever."

Smiling at me, she said, "It sounds like you're ready to go home."

"That's what everyone keeps telling me, but you're all mistaken. I'm sure I'll need private nursing care."

Smiling invitingly, she turned and walked away. "Nurse! Don't leave me," I cried.

That afternoon, walking home, I was astonished by the improvement in my leg. I still limped badly, throwing my hip out to the side whenever I took a step, but I could almost walk without my cane. Maybe there was something to Soc's magic urine treatment or the battery-charge he had given me.

School had begun and I was again surrounded by other students and books and assignments, but that was all secondary to me now. I could play the game without concern. I had much more important things to do in a small gas station west of campus.

After a long nap, I walked to the station. The moment I sat down, Soc said, "Lots of work to do."

"What is it?" I said, stretching and yawning.

"A complete overhaul."

"Oh, a big job."

"Especially big; we're going to overhaul you."

"Oh, yeah?" I said. Oh hell, I thought.

"Like the Phoenix, you're going to throw yourself into the fire and rise from your ashes."

"I'm ready!" I said. "For my new year's resolution, I'm going to give up doughnuts."

Socrates grinned at me, saying, "I wish it were that simple. Right now you're a tangled mass of twisted circuits and outmoded habits. You're going to have to change habits of acting, of thinking, of dreaming, and of seeing the world. Most of what you *are* is a series of bad habits."

He was starting to get to me. "Damn it, Socrates, I've overcome some difficult hurdles, and I'm still doing the best I can. Can't you show me some respect?"

Socrates threw his head back and laughed. Then he walked over to me and pulled my shirt out. As I was tucking it back in, he mussed up my hair. "Listen to me, O great buffoon, everyone wants respect. But it is not just a matter of saying, 'Please respect me.' You must earn respect by acting respectable—and the respect of a warrior is not easily earned."

I counted to ten, then asked, "How then, am I going to earn your respect, O Great and Awesome Warrior?"

"By changing your act."

"What act is that?"

"Your 'poor me' act, of course. Stop being so proud of mediocrity; show some spirit!" Grinning, Socrates jumped up and slapped me playfully on my cheek, then poked me in the ribs.

"Stop it!" I yelled, in no mood for his play. I reached out to grab his arm, but he leaped lightly up on his desk. Then he leaped over my head, spun, and pushed me backwards onto the couch. Climbing angrily to my feet I tried to push him back, but just as I touched him he leaped *backward* over the desk. I fell forwards onto the carpet. "Goddamn it!" I raged, seeing red. He slipped out the door into the garage. I limped after him in pursuit.

Socrates perched on a fender and scratched his head. "Why Dan, you're angry."

"Stunning observation," I fumed, panting heavily.

"Good," he said. "Considering your predicament, you should be angry—but make sure you direct that anger wisely." Soc deftly began to change the spark plugs on a VW. "Anger is one of your main tools to transform old habits"—he removed an old plug with the sparkplug wrench—"and replace them with new ones." He threaded a new plug into the block, tightening it with a firm tug of the wrench.

"Anger can burn away old habits. Fear and sorrow inhibit action, you see; anger generates it. When you learn to make proper use of your anger, you can transmute fear and sorrow to anger, and anger, to action. That's your body's secret of internal alchemy."

Back in the office, Socrates drew some water from the spring water dispenser and put on the evening's tea specialty, rose hips, as he continued. "You have many habits that weaken you. The secret of change is to focus all your energy not on fighting the old, but on building the new."

"How can I control my habits if I can't even control my emotions, Soc?"

He sat back in his chair. "It is like this: When your mind creates a problem, when it resists life as it unfolds in the moment, your body tenses and feels this tension as an 'emotion,' variously interpreted by words like 'fear,' 'sorrow,' or 'anger.' True emotion, Dan, is pure energy, flowing freely in the body."

"Then the warrior never feels the normal upsetting emotions?"

"In a sense, this is true. Yet emotions are a natural human capacity, a form of expression. Sometimes it's appropriate to express fear, sorrow, or anger—but the energy should be directed completely outward, not held in. The expression of emotions should be complete and powerful, then should vanish without a trace. The way to control your emotions, then, is to let them flow and let them go."

I got up, took the whistling kettle off the hot plate, and poured our steaming tea. "Can you give me a specific example, Socrates?"

"All right then," he said. "Spend time with a baby."

Smiling, I blew on my tea. "Funny, I never thought of babies as masters of emotional control."

"When a baby is upset, it expresses itself in banshee wails—pure crying. It doesn't wonder about whether it *should* be crying.

Hold or feed it and within seconds, no more tears. If the baby is angry, then it very definitely lets you know. But this too, it lets go of very quickly; can you imagine a baby's feeling guilty about its anger? Babies let it flow, then let it go. They express themselves fully, then shut up. Infants are fine teachers. And they demonstrate the right use of energy. Learn that, and you can transform any habit."

A Ford Ranchero Wagon pulled into the station. Socrates went around to the driver's seat while I, chuckling, grabbed the gas hose and removed the gas cap. Inspired by his enlightening revelation of how to control emotions, I yelled over the roof of the car, "Just tell me what to do and set me loose, Soc. I'll tear those nasty habits to shreds!" Then I got a look at the passengers—three shocked nuns. I choked on my words and, turning beet-red, busied myself with washing the windows. Socrates just leaned against the pump and buried his face in his hands.

After the Ranchero pulled out, much to my relief, another customer drove in. It was the blond man again—the one with the curly beard. He jumped out of the car and gave Socrates a bear hug. "Good to see you, as always, Joseph," Socrates said.

"Same here . . . *Socrates,* isn't it?" He gave me a beguiling grin.

"Joseph, this young question machine is named 'Dan'. Push a button and he asks a question. Marvelous to have around, really, when I've no one to talk to."

Joseph shook my hand. "Has the old man mellowed in his declining years?" he asked with a broad smile.

Before I could assure him that Soc was probably more ornery than ever, the 'old man' interrupted, "Oh, I've really become lazy; Dan has it much easier than you did."

"Oh, I see," Joseph said, maintaining a serious countenance. "You haven't taken him on any 100-mile runs or worked with the burning coals yet, hmm?"

"No, nothing like that. We're just about to start with the basics, like how to eat, walk, and breathe."

Joseph laughed merrily; I found myself laughing with him. "Speaking of eating," he said, "Why don't both of you come to the café this morning. You'll be my private guests, and I'll whip up something for breakfast."

I was just about to say, "Oh, I'd like to, but I really can't," when Socrates volunteered, "We'd be delighted. The morning shift gets on in half an hour—we'll walk over."

"Great. See you then." He handed Soc a five dollar bill for the gas, and drove off.

I wondered about Joseph. "Is he a warrior, like you, Soc?"

"No one is a warrior like me," he answered, laughing. "Nor would anyone want to be. Each man or woman has natural qualities. For example, while you've excelled in gymnastics, Joseph has mastered the preparation of food."

"Oh, you mean cooking?"

"Not exactly. Joseph doesn't heat food much; it destroys the natural enzymes needed to fully digest the food. He prepares natural foods in a way you'll soon see for yourself. After a taste of Joseph's culinary magic, you'll have no tolerance for fast food joints ever again."

"What's so special about his cooking?"

"Only two things, really—both subtle. First, he gives his complete attention to what he does; second, love is literally one of the primary ingredients in everything he makes. You can taste it afterwards for a long time."

Soc's replacement, a lanky teenager, came in with his usual grunted greeting. We left, crossed the streets, and headed south. My limping pace quickened to keep up with Soc's strides as we took the scenic route down side streets, avoiding early morning rush-hour traffic.

Our feet crunched over dried leaves as we walked past the varied array of dwellings that characterize Berkeley's housing, a mixture of Victorian, Spanish Colonial, neo-alpine funk, and boxlike apartment houses catering to many of the 30,000 students.

While we walked, we talked. Socrates began. "Dan, a tremendous amount of energy is necessary to cut through the mists of your mind and find the gate. So purifying, regenerative practices are essential."

"Could you run that by me again?"

"We're going to clean you out, take you apart, and put you back together again."

"Oh, why didn't you say that in the first place," I teased.

"You're going to readapt your every human function—moving,

sleeping, breathing, thinking, feeling—and eating. Of all the human activities, eating is one of the most important to stabilize first."

"Wait a minute, Socrates. Eating isn't really a problem area for me. I'm slim, I generally feel pretty good, and my gymnastics proves I have enough energy. How is changing a few things in my diet going to make a difference?"

"Your present diet," he said, glancing up through the sunlit branches of a beautiful tree, "may give you a 'normal' amount of energy, but much of what you eat also makes you groggy, affects your moods, lowers your level of awareness, and interferes with your body's optimal vitality. Your impulsive diet results in toxic residues that have a long-range effect on your longevity. Most of your mental and emotional problems could be minimized by simple attention to proper eating."

"How can changing my diet affect my energy?" I argued. "I mean, I take in calories, and they represent a certain amount of energy."

"That is the traditional view, but it is a shallow one; the warrior must recognize more subtle influences. Our primary source of energy in this system," he said, waving his arm to indicate the solar system, "is the sun. But in general, the human being—that's you . . ."

"Thanks for the concession."

". . . in his present state of evolution, has not developed the ability to make direct use of the sun's energy; you cannot 'eat sunlight' except in limited ways. When humanity does develop this ability, the digestive organs will become vestigial and the laxative companies will go out of business. For now, food is the form of stored sunlight which you need.

"A proper diet allows you to make the most direct use of the sun's energy. The ensuing store of energy will open your senses, expand your awareness, and sharpen your concentration into a slashing blade."

"All that is going to happen by eliminating cupcakes from my diet?"

"Yes—by eliminating cupcakes, and a few other odds and ends."

"One of the Japanese Olympic gymnasts once told me that it's not your bad habits that count, but your good ones."

"That means your good habits must become so strong that they dissolve those which are not useful." Socrates pointed ahead to a small café on Shattuck near Ashby. I'd walked by there many times without really noticing it.

"So, you believe in natural foods, Soc?" I said as we crossed the street.

"It's not a matter of believing but of doing. I can tell you this: I eat only what is wholesome, and I eat only as much as I need. In order to appreciate what you call natural foods, you have to sharpen your instincts; you have to become a natural man."

"Sounds positively ascetic to me. Don't you even have a little ice cream now and then?"

"My diet may at first seem spartan compared to the indulgences you call 'moderation', Dan, but the way I eat is actually filled with pleasure, because I've developed the capacity to enjoy the simplest foods. And so will you."

We knocked on the door, and Joseph opened it. "Come in, come in," he said enthusiastically, as if welcoming us to his home. It did, in fact, look like a home. Thick carpets covered the floor of the small waiting room. Heavy, polished, rough-hewn tables were placed around the room, and the soft straight-backed chairs looked like antiques. Tapestries hung on the walls, except for one wall almost completely hidden by a huge aquarium of colorful fish. Morning light poured through a skylight overhead. We sat directly below it, in the warm rays of the sun, occasionally shaded by clouds drifting overhead.

Joseph approached us, carrying two plates over his head. With a flourish, he placed them in front of us, serving Socrates first, then me. "Ah, it looks delicious!" said Socrates, tucking his napkin into the neck of his shirt. I looked down. There before me, on a white plate, were a sliced carrot and a piece of lettuce. I stared at it in consternation.

At my expression, Socrates almost fell out of his chair laughing and Joseph had to lean against a table. "Ah," I said, with a sigh of relief. "It is a joke, then."

Without another word, Joseph took the plates and returned with two beautiful wooden bowls. In each bowl was a perfectly carved, miniature replica of a mountain. The mountain itself was a blended combination of cantaloupe and honeydew melon. Small chunks of walnuts and almonds, individually carved, became brown boulders. The craggy cliffs were made from apples and thin slices of cheese. The trees were made of many pieces of parsley, each pruned to a perfect shape, like bonsai trees. An icing of yogurt capped the peak. Around the base were halved grapes and a ring of fresh strawberries.

I sat and stared. "Joseph, it's too beautiful. I can't eat this; I want to take a picture of it." Socrates, I noticed, had already begun eating, nibbling slowly, as was his manner. I attacked the mountain with gusto and was almost done, when Socrates suddenly started gobbling his food. I realized he was mimicking me.

I did my best to take small bites, breathing deeply between each bit as he did, but it seemed frustratingly slow.

"The pleasure you gain from eating, Dan, is limited to the taste of the food and the feeling of a full belly. You must learn to enjoy the entire process—the hunger beforehand, the careful preparation, setting an attractive table, chewing, breathing, smelling, tasting, swallowing, and the feeling of lightness and energy after the meal. Finally, you can enjoy the full and easy elimination of the food after it's digested. When you pay attention to all these elements, you'll begin to appreciate simple meals; you won't need as much food.

"The irony of your present eating habits is that while you fear missing a meal, you aren't fully aware of the meals you do eat."

"I'm not afraid of missing a meal," I argued.

"I'm glad to hear that. It will make the coming week easier for you. This meal is the last one you'll be having for the next seven days." Soc proceeded to outline a purifying fast that I was to begin immediately. Diluted fruit juice or plain herb teas were to be my only fare.

"But Socrates, I need my protein and iron to help my leg heal; I need my energy for gymnastics." It was no use. Socrates could be a very unreasonable man.

We helped Joseph with a few chores, talked for awhile, thanked him, and left. I was already hungry. While we walked back toward campus, Socrates summarized the disciplines I was to follow until my body regained its natural instincts.

"In a few years, there will be no need for rules. For now, however, you're to eliminate all foods that contain refined sugar, refined flour, meat, and eggs, as well as drugs including coffee, alcohol, tobacco, or any other nonuseful food. Eat only fresh, unrefined, unprocessed foods, without chemical additives. In general, make breakfast a fresh fruit meal, perhaps with cottage cheese or yogurt. Your lunch, your main meal, should be a raw salad, baked or steamed potato, perhaps some cheese, and whole grain bread or cooked grains. Dinner should be a raw salad and, on occasion, lightly steamed vegetables. Make good use of raw, unsalted seeds and nuts at every meal."

"I guess by now you're quite an expert on nuts, Soc," I grumbled.

On the way home, we passed by a neighborhood grocery store. I was about to go inside and get some cookies when I remembered that I was no longer allowed to eat store-bought cookies for the rest of my life! And for the next six days and twenty-three hours, I wouldn't be eating anything at all.

"Socrates, I'm hungry."

"I never said that the training of a warrior would be a piece of cake."

We walked through the campus just between classes, so Sproul Plaza was filled with people. I gazed wistfully at the pretty coeds. Socrates touched my arm. "That reminds me, Dan. Culinary sweets aren't the only indulgence you're going to have to avoid for awhile."

"Oh-oh." I stopped dead in my tracks. "I want to make very sure I don't misunderstand you. Can you be more specific?"

"Sure. While you may of course enjoy intimate, heartfelt relationships, until you're sufficiently mature, you're to refrain completely from your preoccupation with sexual release. To spell it out for you: Keep it in your pants."

"But Socrates," I argued, as if on trial for my life, "that's old-fashioned, puritanical, unreasonable, and unhealthy. Cutting down on food is one thing, but this is different!" I started quoting the "Playboy Philosophy," Albert Ellis, Robert Rimmer, Jacqueline Susann, and the Marquis de Sade. I even threw in *Reader's Digest* and "Dear Abby," but nothing moved him.

He said, "There's no point in my trying to explain my reasons; you're just going to have to find your future thrills in fresh air, fresh food, fresh water, fresh awareness, and sunshine."

"How can I possibly follow every discipline you demand?"

"Consider the final words of advice the Buddha gave to his disciples."

"What did he say?" I awaited inspiration.

" 'Do your best.' " With that, he vanished into the crowd.

The next week, my rites of initiation got under way. While my stomach growled, Soc filled my nights with "basic" exercises, teaching me how to breathe more deeply and slowly—mouth lightly closed and the tongue on the roof of the mouth. I plodded on, doing my best, feeling lethargic, looking forward to my (ugh!) diluted fruit juice and herb tea, dreaming about steaks and sweet rolls. And I didn't even particularly *like* steaks or sweet rolls!

He told me to breathe with my belly one day, and to breathe with my heart the next. He began to criticize my walking, my talking, the way my eyes wandered around the room as my "mind wandered around the universe." Nothing I did seemed to satisfy him.

Over and over he corrected me, sometimes gently, sometimes harshly. "Proper posture is a way of blending with gravity, Dan. Proper attitude is a way of blending with life." And so it went.

The third day of the fast was the hardest. I was weak and cranky; I had headaches and bad breath. "All part of the purification process, Dan. Your body is cleaning out, getting rid of stored toxins." At workout, all I did was lie around and stretch.

I was actually feeling good—even cocky—the seventh day of the fast. I felt I could go longer. My hunger had disappeared; all I felt in its stead was a pleasant lassitude and a feeling of lightness. Workouts actually improved. Limited only by my weak leg, I trained hard, feeling relaxed and more supple than ever.

When I started eating on the eighth day, beginning with very small amounts of fruit, I had to use all my will power not to start gorging myself on whatever I was allowed to eat.

Socrates tolerated no complaints, no back talk. In fact, he didn't want me to talk *at all* unless it was absolutely necessary. "No more idle jabbering," he said. "What comes out of your mouth is as important as what goes into it." I was thus able to censor the inane comments that used to make me appear a fool. It actually felt pretty good to talk less, once I started getting the knack of it. I felt calmer, somehow. But after a few weeks I tired of it.

"Socrates, I'll bet you a dollar that I can make you say more than two words."

He held out his hand, palm up, saying, "You lose."

Because of my gymnastics successes in the past, I was brimming with spirit and confidence the first month or so. But before long I realized that, as Socrates had said, it wasn't going to be a piece of cake.

My main problem was fitting in socially with my friends. Rick, Sid, and I took dates to LaVal's for pizza. Everyone else, including my date, shared an extra-large sausage pizza; I ordered a small, whole wheat, vegetarian special. They had milk shakes or beer; I sipped my apple juice. They wanted to go to Fenton's Ice Cream Parlor afterward. While they ate their sundaes, I sucked on a piece of ice. I looked at them enviously; they looked back with vague resentment. I probably made them feel guilty. My social life was collapsing under the weight of my disciplines.

I would walk blocks out of my way to avoid the doughnut shops, food stands, and outdoor restaurants near campus. My cravings and compulsions were becoming obvious to me, but I fought back. If I turned into a jellyfish over a jelly doughnut, I just wouldn't be able to face Socrates.

As time passed, though, I began to feel a growing resistance. I complained to Socrates, in spite of his dark look, "Soc, you're no fun anymore. You've become an ordinary grumpy old man; you never even glow."

He glowered at me. "No more magic tricks." That was just it—no tricks, no sex, no potato chips, no hamburgers, no candy, no doughnuts, no fun, and no rest; discipline in the station and out.

January had trudged by; February had flown, and now March was nearly over. The team was finishing the season without me.

Again I told Socrates my feelings, but he offered no consolation, no support. "Socrates, I'm a real spiritual boy scout. My friends don't want to go out with me anymore. You're ruining my life! I'm afraid I'll become a dried-up old . . ."

I was interrupted by his laughter. "Dan, I can assure you, if dehydration is what you fear, that my late wife considered me rather juicy."

"Your *wife?*"

He laughed again at my shocked expression. Then he looked at me; I thought he wanted to say something else. But he only resumed his paperwork and said, "Do your best."

"Well, thank you for the stirring pep talk." Deep down, I was offended by having another person—even Socrates—direct my life.

Still, I fulfilled every rule with teeth-clenching determination until one day, during workout, in walked the dazzling nurse who had starred in my erotic fantasies since my stay in the hospital. She sat down quietly, and watched our aerial routines. Almost immediately, I noticed, everyone in the gym was inspired to a new level of energy, and I was no exception.

Pretending to be immersed in practice, I glanced at her every now and then out of the corner of my eyes. Her tight silk pants and halter top had snared my concentration; my mind kept drifting off to more exotic forms of gymnastics. For the rest of workout I was acutely conscious of her attention.

She disappeared just before the end of training. I showered, dressed, and headed up the stairs. There she was, at the top of the staircase, leaning seductively against the bannister. I don't even remember walking up the final flight of stairs.

"Hi, Dan Millman. I'm Valerie. You look much better than when I cared for you in the hospital."

"I am better, nurse Valerie," I grinned. "And I'm so glad you cared." She laughed and stretched invitingly.

"Dan, I wonder if you'd do me a big favor. Would you walk me home? It's getting dark out, and a strange man has been following me."

I was about to point out that it was early April and the sun wouldn't be going down for another hour, but then thought, "What the hell—a petty detail."

We walked, we talked and I ended up having dinner at her apartment. She opened her bottle of "special wine for special occasions." I merely had a sip; but it was the beginning of the end. I was sizzling; hotter than the steak on the grill. There was a moment when a little voice asked, "Are you a man or a jellyfish?" Another little voice answered, "I'm one horny jellyfish." That night I washed out on every discipline I'd been given. I ate whatever she gave me. I started with a cup of clam chowder, then salad and steak. And for dessert, I had several helpings of Valerie.

For the next three days I didn't sleep very well, preoccupied with how to present my true confession to Socrates. I was prepared for the worst.

That night I walked into the office and told him everything, without apology, and waited, holding my breath. Socrates didn't speak for a long time. Finally, he said, "I noticed you haven't learned to breathe yet." Before I could reply, he held up his hand. "Dan, *I* can understand how you might choose an ice cream cone or a fling with a pretty woman over the Way I have shown you—but can *you* understand it?" He paused. "There is no praise, no blame. You now understand the compelling hungers in your belly and your loins. That is good. But consider this: I've asked you to do your best. Was that really your best?"

Socrates turned his eyes on "bright"; they shone through me. "Come back in a month, but only if you've strictly applied the disciplines. See the young woman if you wish; serve her with attention and real feeling, but no matter what urges you may feel, be guided by a superior discipline!"

"I'll do it, Socrates; I swear I will! I really understand now."

"Neither resolutions nor understanding will ever make you strong. Resolutions have sincerity, logic has clarity; but neither has the energy you will need. Let anger be your resolution, your logic. See you next month."

I knew that if I forgot the disciplines again, it would be the end for me and Socrates. With a growing inner resolve, I said, "No seductive woman, doughnut, or piece of roasted cow flesh is going to benumb my will again. I'll master my impulses or die."

Valerie called me the next day. I felt all the familiar stirrings at the sound of her voice, which had moaned in my ear not long before. "Danny, I'd love to see you tonight. Are you available? Oh, good. I get off work at seven. Shall I meet you at the gym? O.K., see you then—bye."

I took her to Joseph's café that night for a supreme salad surprise. I noticed that Valerie was flirting with Joseph. He was his usual warm self, but showed no sign of returning her flirtations.

Later, we returned to her apartment. We sat and talked awhile. She offered wine; I asked for juice. She touched my hair and kissed me softly, murmuring in my ear. I kissed her back with feeling. Then my inner voice came through loud and clear. "Get yourself together. Remember what you must."

I sat up, taking a deep breath. This wasn't going to be easy. She sat up too, straightening herself, patting her hair. "Valerie, you know I find you very attractive and exciting—but I'm involved in some, uh, personal disciplines that no longer allow for what was about to happen. I enjoy your company and want to see you again. But from now on, I suggest you think of me as an intimate friend, a loving p-p-priest." I almost couldn't get it out.

She took a deep breath and smoothed her hair again. "Dan, it's really good to be with someone who isn't interested only in sex."

"Well," I said, encouraged. "I'm glad to hear you feel that way, because I know we can share many things besides a bed."

She looked at her watch. "Oh, will you look at the time—and I have to work early tomorrow, too—so I'll say goodnight, Dan. Thank you for dinner. It was lovely."

I called her the next day, but her phone was busy. I called her the following day and finally reached her. "I'm going to be very busy with nursing exams for the next few weeks."

I saw her one week later when she appeared at the end of practice to meet Scott, one of the other guys on the team. They both walked right by me as I came up the stairs—so close that I could smell her perfume. She nodded politely and said hello.

Scott leered back at me and gave me a meaningful wink. I didn't know a wink could hurt so much.

With a desperate hunger that a raw salad repast couldn't possibly satisfy, I found myself in front of the Charbroiler. I smelled the sizzling hamburgers, basted with special sauce. I remembered all the good times I'd had, eating burgers with lettuce and tomatoes—and friends. In a daze, I went in without thinking, walked right up to the woman behind the counter and heard myself say, "One charbroiled with double cheese, please."

She gave it to me and I sat down, held it to my mouth, and took a huge bite. Suddenly I realized what I was doing; choosing between Socrates and a cheeseburger. I spit it out, threw it angrily in the trash, and walked out. It was over; I was through being a slave to random impulses.

That night marked the beginning of a new glow of self-respect and a feeling of personal power. I knew it would get easier now.

Small changes began to add up in my life. Ever since I was a kid, I'd suffered all kinds of minor symptoms, like a runny nose at night when the air cooled, headaches, stomach upsets and mood swings, all of which I thought were normal and inevitable. Now they had all vanished.

I felt a constant sense of lightness and energy which radiated around me. Maybe that accounted for the number of women flirting with me, the little kids and dogs coming up to me and wanting to play. A few of my teammates started asking for advice about personal problems. No longer a small boat in a stormy sea, I started to feel like the Rock of Gibraltar.

I told Socrates about my experience. He nodded. "Your energy level is rising. People, animals, and even things are attracted to and awed by the presence of an energy field. That's how it works."

"House Rules?" I asked.

"House Rules." Then he added, "On the other hand, it would be premature for self-congratulation. To keep your perspective, you'd better compare yourself to me. Then it will be clear that you've only graduated from kindergarten."

School ended for the year almost without my noticing it. Exams went smoothly; the studies that had always seemed to be a major struggle for me had become a minor piece of business to get out of the way. The team left for a short vacation, then returned for summer workouts. I was beginning to walk without my cane and even tried to run very slowly a few times a week. I continued pushing myself to the limit of pain, discipline, and endurance, and, of course, I continued to do my best with right eating, right moving, and right breathing—but my best was still not very good.

Socrates started to increase his demands on me. "Now that your energy is building, you can begin training in earnest."

I practiced breathing so slowly that it took one minute to complete each breath. When combined with intense concentration and control of specific muscle groups, this breathing exercise heated my body up like a sauna and allowed me to remain comfortable outside, no matter what the temperature.

I was excited to realize that I was developing the same power

Soc had shown me the night we met. For the first time, I began to believe that maybe, just maybe, I could become a warrior of his stature. No longer feeling left out, I now felt superior to my friends. When a friend complained of illness or other problems that I knew could be remedied by simply eating properly, I told him what I'd learned about responsibility and discipline.

I took my newfound confidence with me to the station one night, feeling sure that I was about to learn some ancient and arcane secrets of India, Tibet, or China. Instead, as soon as I stepped through the door, I was handed a mop and told to clean the bathroom. "Make those toilets shine." For weeks afterward, I did so many menial tasks around the station that I had no time for my important exercises. I lifted tires for an hour, then took out the trash. I swept the garage and straightened the tools. I had never imagined it could happen, but being around Socrates was getting boring.

At the same time, it was impossibly demanding. He'd give me five minutes to do a half-hour job, then criticize me mercilessly if it wasn't done thoroughly. He was unfair, unreasonable, and even insulting. As I was considering my disgust with this state of affairs, Socrates stepped into the garage to tell me that I'd left dirt on the bathroom floor.

"But someone used the bathroom after I finished," I said.

"No excuses," he said, and added, "Throw out the garbage."

I was so mad that I gripped my broom handle like a sword. I felt an icy calm. "But I just threw the garbage out five minutes ago, Socrates. Do you remember old man, or are you getting senile?"

He grinned. "I'm talking about this garbage, baboon!" He tapped his head and winked at me. The broom clattered to the floor.

Another evening when I was sweeping the garage, Socrates called me into the office. I sat down, sullen, waiting for more orders. "Dan, you still haven't learned to breathe naturally. You've been indolent and need to concentrate more."

That was the last straw. I screamed at him, "You've been the indolent one—I've been doing all your work for you!"

He paused, and I actually thought I saw pain in his eyes. Softly he said, "It isn't proper, Dan, to yell at your teacher."

Again I remembered that the purpose of his insults had always been to show me my own mental and emotional turbulence, to turn my anger to action, and to help me persevere. Before I could apologize, he said, "Dan you'd better go away, and not come back until you have learned courtesy—and until you can breathe properly. Perhaps an absence will help your mood."

Sadly, I shuffled out, my head down. As I walked home, I considered how patient he had been with my tantrums, complaints, and questions. All his demands had been to serve me. I vowed never to yell at him in anger again.

Alone, I tried harder than ever to correct my tense habits of breathing, but it only seemed to get worse. If I breathed deeply, I'd forget to keep my tongue on the roof of my mouth; if I remembered that, I'd slouch over. I was going crazy.

In frustration, I went back to the station to see Soc and ask for his advice. I found him tinkering in the garage. He took one look at me and said, "Go away." Angry and hurt, I wordlessly limped off into the night. I heard his voice behind me, "After you learn how to breathe, do something about your sense of humor." His laughter seemed to chase me halfway home.

When I reached the front steps of my apartment, I sat down and gazed at the church across the street without really seeing anything in front of my eyes. I said to myself, "I'm going to quit this impossible training." Even so, I didn't believe a word I said. I continued eating my salads, avoiding every temptation; I struggled doggedly with my breathing.

It was almost mid-summer when I remembered Joseph's café. I'd been so busy with training in the day and with Soc at night that I hadn't made time to visit him. Now I thought sadly, my nights were completely free. I walked to his café just at closing time. The place was empty; I found Joseph in the kitchen, lovingly cleaning the fine porcelain dishes.

We were so different, Joseph and I. I was short, muscular, athletic, with short hair and a clean-shaven face; Joseph was tall, lean, even fragile looking, with a soft, curly blond beard. I moved and talked quickly; he did everything with slow-motion care. In spite of our differences, or maybe because of them, I was drawn to him.

We talked into the night as I helped him stack chairs and sweep the floors. Even as I talked, I concentrated as well as I could on my breathing, which made me drop a dish and trip over the carpet.

"Joseph," I asked, "Did Socrates really make you go on 100-mile runs?"

"No, Dan," he laughed. My temperament isn't really suited for athletic feats. Didn't Soc tell you? I was his cook and personal attendant for years."

"No, he never told me. But what do you mean that you were his attendant for years? You couldn't be older than twenty-eight or twenty-nine."

Joseph beamed. "I'm a bit older than that—I'm fifty-two."

"Are you serious?"

He nodded. There certainly was something to all those disciplines.

"But if you didn't do very much physical conditioning, what did you do? What was your training?"

"Dan, I was a very angry and self-centered young man. By making extremely rigorous demands on me for service, he showed me how to give myself away, with real happiness and love."

"And what better place to learn how to serve," I said, "than at a service station!"

Smiling, Joseph said, "He wasn't always a service station attendant, you know. His life has been extremely unusual and varied."

"Tell me about it!" I urged.

"Hasn't Socrates told you about his past?"

"No, he likes to keep it mysterious. I don't even know where he lives."

"Not surprising. Well, I'd better keep it mysterious, too, until he wants you to know."

Hiding my disappointment, I asked, "Did you call him Socrates, too? It seems an unlikely coincidence."

"No, but his new name, like his new student, has spirit," he smiled.

"You said he made rigorous demands on you."

"Yes, very rigorous. Nothing I did was good enough—and if I had a single negative thought, he always seemed to know and would send me off for weeks."

"As a matter of fact, I may not be able to see him ever again."

"Oh? Why so?"

"He said I had to stay away until I could breathe properly—relaxed and natural. I've been trying but I just can't."

"Ah, that," he said, putting down his broom. He came over to me and put one hand on my belly, one on my chest. "Now breathe," he said.

I started breathing deeply, the way Socrates had shown me. "No, don't try so hard." After a few minutes I started to feel funny in my belly and chest. They were warm inside, relaxed, and open. Suddenly, I was crying like a baby, wildly happy and not knowing why. In that moment, I was breathing completely without effort; it felt like I was *being breathed.* It felt so pleasurable, I thought, "Who needs to go to movies to be entertained?" I was so excited I could hardly contain myself! But then I felt the breathing start to tighten again.

"Joseph, I lost it!"

"Don't worry, Dan. You just need to relax a little. I helped you with that. Now you know what natural breathing feels like. To stabilize it, you'll have to *let* yourself breathe naturally, more and more, until it starts to feel normal. Controlling the breath means undoing all your emotional knots and when you do, you're going to discover a new kind of body happiness."

"Joseph," I said, hugging him, "I don't know how you did what you did, but thank you—thank you so much."

He flashed that smile that made me feel warm all over and putting away his broom said, "Give my regards to . . . Socrates."

My breathing didn't improve right away. I still struggled. But one afternoon, after an early workout in the gym, pressing weights with my improving leg, I was walking home and noticed that without my trying, my breathing was completely natural—close to the way it felt at the café.

That night, I burst into the office, ready to regale Socrates with my success and apologize for my behavior. He looked like he'd been expecting me. As I skidded to a halt in front of him, he said calmly, "Okay, let's continue,"—as if I'd just returned from the bathroom, rather than from six weeks of intensive training!

"Have you nothing else to say, Soc? No, 'Well done, lad,' no 'looking good'?"

"There's no praise and no blame on the path you've chosen. Praise and blame are forms of manipulation that you no longer require."

I shook my head in exasperation, then smiled with effort. Although I was going to try my best to be more respectful, I was hurt by his indifference. But at least I was back.

When I wasn't cleaning toilets, I was learning new and more frustrating exercises, like meditating on internal sounds until I could hear several at once. One night, as I practiced that exercise, I found myself drawn into a state of peace and relaxation I'd never known before. For a period of time—I don't know how long—I felt as if I was out of my body. This was the first time that my own efforts and energy resulted in a paranormal experience; I hadn't needed Soc's fingers pressing into my head.

Excited, I told him about it. Instead of congratulating me, he said, "Dan, don't get distracted by your experiences. Cut through the visions and sounds and see the lessons behind them. They are signs of transformation, but if you don't go beyond them you never go anywhere.

"If you want an experience, go see a movie; it's easier than yoga. Meditate all day, if you like; hear sounds and see lights, or even see sounds and hear lights. You'll still remain a jackass if you become trapped by experience. Let it go! I've suggested that you become a vegetarian, not a vegetable."

Frustrated, I said, "I'm only 'experiencing', as you call it, because you told me to!"

Socrates looked at me as if surprised. "Do I have to tell you everything?"

About to get furious, I found myself laughing. He laughed too, pointing at me. "Dan, you just experienced a wondrous alchemical transformation. You've transmuted anger to laughter. This means your energy level is much higher than before. Barriers are breaking down. Maybe you're making a little progress after all." We were still chuckling when he handed me the mop.

The following night, for the first time, Socrates was completely silent about my behavior. I got the message: I was going to have to be responsible for watching myself from now on. That's when I realized the kindness in all of his criticisms. I almost missed them.

I wasn't aware of it then, nor would I realize it until months later, but that evening, Socrates had stopped being my "parent" and started being my friend.

I decided to pay Joseph a visit, and tell him what had happened. As I walked down Shattuck a couple of fire engines wailed by me. I didn't think anything about it until I neared the café and saw the orange sky. I began to run.

The crowd was already dispersing when I arrived. Joseph had just arrived himself and was standing in front of his charred and gutted café. I was still twenty yards away from Joseph when I heard his cry of anguish and saw him drop slowly to his knees and cry. He leaped up with a scream of fury; then he relaxed. He saw me. "Dan! It's good to see you again." His face was serene.

The fire chief came over to him, and told him that the fire had probably started at the dry cleaners next door. "Thank you," Joseph said.

"Oh, Joseph, I'm so sorry." Then my curiosity surfaced. "Joseph, I saw you a minute ago. You were very upset."

He smiled. "Yes, I felt very upset, so I really let it out." I remembered Soc's words, "Let it flow and let it go." Until now, it had just been a nice idea, but here, before the blackened, waterlogged remains of his beautiful cafe, tnis fragile warrior had actually demonstrated complete mastery of his emotions.

"It was such a beautiful place, Joseph," I sighed, shaking my head.

"Yes," he said, wistfully, "wasn't it?"

For some reason, his calm now bothered me. "Aren't you upset now at all?"

He looked at me dispassionately, then said, "I have a story you might enjoy, Dan. Want to hear it?"

"Well—OK."

In a small fishing village in Japan, there lived a young, unmarried woman who gave birth to a child. Her parents felt disgraced and demanded to know the identity of the father. Afraid, she refused to tell them. The fisherman she loved had told her, secretly, that he was going off to seek his fortune and would return to marry her. Her parents persisted. In desperation, she named Hakuin, a monk who lived in the hills, as the father.

Outraged, the parents took the infant girl up to his door, pounded until he opened it, and handed him the baby, saying "This child is yours; you must care for it!"

"Is that so?" Hakuin said, taking the child in his arms, waving good-bye to the parents.

A year passed and the real father returned to marry the woman. At once they went to Hakuin to beg for the return of the child. "We must have our daughter," they said.

"Is that so?" said Hakuin, handing the child to them.

Joseph smiled and waited for my response.

"An interesting story, Joseph, but I don't understand why you're telling it to me now. I mean, your cafe just burned down!"

"Is that so?" he said. Then we laughed as I shook my head in resignation.

"Joseph, you're as crazy as Socrates."

"Why, thank you, Dan—and you're upset enough for both of us. "Don't worry about me, though; I've been ready for a change. I'll probably move south soon—or north. It makes no difference."

"Well don't go without saying good-bye."

"Good-bye, then," he said, giving me one of his hugs that left me glowing. "I'll be leaving tomorrow."

"Are you going to say good-bye to Socrates?"

He laughed, replying, "Socrates and I rarely say hello or good-bye. You'll understand later." With that, we parted. It was the last time I would ever see Joseph.

About 3:00 A.M. Friday morning I passed the clock at Shattuck and Center on my way to the gas station. I was more aware than ever of how much I still had to learn.

I stepped into the office already talking. "Socrates, Joseph's café burned down tonight."

"Strange," he said, "Cafés usually burn *up*." He was making jokes! "Anyone hurt?" he asked, without apparent concern.

"Not that I know of. Did you hear me, aren't you even a little upset?"

"Was Joseph upset when you spoke with him?"

"Well . . . no."

"All right, then." And that topic was simply closed.

Then, to my amazement, Socrates took out a pack of cigarettes and lit one. "Speaking of smoke," he said, "Did I ever mention to you that there's no such thing as a bad habit?"

I couldn't believe my eyes or my ears. This isn't happening, I told myself.

"No, you didn't, and I've gone to great lengths on your recommendation to change my bad habits."

"That was to develop your will, you see, and to give your instincts a refresher course. And we can say that habit itself—any unconscious, compulsive ritual—is negative. But specific activities—smoking, drinking, taking drugs, eating sweets, or asking silly questions—are bad and good; every action has its price, and its pleasures. Recognizing both sides, you become realistic and responsible for your actions. And only then can you make the warrior's free choice—to do or not to do.

"There is a saying: 'When you sit, sit; when you stand, stand; whatever you do, don't wobble.' Once you make your choice, do it with all your spirit. Don't be like the evangelist who thought about praying while making love to his wife, and thought about making love to his wife while praying."

I laughed at this image, while Socrates blew perfect smoke rings.

"It's better to make a mistake with the full force of your being than to carefully avoid mistakes with a trembling spirit. Responsibility means recognizing both pleasure and price, making a choice based on that recognition, and then living with that choice without concern."

"It sounds so 'either-or'. What about moderation?"

"Moderation?" He leaped up on the desk, like an evangelist. "Moderation? It's mediocrity, fear, and confusion in disguise. It's the devil's reasonable deception. It's the wobbling compromise that makes no one happy. Moderation is for the bland, the apologetic, for the fence sitters of the world afraid to take a stand. It's for those afraid to laugh or cry, for those afraid to live or die. *Moderation*"—he took a deep breath, getting ready for his final condemnation—"is *lukewarm tea,* the devil's own brew!"

Laughing, I said, "Your sermons come in like a lion and go out like a lamb, Soc. You'll have to keep practicing."

He shrugged his shoulders, climbing down from the desk. "They always told me that in the seminary." I didn't know whether he was kidding or not. "Soc, I still think smoking is disgusting."

"Haven't I got the message across to you *yet?* Smoking is not disgusting; the habit is. I may smoke one cigarette a day, then not smoke again for six months; I may enjoy one cigarette a day, or one a week, without any unmanageable urges to have another. And when I do smoke, I don't pretend that my lungs won't pay a price; I follow appropriate action afterward to help counterbalance the negative effects."

"I just never imagined a warrior would smoke."

He blew smoke rings at my nose. "I never said that a warrior behaved in a way that you considered perfect, nor do all warriors act exactly as I do. But we all follow the House Rules, you see.

"So whether or not my behavior meets your new standards or not, it should be clear to you that I have mastered all compulsions, all behavior. I have no habits; my actions are conscious, intentional, and complete."

Socrates put out his cigarette, smiling at me. "You've become too stuffy, with all your pride and superior discipline. It's time we did a little celebrating."

Then Socrates pulled out a bottle of gin from his desk. I just sat in disbelief, shaking my head. He mixed me a drink with gin and soda pop.

"Soda pop?" I asked.

"We only have fruit juice here, and don't call me 'Pop'," he said, reminding me of the words he'd spoken to me so long ago. Now here he was, offering me a gin-and-ginger ale, drinking his straight.

"So," he said, drinking the gin quickly, "Time to party, no holds barred."

"I like your enthusiasm, Soc, but I have a hard workout on Monday."

"Get your coat, sonny, and follow me." I did.

The only thing I remember clearly is that it was Saturday night in San Francisco; we started early and never stopped moving. The evening was a blur of lights, tinkling glasses, and laughter.

I do remember Sunday morning. It was about five o'clock. My head was throbbing. We were walking down Mission, crossing Fourth Street. I could barely see the street signs through the thick early-morning fog that had rolled in. Suddenly, Soc stopped and stared into the fog. I stumbled into him, giggled, then woke up quickly; something was wrong. A large dark shape emerged from the mist. My half-forgotten dream flashed into my mind but vanished as I saw another shape, then a third: three men. Two of them—tall, lean, tense—blocked our way. The third approached us and drew a stiletto from his worn leather jacket. I felt my pulse pounding through my temples.

"Give me your money," he commanded.

Not thinking clearly, I stepped toward him, reaching for my wallet, and stumbled forward.

He was startled and rushed toward me, slashing with his knife. Socrates, moving faster than I'd ever seen before, caught the man's wrist, whirled around and threw him into the street, just as another thug lunged for me. He never touched me; Socrates had kicked his legs out from under him with a lightning leg sweep. Before the third attacker could even move, Soc was upon him, taking him down with a wrist lock and a sweeping motion of his arm. He sat down on the man and said, "Don't you think you ought to consider nonviolence?"

One of the men started to get up when Socrates let out a powerful shout and the man fell backward. By then the leader had picked himself out of the street, found his knife, and was limping furiously toward Socrates. Socrates stood up, lifted the man he'd been sitting on, and threw him toward the knife-man, yelling "Catch!" They tumbled to the concrete; then, in a wild rage, all three came screaming at us in a last desperate assault.

The next few minutes were blurred. I remember being pushed by Socrates and falling. Then it was quiet, except for a moan. Socrates stood still, then shook his arms loose, and took a deep breath. He threw the knives into the sewer. Then he turned to me. "You okay?"

"Except for my head."

"You get hit?"

"Only by alcohol. What happened?"

He turned to the three men, stretched out on the pavement, knelt, and felt their pulses. Turning them over, almost tenderly, he gave gentle prodding motions, checking them for injuries. Only then did I realize he was doing his best to heal them! "Call a police ambulance," he said, turning to me. I ran to a nearby phone booth and called. Then we left and walked quickly to the bus station. I looked at Socrates. There were faint tears in his eyes, and for the first time since I'd known him, he looked pale and very tired.

We spoke little on the bus ride home. That was fine with me;

talking hurt too much. When the bus stopped at University and Shattuck, Socrates got off and said, "You're invited to my office next Wednesday, for a few drinks . . ." Smiling at my pained expression, he continued, ". . . of herb tea."

I got off the bus a block from home. My head was ready to explode. I felt like we'd lost the fight, and they were still beating on my head. I tried to keep my eyes closed as much as possible, walking the last block to the apartment house. "So this is what it feels like to be a vampire," I thought. "Sunlight can kill."

Our celebration, steeped in an alcoholic haze, had taught me two things: first, I had needed to loosen up and let loose; second, I was making a responsible choice—no more drinking; it wasn't worth the price. Besides, its pleasure was insignificant compared to what I was beginning to enjoy.

Monday's gymnastics workout, the best in many months, made me even more determined that I would again become physically and spiritually whole. My leg was healing better than I'd had any right to expect; I had been taken under the wing of an extraordinary man.

Walking home, I was so overwhelmed with gratitude that I knelt outside my apartment and touched the earth. Taking a handful of dirt in my hand, I gazed up through emerald leaves shimmering in the breeze. For a few precious seconds, I seemed to slowly melt into the earth. Then, for the first time since I was a tiny child, I felt a life-giving presence without a name.

Then my analytical mind piped in, "Ah, so this is a spontaneous mystical experience," and the spell was broken. I returned to my earthly predicament—I was an ordinary man again, standing under an elm holding dirt in his hand. I entered my apartment in a relaxed daze, read for awhile, and fell asleep.

Tuesday was a day of quiet—the quiet before the storm.

Wednesday morning I plunged into the mainstream of classes. My feelings of serenity, which I thought were permanent, soon gave way to subtle anxieties and old urges. After all my disciplined training, I was profoundly disappointed. Then, something new happened: I felt the awakening of a powerful intuitive wisdom that could be translated into words: "Old urges will continue to arise, perhaps for years. Urges do not matter; actions do. Persist as a warrior."

At first, I thought my mind was playing tricks on me. But it wasn't a thought, it wasn't a voice; it was a *feeling-certainty.* I felt like Socrates was inside me, a warrior within. This feeling was to remain with me.

That evening, I went to the station to tell Socrates about my mind's recent hyperactivity, and about the Feeling. I found him replacing a generator in a battered Mercury. He looked up, greeted me, and said casually, "Joseph died this morning." I fell back against the station wagon behind me, sick at the news of Joseph's death and Soc's callousness.

Finally, I was able to speak. "How did he die?"

"Oh, very well, I imagine," Socrates smiled. "He had leukemia, you see. Joseph had been ill for a number of years; he hung in there for a long time. Fine warrior, that one." He spoke with affection, but almost casually, without a trace of sorrow.

"Socrates, aren't you upset, just a little?" He laid the wrench down.

"That reminds me of a story I heard a long time ago, about a mother who was overcome with grief by the death of her young son.

'I can't bear the pain and sorrow,' she told her sister.

'My sister, did you mourn your son before he was born?'

'No, of course not,' the despondent woman replied.

'Well then, you need not mourn for him now. He has only returned to the same place, his original home, before he was ever born.' "

"Is that story a comfort to you, Socrates?"

"Well, I think it's a good story. Perhaps in time you'll appreciate it," he replied brightly.

"I thought I knew you well, Socrates, but I never knew you could be so heartless."

"There's no cause for unhappiness."

"But, Socrates, he's gone!"

Soc laughed softly. "Perhaps he's gone, perhaps not. Maybe he was never here!" His laughter rang through the garage.

"I want to understand you, but I can't. How can you be so casual about death? Will you feel the same way if I die?"

"Of course!" he laughed. "Dan, there are things you don't understand yet. For now, I can only say that death is a transformation—perhaps a bit more radical than puberty," he smiled, "but nothing to get particularly upset about. It's just one of the body's changes. When it happens, it happens. The warrior neither seeks nor flees from death."

His face grew more somber before he spoke again. "Death is not sad; the sad thing is that most people don't ever really live at all." Then his eyes filled with tears. We sat, two friends in silence, before I walked home. I had just turned down a side street, when the Feeling came again. " 'Tragedy' is very different for the warrior and for the fool." Socrates hadn't been sad because he simply didn't consider Joseph's death a tragedy. I wasn't to realize why that was so until months later, deep within a mountain cave.

Still, I couldn't shake the belief that I— and therefore Socrates— was supposed to be miserable when death struck. With that confusion ringing in my mind, I finally fell asleep.

In the morning, I had my answer. Socrates had simply not met my expectations. Instead, he had demonstrated the superiority of happiness. I was filled with a new resolve; I'd seen the futility of trying to live up to the conditioned expectations of others or of my own mind. I would, like the warrior, choose when, where, and how I would think and act. With that firm decision, I felt I had begun to understand the life of a warrior.

That night, I walked into the station office and said to Socrates, "I'm ready. Nothing can stop me now."

His fierce stare undid all my months of training. I quivered. He whispered, yet his voice seemed piercing. "Do not be so flippant! Perhaps you are ready, perhaps not. One thing is certain: you don't have much time left! Each day that passes is one day closer to your death. We are not playing games here, do you understand that?"

I thought I heard the wind begin to howl outside. Without warning, I felt his warm fingers touch my temple.

I was crouched in the brush. Ten feet away, facing my hiding place, was a swordsman, over seven feet tall. His massive, muscular body reeked of sulfur. His head, even his forehead, was covered by ugly, matted hair; his eyebrows were huge slashes on a hateful, twisted face.

He stared malevolently at a young swordsman who faced him. Five identical images of the giant materialized, and encircled the young swordsman. All six of them laughed at once—a groaning, growling laugh, deep in their bellies. I felt sick.

The young warrior jerked his head right and left, swinging his sword frantically, whirling, dodging, and cutting through the air. He didn't have a chance.

With a roar, all the images leaped toward him. Behind him, the giant's sword cut downward, hacking off his arm. He screamed in pain as the blood spurted, and slashed blindly through the air in a last frenzied effort. The huge sword sliced again, and the young swordsman's head fell from his shoulder and rolled to the earth, a shocked expression on its face.

"Ohhh," I groaned involuntarily, nausea washing over me. The stink of sulfur overwhelmed me. A painful grip on my arm tore me from the bushes and flung me to the ground. When I opened my eyes, the dead eyes of the young swordsman's severed head, inches away from my face, silently warned me of my own impending doom. Then I heard the guttural voice of the giant.

"Say farewell to life, young fool!" the magician growled. His taunt enraged me. I dove for the young warrior's sword and rolled to my feet, facing him.

"I've been called 'fool' by a far better man than you, you slobbering eunuch!" With a scream I attacked, swinging my sword.

The force of his parry knocked me off my feet. Suddenly, there were six of him. I tried to keep my eye on the original as I leaped to my feet, but was no longer sure.

They began a chant, deep in their bellies; it became a low-pitched, horrible death rattle as they crept slowly toward me.

Then the Feeling came to me and I knew what I had to do. *"The giant represents the* source *of all your woes; he is your* mind. *He is the demon you must cut through. Don't be deluded like the fallen warrior: keep your focus!"* Absurdly, my mind commented, "One hell of a time for a lesson." Then I was back to my immediate predicament, feeling an icy calm.

I lay down on my back and closed my eyes, as if surrendering to my fate, the sword in my hands, its blade across my chest and cheek. The illusions could fool my eyes but not my ears. Only the real swordsman would make a sound as he walked. I heard him behind me. He had only two choices—to walk away, or to kill. He chose to kill. I listened intently. Just as I sensed his sword about to cut downward, I drove my blade upward with all my might and felt it pierce, tearing upward through cloth, flesh, and muscle. A terrible scream, and I heard the thud of his body. Face down, impaled on my sword, was the demon.

"You almost didn't come back that time," said Socrates, his brows were knitted.

I ran to the bathroom, where I was immediately, thoroughly sick. When I came out, he had made some chamomile tea with licorice, "for the nerves and the stomach."

I started to tell Socrates about the journey. "I was hiding in the bush behind you, watching the whole thing," he interrupted. "I nearly sneezed once; sure glad I didn't. I certainly wasn't anxious to tangle with that character. For a moment, I thought I was going to have to, but you handled yourself pretty well, Dan."

"Why thanks, Soc." I beamed. "I . . ."

"On the other hand, you seemed to have missed the point that nearly cost you your life."

Now it was my turn to interrupt him. "The main point I was concerned with was at the end of that giant's blade," I joked. "And I didn't miss the point."

"Is that so?"

"Soc, I've been battling illusions my whole life, preoccupied with every petty personal problem. I've dedicated my life to self-improvement without grasping the one problem that sent me seeking in the first place. While trying to make everything in the world work out for me, I always succumbed to my own mind; always preoccupied with me, me, me. The giant is my only real problem in life—it's my mind. And Socrates," I said with growing excitement, just realizing what I'd done, "I cut through it!"

"There was no doubt about that," he said.

"What would have happened if the giant had won; what then?"

"Don't talk of such things," he said darkly.

"I want to know. Would I have really died?"

"Very likely," he said. "At the very least, you would have gone mad."

The tea kettle began to shriek.

5

The Mountain Path

Socrates poured steaming hot tea into our twin mugs and spoke the first encouraging words I'd heard in many months. "Your survival in the duel is real evidence that you're ready to progress further toward the One Goal."

"What's that?"

"When you discover that, you'll already be there. In the meantime, your training can now move to a different arena."

A change! A sign of progress. I was getting excited. Finally we're going to get moving again, I thought. "Socrates," I asked, "What different arena are you referring to?"

"For one thing I'm no longer going to be an answer machine. You're going to have to find the answers from within." "And you begin now. Go out back, behind the station, behind the trash bin. There, in the very corner of the lot, against the wall, you'll find a large flat stone. Sit on that stone until you have something of value to tell me."

I paused. "That's all?"

"That's it. Sit and open your mind to your own inner wisdom."

I went outside, found the rock, and sat in the darkness. First, random thoughts drifted through my mind. Then I thought of all the important concepts I'd learned in my years at school. An hour went by, then two, then three. The sun would rise in another few hours, and I was getting cold. I began to slow my breathing and to vividly imagine my belly as warm. Before long, I felt comfortable again.

Dawn came. The only thing that I could think of to tell him was a realization I'd had during a psychology lecture. I got up on stiff, sore legs and hobbled into the office. Socrates, looking relaxed and comfortable at his desk, said, "Ah, so soon? Well, what is it?"

I was almost embarrassed to say it but hoped he'd be satisfied. "Okay, Soc. Beneath all our apparent differences we all share the same human needs and fears; we're all on the same path together, guiding one another. And that understanding can give us compassion."

"Not bad; back to the rock."

"But it's going to be dawn—you're leaving."

"That's no problem," he grinned. "I'm sure you'll have thought of something by tonight."

"Tonight, I . . ." He pointed out the door.

Sitting on the rock, my whole body aching, I thought back to my childhood. I considered my past, searching for insights. I tried to compress all that had transpired in the months with Socrates into a witty aphorism.

I thought of the classes I was missing and the gymnastics workout I'd have to miss—and the excuse I'd give the coach; maybe I'd tell him I had been sitting on a rock in a gas station. That would be a crazy enough story to make him laugh.

The sun crept with agonizing slowness across the sky. I sat, hungry, irritated, then depressed, as darkness fell. I had nothing for Socrates. Then, just about the time he was due in, it came to me. He wanted something deep, something more cosmic! I concentrated with renewed effort. I saw him walk into the office, waving to me. I redoubled my efforts. Then, about midnight, I had it. I couldn't even walk, so I stretched for a few minutes before shuffling into the office.

"I've seen beneath people's social masks to their common fears and troubled minds, and that has made me cynical, because I haven't yet been able to get beyond all that to see the light within them." I figured that was a revelation of major proportions.

"Excellent," Soc announced. Just as I started to sigh, he added, "but not quite what I had in mind. Can't you bring me something more moving?" I roared with anger at no one in particular and stomped out to my philosopher's stone.

"Something more moving," he had said. Was that a hint? I naturally thought back to my recent workouts in the gymnastics room. My teammates now clucked about me like mother hens. Recently I was doing giant swings around the high bar, missed a pirouette change, and had to jump off from the top of the bar. I knew I was going to land on my feet pretty hard, but before I even hit the ground, Sid and Herb caught me in mid-air and set me down gently. "Be careful, Dan," Sid scolded. "You want to snap your leg before it heals?"

None of that seemed very relevant to my present situation, but I let my awareness relax, hoping that maybe the Feeling would advise me. Nothing. I was getting so stiff and sore I couldn't concentrate anymore. I didn't think it would be cheating to stand on the rock and practice a few flowing movements of t'ai chi, the Chinese form of slow-motion exercise that Soc had shown me.

As I bent my knees and gracefully rocked back and forth, my hips turning and arms floating in the air, I let my breath control the shifting of my weight. My mind emptied, then filled with a scene.

A few days before, I had jogged slowly and carefully to Provo Square, in the middle of Berkeley, across from City Hall and directly adjacent to Berkeley High School. To help relax, I began swaying back and forth in the movements of t'ai chi. I concentrated on softness and balance, feeling like seaweed floating in the ocean.

A few boys and girls from the high school stopped and watched me, but I paid them no attention, letting my concentration flow with the movements. When I finished and walked over to put my sweat pants back on over my running shorts, my ordinary awareness asserted itself: "I wonder if I looked good." My attention was captured by two pretty teenagers who were watching me and giggling. "I guess those girls are impressed," I thought, as I put both legs into one pant leg, lost my balance and fell on my ass.

A few other students joined the girls in their laughter. I felt embarrassed for a moment, but then lay back and laughed with them.

I wondered, still standing on the rock, why that incident could be important. Then it hit me; I knew I had something of value to tell Socrates.

I walked into the office, stood before Soc's desk, and said, "There are no ordinary moments!"

Soc smiled. "Welcome back." I collapsed on the couch and he made tea.

After that, I treated every moment in the gym—on the ground as well as in the air—as special, worthy of my full attention. Further lessons would be necessary though, for as Socrates had explained to me more than once, the ability to extend razor-sharp attention to every moment in my daily life would require much more practice.

The next day in the early afternoon before workout, I took advantage of the blue sky and warm sunshine to sit shirtless in the redwood grove and meditate. I hadn't been sitting for more than ten minutes when someone grabbed me and started shaking me back and forth. I rolled away, panting, and stood in a crouch. Then I saw who it was.

"Socrates, you have absolutely no manners sometimes."

"Wake up!" he said. "No more sleeping on the job. There's work to be done."

"I'm off duty now," I teased. "Lunch hour, see the next clerk."

"It's time to get moving, Chief Sitting Bull. Go get your running shoes and meet me back here in ten minutes.

I went home and put on my old Adidas shoes, and hurried back to the redwood grove. Socrates was nowhere in sight. Then I saw her.

"Joy!" She was wearing blue satin running shorts, yellow Tiger shoes, and a T-shirt tied at the waist. I ran up to her and hugged her. I laughed, I tried to push her, to wrestle her to the ground, but she was no push-over. I wanted to talk, to tell her my feelings, my plans, but she held her fingers to my lips, and said, "There will be time to talk later, Danny. Now, just follow me."

She demonstrated a tricky warm-up; a combination of t'ai chi movements, visualizations, calisthenics, and coordination exercises to "warm up the mind as well as the body." In a few minutes, I felt light, loose, and full of energy.

Without warning, I heard Joy say "On your mark, get set, go!" She took off, running upward through campus, toward the hills of Strawberry Canyon. I followed, huffing and puffing. Not yet in running shape, I began to trail far behind. Angrily I pushed harder, my lungs burning. Up ahead, Joy had stopped at the top of the rise overlooking the football stadium. I could hardly breathe by the time I reached her.

"What took you so long, sweetheart?" she said, hands on her hips. Then she bounced off again, up the canyon, heading for the base of the fire trails, narrow dirt roads that wound up through the hills. Doggedly I pursued her, hurting as I hadn't hurt in a long time but determined to run her down.

As we neared the trails, she slowed down and began running at a humane pace. Then, to my dismay, she reached the base of the lower trails and instead of turning around, led me up another grade, far into the hills.

I offered up a silent prayer of thanks as she turned around at the end of the lower trails, instead of heading up the agonizingly steep, quarter-mile "connector" that joined the lower and upper trails. As we ran more easily back down a long grade, Joy began to talk. "Danny, Socrates asked me to introduce you to your new phase of training. Meditation is a valuable exercise. But eventually you have to open your eyes and look around. The warrior's life," she continued, "is not a sitting practice; it is a moving experience. As Socrates has told you," she said, as we rounded a curve and began a steep downgrade, "this way is a way of action—and action is what you'll get!"

I, meanwhile, had been listening thoughtfully, staring at the ground. I answered, "Yes, I understand that, Joy, that's why I train in gym . . ." I looked up just in time to see her lovely figure disappear in the distance.

I was completely drained when, later that afternoon, I walked into the gym. I lay on the mat and stretched and stretched, and stretched, until the coach came over and asked, "Are you going to stretch all day, or would you like to try one of the other nice activities we have for you—we call them 'gymnastics' events."

"Okay, Hal," I smiled. I tried some very simple tumbling moves for the first time, testing my leg. Running was one thing; tumbling was another. Advanced tumbling moves could exert as much as sixteen hundred pounds of force as the legs drove into the ground, thrusting the body skyward. I also began to test my trampoline legs for the first time in a year. Bouncing rhythmically into the air, I somersaulted again and again. "Whoopie, ya-hoo!"

Pat and Dennis, my two trampoline mates, yelled, "Millman, will you take it easy? You know your leg isn't healed yet!" I wondered what they'd say if they knew I had just run for miles in the hills.

Walking to the station that night, I was so tired I could hardly keep my eyes open. I stepped out of the cool October air into the office, ready for some soothing tea and relaxing talk. I should have known better.

"Come over here and face me. Stand like this," Socrates demonstrated, his knees half bent, his hips forward, and his shoulders back. He put his hands out in front of him, as if holding an invisible beach ball. "Hold that position without moving and breathe slowly, while I tell you a few things you need to know about proper training."

He sat down behind his desk and watched me. Right away my legs started to ache and tremble. "How long do I have to stay this way?" I groaned.

Ignoring my question, he said, "You move well, Dan, compared to the average man, but your body is nevertheless full of knots. Your muscles hold too much tension, and tense muscles require more energy to move. So first of all, you have to learn how to release stored tensions."

My legs were starting to shake with pain and fatigue. "It hurts!"

"It only hurts because your muscles are like rocks."

"All right, you've made your point!"

Socrates only smiled and left the office abruptly, leaving me standing, bent-legged, sweating and shaking. He came back with a wiry grey tomcat who had obviously seen some action on the front lines.

"You need to develop muscles like this cat so that you can move like *us*," he said, scratching the purring feline behind the ears.

My forehead was beaded with perspiration. The pain in my shoulders and legs was intense. Finally, Socrates said, "at ease." I stood up immediately, wiping my forehead and shaking loose. "Come over here and introduce yourself to this cat." It purred with delight as Soc scratched it behind the ears. "We're both going to serve as your coaches, aren't we, puss?" The cat meowed loudly and I patted it. "Now squeeze its leg muscles, slowly, to the bone."

"I might hurt it."

"Squeeze!"

I pressed deeper and deeper into the cat's muscle until I felt the bone. The cat watched me with curiosity and kept purring.

"Now squeeze my calf muscle," Soc said.

"Oh, I couldn't, Soc. We don't know each other well enough."

"Do it, Dumbo." I squeezed and was surprised to feel that his muscles felt just like the cat's, yielding like firm jelly.

"Your turn," he said, reaching down and squeezing my calf muscle.

"Ow!" I yelped. "I'd always thought hard muscles were normal," I said, rubbing my calves.

"They are normal, Dan, but you must go far beyond normal, beyond usual, beyond common and reasonable, into the realm of the warrior. You've always tried to become superior in an ordinary realm. Now you're going to become ordinary in a superior realm."

Socrates petted the cat once more and let it go out the door. It hung around for a moment, then wandered off. He then began my introduction to the subtle elements of physical training. "By now you can appreciate how the mind imposes tension on the body. You've accumulated worries and concerns and other mental debris for years. Now it's time for you to release old tensions that have become locked into the muscles."

Socrates handed me a pair of running shorts and told me to change into them. When I returned, he was in trunks, too, and had spread a white sheet on the carpet. "What are you going to do if a customer comes?" He pointed to his overalls hanging by the door.

"Now, do exactly as I do." He began by rubbing a sweet-scented oil over his left foot. I copied every step, as he squeezed, pressed, and dug very deeply into the bottom, top, sides, and between the toes, stretching, pressing and pulling.

"Massage the bones, not just the flesh and muscle—*deeper*," he said. Half an hour later, we were through with the left foot. We repeated the same process with the right foot. This process went on for hours, covering every part of the body. I learned things about my muscles I'd never known before. I could feel where they were attached; I could feel the shape of the bones. It was amazing that I, an athlete, was so unfamiliar with my body.

Socrates had quickly slipped into his overalls a few times when the bell clanged, but otherwise, we were undisturbed. When I donned my clothes five hours later, it felt as if I had also donned a new body. Returning from a customer, Soc said, "You've cleaned many old fears from your body. Take the time to repeat this process at least once a week for the next six months. Pay attention to your legs; work on the site of your injury every day for two weeks."

"More homework," I thought. The sky began to grow light. I yawned. Time to go home. As I was walking out the door, Socrates told me to be at the base of the fire trails at 1 P.M. sharp, that afternoon.

I arrived early at the trails. I stretched and warmed up lazily; my body felt very loose and light after the "bone massage," but with only a few hours sleep I was still tired. A light drizzle had begun; all in all, I didn't feel like running anywhere, with anyone. Then I heard a rustling in the bushes nearby. I stood quietly and watched, expecting to see a deer emerge from the thicket. Out of the foliage stepped Joy, looking like an elf princess, wearing dark green shorts and a lime T-shirt emblazoned with the words, "Happiness is a full tank." A gift from Socrates, no doubt.

"Joy, before we run, let's sit down and talk; there's so much I want to tell you." She smiled and sped away.

As I pursued her up around the first curve, almost slipping on the wet clay earth, I felt the weakness in my legs after yesterday's exercise. I was soon winded and my right leg throbbed, but I didn't complain. I was thankful that she kept her pace slower than yesterday's.

We approached the end of the lower trail without talking. My breathing was labored, and I had no energy left. I started to turn around when she said, "Upsy daisy," and started up the connector. "No!" my mind screamed. "Definitely not" said my weary muscles. Then I looked at Joy, bounding lightly up the hill as if it were level.

With a rebel yell, I took the hill. I looked like a drunken gorilla, hunched over, grunting, panting, blindly clambering up, two steps forward, sliding one step back.

At the top, it levelled off. Joy was standing there, smelling the wet pine needles, looking as peaceful and content as Bambi. My lungs were begging for more air. "I have an idea," I panted. "Let's walk the rest of the way—no, let's crawl—it gives us more time to talk. How does that sound, pretty good?"

"Let's go," she said merrily.

My chagrin turned to anger. I'd run her to the ends of the earth! I stepped into a puddle, slipped through the mud, and ran into a small tree branch, nearly knocking myself over the side of the hill.

"Goddamn-it-shit-son-of-a-bitch!" My words emerged a hoarse whisper. I had no energy left to talk.

I struggled over a small hill that seemed like the Colorado Rockies and saw Joy squatting, playing with some wild rabbits as they hopped across the trail. When I stumbled up to her, the rabbits leaped into the bushes. Joy looked up at me, smiling, and said, "Oh, there you are." By some heroic effort, I leaned forward and managed to accelerate past her, but she just shot ahead and disappeared again.

We had climbed eleven hundred feet. I was now high above the Bay and could see the University below me. I was, however, in no condition or state of mind to appreciate the view. I felt very close to passing out. I had a vision of me buried on the hill, under the wet earth, with a marker: "Here lies Dan. Nice guy, good try."

The rain had increased, but I ran on as if in a trance, leaning forward, stumbling, pulling one leg forward after the other. My shoes felt like iron boots. Then I rounded a corner and saw a final hill that looked nearly vertical. Again my mind refused; my body stopped, but up there, at the top of the hill, stood Joy, with her hands on her hips as if challenging me. Somehow I managed to tip forward and start my legs moving again. I plodded, I pushed, I strained and groaned up the last endless steps until I ran right into her.

"Whoa, boy, whoa," she laughed. "You're finished, all done."

Between gasps, as I leaned against her, I wheezed, "You—can—say—that—again."

We walked back down the hill, giving me welcome time to recover and talk. "Joy, it seems like pushing this hard this fast isn't natural. I wasn't properly prepared to run this far; I don't think it's very good for the body."

"You're right," she said. "This wasn't a test of your body, but of your spirit—a test to see if you would go on—not just with the hill, but with your training. If you had stopped, it would have been the end. But you passed, Danny, you passed with flying colors."

The wind began to blow, and the rain poured, drenching us. Then Joy stopped, and took my head in her hands. Water dripped from our sopping hair and ran down our cheeks. I reached around her waist, and was drawn into her shining eyes, and we kissed.

I was filled with a new energy. I laughed at the way we both looked, like sponges that needed to be wrung out, and said, "I'll race you to the bottom!" I took off and got a good head start. "What the hell," I figured. "I can *roll* down these damn trails!" She won, of course.

Later that afternoon, dry and warm, I stretched lazily in the gym with Sid, Gary, Scott, and Herb. The warmth of the gym was a pleasurable shelter from the pounding rain outside. In spite of my grueling run, I still had a reserve of energy.

But by the time I stepped into the office that evening and took off my shoes, the reservoir had evaporated. I wanted to flop my aching body down on the couch and take a nap for ten or twelve hours. Resisting the urge, I settled as gracefully as I could manage and faced Socrates.

I was amused to see that he'd rearranged the decor. Pictures of golfers, skiers, tennis players, and gymnasts were up on the wall; on his desk sat a baseball mitt and a football. Socrates even wore a sweatshirt that said, "Ohio State Coaching Staff." It seemed that we'd entered the sports phase of my training.

While Soc made us some of his special wake-up tea he called "Thundering Tarnation," I told him about my gymnastics progress. He listened, nodding with clear approval. And his following words intrigued me.

"Gymnastics can be even more than you've yet comprehended. To help you understand this, you need to see precisely why you enjoy your acrobatic art."

"Can you explain that?"

He reached into his desk and took out three lethal-looking daggers. "Never mind, Soc," I said, "I don't really need an explanation."

"Stand up," he ordered. When I did, he casually threw a knife, underhand, straight toward my chest.

I leaped aside, falling onto the couch as the knife dropped soundlessly to the carpet. I lay there, shocked, my heart beating overtime.

"Good," he said. "You overreacted a bit, but good. Now stand up and catch the next one."

Just then, the kettle started whistling; a reprieve. "Well," I said, rubbing my sweaty palms together, "tea time."

"It will keep," he said. "Watch me closely." Soc tossed a glittering blade straight into the air. I watched it spin and drop. As it fell, he matched the speed of the blade with the downward motion of his hand and grasped the handle between his thumb and fingers, like a pincer, gripping firmly.

"Now you try. Notice how I caught it so that even if I happened to grab the blade, it wouldn't slice me." He tossed another knife toward me. More relaxed, I stepped out of the way and made only a feeble attempt at catching it.

"If you drop the next one, I'm going to start throwing overhand," he promised.

This time my eyes were glued to the handle; as it came near, I reached out. "Hey, I did it!"

"Aren't sports wonderful?" he said. For awhile we became totally immersed in throwing and catching. Then he paused.

"Now let me tell you about *satori,* a Zen concept. *Satori* is the warrior's state of being; it occurs at the moment when the mind is free of thought, pure awareness; the body is active, sensitive, relaxed; and the emotions are open and free: satori is what you experienced when the knife was flying toward you."

"You know, Soc, I've had that feeling many times, especially during competitions. Often I'm concentrating so hard, I can't even hear the applause."

"Yes, that is the experience of satori. And now, if you grasp what I say next, you'll understand the right use of sports—or painting, or music—or any other active or creative gateway to satori. You imagine that you love gymnastics, but it's merely the wrapping for the gift within: satori. The right use of gymnastics is to focus your full attention and feeling on your actions; then you will achieve satori. Gymnastics draws you into the moment of truth, when your life is on the line, like a dueling samurai. It demands your full attention: satori or die!"

"Like in the middle of a double somersault."

"Yes, that's why gymnastics is a warrior's art, a way to train mind and emotions as well as the body; a doorway to satori. The final step for the warrior is to expand his clarity into daily life. Then satori will become your reality, your key to the gate; only then we will be equals."

I sighed. "It seems like such a distant possibility, Socrates."

"When you ran up the hill after Joy," he grinned, "you didn't look wistfully at the top of the mountain, you looked directly in front of you and took one step at a time. That's how it works."

"The House Rules, right?" He smiled in answer.

I yawned, and stretched. Socrates advised, "You'd better get some sleep. You're beginning special training tomorrow morning at 7:00 at the Berkeley High School track."

When my alarm rang at 6:15, I had to drag myself out of bed, submerge my head in cold water, do some deep breathing by the open window, then scream into my pillow to wake up.

I was alert by the time I hit the streets. I jogged slowly, crossing Shattuck, and cut down Allston Way past the Berkeley YMCA, the post office, then across Milvia, onto the high school grounds where Soc was awaiting me.

I soon discovered that he had a regular program planned for me. It started with a half hour in that unbearable crouching position he'd shown me in the gas station. Then we worked with some basic principles of the martial arts. "The true martial arts teach harmony, or nonresistance—the way of the trees bending in the wind, for example. This attitude is far more important than physical technique."

Using the principles of Aikido, Socrates was able to throw me without any apparent effort, no matter how I tried to push him, grab him, punch him, or even tackle him. "Never struggle with anyone or anything. When you're pushed, pull; when you're pulled, push. Find the natural course and bend with it; then you join with nature's power." His actions were the proof of his words.

Soon it was time to go. "See you tomorrow, same time, same place. Stay home tonight and practice your exercises. Remember, make your breathing so slow that it wouldn't disturb a feather in front of your nose." He moved off as if on roller skates, and I ran toward my apartment, so relaxed that I felt like the wind was blowing me home.

In the gym that day, I did my best to apply what I'd learned, "letting movements happen" instead of trying to do them. My giant swings on the high bar seemed to go around by themselves; I swung, hopped, and somersaulted to handstand after handstand on the parallel bars; my circles, scissors, and pommel work on the horse felt as if I were supported by strings from the ceiling, weightless. And, finally, my tumbling legs were returning!

Soc and I met just after sunrise every morning. I would stride along, and Soc would run leaping like a gazelle. Each day I grew more relaxed and my reflexes became lightning quick.

One day, when we were in the middle of our warm-up run, he suddenly stopped, looking paler than I'd ever seen him before.

"I'd better sit down," he said.

"Socrates—can I do anything?"

"Yep," it seemed difficult for him to talk. "Just keep running, Dan. I'll just sit quietly." I did as he asked, but kept my eyes on his still figure, sitting with eyes closed looking proud and straight, but older somehow.

As we'd agreed weeks before, I didn't come to see him in the evening at the station, but I called to see how he was. I was relieved when Socrates answered.

"How's it going, Coach?" I asked.

"In the pink," he said, "but I've hired an assistant to take over for a few weeks."

"OK, Soc, take care of yourself."

The next day I saw my assistant coach run onto the track and literally jumped for Joy. I held her gently, hugging her and whispering in her ear; she threw me just as gently, head over heels onto the lawn. If that wasn't mortifying enough, she beat me kicking field goals, then batted the balls I pitched fifty yards over my head. Whatever we did, no matter what game, she played flawlessly, making me, a world champion, blush with shame—and anger.

I doubled the number of exercises Socrates had given me. I trained with a greater concentration than ever before. I awoke at 4:00 A.M., practiced t'ai chi until dawn, and ran into the hills before meeting Joy each day. I said nothing about my extra training.

I carried her image with me into my classes and into the gym. I wanted to see her, to hold her; but first I had to catch her. For the present, the most I could hope for was to beat her at her own games.

A few weeks later, I was back running, skipping, and leaping around the track with Socrates, who was back in action. My legs felt filled with power and spring.

"Socrates," I said, sprinting ahead and falling behind, playing tag with him, "You've been pretty close-mouthed about your daily habits. I've no idea what you're like when we're not together. Well?"

Grinning at me, he leaped forward about ten feet, then sprinted off around the track. I took off after him, until I was within talking range.

"Are you going to answer me?"

"Nope," he said. The subject was closed.

When we finally finished our stretching and meditation exercises for the morning, Socrates came up to me, put his arm around my shoulders, and said, "Dan, you've been a willing and apt pupil. From now on, you're to arrange your own schedule; do the exercises as you feel they're needed. I'm going to give you something extra, because you've earned it. I'm going to coach you in gymnastics."

I had to laugh. I couldn't help it. "You're going to coach *me*—in gymnastics? I think you're overreaching yourself this time, Soc." I ran quickly down the turf, and snapped into a roundoff, back handspring, and a high layout somersault with a double twist.

Socrates walked over to me, and said, "You know, I can't do that."

"Hot dog!" I yelled. "I've finally found something I can do that you can't."

"I did notice, though," he added, "that your arms need to stretch more when you set for the twist—oh, and your head is too far back on take-off."

"Soc, you old bluffer . . . you're right," I said, realizing that I had set my head back too far, and my arms did need to stretch more.

"Once we straighten out your technique a bit, we can work on your attitude," he added, with a final twist of his own. "I'll be seeing you in the gym."

"But Socrates, I already have a coach and I don't know if Hal or the other gymnasts will take to your wandering around the gymnastics room."

"Oh, I'm sure you'll think of something to tell them." I certainly would.

That afternoon, during the team meeting prior to workout, I told the coach and team that my eccentric grandfather from Chicago, who used to be a member of the Turners Gymnastics Club, was visiting for a couple of weeks and wanted to come watch me. "He's a nice old guy, really spry; he fancies himself quite a coach. If you all wouldn't mind and would be willing to humor him a little—he's not quite playing with a full deck, if you know what I mean—I'm sure he won't disrupt workout too much."

The consensus was favorable. "Oh, by the way," I added. He likes to be called Marilyn." I could hardly keep a straight face.

"Marilyn?" everyone echoed.

"Yeah. I know it's kind of bizarre, but you'll understand when you meet him."

"Maybe seeing 'Marilyn' in action will help us understand *you*, Millman. They say it's hereditary." They laughed and started warm-up. Socrates was entering my domain this time, and I'd show him. I wondered if he'd like his new nickname.

Today, I had a little surprise planned for the whole team. I'd been holding back in the gym, and they had no idea that I'd recovered so fully. I arrived at the gym early, and walked into the coach's office. He was shuffling through papers scattered on the desk when I spoke.

"Hal," I said, "I want to be in the intersquad competition."

Peering above his glasses he said sympathetically, "You know you're not fully healed yet. I've talked to the team doctor, and he said your leg will need at least three more months."

"Hal," I pulled him aside and whispered, "I can do it today, now! I've been doing some extra work outside the gym. Give me a chance!"

He hesitated. "Well, okay, one event at a time, and we'll see how it goes."

We all warmed up together, from event to event, around the small gymnastics room, swinging, tumbling, vaulting, pressing to handstands. I started out performing moves I hadn't done in over a year. I was saving the real surprises for later.

Then the first event came—floor exercise. Everyone waited, staring at me as I stood ready to begin my routine, as if wondering whether my leg would stand the strain.

Everything clicked; the double back, a smooth press to handstand, keeping a light rhythm going on the dance elements and turns I'd created, another sky-high tumbling pass, then a final aerial sequence. I landed lightly, under perfect control. I became aware of the whistling and applauding. Sid and Josh looked at one another in amazement. "Where'd the new guy come from?" "Hey, we'll have to sign him up for the team."

Next event. Josh went first on rings, then Sid, Chuck, and Gary. Finally, it was my turn. I adjusted my handguards, made sure the tape on my wrists was secure, and jumped up to the rings. Josh stilled my swing, then stepped back. My muscles twitched with anticipation. Inhaling, I pulled up to an inverted hang, then slowly pulled and pressed my body up to an iron cross.

I heard muffled tones of excitement as I swung smoothly down, then up again to a front uprise. I pressed slowly to a handstand with straight arms and straight body. "Well I'll be damned," Hal said, using the strongest language I'd ever heard him use. Bailing out of the handstand, I did a fast, light giant swing and locked it without a tremor. After a high double somersault dismount, I landed with only a small step. Not a bad job.

And so it went. After completing my final routine, again greeted by hoots and shouts of surprise I noticed Socrates, sitting quietly in the corner, smiling. He must have seen it all. I waved to him to come on over.

"Guys, I'd like to introduce my grandfather." I said, "This is Sid, Tom, Herb, Gary, Joel, Josh. Guys, this is . . ."

"We're pleased to meet you, Marilyn," they said in chorus. Socrates looked puzzled for the merest moment, then said, "Hello, I'm glad to meet you, too. I wanted to see what kind of crowd Dan runs around with." They grinned, probably deciding they liked him.

"I hope you don't think it's too strange, my being called Marilyn," he said casually. "My real name is Merrill, but I got stuck with the nickname. Did Dan ever tell you what he was called at home?" he chuckled.

"No," they said eagerly. "What?"

"Well, I'd better not say. I don't want to embarrass him. He can always tell you if he wants to." Socrates, the fox, looked at me and solemnly said, "You don't have to be ashamed of it, Dan."

As they walked off, they said to me, "Bye, Suzette," "Bye, Josephine," "See you later, Geraldine."

"Oh, hell, look what you've started, Marilyn!" I stomped down to the showers.

For the rest of that week, Socrates never took his eyes off me. Occasionally, he'd turn to another gymnast and offer some superb advice, which always seemed to work. I was astonished at his knowledge. Tirelessly patient with everyone else, he was much less so with me. One time I finished my best-ever pommel horse routine and walked over happily to take the tape off my wrists. Soc beckoned me and said, "The routine looked satisfactory, but you did a very sloppy job taking the tape off. Remember, *every-moment* satori."

After high bar, he said, "Dan, you must still learn to meditate your actions."

"What do you mean, meditate an action?"

"Meditating an action is different from doing it. To do, there must be a doer, a self-conscious someone performing. But when you meditate an action, you've already released all thoughts, even the thought, 'I'. There's no 'you' left to do it. In forgetting yourself, you become what you do, so your action is free, spontaneous, without ambition, inhibition, or fear."

On and on it went. He watched every expression on my face, listened to every comment I made. He told me to constantly pay more attention to my mental and emotional form.

Some people heard that I was back in shape. Susie came by to watch, bringing with her Michelle and Linda, two new friends. Linda immediately caught my eye. She was a slim red-haired woman with a pretty face behind horn-rimmed glasses, wearing a simple dress that suggested pleasing curves. I hoped to see her again.

The next day, after a very disappointing workout when nothing seemed to go well, Socrates called me over to sit with him on a crash pad. "Dan," he said, "You've achieved a high level of skill. You're an expert gymnast."

"Why thank you, Socrates."

"It wasn't necessarily a profound compliment." He turned to face me more directly. "An expert trains the physical body with the purpose of winning competitions. Someday, you may become a master gymnast. The master dedicates his training to life; therefore, he constantly places emphasis on the mind and emotions."

"I understand that, Soc. You've told me a number . . ."

"I know you understand it. What I am telling you is that you haven't yet realized it; you don't yet live it. You persist in gloating over a few new physical skills, then become depressed if the physical training doesn't go well one day. But when you really acknowledge and aim toward mental and emotional form—the warrior's practice—then the physical ups and down won't matter. Look, what happens if you have a sore ankle one day?"

"I work something else, some other area."

"It's the same with your three centers. If one area isn't going well, it's still an opportunity to train the others. On some of your weakest physical days, you can learn the most about your mind." He added, "I won't be coming into the gym again. I've told you enough. I want you to feel that I'm inside you, watching and correcting every error, no matter how small."

The next few weeks were intense. I'd rise at 6:00 A.M. stretch, then meditate before class. I went to class most of the time and completed homework quickly and easily. Then I'd sit and just do nothing for about half an hour before workout.

During this period I began seeing Susie's friend Linda. I was very attracted to her but had no time or energy to do more than talk to her for a few minutes before or after workout. Even then, I thought about her a lot—then about Joy—then about her, between my daily exercises.

The team's confidence and my abilities were building with each new victory. It was clear to everyone that I had more than recovered. Though gymnastics was no longer the center of my life, it was still an important part, so I did my very best.

Linda and I went out on a few dates and hit it off very well. She came to talk with me about a personal problem one evening and ended up staying the night, a night of intimacy, but within the conditions imposed by my training. I was growing close to her so quickly that it scared me. She was not in my plans. Still, my attraction to her grew.

I felt "unfaithful" to Joy, but I never knew when that enigmatic young woman would appear again, if ever. Joy was the ideal who flitted in and out of my life. Linda was real, warm, loving—and there.

The coach was getting more excited, more careful, and more nervous, as each passing week brought us closer to the 1968 National Collegiate Championships in Tucson, Arizona. If we won this year, it would be a first for the University, and Hal would realize a goal of twenty years' standing.

Soon enough, we were out on the floor for our three-day contest against Southern Illinois University. By the final night of the team championships, Cal and SIU were running neck-and-neck, in the fiercest race in gymnastics history. With three events still to go, Southern had a three point lead.

This was a critical point. If we were going to be realistic, we could resign ourselves to a respectable second place finish. Or we could go for the impossible.

I, for one, was going for the impossible; my spirit was on the line. I faced Hal and the team—my friends. "I'm telling you, we are going to win. Nothing is going to stop us this time. Let's do it!"

My words were ordinary, but whatever I was feeling—the electricity—call it absolute resolve, generated power in each man on the team.

Like a tidal wave, we began to pick up momentum, speeding faster and more powerfully with each performer. The crowd, almost lethargic before, started to stir with excitement, leaning forward in their seats. Something was going on; everyone could feel it.

Apparently, Southern was feeling our power too, because they started to tremble in handstands and bobble on landings. But by the last event of the meet, they still had a full point lead, and the high bar was always a strong event for them.

Finally there were two Cal gymnasts left—Sid and I. The crowd was hushed. Sid walked to the bar, leaped up, and did a routine which made us hold our breath. He ended with the highest double flyaway anyone in that gym had ever seen. The crowd went wild. I was the last man up on our team—the anchor position, the pressure spot.

Southern's last performer did a fine job. They were almost out of reach; but that "almost" was all I needed. I was going to have to do a 9.8 routine just to tie, and I'd never scored even close to that.

Here it was, my final test. My mind was awash with memories: that night of pain when my thigh bone was splintered; my vow to recover; the doctor's admonition to forget about gymnastics; Socrates and my continual training; that endless run in the rain, far up into the hills. And I felt a growing power, a wave of fury at all those who said I'd never perform again. My passion turned to icy calm. There, in that moment, my fate and future seemed in balance. My mind cleared. My emotions surged with power. Do or die.

With the spirit and determination I'd learned in that small gas station over the past months, I approached the high bar. There was not a sound in the gym. The moment of silence, the moment of truth.

I chalked up slowly, adjusting my handguards, checking my wrist straps. I stepped forward and saluted the judges. My eyes shone with a simple message as I faced the head judge: "Here comes the best damn routine you ever saw."

I leaped up to the bar and drove my legs upward. From a handstand I began swinging. The only sound in the gym was that of my hands, revolving around the bar, releasing, vaulting, catching, kipping, twisting.

Only movement, nothing else. No oceans, no world, no stars. Only the high bar and one mindless performer—and soon, even they dissolved into a unity of motion.

Adding a move I'd never done in competition before, I continued on, reaching past my limit. Around and around I swung, faster and faster, getting ready for the dismount, a piked double flyaway.

I whipped around the bar, preparing to release and go flying into space, floating and twirling in the hands of a fate that I'd chosen for myself. I kicked and snapped my legs, spun 'round once, then twice, and kicked open, stretching my body for the landing. The moment of truth had arrived.

I made a perfect landing that echoed through the arena. Silence—then pandemonium broke loose. A 9.85: we were champions!

My coach appeared out of nowhere, grabbing my hand and shaking it wildly, refusing to let go in his rapture. My teammates, jumping and screaming, surrounded and hugged me; a few of them had tears in their eyes. Then I heard the applause thundering in the distance, growing louder. We could hardly contain our excitement during the awards ceremony. We celebrated all night, recounting the meet until morning.

Then it was over. A long awaited goal was accomplished. Only then did I realize that the applause, the scores and victories were not the same anymore. I had changed so much; my search for victory had finally ended.

It was early spring, 1968. My college career was drawing to a close. What would follow, I knew not.

I felt numb as I said farewell to my team in Arizona and boarded a jet, heading back to Berkeley, and Socrates—and Linda. I looked aimlessly at the clouds below, drained of ambition. All these years I had been sustained by an illusion—happiness through victory—and now that illusion was burned to ashes. I was no happier, no more fulfilled, for all my achievements.

Finally I saw through the clouds. I saw that I had never learned how to enjoy life, only how to achieve. All my life I had been busy seeking happiness, but never finding or sustaining it.

I put my head back on the pillow as the jet started its descent. My eyes misted with tears. I had come to a dead end; I didn't know where to turn.

6

Pleasure Beyond the Mind

Carrying my suitcase, I went straight to Linda's apartment. Between kisses I told her about the championship, but said nothing of my recent depressing insights.

Linda then told me about a personal decision she had made, drawing me, for the moment, out of my own concerns. "Danny, I'm dropping out of school. I've thought about it a lot, of course. I'll get a job, but I don't want to go back home and live. Do you have any ideas?"

Immediately I thought of the friends I had stayed with after the motorcycle accident. "Linda, I could call Charlotte and Lou in Santa Monica. They're wonderful—you remember I told you about them—and I bet they'd love to have you stay with them."

"Oh, that would be wonderful! I could help around the house and get a job to help with groceries."

A five-minute phone call later, Linda had a future. I only wished it would be that simple for me.

Remembering Socrates, I abruptly told a very puzzled Linda that I had to go somewhere.

"After midnight?"

"Yes. I have . . . some unusual friends who stay up most of the night. I really have to go." Another kiss, and I was gone.

Still carrying my suitcase, I stepped into the office.

"Moving in?" Soc joked.

"I don't know what I'm doing, Socrates."

"Well, you apparently knew what you were doing at the Championships. I read a news report. Congratulations. You must be very happy."

"You know very well what I'm feeling, Soc."

"I certainly do," he said lightly as he walked into the garage to resurrect an old VW transmission. "You're making progress—right on schedule."

"Delighted to hear it," I answered without enthusiasm. "But on schedule to where?"

"To the gate! To real pleasure, to freedom, to enjoyment, to unreasonable happiness! To the one and only goal you've ever had. And to begin, it's time to awaken your senses once again."

I paused, digesting what he had said. "Again?" I asked.

"Oh, yes. You once were bathed in brightness, and found pleasure in the simplest things."

"Not recently, I'd venture."

"No, not recently," he answered, taking my head in his hands, sending me back to my infancy.

My eyes open wide, staring intently at shapes and colors beneath my hands as I crawl on the tiled floor. I touch a rug and it touches me back. Everything is bright and alive.

I grasp a spoon in one tiny hand and bang it against a cup. The clinking noise delights my ears. I yell with power! Then I look up to see a skirt, billowing above me. I'm lifted up, and make cooing sounds. Bathed in my mother's scent, my body relaxes into hers, and I'm filled with bliss.

Some time later. Cool air touches my face as I crawl in a garden. Colorful flowers tower around me, and I'm surrounded by new smells. I tear one and bite it; my mouth is filled with a bitter message. I spit it out.

My mother comes. I hold out my hand to show her a wiggly black thing that tickles my hand. She reaches down and knocks it away. "Nasty spider!" she says. Then she holds a soft thing to my face; it talks to my nose. "Rose," she says, then makes the same noise again. "Rose." I look up at her, then around me, and drift again into the world of scented colors.

I'm looking at Soc's ancient desk, down at the yellow rug. I shake my head. All of it seems hazy; there's no brightness to it. "Socrates, I feel half asleep, like I need to douse myself with cold water and wake up. Are you sure that last journey didn't do some damage?"

"No, Dan, the damage was done over the years, in ways you'll soon see."

"That place—it was my grandfather's garden, I think. I remember it; it was like the Garden of Eden."

"That is entirely accurate, Dan. It *was* the Garden of Eden. Every infant lives in a bright Garden where everything is sensed directly, without the interference of thought.

"The 'fall from grace' happens to each of us when we start thinking, when we become namers and knowers. It's not just Adam and Eve, you see, it's all of us. The birth of the mind is the death of the senses—it's not that we eat an apple and get a little sexy!"

"I wish I could go back," I sighed. "It was so bright, so clear, so enjoyable."

"What you enjoyed as a child can be yours again. Jesus of Nazareth, one of the Great Warriors, once said that you must be like a little child to enter the Kingdom of Heaven. Now you understand."

"Before you leave tonight, Dan," he said filling his mug from the dispenser, "would you like some more tea?"

"No, thanks, Soc. My tank is full for tonight."

"Okay then, I'll meet you tomorrow morning at 8 A.M. at the Botanical Gardens. It's time we went on a nature hike."

I left, already looking forward to it. I awoke after a few hours' sleep, refreshed and excited. Maybe today, maybe tomorrow, I'd discover the secret of enjoyment.

I jogged up into Strawberry Canyon, and was waiting for Soc at the entrance to the Gardens. When he arrived we walked through green acres of every kind of imaginable tree, bush, plant, and flower.

We entered a giant greenhouse. The air was warm and humid, contrasting with the cool morning air outside. Soc pointed to the tropical foliage that towered over us. "As a child, all this would appear before your eyes and ears and touch as if for the first time. But now you've learned names and categories for everything. 'That's good, that's bad, that's a table, that's a chair, that's a car, a house, a flower, dog, cat, chicken, man, woman, sunset, ocean, star.' You've become bored with things because they only exist as names to you. The dry concepts of the mind obscure your vision."

Socrates waved his arm in a sweeping gesture, taking in the

palms high above our heads that nearly touched the plexiglass canopy of the geodesic dome. "You now see everything through a veil of associations *about* things, projected over a direct, simple awareness. You've 'seen it all before'; it's like watching a movie for the twentieth time. You see only memories of things, so you become bored. Boredom, you see, is fundamental nonawareness of life; boredom is awareness, trapped in the mind. You'll have to lose your mind before you can come to your senses."

The next night Socrates was already putting the kettle on when I stepped into the office, carefully removed my shoes, and put them on the mat beneath the couch. With his back still turned, he said, "How about a little contest? You do a stunt, then I'll do a stunt, and we'll see who wins."

"Well, okay, if you really want to." I didn't want to embarrass him, so I just did a one-arm handstand on the desk for a few seconds, then stood on it and did a back somersault off, landing lightly on the carpet.

Socrates shook his head, apparently demoralized. "I thought it might be a close contest, but I can see that it's not going to be."

"I'm sorry, Soc, but after all, you aren't getting any younger, and I am pretty good at this stuff."

"What I meant to say," he grinned, "is that you don't stand a chance."

"What?"

"Here goes," he said. I watched him as he slowly turned around and walked deliberately into the bathroom. I moved toward the front door in case he came running out with a sword again. But he only emerged with his mug. He filled it with water, smiled at me, held the water up as if to toast me, and drank it slowly.

"Well?" I said.

"That's it."

"That's what? You didn't do a damn thing."

"Ah, but I did. You just don't have the eyes to appreciate my feat. I was feeling a slight toxicity in my kidneys; in a few days, it might have begun to affect my entire body. So before any symptoms could arise, I located the problem and flushed out my kidneys."

I had to laugh. "Soc, you're the greatest, most silver-tongued con man I've ever met. Admit defeat—you're bluffing."

"I am completely serious. What I've just described did, in fact, take place. It requires sensitivity to internal energies and the voluntary control of a few subtle mechanisms.

"You, on the other hand," he said, rubbing salt in the wound, "are only vaguely aware of what's going on inside that bag of skin. Like a balance beam performer just learning a handstand, you're not yet sensitive enough to detect when you're out of balance, and you can still 'fall' ill."

"The thing is, Soc, I've developed a very sensitive balance in gymnastics. One has to, you see, to do some of the advanced . . ."

"Nonsense. You've only developed a gross level of awareness; sufficient to perform some elementary movement patterns, but nothing to write home about."

"You sure take the romance out of a triple somersault, Soc."

"There is no romance in it; it's a stunt that requires some ordinary qualities. When you can feel the flow of energies in your body and do a minor tune-up—*then* you'll have your 'romance'. So keep practicing, Dan. Refine your senses a little more each day; stretch them, as you would in the gym. Finally, your awareness will pierce deeply into your body and into the world. Then you'll think about life less and feel it more. Then you'll enjoy even the simplest things in life—no longer addicted to achievement or expensive entertainments. Next time," he laughed, "perhaps we can have a real competition."

I warmed up the tea water again. We sat quietly for a while, then went into the garage, where I helped Soc pull an engine from a VW and take apart another ailing transmission.

We went out to service a huge black limousine. When we returned later to the office, I asked Soc whether he thought rich people are any happier than "poor stiffs like us."

His response, as usual, shocked me. "I am not poor, Dan, I'm extremely wealthy. And as a matter of fact, you must become rich to be happy." He smiled at my dumbfounded expression, picked up a pen from his desk, and wrote on a clean white sheet of paper:

$$\text{Happiness} = \frac{\text{Satisfaction}}{\text{Desires}}$$

"If you have enough money to satisfy your desires, Dan, you are rich. But there are two ways to be rich: You can earn, inherit, borrow, beg, or steal enough money to meet expensive desires; or, you can cultivate a simple lifestyle of few desires; that way you always have more than enough money.

"Only the warrior has the insight and discipline to make use of that second way. Full attention to every moment is my desire and my pleasure. Attention costs no money; your only investment is training. That's another advantage of being a warrior, Dan—it's cheaper! The secret of happiness, you see, is not found in seeking more, but in developing the capacity to enjoy less."

I felt content, listening to the spell he wove. There were no complications, no pressing searches, no desperate enterprises that had to be done. Socrates showed me the treasure trove of wealth within the body.

Socrates must have noticed me daydreaming, because suddenly he grabbed me under the arms, picked me up, and threw me straight up into the air, so high, my head almost hit the ceiling! When I came down, he slowed my descent, setting me back down on my feet.

"I just want to make sure I have your attention for this next part. What time is it?"

Shaken by my brief flight, I responded, "Um, it's right on the garage clock—2:35."

"Wrong! The time always was, is, and always will be *now! Now* is the time; the time is *now*. Is it clear?"

"Well, yeah, it's clear."

"Where are we?"

"We're in the gas station office—say, didn't we play this game a long time ago?"

"Yes we did, and what you learned is that the only thing you know absolutely is that you are here, wherever here may be. From now on, whenever your attention begins to drift off to other times and places, I want you to snap back. Remember, the time is now and the place is here."

Just then, a college student burst into the office, dragging a friend with him. "I couldn't believe it!" he said to his friend, pointing to Socrates, then speaking to him. "I was walking by on the street, when I glanced over here and saw you throw that guy to the ceiling. Who *are* you, anyway?"

It looked as if Socrates was about to blow his cover. He looked at the student blankly, then laughed. "Oh," Soc laughed again, "Oh, that's good! No, we were just exercising to pass the time. Dan here is a gymnast—aren't you, Dan?" I nodded. The student's friend said he remembered me; he'd watched a couple of gymnastics meets. Soc's story was becoming credible.

"We have a little trampoline behind the desk there." Socrates went behind the desk, where, to my complete stupefaction, he "demonstrated" the nonexistent mini-trampoline so well I began to believe it was behind the desk. Jumping higher and higher until he could almost reach the ceiling, Soc then "bounced" lower, bobbing up and down, and finally stopped, bowing. I clapped.

Confused but satisfied, they left. I ran around to the other side of the desk. There was, of course, no trampoline. I laughed hysterically. "Socrates, you're incredible!"

"Yep," he said, never one for false modesty.

By this time the sky was showing the faint light of dawn as Socrates and I got ready to leave. Zipping up my jacket, I felt as if it was a symbolic dawn for me.

Walking home, I thought of the changes that were showing up, not so much on the outside, but on the inside. I felt a new clarity about where my path lay and what my priorities were. As Soc had demanded of me long ago, I'd finally released my expectation that the world could fulfill me; therefore my disappointments had vanished, too. I would continue to do whatever was necessary to live in the everyday world, of course, but on my own conditions. I was starting to feel free.

My relationship with Socrates had changed, too. For one thing, I had fewer illusions to defend. If he called me a jackass, I could only laugh, because I knew that by his standards at least, he was right. And he rarely frightened me anymore.

As I passed Herrick Hospital on my walk home, a hand grasped my shoulder and I slipped instinctively under it, like a cat that didn't want to be patted. Turning, I saw a grinning Socrates.

"Ah, you're not such a nervous fish anymore, are you?"

"What are you doing here, Soc?"

"Going for a walk."

"Well, it's great to have you along."

We walked in silence for a block or two, then he asked, "What time is it?"

"Oh, it's about . . ." Then I caught myself. ". . . about *now.*"

"And where are we?"

"Here."

He said nothing else, and I felt like talking, so I told him about my new feelings of freedom, my plans for the future.

"What time is it?" he asked.

"Now," I sighed. "You don't have to keep . . ."

"Where are we?" he asked innocently.

"Here, but . . ."

"Listen to me," he interrupted. "Stay in the present. You can do nothing to change the past, and the future will never come exactly as you plan or hope for. There have never been past warriors, nor will there be future ones, either. The warrior is *here, now.* Your sorrow, your fear and anger, regret and guilt, your envy and plans and cravings live only in the past, or in the future."

"Hold on, Socrates. I distinctly remember being angry in the present."

"Not so," he said. "What you mean is that you *acted* angry in a present moment. This is natural; action is always in the present, because it is an expression of the body, which can only exist in the present. But the mind, you see, is like a phantom, and, in fact, never exists in the present. Its only power over you is to draw your attention out of the present."

I bent over to tie my shoe when I felt something touch my temples.

I finished tying my shoe and stood up, finding myself standing alone in a musty old attic without windows. In the dim light I discerned a couple of old trunks, shaped like vertical coffins, in the corner of the room.

I felt very frightened all at once, especially when I realized that, in the stillness of the air, I could hear nothing at all, as if all sound was muffled by the stale dead air. Taking a tentative step, I noticed that I was standing within a pentacle, five-pointed star, painted in brownish red, on the floor. I looked closer. The brownish red color was from dried—or drying—blood.

Behind me I heard a growling laugh, so sickening, so horrifying that I had to swallow the rising metallic taste in my mouth. Reflexively, I turned to face a leprous, misshapen beast. It breathed in my face and the sickeningly sweet stench of the long-dead hit me full force.

Its grotesque cheeks pulled back to reveal black fangs. Then it spoke: "Commme to mmeeee." I felt impelled to obey, but my instincts held. I stayed put.

It roared with fury. "My children, take him!" The trunks in the corner began moving slowly toward me and opened to reveal loathsome, decaying human corpses, which stepped out and advanced steadily. I gyrated wildly within the pentacle, seeking a place to run, when the attic door opened behind me and a young woman of about nineteen stumbled into the room and fell just outside the pentacle. The door remained ajar, and a shaft of light fell through.

She was beautiful, dressed in white. She moaned, as if hurt, and said in a faraway voice, "Help me, please help me." Her eyes were tearfully pleading, yet held a promise of gratitude, reward, and unquenchable desire.

I looked at the advancing figures. I looked at the woman and at the door.

Then the Feeling came to me: *"Stay where you are. The pentacle is the present moment. There, you're safe. The demon and his attendants are the past. The door is the future. Beware."*

Just then, the girl moaned again and rolled over on her back. Her dress slid up one leg, almost to her waist. She reached out to me pleading, tempting, "Help me. . . ."

Drunk with desire, I lunged out of the pentacle.

The woman snarled at me, showing blood-red fangs. The demon and his entourage yelped in triumph and leaped toward me. I dove for the pentacle.

Huddled on the sidewalk, shaking, I looked up at Socrates.

"If you're sufficiently rested now, would you like to continue?" he said to me, as some early morning joggers ran by with amused looks on their faces.

"Do you have to scare me half to death every time you want to make a point?" I screeched.

"I should say so," he replied, "when it is a very important point."

After a few moments' silence I asked sheepishly, "You wouldn't have that girl's phone number, would you?" Socrates slapped his forehead and looked to the heavens.

"I will presume you did get the point of that little melodrama?"

"In summation," I said, "stay in the present: it's safer. And don't step outside a pentacle for anyone with fangs."

"Right you are," he grinned. "Don't let anybody or anything, least of all your own thoughts, draw you out of the present. Surely you have heard the story of the two monks:

Two monks, one old, one very young, walked along a muddy path in a rain forest, on their way back to a monastery in Japan. They came upon a lovely woman who stood helplessly at the edge of a muddy, fast-flowing stream.

Seeing her predicament, the older monk swept her up in his strong arms and carried her across. She smiled at him, her arms around his neck, until he put her gently down on the other side. Thanking him, she bowed, and the monks continued on their way in silence.

As they neared the monastery gates, the young monk could no longer contain himself. "How could you carry a beautiful woman in your arms? Such behavior does not seem proper for a priest."

The old monk looked at his companion, replying, "I left her back there. Are you still carrying her?"

"Looks like more work ahead," I sighed, "just when I thought I was getting somewhere."

"Your business is not to 'get somewhere'—it is to be here. Dan, you still hardly ever live fully in the present. You've only focused your mind here and now when you're doing a somersault or being badgered by me. It's time now to apply yourself like never before, if you're to have a chance of finding the gate. It is here, before you; open your eyes, now!"

"But how?"

"Just keep your attention in the present moment, Dan, and you'll be free of thought. When thoughts touch the present, they dissolve." He prepared to leave.

"Wait, Socrates. Before you go, tell me—were you the older monk in the story—the one who carried the woman? That sounds like something you would have done."

"Are you still carrying her?" He laughed as he glided away and disappeared around the corner.

I jogged the last few blocks home, took a shower, and fell sound asleep.

When I awoke I went for a walk, continuing to meditate in the way Socrates had suggested, focusing my attention more and more in the present moment. I was awakening to the world and, like a child once again, was coming to my senses. The sky seemed brighter, even on the foggy days of May.

I said nothing to Socrates about Linda, perhaps for the same reason I never told her about my teacher. They were different parts of my life; and I sensed that Socrates was more interested in my inner training than my worldly relations.

I never heard from Joy, it seemed, unless she stepped from the shadows, or appeared in a dream. Linda wrote to me almost every day, and sometimes called, since she worked at Bell Telephone.

Classes rolled by smoothly as the weeks went on. My real school room, however, was Strawberry Canyon, where I ran like the wind through the hills, losing track of the distance, racing by jackrabbits. Sometimes I would stop to meditate beneath the trees or just smell the fresh breeze coming off the sparkling bay far below. I would sit for half an hour, watching the water's shimmer, or the clouds drifting overhead.

I had been released from all the "important goals" of my past. Only one remained: the gate. Sometimes even that was forgotten in the gym, when I played ecstatically, soaring high into the air on the trampoline, turning and twisting, floating lazily, then snapping into double somersaults and driving skyward again.

Linda and I continued to correspond, and our letters became poetry. But Joy's image would float before my eyes, smiling mischievously, knowingly, until I wasn't sure of what, or whom, I really wanted.

Then, before I knew it, my last year at the university was drawing to a close. Final exams were just a formality. Writing answers in the familiar blue books, I knew my life had changed as I delighted in the smooth blue ink emanating from the point of my pen. Even the lines on the paper seemed a work of art. The ideas just rolled out of my head, unobstructed by tension or concern. Then it was over, and I realized I'd finished my university education.

I brought fresh apple juice to the station to celebrate with Socrates. As we sat and sipped, my thoughts slipped out from under my attention and drifted into the future.

"Where are you?" Soc asked. "What time is it?"

"Here, Soc, now. But my present reality is that I need a career. Have any advice?"

"My advice is: do what you will."

"That's not entirely helpful. Can you add anything?"

"Okay, do what you must."

"But what?"

"It doesn't matter what you do, only how well you do it. By the way," he added, "Joy will be visiting this weekend."

"Wonderful! How about us going on a picnic this Saturday? Does 10 A.M. sound good?"

"Fine, we'll meet you here."

I said goodnight, and stepped out into a cool June morning, under sparkling stars. It was about 1:30 A.M. as I turned from the station and walked to the corner. Something made me turn around, and I looked up on the roof. There he was, the vision I'd seen so many months ago, standing very still, a soft light glowing around his body as he looked up into the night. Even though he was sixty feet away and speaking softly, I heard him as if he were next to me. "Dan, come here."

I walked quickly around back in time to see Socrates emerge from the shadows.

"Before you leave tonight there is one final thing you should see." He pointed his two index fingers toward my eyes, and touched me just above the brows. Then he simply stepped away and leaped straight up, landing on the roof. I stood, fascinated, not believing what I'd seen. Soc jumped down, landing with very little sound. "The secret," he grinned, "is very strong ankles."

I rubbed my eyes. "Socrates, was it real? I mean, I saw it; but you touched my eyes first."

"There are no well-defined edges of reality, Dan. The earth isn't solid. It is made of molecules and atoms, tiny universes filled with space. It is a place of light, and of magic, if you only open your eyes."

We said goodnight.

Saturday finally arrived. I walked into the office and Soc rose from his chair. Then I felt a soft arm wrap around my waist and saw Joy's shadow move next to mine.

"I'm so happy to see you again," I said, hugging her.

Her smile was radiant. "Ooh," she squeaked. "You *are* getting strong. Are you training for the Olympic Games?"

"As a matter of fact," I answered seriously, "I've decided to retire. Gymnastics has taken me as far as it can; it's time to move on." She nodded without comment.

"Well, let's be off," said Socrates, carrying the watermelon he'd brought. I had the sandwiches in my backpack.

Up we rode, into the hills, on a day that couldn't have been more beautiful. After lunch, Soc decided to leave us alone and "go climb a tree."

Later, he climbed down to hear us brainstorming.

"I'm going to write a book someday about my life with Socrates, Joy."

"Maybe they'll make a movie out of it," she said, as Soc listened, standing by the tree.

I was getting enthusiastic now. "And they'll have warrior T-shirts. . . ."

"And warrior soap," Joy cried.

"And warrior decals."

"And bubble gum!"

Socrates had heard enough. Shaking his head, he climbed back up the tree.

We both laughed, rolling in the grass, and I said with practiced casualness, "Hey, why don't we have a little race to the Merry-Go-Round and back?"

"Dan, you must be a glutton for punishment," Joy boasted. "My father was an antelope, my mother a cheetah. My sister is the wind, and . . ."

"Yeah, and your brothers are a Porsche and a Ferrari." She laughed as she slipped into her sneakers.

"The loser cleans up the garbage," I said.

Doing a perfect imitation of W. C. Fields, Joy said, "There's a sucker born every minute." Then, without warning, she took off. I yelled after her, putting on my shoes, "And I suppose your uncle was Peter Rabbit!" I called up to Socrates, "Be back in a few minutes," and sprinted after Joy, now far ahead, running for the Merry-Go-Round about a mile away.

She was fast, all right—but I was faster, and I knew it. My training had honed me to an edge sharper than I'd ever imagined.

Joy looked back as her arms and legs pumped smoothly, and was surprised—might I say shocked?—to see me running right behind her, breathing easy.

She pushed even harder and looked back again. I was close enough to see beads of perspiration dripping down her soft neck. As I pulled up alongside her, she puffed, "What did you do, hitch a ride on the back of an eagle?"

"Yes," I smiled at her. "One of my cousins." Then I blew her a kiss and took off.

I was already around the Merry-Go-Round and halfway back to the picnic spot when I saw that Joy had fallen a hundred yards behind. It looked like she was pushing hard and getting tired. I felt sorry for her, so I stopped, sat down, and picked a wild mustard flower growing by the path. When she approached me, she slowed down to see me sniffing the flower. I said, "Lovely day, isn't it?"

"You know," she said, "this reminds me of the story of the tortoise—and the hare." With that, she accelerated in a burst of incredible speed.

Surprised, I jumped up and took off after her. Slowly but surely I gained on her, but now we were nearing the edge of the meadow, and she had a good lead. I edged closer and closer until I could hear her sweet panting. Neck and neck, shoulder to shoulder, we raced the last twenty yards. Then she reached out and took my hand; we slowed down, laughing, and fell right on top of the watermelon slices which Soc had prepared, sending seeds flying in every direction.

Socrates, back down from his tree, applauded as I slid, face first, into a slice of melon which smeared all over my cheeks.

Joy looked at me, and simpered, "Why honey, y'all don't need to blush like that. After all, y'all almos' *did* beat lil' ol' me."

My face was dripping wet; I wiped if off and licked the melon juice from my fingers. I answered, "Why honey chile, even a lil' ol' fool could plainly see that I won."

"There's only one fool around here," Soc grumbled, "and he just demolished the melon."

We all laughed, and I turned to Joy with love shining in my eyes. But when I saw how she was staring at me, I stopped laughing. But she took my hand and led me to the edge of the meadow, overlooking the rolling green hills of Tilden Park.

"Danny, I have to tell you something. You're very special to me. But from what Socrates says"—she looked back at Socrates, who was shaking his head slowly from side to side—"your path doesn't seem to be wide enough for me, too—at least that's how it looks. And I'm still very young, Danny—I also have many things I must attend to."

I was trembling. "But Joy, you know I want you to be with me always. I want to have children with you and keep you warm at night. Our life could be so fine together."

"Danny," she said, "there's something else I should have told you before. I know I look and act—well, the age you might expect me to be. But I'm only fifteen years old."

I stared at her, my jaw slack. "That means that for months I've had an awful lot of illegal fantasies."

All three of us laughed, but my laughter was hollow. A piece of my life had fallen and broken. "Joy, I'll wait. There's still a chance."

Joy's eyes filled with tears. "Oh, Danny, there is always a chance—for anything. But Socrates has told me that it's best if you forget."

Silently, Socrates approached me from behind as I looked into Joy's luminous eyes. I was reaching out for her when he touched me lightly at the base of my skull. The lights went out, and I immediately forgot I ever knew a woman named Joy.

BOOK THREE

UNREASONABLE HAPPINESS

7

The Final Search

When my eyes opened, I was lying on my back looking up at the sky.

I must have dozed off. Stretching, I said, "The two of us should get out of the station and picnic more often, don't you think?"

"Yes," he nodded slowly. "Just the two of us."

We collected our gear and walked a mile or so through the wooded hills before catching the bus. All the way down the hill, I had a vague feeling that I'd forgotten to say or do something—or maybe I'd left something behind. By the time the bus reached the lowlands, the feeling had faded.

Before he stepped off the bus, I asked, "Hey, Soc, how about going for a run with me sometime tomorrow?"

"Why wait?" he answered. "Meet me tonight on the bridge over the creek at 11:30. We can go for a nice long midnight run up the trails."

That night the full moon gave a silver sheen to the tops of the weeds and bushes as we started up the trails. But I knew every foot of the five-mile climb and could have run the trails in complete darkness.

After a steep climb on the lower trails, my body was toasty warm. Soon we had reached the connector and started up. What had seemed like a mountain many months ago was now hardly any strain for me. Breathing deeply, I sprinted up and hooted at Socrates trailing behind, wheezing, clowning around. "Come on, old geezer—catch me if you can!"

On a long straight stretch I looked back, expecting to see Soc bouncing along. He was nowhere in sight. I stopped, chuckling, suspecting an ambush. Well, I'd let him wait up ahead and wonder where *I* was. I sat on the edge of a hill and looked out over the bay to the city of San Francisco glittering in the distance.

Then the wind began to whisper, and suddenly I knew that something was wrong—very wrong. I leaped up and raced back down the trails.

I found Socrates just around the bend, lying face down on the cold earth. I knelt down quickly, tenderly turning him over and holding him, and put my ear to his chest. His heart was silent. "My God, oh my God," I said as a shrill gust of wind howled up the canyon.

Laying Soc's body down, I put my mouth over his and blew into his lungs; I pumped his chest madly in a growing panic.

Finally, I could only murmur softly to him, cradling his head in my hands. "Socrates, don't die—please, Socrates." It had been my idea to run. I remembered how he had fought his way up the connector, wheezing. If only . . . Too late. I was overcome with anger at the injustice of the world; I felt a rage greater than any I had ever known.

"NOOOOOOOOOOO!" I screamed, and my anguish echoed down the canyon, sending birds soaring from their nests into the safety of the air.

He would not die—I would not let him! I felt energy surging through my arms, legs, and chest. I would give it all to him. If it meant my life, it was a price I would gladly pay. "Socrates, live, *live!*" I grabbed his chest in my hands, digging my fingers into his ribs. I felt electrified, saw my hands glowing, as I shook him, willing his heart to beat. "Socrates!" I commanded. "Live!"

But there was nothing . . . nothing. Uncertainty entered my mind and I collapsed. It was over. I sat still, with tears running down my cheeks. "Please," I looked upward, into the silver clouds drifting across the moon. "Please," I said to the God I'd never seen. "Let him live." Finally I stopped struggling, stopped hoping. He was beyond my powers. I had failed him.

Two small rabbits hopped out of the bush to see me, gazing down at the lifeless body of an old man which I held tenderly in my arms.

That's when I felt it—the same Presence I had known many months before. It filled my body. I breathed It; It breathed me. "Please," I said one last time, "take me instead." I meant it. And in that moment, I felt a pulse begin to throb in Soc's neck. Quickly, I put my head against his chest. The strong, rhythmic beat of that old warrior's heart pounded against my ear. I breathed life into him, then, until his chest rose and fell of its own accord.

When Socrates opened his eyes, he saw my face above his, laughing, crying softly with gratitude. And the moonlight bathed us in quicksilver. The rabbits, their fur shining, gazed at us. Then, at the sound of my voice, they retreated into the bush.

"Socrates, you're alive."

"I see that your powers of observation are at their usual razor-sharp keenness," he said weakly.

He tried to stand, but he was very shaky, and his chest hurt, so I lifted him on my shoulders, firefighter style, and began carrying him up toward the end of the trails, two miles away. From the Lawrence Science Lab, the night watchman could call an ambulance.

He rested quietly on my shoulders most of the way as I fought fatigue, sweating under his weight. Now and then he would say, "The only way to travel—let's do this more often"—or "Giddyup."

I returned home only after he was settled into the intensive care unit at Herrick Hospital. That night the dream returned. Death reached out for Socrates; with a cry, I awoke.

I sat with him during the next day. He was asleep most of the time, but late in the afternoon he wanted to talk.

"Okay—what happened?"

"I found you lying there. Your heart had stopped and you weren't breathing. I—I willed you to live."

"Remind me to put you in my will, too. What did you feel?"

"That was the strange part, Soc. At first I felt energy course through me. I tried to give it to you. I had nearly given up, when . . ."

"Never say die" he proclaimed.

"Socrates, this is serious!"

"Continue—I'm rooting for you. I can't wait to find out how it all came out."

I grinned, "You know damn well how it came out. Your heart started beating again—but only after I stopped trying. That Presence I once felt—*It* started your heartbeat."

He nodded. "You were feeling *It*." It wasn't a question, but a statement.

"Yes."

"That was a good lesson," he said, stretching gently.

"A lesson! You had a heart attack and it was a nice little lesson for me? That's how you see it?"

"Yes," he said. "And I hope you make good use of it. No matter how strong we appear, there is always a hidden weakness which may be our ultimate undoing. House Rules: For every strength there is a weakness—and vice versa. Of course, even as a child, my weakness has always been my heart. You, my young friend, have another kind of 'heart trouble'."

"*I* do?"

"Yes. You haven't yet opened your heart in a natural way, to bring your emotions to life in the way that you did last night. You've learned body control and even some mind control, but your heart has not yet opened. Your goal is not invulnerability, but vulnerability—to the world, to life, and therefore, to the Presence you felt.

I've tried to show you by example that a warrior's life is not about imagined perfection or victory; it is about love. Love is the warrior's sword; wherever it cuts, it gives life, not death."

"Socrates, tell me about love. I want to understand it."

He laughed softly. "It is not something to be understood; it can only be felt."

"Well then, what about feeling?"

"You see?" he said. "You want to turn it into a mental concept. Just forget yourself and feel!"

I looked down at him, realizing the extent of his sacrifice—how he had trained with me, never holding back, even though he knew he had a heart condition—all, just to keep my interest. My eyes filled with tears. "I do feel, Soc . . ."

"Bullshit! Sorrow is not good enough."

My shame turned to frustration. "You can be infuriating sometimes, you old wizard! What do you want from me, blood?"

"Anger is not good enough," he intoned dramatically, pointing at me with his eyes popping out like an old-fashioned movie villain.

"Socrates, you're completely loony," I laughed.

"That's *it*—laughter *is* good enough!"

Socrates and I both laughed with delight; then, chuckling softly, he fell asleep. I left quietly.

When I came to visit the next morning, he appeared stronger. I took him to task right away. "Socrates, why did you persist in running with me and, furthermore, doing all those leaps and bounds when you knew that they might kill you at any time?"

"Why worry? Better to live until you die. I am a warrior; my way is action," he said. "I am a teacher; I teach by example. Someday you too may teach others as I have shown you—then you'll understand that words are not enough; you too must teach by example, and only what you've realized through your own experience."

Then he told me a story:

A mother brought her young son to Mahatma Gandhi. She begged, "Please, Mahatma. Tell my son to stop eating sugar."

Gandhi paused, then said, "Bring your son back in two weeks." Puzzled, the woman thanked him and said that she would do as he had asked.

Two weeks later, she returned with her son. Gandhi looked the youngster in the eye and said, "Stop eating sugar."

Grateful but bewildered, the woman asked, "Why did you tell me to bring him back in two weeks? You could have told him the same thing then."

Gandhi replied, "Two weeks ago, *I* was eating sugar."

"Dan, embody what you teach, and teach only what you have embodied."

"What would I teach other than gymnastics?"

"Gymnastics is enough, as long as you use it as a medium for conveying more universal lessons," he said. "Respect others. Give them what they want at first and, perhaps eventually, a few of them will want what you want to give them. Be content to teach flips until someone asks for more."

"How will I know if they want something more?"

"You'll know."

"But Socrates, are you sure I'm destined to be a teacher? I don't feel like one."

"You appear to be headed in that direction."

"That brings me to something I've wanted to ask you for a long time—you often seem to read my thoughts or to know my future. Will I someday have these kinds of powers?" Upon hearing this, Soc reached over and clicked the TV on and started to watch cartoons. I clicked it back off.

He turned to me and sighed. "I was hoping you would completely bypass any fascination with powers. But now that it's come up, we might as well get it out of the way. All right, what do you want to know?"

"Well, for starters, foretelling the future. You seem to be able to do it sometimes."

"Reading the future is based on a realistic perception of the present. Don't be concerned about seeing the future until you can clearly see the present."

"Well, what about mind-reading?" I asked.

Socrates sighed. "What about it?"

"You seem to be able to read my mind most of the time."

"Yes, as a matter of fact," he admitted, "I do know what you're thinking most of the time. Your 'mind' is easy to read, because it's written all over your face."

I blushed.

"See what I mean?" he laughed, pointing to my rouge complexion. "And it doesn't take a magician to read faces; poker players do it all the time."

"But what about *real* powers?"

He sat up in bed and said, "Special powers do in fact exist. But for the warrior, such things are completely beside the point. Don't be deluded. Happiness is the only power that counts. And you cannot attain happiness; it attains you—but only after you surrender everything else."

Socrates seemed to grow weary. He gazed at me for a moment, as if making a decision. Then he spoke in a voice both gentle and firm, saying the words I had most feared. "It's clear to me that you are still trapped, Dan—still searching somewhere else for happiness. So be it. You shall search until you tire of it altogether. You are to go away for awhile. Seek what you must, and learn what you can. Then we shall see."

My voice quavered with emotion. "How—how long?"

His words jolted me. "Nine or ten years should be sufficient."

I was terrified. "Socrates, I'm not really that interested in powers. I honestly understand what you've said. Please, let me stay with you."

He closed his eyes, and sighed. "My young friend, have no fear. Your path will guide you; you cannot lose your way."

"But when can I see you again, Socrates?"

"When your search is finished—really finished."

"When I become a warrior?"

"A warrior is not something you become, Dan. It is something you either are, in this moment, or something you are not. The Way itself creates the warrior. And now you must forget me altogether. Go, and come back radiant."

I had grown to depend so much on his counsel, on his certainty. Still trembling, I turned and walked to the door. Then I looked one last time into those shining eyes. "I'll do all that you've asked, Socrates—except one. I'll never forget you."

I walked down the stairs, out into the city streets, and up the winding roads through campus into an uncertain future.

I decided to move back to Los Angeles, my hometown. I took my old Valiant out of storage and spent my last weekend in Berkeley packing for my departure. Thinking of Linda, I walked to the corner phone booth and dialed the number of her new apartment. When I heard her sleepy voice, I knew what I wanted to do.

"Sweetheart, I have a couple of surprises. I'm moving to L.A.; will you fly up to Oakland as soon as you can tomorrow morning? We could drive down south together; there's something we need to talk about."

There was a pause on the other end. "Oh, I'd love to! I'll be on the 8 A.M. plane. "Um"—a longer pause—"What do you want to talk about, Danny?"

"It's something I should ask you in person, but I'll give you a hint: It's about sharing our lives, and about babies, and waking up in the mornings hugging." A longer pause ensued. "Linda?"

Her voice quivered. "Dan—I can't talk now. I'll fly up early tomorrow."

"I'll meet you at the PSA gate. 'Bye, Linda."

" 'Bye, Danny." Then there was the lonely buzz on the line.

I arrived at the gate by 8:45 A.M. She was already standing there, bright-eyed, a beauty with dazzling red hair. She ran up to me, laughing, and threw her arms around me. "Ooh, it's good to hold you again, Danny!"

I could feel the warmth of her body radiate into mine. We walked quickly to the parking lot, not finding any words at first.

I drove back up to Tilden Park and turned right, climbing to Inspiration Point. I had it all planned. I asked her to sit on the fence and was about to pop the question, when she threw her arms around me and said "Yes!" and began to cry. "Was it something I said?" I joked feebly.

We were married in the Los Angeles Municipal Courthouse in a beautiful private ceremony. Part of me felt very happy; another part was unaccountably depressed. I awoke in the middle of the night and gently tiptoed out to the balcony of our honeymoon suite. I cried soundlessly. Why did I feel as if I had lost something, as if I had *forgotten something important?* The feeling was never to leave me.

We soon settled into a new apartment. I tried my hand at selling life insurance; Linda got a part-time job as a bank teller. We were comfortable and settled, but I was too busy to devote much time to my new wife. Late at night, when she was sleeping, I sat in meditation. Early in the morning I would do a few exercises. But before long my job responsibilities left me little time for such things; all my training and discipline began to fade.

After six months of sales work, I had had enough. I sat down with Linda for our first good talk in many weeks.

"Honey, how do you feel about moving back up to Northern California and looking for different work?"

"If that's what you want to do, Dan, it's OK with me. Besides, it might be nice to be near my folks. They're great babysitters."

"Babysitters?"

"Yes. How do you feel about being a father?"

"You mean a baby? You—me—a baby?" I hugged her very gently for a long time.

I couldn't make any wrong moves after that. The second day up North Linda visited her folks and I went job-hunting. I learned from my ex-coach Hal that the men's coaching position for gymnastics was open at Stanford University. I interviewed for the job that day and drove up to my in-laws' to tell Linda the news. When

I arrived, they said I had received a call from the Stanford Athletic Director and had been offered the coaching job, to begin in September. I accepted; I'd found a career, just like that.

In late August, our beautiful daughter, Holly, was born. I drove all our belongings up to Menlo Park and moved us into a comfortable apartment. Linda and the baby flew up two weeks later. We were contented, for a time, but I was soon immersed in my job, developing a strong gymnastics program at Stanford. I ran for miles through the golf course early each morning and often sat alone on the shore of Lake Lagunita. Again, my energies and attention flew in many directions, but sadly, not in Linda's.

A year went by almost without my noticing it. Everything was going so well; I couldn't understand my persistent feeling that I had lost something, a long time ago. The sharp images of my training with Socrates—running into the hills, the strange exercises late at night, the hours of talking and listening and watching my enigmatic teacher—were fading memories.

Not long after our first anniversary, Linda told me she wanted us to see a marriage counselor. It came as a complete shock, just when I felt we'd be able to relax and have more time together.

The marriage counselor did help, yet a shadow had come between Linda and me—maybe it had been there since our wedding night. She had grown quiet and private, drawing Holly with her into her own world. I came home from work each day totally spent, with too little energy left for either of them.

My third year at Stanford, I applied for the position of Faculty Resident in one of the university residence halls so that Linda could be with other people. It soon became apparent that this move had worked only too well, especially in the arena of romance. She had formed her own social life, and I had been relieved of a burden I could not, or would not, fulfill. Linda and I were separated in the spring of my third year at Stanford. I delved even deeper into my work, and began my inner search once again. I sat with a Zen group in the mornings in our gym. I began to study Aikido in the evenings. I read more and more, hoping to find some clues or directions or answers to my unfinished business.

When I was offered a faculty position at Oberlin College, a residential liberal arts college in Ohio, it seemed like a second chance for us. But there I only pursued my personal search for happiness with more intensity. I taught more gymnastics, and developed two courses—"Psycho-physical Development" and "Way of the Peaceful Warrior"—which reflected some of the perspectives and skills I'd learned from Socrates. At the end of my first year there, I received a special grant from the college to travel and do research in my chosen field.

After a troubled marriage, Linda and I separated. Leaving her and my young daughter behind, I set off on what I hoped would be my final search.

I was to visit many places around the world—Hawaii, Japan, Okinawa, India, and elsewhere, where I encountered some extraordinary teachers, and schools of yoga, martial arts, and shamanism. I had many experiences, and found great wisdom, but no lasting peace.

As my travels neared their conclusion, I became even more desperate—compelled toward a final confrontation with the questions that rang out in my mind: "What is enlightenment? When will I find peace?" Socrates had spoken of these things, but at the time, I didn't have the ears to hear him.

When I arrived in the village of Cascais on the coast of Portugal, the last stop on my journey, the questions continued to replay themselves endlessly, burning deeper into my mind.

One morning I awoke on an isolated stretch of beach where I had camped for a few days. My gaze drifted to the water, where the tide was devouring my painstakingly constructed castle of sand and sticks.

For some reason, this reminded me of my own death, and what Socrates had tried to tell me. His words and gestures played back in bits and pieces, like the twigs from my castle, now scattered and floating in the shallow surf: "Consider your fleeting years, Danny. One day you'll discover that death is not what you might imagine; but then, neither is life. Either may be wondrous, filled with change; or, if you do not awaken, both may turn out to be a considerable disappointment."

His laughter rang out in my memory. Then I remembered an incident in the station: I had been acting lethargic; Socrates suddenly grabbed me and shook me. "Wake up! If you knew for certain that you had a terminal illness—if you had little time left to live—you would waste precious little of it! Well, I'm telling you, Dan—you *do* have a terminal illness: It's called birth. You don't have more than a few years left. No one does! So be happy *now*, without reason—or you never will be at all."

I began to feel a terrible sense of urgency, but there was nowhere to go. So I stayed, a beachcomber who never stopped combing through his own mind. "Who am I? What is enlightenment?"

Socrates had told me, long ago, that even for the warrior, there is no victory over death; there is only the realization of Who we all really are.

As I lay in the sun, I remembered peeling away the last layer of the onion in Soc's office to see "who I was." I remembered a character in a J. D. Salinger novel, who, upon seeing someone drink a glass of milk, said, "It was like pouring God into God, if you know what I mean."

I remembered Lao Tzu's dream:

Lao Tzu fell asleep and dreamt he was a butterfly. Upon awakening, he asked himself, "Am I a man who has just been dreaming that he was a butterfly, or a sleeping butterfly, now dreaming that he is a man?"

I walked down the beach, singing the children's nursery rhyme over and over:

"Row, row, row your boat, gently down the stream,
Merrily, merrily, merrily, merrily, life is but a dream."

After one afternoon walk, I returned to my sheltered campsite, hidden behind some rocks. I reached into my pack and took out an old book I'd picked up in India. It was a ragged English translation of spiritual folk tales. Flipping through the pages, I came upon a story about enlightenment:

"Milarepa had searched everywhere for enlightenment, but could find no answer—until one day, he saw an old man walking slowly down a mountain path, carrying a heavy sack. Immediately, Milarepa sensed that this old man knew the secret he had been desperately seeking for many years.

" 'Old man, please tell me what you know. What is enlightenment?'

"The old man smiled at him for a moment, and swung the heavy burden off his shoulders, and stood straight.

" 'Yes, I see!' cried Milarepa. 'My everlasting gratitude. But please, one question more. What is *after* enlightenment?'

"Smiling again, the old man picked up the sack once again, slung it over his shoulders, steadied his burden, and continued on his way."

That same night I had a dream:

I am in darkness at the foot of a great mountain, searching under every stone for a precious jewel. The valley is covered in darkness, so I cannot find the jewel.

Then I look up at the shining mountain peak. If the jewel is to be found, it must be at the top. I climb and climb, beginning an arduous journey that takes many years. At last I reach my journey's end. I stand bathed in the bright light.

My eyesight is clear now, yet the jewel is nowhere to be found. I look upon the valley far below, where I began the climb many years ago. Only then do I realize that the jewel had always been within me, even then, and that the light had always shined. Only my eyes had been closed.

I awoke in the middle of the night, under a shining moon. The air was warm and the world was silent, except for the rhythmic wash of the tides. I heard Soc's voice but knew that it was only another memory: "Enlightenment is not an attainment, Dan; it is a realization. And when you wake up, everything changes and nothing changes. If a blind man realizes that he can see, has the world changed?"

I sat and watched the moonlight sparkling on the sea and capping the distant mountains with silver. "What was that saying about mountains, and rivers, and the great search?" "Ah, yes," I remembered:

"First mountains are mountains and rivers are rivers.

"Then mountains are no longer mountains and rivers are no longer rivers.

"Finally, mountains are mountains and rivers are rivers."

I stood, ran down the beach, and dove into the dark ocean, swimming out far beyond the surf. I had stopped to tread water when I suddenly sensed a creature swimming through the black depths somewhere below my feet. Something was coming at me, very rapidly: it was Death.

I flailed wildly to the shore and lay panting on the wet sand. A small crab crawled in front of my eyes and burrowed into the sand as a wave washed over it.

I stood, dried myself, and slipped into my clothes. I packed by the light of the moon. Then, shouldering my knapsack, I said to myself,

"Better never begin; once begun, better finish."

I knew it was time to go home.

As the jumbo jet settled onto the runway at Hopkins Airport in Cleveland, I felt a growing anxiety about my marriage and my life. Over six years had passed. I felt older, but no wiser. What could I say to my wife and my daughter? Would I ever see Socrates again—and if I did, what could I bring to him?

Linda and Holly were waiting for me when I got off the plane. Holly ran to me squealing with delight, and hugged me tight. My embrace with Linda was soft and warm, but empty of real intimacy, like hugging an old friend. It was obvious that time and experience had drawn us in different directions.

Linda drove us home from the airport. Holly slept contentedly on my lap.

Linda had not been lonely in my absence, I learned. She had found friends—and intimacies. And as it happened, soon after my return to Oberlin I met someone very special; a student, a sweet young woman named Joyce. Her short black hair hung in bangs over a pretty face and bright smile. She was small, and full of life. I felt intensely attracted to her, and we spent every available hour together, walking and talking, strolling through the Arboretum grounds, around the placid waters. I was able to talk with her in a way I'd never been able to speak with Linda—not because Linda couldn't understand, but because her paths and interests lay elsewhere.

Joyce graduated in the spring. She wanted to stay near me, but I felt a duty to my marriage, so we sadly parted. I knew I'd never forget her, but my family had to come first.

In the middle of next winter, Linda, Holly and I moved back to Northern California. Perhaps it was my preoccupation with my work and with myself that was the final blow to our marriage, but no omen had been so sad as the continual nagging doubt and melancholy I first felt on our wedding night—that painful doubt, that sense of something I should remember, something I'd left behind me years ago. Only with Joyce had I felt free of it.

After the divorce, Linda and Holly moved into a fine old house. I lost myself in my work teaching gymnastics and Aikido at the Berkeley YMCA.

The temptation to visit the gas station was agonizing, but I would not go until I was called. Besides, how could I go back? I had nothing at all to show for my years.

I moved to Palo Alto and lived alone, as lonely as I had ever been. I thought of Joyce many times, but knew I had no right to call her; I still had unfinished business.

I began my training anew. I exercised, read, meditated, and continued driving questions deeper and deeper into my mind, like a sword. In a matter of months, I started to feel a renewed sense of well-being that I hadn't felt in years. During this time, I started writing, recording volumes of notes from my days with Socrates. I hoped my review of our time together would give me a fresh clue. Nothing had really changed—at least nothing I could see—since he had sent me away.

One morning, I sat on the front steps of my small apartment, overlooking the freeway. I thought back over the past eight years. I had begun as a fool and had almost become a warrior. Then Socrates had sent me out into the world to learn, and I'd become a fool again.

It seemed a waste—all eight years. So here I sat on the front steps, gazing over the city to the mountains beyond. Suddenly my attention narrowed, and the mountains began to take on a soft glow. In that instant, I knew what I would do.

I sold what few belongings I had left, strapped my pack to my back, and hitchhiked south toward Fresno, then headed east into the Sierra Nevadas. It was late summer—a good time to get lost in the mountains.

8

The Gate Opens

On a narrow road somewhere near Edison Lake, I started hiking inward to an area Socrates had once mentioned—inward and upward, toward the heart of the wilderness. I sensed that here in the mountains I would find the answer—or die. In a way, I was right on both counts.

I hiked up through alpine meadows, between granite peaks, winding my way through thick groves of pine and spruce, up into the high lake country, where people were scarcer than the puma, deer, and small lizards that scurried under rocks as I approached.

I made camp just before dusk. The next day I hiked higher, across great fields of granite at the edge of the timberline. I climbed over huge boulders, cut through canyons and ravines. In the afternoon I picked edible roots and berries, and lay down by a crystal spring. For the first time in years, it seemed, I was content.

Later in the afternoon, I walked alone in the wilds, down through the shade of tangled forests, heading back to base camp. Then I prepared wood for the evening fire, ate another handful of food, and meditated beneath a towering pine tree, surrendering myself to the mountains. If they had anything to offer me, I was ready to accept it.

After the sky turned black, I sat warming my hands and face over the crackling fire, when out of the shadows stepped Socrates!

"I was in the neighborhood, so I thought I'd drop in," he said.

In disbelief and delight, I hugged him and wrestled him to the ground, laughing and getting both of us thoroughly dirty. We brushed ourselves off and sat by the fire. "You look almost the same, old warrior—not a year over a hundred." (He did look older, but his grey-speckled eyes still had their twinkle.)

"You, on the other hand," he grinned, looking me over, "look a lot older, and not much smarter. Tell me, did you learn anything?"

I sighed, staring into the fire. "Well, I learned to make my own tea." I put a small pot of water on my makeshift grill and prepared the spicy tea, using herbs I'd found on my hike that day. I hadn't been expecting company; I handed him my cup, and poured my tea into a small bowl. Finally, the words poured forth. As I spoke, the despair that I'd held off for so long finally caved in on me.

"I have nothing to bring you, Socrates. I'm still lost—no closer to the gate than I was when we first met. I've failed you, and life has failed me; life has broken my heart."

He was jubilant. "Yes! Your heart has been broken, Dan—broken open to reveal the gate, shining within. It's the only place you haven't looked. Open your eyes, buffoon—you've almost arrived!"

Confused and frustrated, I could only sit there helplessly.

Soc reassured me. "You're almost ready—you're very close."

I pounced on his words eagerly. "Close to what?"

"To the end." Fear crept up my spine for a moment. I crawled quickly into my sleeping bag, and Socrates unrolled his. My last impression that night was of my teacher's eyes, shining, as if he were looking through me, through the fire, into another world.

In the first direct rays of the morning sun, Socrates was already up, sitting over by a nearby stream. I joined him for awhile in silence, tossing pebbles into the running water, and listening to the plop. Silent, he turned and watched me closely.

That night, after a carefree day of hiking, swimming, and sunning, Socrates told me that he wanted to hear about everything I could remember feeling since I had seen him. I talked for three days and three nights—I'd exhausted my store of memories. Socrates had hardly spoken the whole time, except to ask a brief question.

Just after the sun had set, he motioned for me to join him by the fire. We sat very still, the old warrior and I, our legs crossed on the soft earth, high in the Sierra Nevadas.

"Socrates, all my illusions have shattered, but there seems nothing left to take their place. You've shown me the futility of searching. But what about the way of the peaceful warrior? Isn't that a path, a search?"

He laughed with delight and shook me by my shoulders. "After all this time, you finally come up with a juicy question! But the answer is right in front of your nose. All along I have shown you the way *of* the peaceful warrior, not the way *to* the peaceful warrior. As long as you tread the way, you *are* a warrior. These past eight years you have abandoned your "warriorship" so you could search for it. But the way is *now;* it always has been."

"What do I do then, now? Where do I go from here?"

"Who cares?" he yelled gleefully. "A fool is 'happy' when his cravings are satisfied. A warrior is happy without reason. That's what makes happiness the ultimate discipline—above all else I have taught you."

As we climbed into our sleeping bags once more, Soc's face shone at me in the red glow of the fire. "Dan," he said softly, "this is the final task I will ever give you, and it goes on forever. Act happy, feel happy, be happy, without a reason in the world. Then you can love, and do what you will."

I was growing drowsy. As my eyes closed, I said softly, "But Socrates, some things and people are very difficult to love; it seems impossible to always be happy."

"Nevertheless, Dan, that is what it means to be a warrior. I am not telling you how to be happy, you see, I am just telling you to be happy." With these final words, I slept.

Socrates shook me gently awake just after dawn. "We have a long hike ahead," he said. Soon we set off into the high country.

The only sign of Soc's age or susceptible heart was the slowed pace of his climb. Once again I was reminded of my teacher's vulnerability and his sacrifice. I could never again take my time with him for granted. As we climbed higher, I remembered a strange story that I had never understood until now.

A saintly woman was walking along the edge of a cliff. Several hundred feet below her, she saw a dead mother lion, surrounded by crying cubs. Without hesitation, she leaped off the cliff so that they would have something to eat.

Perhaps in another place, another time, Socrates would have done the same thing.

We climbed higher and higher, mostly in silence, through sparsely wooded rocky ground, then up to the peaks above the timberline.

"Socrates, where are we headed?" I asked as we sat for a brief rest.

"We're going to a special mound, a holy place, the highest plateau in many miles. It was a burial site for an early American tribe so small that the history books do not record its existence, but these people lived and worked in solitude and in peace."

"How do you know this?"

"I had ancestors who lived among them. Let's move on now; we must reach the plateau before dark."

At this point I was willing to trust Socrates with anything—yet I had an unsettling feeling that I was in grave danger and that he wasn't telling me something.

The sun was ominously low; Socrates increased his pace. We were breathing hard now, leaping and clambering from one huge boulder to the next, deep in shadow. Socrates disappeared into a crack between two boulders and I followed him down a narrow tunnel formed by the huge rocks, and out again in the open. "In case you come back alone, you'll need to use this passageway," Socrates told me. "It's the only way in or out." I started to question him, but he silenced me.

The light was fading from the sky when we climbed over a final rise. There below us lay a bowl-shaped depression surrounded by soaring cliffs, now covered in shadow. We headed down into the bowl, straight for a jagged peak.

"Are we near the burial site yet?" I asked nervously.

"We are standing on it," he said, "standing among the ghosts of an ancient people, a tribe of warriors."

The wind began to buffet us, as if to add emphasis to his words. Then came the most eerie sound I'd ever heard—like a human voice, moaning.

"What the hell kind of wind is that?"

Without responding, Socrates stopped before a black hole in the face of the cliff and said "Let's go in."

My instincts were wildly signalling danger, but Soc had already entered. Clicking my flashlight on, I left the moaning wind behind me and followed his faint light deeper into the cave. The flickering beam of my light showed pits and crevices whose bottoms I couldn't see.

"Soc, I don't like being buried this far back in the mountain." He glared at me. But to my relief he headed out toward the mouth of the cave. Not that it mattered; it was as dark outside as inside. We made camp, and Socrates took a pile of small logs out of his pack. "Thought we might need these," he said. The fire was soon crackling. Our bodies cast bizarre, twisted shadows, dancing wildly on the cave wall in front of us, as the flames consumed the logs.

Pointing to the shadows, Socrates said, "These shadows in the cave are an *essential image* of illusion and reality, of suffering and happiness. Here is an ancient story popularized by Plato:

There once was a people who lived their entire lives within a Cave of Illusions. After generations, they came to believe that their own shadows, cast upon the walls, were the substance of reality. Only the myths and religious tales spoke of a brighter possibility.

Obsessed with the shadow-play, the people became accustomed to and imprisoned by their dark reality.

I stared at the shadows and felt the heat of the fire upon my back as Socrates continued.

"Throughout history, Dan, there have been blessed exceptions to the prisoners of the Cave. There were those who became tired of the shadow play, who began to doubt it, who were no longer fulfilled by shadows no matter how high they leaped. They became seekers of light. A fortunate few found a guide who prepared them and who took them beyond all illusion into the sunlight."

Captivated by his story, I watched the shadows dance against the granite walls in the yellow light. Soc continued:

"All the peoples of the world, Dan, are trapped within the Cave of their own minds. Only those few warriors who see the light, who cut free, surrendering everything, can laugh into eternity. And so will you, my friend."

"It sounds unreachable, Soc—and somehow frightening."

"It is beyond searching and beyond fear. Once it happens, you will see that it is only obvious, simple, ordinary, awake, and happy. It is only reality, beyond the shadows."

We sat in a stillness broken only by the sound of crackling logs. I watched Socrates, who appeared to be waiting for something. I had an uneasy feeling, but the faint light of dawn, revealing the mouth of the cave, revived my spirits.

But then the cave was again shrouded in darkness. Socrates stood quickly and walked to the entrance with me right behind. The air smelled of ozone as we stepped outside. I could feel the static electricity raise the hairs on the back of my neck. Then the thunderstorm struck.

Socrates whirled around to face me. "There's not much time left. You must escape the cave; eternity is not so far away!"

Lightning flashed. A bolt struck one of the cliffs in the distance. "Hurry!" Socrates said, with an urgency I'd not heard before. In that moment, the Feeling came to me—the feeling that had never been wrong—and it brought me the words, "Beware—Death is stalking."

Then Socrates spoke again, his voice ominous and strident. "There's danger here. Get further back into the cave." I started to look in my pack for my flashlight, but he barked at me, "Move!"

I retreated into the blackness and pressed against the wall. Hardly breathing, I waited for him to come get me, but he had disappeared.

As I was about to call out to him, I was jarred almost unconscious as something vise-like suddenly gripped me behind my neck with crushing force and dragged me back, deeper into the cave. "Socrates!" I screamed. "Socrates!"

The grip on my neck released, but then a far more terrible pain began: my head was being crushed from behind. I screamed, and screamed again. Just before my skull shattered with the maddening pressure, I heard these words—unmistakably the voice of Socrates: "This is your final journey."

With a horrible crack, the pain vanished. I crumpled, and hit the floor of the cavern with a soft thud. Lightning flashed, and in its momentary glare I could see Socrates standing over me, staring down. Then came the sound of thunder from another world. That's when I knew I was dying.

One of my legs hung limp over the edge of a deep hole. Socrates pushed me over the precipice, into the abyss, and I fell, bouncing, smashing against the rocks, falling down into the bowels of the earth, and then dropping through an opening, I was released by the mountain out into the sunlight, where my shattered body spun downward, finally landing in a heap in a wet green meadow, far, far below.

The body was now a broken, twisted piece of meat. Carrion birds, rodents, insects, and worms came to feed on the decomposing flesh that I had once imagined to be "me." Time passed faster and faster. The days flashed by and the sky became a rapid blinking, an alternation of light and darkness, flickering faster and faster into a blur; then the days turned to weeks, and the weeks became months.

The seasons changed, and the remains of the body began to dissolve into the soil, enriching it. The frozen snows of winter preserved my bones for a moment in time, but as the seasons flashed by in ever more rapid cycles, even the bones became dust. From the nourishment of my body, flowers and trees grew and died in that meadow. Finally even the meadow disappeared.

I had become part of the carrion birds that had feasted on my flesh, part of the insects and rodents, and part of their predators in a great cycle of life and death. I became their ancestors, until ultimately, they too were returned to the earth.

The Dan Millman who had lived long ago was gone forever, a flashing moment in time—but *I* remained unchanged through all the ages. I was now Myself, the Consciousness which observed all, was all. All my separate parts would continue forever; forever changing, forever new.

I realized now that the Grim Reaper, the Death Dan Millman had so feared, had been his great illusion. And so his life, too, had been an illusion, a problem, nothing more than a humorous incident when Consciousness had forgotten Itself.

While Dan had lived, he had not passed through the gate; he had not realized his true nature; he had lived in mortality and fear, alone.

But *I* knew. If he had only known then what I know now.

I lay on the floor of the cave, smiling. I sat up against the wall then gazed into darkness, puzzled, but without fear.

My eyes began to adjust, and I saw a white-haired man sitting near me, smiling. Then, from thousands of years away, it all came back, and I felt momentarily saddened by my return to mortal form. Then I realized that it didn't matter—nothing could possibly matter!

This struck me as very funny; everything did, and so I started to laugh. I looked at Socrates; our eyes gleamed ecstatically. I knew that he knew what I knew. I leaped forward and hugged him. We danced around the cavern, laughing wildly at my death.

Afterward, we packed and headed down the mountainside. We cut through the passageway, down through ravines and across fields of boulders toward our base camp.

I didn't speak much, but I laughed often, because every time I looked around—at the earth, the sky, the sun, the trees, the lakes, the streams—I remembered that it was all Me!

All these years Dan Millman had grown up, struggling to "be a somebody." Talk about backwards! He had been a somebody, locked into a fearful mind and a mortal body.

"Well," I thought, "Now I am playing Dan Millman again, and I might as well get used to it for a few more seconds in eternity, until it too passes. But now I know that I am not only the single piece of flesh—and that secret makes all the difference!"

There was no way to describe the impact of this knowledge. I was simply awake.

And so I awoke to reality, free of any meaning or any search. What could there possibly be to search for? All of Soc's words had come alive with my death. This was the paradox of it all, the humor of it all, and the great change. All searches, all achievements, all goals, were equally enjoyable, and equally unnecessary.

Energy coursed through my body. I overflowed with happiness and burst with laughter; it was the laugh of an unreasonably happy man.

And so we walked down, past the highest lakes, past the edge of the timberline, and into the thick forest, heading down to the stream where we'd camped two days—or a thousand years—ago.

I had lost all my rules, all my morals, all my fear back there on the mountain. I could no longer be controlled. What punishment could possibly threaten me? Yet, though I had no code of behavior,

I felt what was balanced, what was appropriate, and what was loving. I was capable of loving action, and nothing else. He had said it; what could be a greater power?

I had lost my mind and fallen into my heart. The gate had finally opened, and I had tumbled through, laughing, because it too, was a joke. It was a gateless gate, another illusion, another image that Socrates had woven into the fabric of my reality, as he'd promised long ago. I had finally seen what there was to see. The path would continue, without end; but now, it was full of light.

It was turning dark by the time we reached our camp. We made a fire, and ate a small meal of dried fruit and sunflower seeds, the last of my stores. Only then, as the firelight flickered against our faces, did Socrates speak.

"You'll lose it, you know."

"Lose what?"

"Your vision. It is rare—only possible through an unlikely set of circumstances—but it is an experience, so you'll lose it."

"Perhaps that's true, Socrates, but who cares?" I laughed. "I've also lost my mind and can't seem to find it anywhere!"

He raised his eyebrows in pleased surprise. "Well, then, it appears that my work with you is complete. My debt is paid."

"Wow! I grinned. "Do you mean this is graduation day for me?"

"No, Dan, this is graduation day for *me*."

He stood, put his pack on his shoulders, and walked off, melting into the shadows.

It was time to return to the station, where it had all begun. Somehow, I had a feeling that Socrates was already there, waiting for me. At sunrise, I packed my knapsack and started down the mountain.

The trip out of the wilderness took several days. I caught a ride into Fresno, then followed 101 up into San Jose, then back to Palo Alto. It was hard to believe that I'd only left the apartment a few weeks ago, a hopeless "somebody."

I unpacked and drove to Berkeley, arriving in the familiar streets at three in the afternoon, long before Socrates came on duty. I parked up on Piedmont and walked down through campus. School had just begun and students were busy being students. I walked down Telegraph Avenue and watched the shopkeepers playing per fect shopkeepers. Everywhere I visited—the fabric shops, the markets, the movie theaters and massage parlors—everyone was perfectly being what they believed they were.

I walked up University, then along Shattuck, passing through the streets like a happy phantom, the Buddha's ghost. I wanted to whisper in peoples' ears, "Wake up! Wake up! Soon the person you believe you are will die—so now, wake up and be content with this knowledge: *There is no need to search; achievement leads to nowhere. It makes no difference at all, so just be happy now! Love is the only reality of the world, because it is all One, you see. And the only laws are paradox, humor, and change. There is no problem, never was, and never will be. Release your struggle, let go of your mind, throw away your concerns, and relax into the world. No need to resist life; just do your best. Open your eyes and see that you are far more than you imagine. You are the world, you are the universe; you are yourself and everyone else, too! It's all the marvelous Play of God. Wake up, regain your humor. Don't worry, just be happy. You are already free!*

I wanted to say it to everyone I met, but if I had, they might have considered me deranged or even dangerous. I knew the wisdom of silence.

The shops were closing. In a few hours it would be time for Soc's shift at the station. I drove to the hills, left my car, and sat on a cliff overlooking the Bay. I looked down upon the city of San Francisco in the distance, and at the Golden Gate. I could feel it all, the birds nestled in their nests in the woods of Tiburon, Marin, and Sausalito. I felt the life of the city, the lovers embracing, the criminals at work, the social volunteers giving what they could. And I knew that all of it, the goods and bads, the high and low, sacred and profane, were all a perfect part of the Play. Everyone played their roles so well! And I was all of it, every smidgen of it. I gazed to the ends of the world, and loved it all.

I closed my eyes to meditate, but realized that I was always meditating now, with my eyes wide open.

After midnight I drove into the station; the bell clanged my arrival. Out of the warmly lit office came my friend, a man who looked like a robust fifty year old; slim, leathery, graceful. He came around to the driver's side, grinning, and said, "Fill 'er up?"

"Happiness is a full tank," I answered, then paused. Where had I seen that saying before? What was it I needed to remember?

While Soc pumped gas, I did the windows; then I parked the car behind the station and entered the office for the last time. It was like a holy place for me—an unlikely temple. Tonight the room seemed electrified; something was very definitely up, but I had no idea what.

Socrates reached into his drawer and handed me a large notebook, cracked and dried with age. In it were notes written in a careful, finely wrought hand. "This is my journal—entries of my life, since I was young. It will answer all your unasked questions. It is yours now, a gift. I've given everything I can. Now it's up to you. My work is done, but you have work still to do."

"What could there possibly be left?" I smiled.

"You will write and you will teach. You will live an ordinary life, learning how to remain ordinary in a troubled world to which, in a sense, you no longer belong. Remain ordinary, and you can be useful to others."

Socrates rose from his chair and aligned his mug carefully on the desk, next to mine. I looked at his hand. It was shining, glowing brighter than ever before.

"I'm feeling very strange," he said in a tone of surprise. "I think I have to go."

"Is there anything I can do?" I said, thinking he had an upset stomach.

"No." Gazing into space as if the room and I no longer existed, he walked slowly to the door marked "Private," pushed it open, and stepped inside.

I wondered if he'd be all right. I sensed that our time in the mountains had drained him, yet he was shining now as never before. As usual, Socrates didn't make sense.

I sat there on the couch and watched the door, waiting for his return. I yelled through the door, "Hey, Socrates, you're glowing like a lightning bug tonight. Did you eat an electric eel for dinner? I must have you over for dinner this Christmas; you'd make a wonderful decoration for my tree."

I thought I saw a flash of light under the crack in the door. Well, a blown lightbulb might hasten his business. "Soc, are you going to spend all evening in there? I thought warriors didn't get constipated."

Five minutes passed, then ten. I sat holding his prized journal in my hands. I called him, then called again, but I was answered by silence. Suddenly I knew; it wasn't possible, but I knew it had happened.

I leaped to my feet and ran to the door, pushing it open so hard it struck the tile wall with a metallic clang that echoed hollowly in the empty bathroom. I remembered the flash of light, minutes ago. Socrates had walked, glowing, into this bathroom, and disappeared.

I stood there a long time, until I heard the familiar station bell, then a honking horn. I walked outside and mechanically filled the tank, taking the money and giving change out of my own pocket. When I returned to the office, I noticed that I hadn't even put my shoes on. I began to laugh; my laughter became hysterical, then quieted. I sat back on the couch, on the old Mexican blanket now tattered, disintegrating, and looked around the room at the yellow carpet, faded with age, at the old walnut desk, and the water cooler. I saw the two mugs—Soc's and mine—still sitting on the desk, and last of all, his empty chair.

Then I spoke to him. Wherever that mischievous old warrior was, I'd have the last word.

"Well, Soc, here I am, between past and future, again, floating between heaven and earth. What can I say to you that would be enough? Thank you my teacher, my inspiration, my friend. I'll miss you. Farewell."

I left the station for the last time feeling only wonder. I knew that I'd not lost him, not really. It had taken me all these years to see the obvious, that Socrates and I had never been different. All this time, we had been one and the same.

I walked through the tree-lined paths of campus, across the creek, and beyond the shady groves out into the city—continuing on the Way, the way toward home.

EPILOGUE
LAUGHTER IN THE WIND

I'd passed through the gate; seen what there was to see; realized, high on a mountain, my true nature. Yet, like the old man who shouldered his burden and continued on his way, I knew that though everything had changed, nothing had changed.

I was still living an ordinary human life with ordinary human responsibilities. I would have to adapt myself to living a happy, useful life in a world which was offended by one who is no longer interested in any search or problem. An unreasonably happy man, I learned, can grate on people's nerves! There were many occasions when I began to understand and even envy the monks who set up housekeeping in faraway caves. But I had been to my cave. My time for receiving was finished; now it was time for giving.

I moved from Palo Alto to San Francisco, and began working as a house painter. As soon as I was settled into a house, I attended to some unfinished business. I hadn't spoken with Joyce since Oberlin. I found her number in New Jersey and called her.

"Dan, What a surprise! How are you?"

"Very well, Joyce. I've been through a lot recently."

There was a pause on the line. "Uh, how is your daughter—and your wife?"

"Linda and Holly are doing fine. Linda and I were divorced some time ago."

"Dan"—there was another pause—"Why did you call?"

I took a deep breath. "Joyce, I want you to come to California and live with me. I have no doubts at all about you—about us. There's plenty of room here. . . ."

"Dan," Joyce laughed. "You're going much too fast for me! When do you propose this little adjustment should take place?"

"Now, or as soon as you can. Joyce, there's so much to tell you—things I've never told anyone. I've held it in so long. Will you call me as soon as you've decided?"

"Dan, are you sure of this?"

"Yes, believe me, and I'll be waiting here every evening for your call."

About two weeks later, I received a call at 7:15 P.M.

"Joyce!"

"I'm calling from the airport."

"From Newark Airport? You're leaving? You're coming?"

"From San Francisco Airport. I've arrived."

For a moment, I didn't get it. "San Francisco Airport?"

"Yes," she laughed. "You know, that landing strip south of the city? Well? Are you going to meet me, or shall I hitchhike?"

In the days that followed we spent every free moment together. I'd quit my painting job and was teaching in a small gymnastics studio in San Francisco. I told her about my life, much as is written here, and all about Socrates. She listened intently.

"You know Dan, I get a funny feeling when you tell me about that man—as if I know him."

"Well, anything's possible," I smiled.

"No, really, like I knew him! What I never told you before, Danny, is that I left home just before starting high school."

"Well," I responded, "that's unusual, but not too strange."

"The strange part is that the years between my leaving home and coming to Oberlin are a complete blank in my memory. And that's not all. At Oberlin, before you came, I remember having dreams, very strange dreams, about someone like you—and about a white-haired man! And my parents—my parents, Danny . . ." Her large, luminous eyes opened wide and filled with tears. ". . . my parents always called me by my nickname . . ." I held her shoulders and looked into her eyes. In the next moment, like an electric shock, a place in our memories opened up as she said, ". . . my nickname was *Joy*."

We were married among our friends, in the mountains of California. It was a moment I would have given anything to share with the man who had begun it all, for both of us. Then I remembered the card he had given me—the one I was to use if I ever really needed him. I figured now was the time.

I slipped away for a moment, and walked across the road to a small mound of earth, overlooking the woods and rolling hills. There was a garden there with a single elm tree, almost hidden among the grape arbors. I reached into my wallet and found the card there among my other papers. It was dog-eared, but still glowing.

Warrior, Inc.
Socrates, Prop.
Specializing in:
Paradox, Humor,
and Change
Emergencies Only!

I held it in both hands and spoke softly. "All right, Socrates, you old wizard. Do your stuff. Come visit us, Soc!" I waited and tried again. Nothing happened. Nothing at all. The wind gusted for a moment—that was all.

My disappointment surprised me. I had held to a secret hope that he might somehow return. But he wasn't coming; not now, not ever. My hands dropped to my sides, and I looked down at the earth. "Goodbye, Socrates. Goodbye, my friend."

I opened my wallet to slip the card back in, glancing again at its lingering glow. The card had changed. In place of "Emergencies Only" was a single word, glowing brighter than the rest. It said, "Happiness." His wedding gift.

In that moment, a warm breeze caressed my face, mussed my hair, and a falling leaf slapped my cheek as it floated down from the elm.

I threw my head back, laughing with delight, and looked up through the elm's outstretched branches, into the clouds drifting lazily by. I gazed above the stone fence, out over the houses dotted in the green forest below. The wind gusted again, and a lone bird soared by.

Then I felt the truth of it. Socrates hadn't come, because he had never left. He was only changed. He was the elm above my head; he was the clouds and the bird and the wind. They would always be my teachers, my friends.

Before walking back to my wife, my home, my friends, and my future, I surveyed the world around me. Socrates *was* here. He was everywhere.

SACRED JOURNEY OF THE PEACEFUL WARRIOR

Contents

Contents

Preface

What if you slept,
and what if in your sleep you dreamed,
and what if in your dream you went to heaven
and there you plucked a strange and beautiful flower,
and what if when you awoke you had
the flower in your hand?
Oh, what then?
Samuel Taylor Coleridge

My first book, *Way of the Peaceful Warrior,* relates a story based on experiences that opened my eyes and heart, and expanded my view of life. Readers of that book will remember that in 1968, after a period of training and testing with Socrates—the old "gas station warrior" who became my mentor—I was sent away for eight years to assimilate his teachings and prepare myself for the final confrontation described at the end of that book.

Sacred Journey of the Peaceful Warrior is, in a sense, a sequel to my first book, but unlike most sequels it does not begin at the end, but rather focuses on a period *within* my first book—after Socrates sent me away—during travels around the world and my initiation into the peaceful warrior's way.

I wrote little about these years in *Way of the Peaceful Warrior,* choosing not to reveal their content until I understood more fully the significance of what had occurred.

I refer to that period as "the lost years," because they began with personal struggles and broken dreams—a period of disorientation and disillusion that sent me on a journey to find myself and to reawaken the vision, purpose, and faith I had found with Socrates, then somehow lost.

Preface

This book relates the first steps on that journey. It began in 1973; I was twenty-six years old. I did, in fact, travel around the world, have unusual experiences, and meet remarkable people, but in this narrative I blend fact and imagination, weaving threads from the fabric of my life into a quilt that stretches across different levels of reality.

By presenting mystical teachings in story form, I hope to breathe new life into ancient wisdom, and to remind the reader that *all* our journeys are sacred, and all our lives, adventures.

Dan Millman
San Rafael, California
Winter 1991

Dedication

To my wife, Joy,
for her constant guidance and support,
and to my daughters, Holly, Sierra, and China,
who remind me about the important things.

Acknowledgments

My deepest appreciation to the following people who contributed, directly or indirectly, to this manuscript: Michael Bookbinder, for his practical wisdom, clear sight, and strong spirit; Sandra Knell, my research assistant; Hawaii historian Richard Marks; Carl Farrell, David Berman, M.D., and Tom McBroom, for their expertise; Wayne Guthrie and Bella Karish, for lighting the path; and Serge Kahili King, urban shaman.

Special thanks to my editor and sometimes counselor, Nancy Grimley Carleton. My thanks also to Linda Kramer, Joy Millman, John Kiefer, Ed Kellogg III, Jan Shelley, and Michael Guenley, for reviewing the third draft. Finally, my deepest gratitude to my publishers and friends, Hal and Linda Kramer, for their encouragement and enthusiasm.

Prologue

A Suggestion From Socrates

Free will does not mean
that you establish the curriculum;
only that you can elect what you want to take
at a given time.
A Course in Miracles

Late at night in an old Texaco service station, during training sessions that ranged from meditation to cleaning toilets, from deep self-massage to changing spark plugs, Socrates would sometimes mention people or places I might someday visit for my "continuing education."

Once he spoke of a woman *shaman** in Hawaii; another time he referred to a special school for warriors, hidden somewhere in Japan. He also told of a sacred book of wisdom, somewhere in the desert.

Naturally, these things intrigued me, but when I asked for details he would change the subject, so I was never certain whether the woman, the school, or the book actually existed.

In 1968, just before he sent me away, Socrates again spoke of the woman shaman. "I wrote to her about a year ago, and I mentioned you," he said. "She wrote back—said she might be willing to instruct you. Quite an honor," he

*A *shaman* uses magical elements to heal the sick, divine the hidden, and control events that affect the welfare of the people. Shamans also use trance states to communicate with nature spirits and other unseen allies and foes.

added, and suggested that I look her up when the time felt right.

"Well, where do I find her?" I asked.

"She wrote the letter on bank stationery."

"What bank?" I asked.

"I don't recall. Somewhere in Honolulu, I think."

"Can I see the letter?"

"Don't have it anymore."

"Does she have a name?" I asked, exasperated.

"She's had several names. Don't know what she's using right now."

"Well, what does she look like?"

"Hard to say; I haven't seen her in years."

"*Socrates,* help me out here!"

With a wave of his hand, he said, "I've told you, Danny—I'm here to support you, not to make it easy on you. If you can't find her, you're not ready anyway."

I took a deep breath and counted to ten. "Well, what about those *other* people and places you mentioned?"

Socrates glared at me. "Do I look like a travel agent? Just follow your nose; trust your instincts. Find her *first;* then one thing will lead to the next."

Walking back toward my apartment in the silence of the early morning hours, I thought about what Socrates had told me—and what he hadn't: *If* I was "ever in the neighborhood," he had said, I *might* want to contact a nameless woman, with no address, who *might* still work at a bank somewhere in Honolulu; then again, she might not. *If* I found her, she *might* have something to teach me, and *might* direct me to the other people and places Socrates had spoken of.

As I lay in bed that night, a part of me wanted to head straight for the airport and catch a plane to Honolulu, but more immediate issues demanded my attention: I was about to compete for the last time in the National Collegiate Gymnastics Championships, then graduate from college and get married—hardly the best time to run off to Hawaii on a wild goose chase. With that decision, I fell asleep—in a sense, for five years. And before I awakened, I was to discover that in spite of all my training and spiritual sophistication, I remained unprepared for what was to follow, as I leaped out of Soc's frying pan and into the fires of daily life.

Book One
Where Spirit Leads

The important thing is this:
To be ready at any moment
to sacrifice what you are
for what you could become.
Charles Dubois

1

Out of the Frying Pan

Enlightenment consists
not merely in the seeing of
luminous shapes and visions,
but in making the darkness visible.
The latter procedure is more difficult,
and therefore, unpopular.
Carl Jung

I cried on my wedding night. I remember it clearly: Linda and I had married during my senior year at Berkeley. I awoke just before dawn, unaccountably depressed, slipped out from under the rumpled covers while the world was still cloaked in darkness, and stepped out into the cool air. I closed the sliding glass door so as not to disturb my sleeping wife, then felt my chest begin to heave. I cried for a long time, but I didn't know why.

How could I feel so miserable when I should feel happy? I asked myself. My only answer was a deeply troubling intuition that I had forgotten something important, and had somehow drifted off my life's course. That feeling would cast a shadow over our entire marriage.

After graduation, I left behind the success and adulation that went with being a star athlete, and adjusted to relative anonymity. Linda and I moved to Los Angeles, where, for the first time, I faced real-world responsibilities. I had a colorful past, a college degree, and a pregnant wife. It was time to look for a job.

After short-lived attempts to sell life insurance, find work as a Hollywood stuntman, and become an instant author, I managed to secure a position as gymnastics coach at Stanford University.

In spite of this good fortune, along with the birth of our lovely daughter, Holly, I was still plagued by the recurring feeling that I was missing something important. Unable to justify or even articulate this feeling to Linda, and missing the guidance of Socrates, I pushed my doubts aside and tried to fulfill the roles of "husband" and "father," which felt like job descriptions that never quite fit, like a suit that was too tight.

Four years passed. The Vietnam War, the moon landing, and Watergate served as a backdrop to my smaller world of university politics, professional aspirations, and family responsibilities.

During my college days, life had seemed much simpler: studies, workouts, recreation, and romance; I knew the rules of the game. But now the rules had changed; daily life gave the exams, and no amount of cleverness could fool the teacher. I could only fool myself, and I proceeded to do so with dogged determination.

Focusing on visions of a white picket fence and two cars in the garage, I continued to deny my confused inner longings, and resolved to make things work. After all, Linda did have many fine qualitites—I'd be a fool to throw all that away. And I had my daughter to think of.

As my entrenchment in the "real world" hardened like concrete, my lessons and experiences with Socrates began to fade like nostalgic pictures in a scrapbook—a set of hazy images from another time, another realm—a dream of long ago. With each passing year, Socrates' words about the woman in Hawaii, the school in Japan, and the book in the desert became less real to me—until I forgot all about them.

I left Stanford to accept a position at Oberlin College in Ohio, hoping that this change might strengthen my relationship with Linda, but our new surroundings only served to clarify our diverging values: Linda liked to cook and enjoyed meat; I preferred a mostly raw vegetarian cuisine. She enjoyed furniture; I was into Zen simplicity and preferred a mattress on the floor. She liked to socialize; I liked to work. She was the all-American wife; I seemed like a metaphysical oddball to her friends, and kept mostly to myself. She lived comfortably in a conventional world that repelled me; yet I envied her comfort.

Linda sensed my discontent, and her frustration grew. Within the year, I found my personal life in a shambles, and my marriage deteriorating before my eyes. I could no longer deny it.

I had believed my time with Socrates would make my life easier, but it only seemed to get worse. The tidal waves of work, family, faculty meetings, and personal concerns washed away nearly everything Socrates had taught me.

Despite his reminder that "the warrior is completely open, like a child," I lived in my own private, self-protected world. I believed that no one, including Linda, really knew or understood me. I felt isolated—no longer good company, even for myself.

And even though Socrates had taught me about "letting go of the mind and living in the present moment," my mind still buzzed with anger, guilt, regrets, and anxiety.

Socrates' cleansing laughter, which once rang inside me like a crystal chime, was now a muffled echo, a distant memory.

Overstressed and out of shape, I had little time or energy for my young daughter. I had put on weight, losing both my edge and my self-respect. Worst of all, I had lost the thread of my life, the deeper purpose of my existence.

I looked at myself in the mirror of my relationships, and didn't like what I saw. I had always been the center of my world. I had never learned to give attention; I had only learned to receive it. I remained either unwilling or unable to sacrifice my own goals and priorities for those of Linda and Holly, or anyone else.

Disturbed by the dawning realization that I might be the *most* self-centered person I'd ever known, I clung even more tenaciously to my disintegrating self-image. By virtue of my past training and accomplishments, I still saw myself as a knight in shining armor, but now the armor had rusted, and my self-esteem sank to an all-time low.

Socrates had once said, "Embody what you teach, and teach only what you have embodied." While pretending to be the bright, even wise, teacher, I felt like a charlatan and a fool. This became painfully obvious as time passed.

Feeling like a failure, I turned toward the coaching and teaching activities that made me feel successful, and avoided the frustrating arena of relationship that most needed my attention.

Linda and I drifted farther apart. She developed other relationships and so did I, until the weakening thread that held us together finally snapped, and we decided to separate.

I moved out on a cold day in March. The snow had turned to slush as I carried my few possessions to a friend's van and found a room in town. My mind said it was the best thing, but my body spoke a different language: Stomach upsets plagued me, and I began to experience muscle spasms. Even a small paper cut or hangnail quickly became infected.

For the next few weeks, due to sheer momentum, I continued to function, going through the motions at work each day. But my identity, and the life I had envisioned for myself, had disintegrated. Lost and miserable, I didn't know where to turn.

Then, one day, while checking my mailbox in the physical education office, a faculty newsletter slipped from my hands and fell open on the floor. As I reached down to pick it up, my eyes skimmed across an announcement: "All faculty members are invited to apply for a Powers Travel Grant, for cross-cultural research in areas of professional interest."

A sudden, gut-level sense of destiny coursed through me; I knew I would apply for that grant, and that somehow I would get it.

Two weeks later, I found the committee's response letter in my mailbox, tore it open, and read: "The Executive

Committee for the Board of Trustees is happy to announce that you have been awarded a Powers Travel Grant, in the amount of two thousand dollars, for research and travel relevant to your academic area, such travel to be taken in the summer of 1973 and, if you choose, during your upcoming six-month sabbatical leave. . . ."

A window had opened; I had a direction once more.

But where would I travel? The answer came during a yoga class I had joined to bring my body back into balance. Some of the breathing and meditative exercises reminded me of techniques I had learned from Joseph, one of Socrates' old students who had run a small café in Berkeley. How I missed his bushy beard and gentle smile!

Joseph had been to India and had spoken positively of his experiences there. I had also read a number of books on Indian saints, sages, and gurus, as well as on yogic philosophy and metaphysics. Surely, in India, I might learn the secret doctrines and practices that would set me free—or at least put me back on course.

Yes, I would go to India; it was the obvious choice. And I would travel light, taking only a small backpack and an open airline ticket for maximum flexibility. I studied maps, did some research, and got a passport and shots.

My plans laid, I told Linda the news and explained that I would try to send Holly a postcard now and then, but that for long periods I might be out of touch.

She said that was nothing new.

On a warm spring morning just before the school year ended, I sat on the lawn with my four-year-old daughter as I struggled to explain my decision. "Sweetheart, I have to go away for a while."

"Where are you going, Daddy?"

"To India."

"Where they have elephants?"

"Yes."

"Can Mommy and me go with you?"

"Not this time, but someday we'll go on a trip together—just you and me. Okay?"

"Okay." She paused. "Which way is India?"

"That way," I pointed.

"Will you be gone a long time?"

"Yes, Holly," I replied honestly. "But wherever I am, I'll be loving you and remembering you. Will you be remembering me?"

"Yes. Do you have to go, Daddy?" The very question I had asked myself many times.

"Yes, I do."

"Why?"

I searched for the right words. "There are some things you won't understand until you're older, but I just have to—even though I'm going to miss you very much while I'm gone."

When Linda and I had decided to separate and I was moving out, Holly had clung to my leg and wouldn't let go, crying, "Don't go, Daddy! *Please*! Don't go!" Pulling her gently but firmly from my leg, hugging her, and then holding her back so I could leave was one of the hardest things I had ever done.

Now, when I told her I was going away, Holly didn't cry; she didn't plead with me to stay. She just looked down at the grass. That hurt the worst, because I could feel what was inside her: She had just given up.

A week later, the school year ended. After a bittersweet good-bye to Linda, I hugged my little daughter and walked outside. The taxi door slammed shut. As the car pulled away, I looked back through the rear window to see my home and familiar world growing smaller, until only my own reflection remained, staring back at me in the rear window. With a mixture of deep regret and keen anticipation, I turned to the driver. "Hopkins Airport."

I had the summer and then a six-month sabbatical leave—nine months in all—to search, and see what would unfold.

2

The Journey

A ship is safe in harbor –
but that's not what ships are for.
John A. Shedd

Resting between heaven and earth, I gazed out the window of the 747, down into the blanket of clouds covering the Indian Ocean, and wondered if the answers I sought lay somewhere below.

As I watched these thoughts float by, my eyelids slowly closed. Moments later it seemed, I was startled awake as the jet's wheels touched down.

I arrived in the humid monsoon season. Constantly drenched by rain or sweat, I traveled by antique taxis, rickshaws, buses, and trains. I walked along muddy roads and through noisy bazaars, where Hindu fakirs demonstrated unusual powers, severe disciplines, and austerities.

Cities, towns, and villages; colors and smells; oppressive heat; incense and cow dung; Calcutta to Madras to Bombay. People everywhere – moving throngs, milling crowds. Sacred India, overburdened with people, compressing souls into every square mile, every square foot, every square inch.

Unfamiliar sights and smells flooded my senses; half the time, I stared, fascinated, and, the other half, I floated as if in a dream. But I hadn't come for a vacation.

With unwavering intensity and heartfelt inquiries, I found my way into numerous schools of yoga, where I learned a variety of postures, breathing systems, and meditations, like those shown to me by Socrates and Joseph.

In Calcutta, I saw the poorest of the poor, living in squalor. Everywhere I turned, I met beggars—men, women, crippled children in ragged clothing. If I gave one a coin, ten more took his place—a dramatic contrast to the grandeur of the Taj Mahal and other temples of beauty and spiritual balance, as well as lesser-known retreats potent with spiritual force.

I made a pilgrimage to the ashrams and met sages filled with the nondualistic wisdom of Advaita Vedanta, which teaches that samsara and nirvana, flesh and spirit, are not separate. I learned of the Godhead and the holy trinity of Brahma the Creator, Vishnu the Sustainer, and Shiva the Destroyer.

I sat at the feet of gurus who spoke simple wisdom and emanated a loving and powerful presence. I felt the deep devotional fervor of holy men and women saints. I even trekked with Sherpa guides to Tibet, Nepal, and the Pamir region, where I met ascetics and hermits. I breathed the rarefied air, sat in the caves, and meditated.

But I grew more dejected each day, because I never found a teacher quite like Socrates, nor did I learn anything that wasn't available in a West Coast bookstore. I felt as if I'd gone searching for the mysterious East only to learn that it was away, visiting relatives in California.

I have the greatest respect for the spiritual traditions of India; I honor its cultural heritage and human treasures. But everywhere I went, I felt as if I were on the outside, looking in. Nothing, and no one, touched me. It wasn't India's failing; it was mine. Realizing this, disheartened but resolute, I decided to return home and try to put our family back together. It was the right thing to do, the responsible thing.

I planned to take the eastern route home, flying directly to Hawaii for a few days rest, then back to Ohio—to Holly and Linda. I missed them both. Somehow, things might still work out.

Maybe coming up empty in India was a sign, I told myself.

Perhaps my time with Socrates was all the spiritual training I was meant to have. But if that were true, why was this restless feeling growing stronger?

The departing jet flew through the night, its wing lights flashing like tiny stars as we passed over a sleeping world. I tried to read, but couldn't concentrate. I tried to sleep, but dreams assailed me. Socrates' face kept popping up, along with fragments of things said long ago. By the time we landed in Hawaii, the "pay-attention-there's-something-you're-missing" feeling became intolerable, like a fire in my belly. I was burning up! I felt like screaming, What is it I'm supposed to *do?*

As I emerged from the 747, stretching in the bright sun, the moist Hawaiian breezes calmed me for the moment.

Legend has it that these islands, born of earth, air, fire, and water, had radiated a powerful healing energy long before sailors, priests, developers, and history transformed Hawaii into a tourist resort. I hoped that beneath the veneer of civilization some of the healing energy remained, and that it might quiet that barking dog inside me that wouldn't let up.

After a snack at the airport, a noisy bus ride through the busy streets of Waikiki, and an hour on foot, I found a small room off the beaten path. I tested the leaky toilet, then quickly unpacked the few belongings I'd stored in my old backpack. The half-open drawer of the nightstand revealed a dog-eared phone directory and barely used Bible. The room would do for a few days.

Suddenly tired, I lay back on the too-soft bed that squeaked rhythmically as I bounced, and remembered nothing more—until my eyes snapped open and I jolted upright. "The woman shaman!" I yelled out loud, hardly knowing what I was saying. "How could I have forgotten?" I pounded my forehead. "Think!" What had Socrates told me? First one memory surfaced, then another. He had urged me to find someone in Hawaii, and he had mentioned a school in—where was it?—

Japan. And something about a sacred book in the desert—a book about the purpose of life!

I wanted to find the book and the school, but first I had to find the woman. *That* was why I was here; *that* was the sense of destiny I'd felt; *that* was the reason I'd taken this journey.

With this realization, my belly relaxed, and the ache inside changed to excitement. I could hardly contain myself. My mind raced: What had he told me about her? She wrote to him on some kind of stationery—*bank* stationery, that was it!

I grabbed the yellow pages and looked up "Banks"; I counted twenty-two of them in Honolulu alone. "Who am I kidding?" I muttered to myself. He hadn't told me her name or address, or what she looked like. I had almost nothing to go on. It seemed impossible.

Then the sense of destiny filled me again. No, this couldn't all be for nothing. I was here! And somehow, I would find her. I looked at my watch. If I rushed, I could check out a few banks before closing time.

But this was Hawaii, not New York City; people here didn't rush anywhere. And what would I do at the first bank anyway—walk in wearing a signboard that said, "Looking for someone special"? Would I whisper, "Socrates sent me" to every teller? And maybe this woman didn't even call him Socrates—*if* she still worked at a bank, *if* she existed.

I stared out the window at a brick wall across the alley. The beach was only ten blocks away; I'd get some dinner, go for a walk in the sand, and decide what to do. I made it to the water's edge just in time for sunset, only to discover that the sun set on the other side of the island. "Terrific," I said under my breath. "How am I going to find my mystery woman if I can't even find the sunset?"

I lay down on the soft sand, still warm in the evening air, and gazed up at a palm tree overhead. Watching its green fronds swaying in the soft breeze, I searched through my mind for a plan.

The next day, as I walked by the office of a local newspaper, it came to me. I entered the building, and quickly composed an ad to appear in the "Personals" column. It read: "Young peaceful warrior, friend of Socrates, seeking likeminded female banker. Let's make change together." I added my motel phone number. Probably a lame idea, with about the same odds of success as stuffing a note in a bottle and tossing it into the sea. A definite long shot, but at least a shot.

Several days passed. I visited art galleries, went snorkeling, and lay on the beach—waiting, just waiting. My personal ad had come up empty, and pounding the pavement seemed like an exercise in futility. Discouraged, I called the airport and booked a flight home. I was ready to call it quits.

On the bus ride to the airport, I sat in a kind of stupor, unaware of my surroundings. I found myself standing in front of the airline counter. Then, in the boarding lounge, as the agent called my flight, a voice inside me said, No. And I knew I couldn't give up. Not now, not ever. No matter what. I had to find her.

I cancelled my reservation, bought a city map, and caught the next bus back to Honolulu. On the way, I marked the location of every bank.

I was relieved to find the first bank, featuring generic bank decor, nearly empty this time of day. Scanning the room, I spotted a good possiblity right away—a slender, athletic-looking woman, maybe in her midforties. She turned and gave me a brief smile. When our eyes met, I experienced a flash of intuition—this was incredible! Why hadn't I trusted myself from the start?

She finished talking to one of the bank officers and returned to her desk by the safety deposit boxes and the vault. I waited patiently for the right moment; then, taking a deep breath, I walked up to her.

"Excuse me," I said, wearing my brightest, clearest, most

alert smile so I wouldn't appear totally crazy. "I'm looking for a woman—no, let me rephrase that—I'm looking for someone who happens to be female, but I don't know her name. You see, an old gentlemen—well, he's not exactly a gentleman—uh, an old man named Socrates suggested I find her. Does that name mean anything to you?"

"Socrates?" she said. "Isn't he a Greek or Roman guy—in history?"

"Yes, he is—was—" I answered, my hope dampened. "Maybe you don't know him by that name. He's a teacher of mine; I met him in a *gas station*"—I whispered emphatically—"a gas station in *California*." Then I waited, and held my breath.

Slowly, her eyes grew wider and then a light went on. "Yes! I had a boyfriend once who worked in a station in California. But his name was Ralph. Do you think it could have been Ralph?"

"Uh, no," I answered, disappointed. "I don't think so."

"Yeah, well, I gotta get back to work. I hope you find Archimedes—"

"*Socrates*," I corrected her. "And I'm not looking for him; I'm looking for a *woman!*"

I felt a chill, and her tone shifted. "Excuse me, I have to go. I hope you find a woman *soon*." I felt her gaze on the back of my neck as I walked over to another bank employee and did a variation of the same routine with a woman about fifty years old wearing heavy pancake makeup and rouge. Not a likely candidate, but I had to be thorough. She exchanged glances with the first teller, then looked back at me, her eyes filled with suspicion. "Can I help you?" she asked.

They must learn some kind of bank telepathy, I thought.

"I'm looking for a woman who works at the bank," I explained, "but I've misplaced her name. You wouldn't happen to know anyone named Socrates—"

"Perhaps you'd better talk to an officer," she interrupted. At first I thought she was referring to a security officer, but she pointed to a third woman in a dark suit, sitting behind a desk, just getting off the phone.

With a quick nod of thanks, I walked over to the officer, looked her in the eyes, and declared, "Hi, I'm a peaceful warrior looking for a friend of Socrates."

"*What?*" she replied, glancing toward the security guard.

"I said I'm a *potential customer looking for a fund of securities.*"

"*Oh,*" she said, smiling and straightening her coat. "Then I think we can help you."

"Oh, gosh, will you look at the time!" I said, looking at my watch. "I'll get back to you. We'll do lunch. Good-bye, ciao, aloha, cheers." I left.

I used the same peaceful warrior/potential customer line the rest of the afternoon. Then I found a bar and had my first beer in a long time. And I don't even *like* beer.

Eight banks later, I sat against the wall of yet another institution of higher finance and reminded myself, Never, *ever*, even *think* about becoming a private investigator! My back ached and I felt like I was developing an ulcer. The whole thing seemed crazy. Maybe someone had *given* the woman the bank stationery. Why would a shaman work at a bank? But, then, why would an old warrior like Socrates choose to work at a gas station?

More confused and discouraged than ever, I had no more illusions about magically bumping into a shaman in a bank who would immediately recognize me as her prodigal son. Any remaining faith in my intuition was smashed as flat as the soda can near me on the sidewalk. I picked it up, stood, and tossed the can in the trash—a good deed. At least the entire day wouldn't be wasted.

That night, I slept like a dead man—which wasn't far from the truth.

The next day, and rounds at another ten banks, left me exhausted and numb. I had been asked to leave by two savings and loans. I had almost gotten arrested at the last bank when I became belligerent. My nerves frazzled, I decided to call it a day.

That night, I dreamed I kept walking right past the woman I was seeking, narrowly missing her—like a scene in the movies when the two main characters are about to meet but turn their backs at the last minute and miss each other. This scene kept repeating itself in a maddening series of retakes.

I woke up tired. I was ready and willing to do *anything* that day—anything at all—except search for a nameless female bank employee. But somehow—and here, my training with Socrates really paid off—I willed myself to get up, get dressed, and get going. Little disciplines like that can make all the difference in the world.

The third day of my search tested my limits. I did find one bright spot, however, an oasis in a sea of frowning faces: At the fourth bank of the day, I met an extraordinarily pretty teller, about my age. When I told her I was looking for a *specific* woman, she asked, with a dimpled smile, "Am *I* specific enough?"

"I . . . uh . . . as a matter of fact, you are one of the most specific women I've seen in a long time," I grinned. I certainly doubted she was the woman shaman, but stranger things had happened, and with Socrates—well, you never knew.

She stared into my eyes, as if waiting for something. Maybe she was just flirting. Maybe she wanted me to make a deposit in her bank. Or maybe she knew something. For all I knew, she could be the shaman's daughter. Or something. I couldn't afford to pass up any lead, I told myself. Anyway, I could stand a little fun.

"Do you know who I am?" I asked.

"You do look familiar," she answered.

Damn. Did she know or didn't she? "Look, uh,"—I glanced at her name plate on the counter—"Barbara. My name's Dan; I'm a college professor visiting Honolulu, and well, it's kind of lonely, vacationing by yourself. I know we just met, but would you consider having dinner with me after work? Maybe you could show me where the sun sets, or we could talk about gas stations and old teachers."

She smiled again—definitely a good sign. "If that's a line," she said, "at least it's original. I get off at five; I'll meet you out front."

"Hey, that's terrific! See you then."

I walked out of the bank feeling good. I had a date, maybe even a lead. But then why did a little voice inside me say, *Idiot!* What are you *doing?* Socrates sends you on a quest and you pick up a bank teller?

"Oh, shut up!" I said aloud as a passerby turned and gave me a look.

My watch read 2:35. I could still make it to two, maybe three, more banks before five o'clock. I looked at my street map, now speckled with crossed-out bank sites; the First Bank of Hawaii was right around the corner.

3

Fool's Gold

When one
is willing and eager,
the gods join in.
Aeschylus

As soon as I entered the lobby, the guard glanced in my direction, started toward me, then walked right by; I let out my breath and glanced up at the cameras: they all seemed focused on me. With a businesslike air, I walked over to a counter, pretended to fill out a deposit slip, and cased the joint.

A few feet away sat a functional desk, behind which sat a functional bank officer—a tall, aristocratic-looking woman in her fifties. She glanced up at me as I approached. But before I could ask her anything, she stood up. "I'm sorry—I'm taking a late lunch—but I think Mrs. Walker can help you," she said, pointing back toward the other desk. Then she turned, and left.

"Uh, thanks," I mumbled after her.

Mrs. Walker offered no help, nor did any of the other tellers or officers at that or the next bank, where I was helped outside by the security officer, who invited me not to come back.

Ready to laugh—or cry—I slumped against the last bank's polished stone exterior and slid to a sitting position on the sidewalk. "I've had it," I said out loud. "That's it, forget it, no more banks."

I understood the importance of persevering, but there's a point to stop banging your head against a wall. And this just wasn't working out. I would go on my date, watch the sun set, and then head back to Ohio.

As I sat there feeling sorry for myself, I heard a voice ask, "Are you all right?" I looked up to see a small but plump Asian woman with silver hair, wearing an oversized muumuu, holding a bamboo cane. She looked to be about sixty years old, and she smiled down at me with an expression of maternal concern.

"I'm okay, thanks," I replied, standing up with some effort.

"You don't look okay," she said. "You look tired."

Irritable, I almost snapped, What business is it of yours? But I took a deep breath instead. "You're right," I confessed. "I am tired. But I've been tired before; I'll be fine, thanks." I expected her to nod and walk away, but she stood there, staring at me.

"Just the same," she said, "I'll bet you could use a glass of juice."

"Are you a doctor or something?" I asked, half in fun.

"No," she smiled. "Not really. But Victor—my godson—he burns it at both ends, too." Seeing my puzzled look, she quickly added, "You know, his candle."

"Oh," I replied, smiling. She seemed like a nice lady. "Well, I guess I could stand a glass of juice. Can I get you one, too?"

"That's very nice of you," she said as we entered a sidewalk café next door to the bank. I noticed she walked with a pronounced limp.

"My name's Ruth Johnson," she informed me, leaning her old bamboo cane against the counter and reaching out to shake hands. Johnson—it wasn't your typical Asian surname; I guessed she was married to a Caucasian.

"Dan Millman," I said in return, shaking her hand. I ordered a carrot juice.

"The same," said Mrs. Johnson. As she turned her head toward the waitress, I studied her face—part Hawaiian, I guessed, or maybe Japanese or Chinese, with an overlay of tan.

The waitress set our juices down on the counter. I picked mine up, then noticed Mrs. Johnson staring at me. Her eyes caught mine, and held them. She had deep eyes, like Socrates. Oh, come *on*, I thought. Stop imagining things.

She continued to stare. "Do I know you from somewhere?"

"I don't think so," I said. "This is my first time here."

"In Honolulu?"

No, on planet earth, I thought. "Yes," I said aloud.

She examined me intently for another moment, then remarked, "Well, then, it must be my imagination. So, you're visiting?"

"Yes, I'm on the faculty at Oberlin College—here on a research trip," I replied.

"No, go on! Oberlin? One of my nieces went to Oberlin!"

"Oh, really," I said, looking at my watch.

"Yes. And my godson, Victor—he's considering it for next year. He just graduated from Punaho School. Say, why don't you come over to the house tonight? You could meet Victor; he'd be *thrilled* to talk with an Oberlin professor!"

"Oh, well, I appreciate the invitation, but I have other plans."

Not at all discouraged, but with a trembling hand, she scrawled an address on a piece of paper and handed it to me. "If you change your mind."

"Thanks again," I said, standing to leave.

"Thank *you*," she said, "for the juice."

"My pleasure," I answered, tossing a five-dollar bill on the counter. I hesitated for a moment, then asked, "You don't happen to work in a bank, do you?"

"No," she answered. "Why?"

"Oh, it's nothing."

"Well then, aloha," she waved. "Create a nice day."

I stopped and turned back toward her. "What was that you said—'*Create* a nice day'?"

"Yes."

"Well, most people say, '*Have* a nice day.'"

"I suppose they do."

"It's just that an old teacher of mine—he used to say that."

"Really," she nodded, smiling at me in a funny kind of way. "How interesting."

My reality meter started buzzing; my tongue went a little numb. Was something a little off?

She stared at me again, then impaled me with a look so intense the café disappeared. "I know you," she said.

Suddenly, everything grew brighter. I felt my face flush, and my hands started to tingle. Where had I last felt like this? Then I remembered. An old gas station, one starry night.

"You know me?"

"Yes. I wasn't sure at first, but now I recognize you as a good-hearted person, but I think a little hard on yourself."

"That's it?" I said, let down. "That's what you meant?"

"And I can tell that you're lonely, and that you need to relax a little more. A barefoot walk in the surf would relax you—yes, you need a barefoot walk in the surf," she whispered.

Dazed, I heard myself ask, "A barefoot walk in the surf?"

"Exactly."

In a fog, I started toward the exit, when I heard her say, "See you tonight—about seven o'clock."

I don't clearly remember leaving the café. The next thing I knew, I found myself carrying my shoes, walking along the clean, wet sand of Waikiki, my feet washed by the shallow surf.

Some time later, a sea gull landed nearby. I glanced at it, then suddenly looked up and around as if waking up. *What was I doing here?* In a moment it came back to me: Ruth Johnson . . . the café . . . her house . . . seven o'clock. I looked at my watch; it said 6:15.

A quarter after six, a quarter after six, I repeated to myself, as if that meant something. Then it dawned on me: I had just stood up Barbara, the pretty bank teller.

I felt pretty, too—pretty stupid.

And so, with nothing else to do, I caught a bus to an attractive suburb of Honolulu, then walked until I found the address Ruth Johnson had written down. At least I thought I had found the right address; her handwriting wasn't very clear.

At 7:15, I walked up the driveway of a well-kept home. Cars filled the driveway, dance music poured out of the open doorway, and an older woman sat on a porch swing, gliding in and out of the moonlight. I climbed the steps and saw that she wasn't Ruth Johnson. Inside I heard people talking loudly. Someone laughed. I had a sinking feeling that this was the wrong place.

The woman on the swing said, "Aloha! Go on in!"

I nodded to her and entered the house, surveying the large living room, crowded with teenagers and a few older men and women—dancing, talking, eating—the women in flowered dresses or halter tops, and the men in jeans, T-shirts, and tank tops.

The music stopped for a moment; I heard a splash as someone jumped, or fell, into the swimming pool just visible through sliding glass doors. Loud laughter followed.

I tapped a young woman on the shoulder just as a rock-'n'-roll tune started; I had to yell to be heard above the music. "I'm looking for Ruth Johnson."

"Who?" she yelled back.

"Ruth Johnson!" I yelled louder.

"I don't know too many people here," she shrugged. "Hey, Janet!" she called to someone else. "You know any Ruth Johnson?"

Janet said something I couldn't hear. "Never mind," I said, and headed for the door.

Walking down the front steps, I stopped, and gave it one last try. Turning to the woman on the swing, I asked, "Does Ruth Johnson live here?"

"No," she said.

"Oh." Depressed, I turned to leave. Couldn't I do *anything* right?

"Ruthie's staying with her sister down the street," the woman added. "She went to buy more soda."

Just then, a car pulled up in front.

"There she is now," the woman pointed.

No one got out of the car at first. Then I saw Ruth Johnson climb slowly to her feet. I quickly ran down the steps to meet her, anxious to get to the bottom of all this, one way or the other.

She was reaching to pick up a grocery bag when I said from behind her, "Let me help you with that." She turned and looked delighted—but not surprised—to see me.

"*Mahalo!* Thank you!" she said. "You see, I was right about your being a kind person."

"Maybe not as kind as you think," I said, as a picture of my young daughter, and the wife I'd left behind, flashed through my mind.

I walked slowly up the front steps to keep pace with her. "So, why did you really invite me here?" I asked.

"Sorry to slow you down," she said, ignoring my question. "I had a small—well, stroke, you could say. But I'm getting better all the time."

"Mrs. Johnson, can we get to the point?"

"I'm glad you found the house," she said.

"I've come a long way—"

"Yes, people come from all over for one of our parties. We really know how to have a good time!"

"You don't really know who I am."

"I don't imagine anyone really knows who anyone really is. But here we are anyway!" she said brightly. "And while you're here, why don't you come in, meet Victor, and enjoy the party?"

Disappointed, I leaned up against the wall and stared at the ground.

"Are you all right?" she asked, concerned.

"I'm okay."

"Hey, Ruthie!" someone yelled from inside. "Did you bring the soda and chips?"

"Have them right here, Bill!"

She turned to me. "Uh, what did you say your name was?"

I looked up at her. "Dan." It came out like "damn."

"Well, Dan, come on in, dance a little, meet some people. That should perk you up."

"Look, I appreciate the offer—you seem like a nice lady—but I'd better be going; I have a lot to do tomorrow." Suddenly tired, I took a deep breath and stood. "Have a nice party, and thanks—uh, mahalo—for your kindness." I turned toward the street.

"Wait a moment," she said, limping after me. "Look, it was my mistake, having you come all the way out here. Let me give you something for the road." She reached into her purse.

"No, really, I couldn't. I don't need—"

She grabbed my hand and looked me in the eyes; the world started spinning. "You take this," she said, pushing what looked like crumpled bills into my hand. "Maybe we'll meet again."

She turned abruptly and entered the house. The sound of music grew louder, then suddenly quiet as the door slammed shut.

Clenching the money in my fist, I shoved it into my pocket and walked on, into the warm night.

Coconut and banyan trees and landscaped lawns faintly shone under the light of a street lamp near a bus stop, where I collapsed to a sitting position, trying to clear my head. Something was off here; nothing made sense. It *had* to be her, but it wasn't. I was back to zero.

I didn't know if I could bring myself to visit another bank; I was tired of getting treated like a nut case. Maybe it was hopeless; maybe I was just a strange person, as my wife had said. Maybe she was right about everything. Why couldn't I just be a normal guy and go to ball games and movies and have barbecues on Sunday?

I was seriously considering flying home the next day and seeing a good therapist when the bus arrived with a sighing of air brakes. The door opened; I got to my feet and reached into my pocket for the money—and saw that Ruth Johnson hadn't given me any money after all.

"Hey, buddy," the bus driver said. "You getting on or not?"

Intent on opening the crinkled pieces of paper, I hardly heard him, and didn't answer. Then my eyes opened wide and I stopped breathing. Vaguely aware of the bus pulling away without me, I stared at the two pieces of paper in my hands: The first was a newspaper ad, clipped from the "Personals" section. It began, "Young peaceful warrior, friend of Socrates." I heard myself breathing rapidly; my whole body trembled.

On the second piece of paper, I found a note Mrs. Johnson had scrawled in a shaky, nearly illegible hand. It read:

I'm from the old school—the hard school. Nothing is given without desire, preparation, and initiation. There is a question of trust, and faith. On Thursday evening, three nights from now, the currents will be exactly right. If you wish to continue, follow all these instructions precisely: Go to Makapuu Beach in the early evening.

I turned the note over. It continued:

You will see a rocky area toward Makapuu Point. Walk toward the point until you find a small shed. One side is caved in. Behind it, you'll see a large surfboard. When you are alone—at dusk, not before—take the board and paddle out beyond the surf. A strong tide will be going out; let the currents take you. Be sure . . .

Strange—that was all. "*Be sure . . .*" The note ended there. What did she mean by that? I wondered, stuffing the note back into my pocket.

Then my wonder changed to excitement and a profound sense of relief. My search was over. I'd found her! A fountain of energy welled up inside me. My senses opened; I felt the temperature of the air, heard faraway crickets, and smelled the fresh aroma of newly mowed lawns, wet from an earlier rain. I walked all the way back to my motel. By the time I arrived, it was nearly dawn.

I fell onto the bed with a bounce and a squeak and stared at the ceiling. Much later, I drifted to sleep.

That night, I dreamed of skeletons—hundreds of them—bleached white by the sun, washed up on the rocky shore, lying askew on black lava rock. A wave crashed, and the shore was washed clean, leaving only the lava, black as night. The blackness swallowed me. I heard a roar, soft at first, then growing louder.

Awakened by the whine of a garbage truck outside, I opened my eyes and stared at the ceiling—but the stark images of skeletons remained in my mind, along with a sense of awe and foreboding. Thursday evening, it would begin.

Things were definitely picking up; a new wave was rising. Just like the old days—I felt so alive! This feeling made me realize how easy life had been these past few years: I had become an armchair warrior whose battles were championed by alter egos on TV or at the movies. Now I was on my feet, waiting for the bell.

4

A Fire at Sea

What is to give light
must endure burning.
Viktor Frankl

I had made no special preparations, because apparently none were called for—just find a big surfboard and go for a paddle.

Thursday afternoon, I checked out of my hotel, ready to camp on the beach, ready for a change, ready for anything. Or so I thought. I carried my belongings, stuffed into my backpack, down to Makapuu Beach. Breathing in the fresh, salty air, I walked toward the point. In the distance ahead, atop a mound of lava rock, I saw an old lighthouse standing starkly against a crimson sky.

The walk was farther than I'd thought; it was nearly dark before I found the shed. The surfboard was there, just as she'd said. It wasn't the streamlined fiberglass I'd expected, but a massive, old-fashioned slab of wood, like the boards used by the ancient Hawaiian kings—I'd seen a picture of one in *National Geographic.*

I looked out over the deserted beach and calm ocean. In spite of the setting sun, the balmy air was comfortable. I stripped to my nylon trunks, stuffed my clothing and wallet into my pack, and hid my pack in the bushes. Then I carried the heavy board out into thigh-deep surf and set it down with a loud slap on the glassy surface.

With a last look down the beach, I pushed off, and glided out, paddling awkwardly through the waves.

Panting, I resolved to get in better shape as I broke through the last phosphorescent whitecap, barely illuminated by a waning moon that appeared and disappeared as clouds passed overhead. Resting on the ocean's gentle rise and fall, I wondered about this strange initiation. Pleasant enough, but how long did Ruth Johnson want me to float out here before coming back in. All night?

The rhythmic ocean swells soothed me into a pleasant lassitude. I lay on my back and gazed up into the constellations of Scorpio and Sagittarius. My eyes scanned the heavens and my thoughts drifted with the current as I waited for who knows what—maybe further instructions from a spaceship for all I knew.

I must have fallen asleep, because I sat up, suddenly awake, straddling the board as it rocked back and forth. Until I awoke, I hadn't realized that I'd been asleep. I wondered if enlightenment was like that.

I was looking around, trying to make out the coastline in the darkness when it struck me: the current. She had written something about the current being "exactly right." For what? I scanned the horizon in every direction, but with the sea's rise and fall, and the cloud cover, I was effectively blind until dawn; I saw no stars, no land.

I had left my watch on shore and had no sense of time or bearings. How long had I drifted? And where? With a chill, I realized I might be drifting straight out to sea! Panic hit me like a punch.

Paranoid fantasies played themselves out in the theater of my imagination: What if this old woman is an eccentric, or even crazy? What if she has a score to settle with Socrates? Would she deliberately . . . ? No! It couldn't be! I thought. My usual methods of reality testing weren't helping me here.

As soon as I fought off one wave of fear, another would roll in. My mind sank beneath the surface of the sea, and I shuddered as I imagined huge, dark shapes swimming beneath me. I felt small and alone, a floating speck in the ocean, thousands of feet above the ocean floor.

Hours passed, as far as I could reckon. I lay still, listening for the sound of a Coast Guard boat, scanning the heavens for signs of a rescue copter. But no one knew where I was—no one except Ruth Johnson.

The clouds blotted out the moon and stars, leaving the sky so dark I couldn't tell whether my eyes were open or closed. I drifted in and out of consciousness, afraid to sleep. But the gentle, lullaby rise and fall of the ocean swells won out, and I plunged down, slowly, into silence, like a rock sinking into the depths of the sea.

I awoke with the first light of dawn, realized where I was, sat up suddenly, and fell off the board. Sputtering and spitting out saltwater, I climbed back on the board and looked around hopefully—then with rising apprehension. I saw nothing but ocean; the clouds still obscured any sight of land. For all I knew, I was far out in the Pacific. I'd heard about strong currents that could pull someone straight out to sea. I could paddle, but in what direction? Fighting off panic, I forced myself to take a deep, calming breath.

Then an even more disturbing revelation dawned on me: I had no shirt or sunscreen, no food, no water. For the first time, it occurred to me that I might really die out here—that this was no middle-class adventure. I might have made a very big mistake.

Ruth Johnson had written that it was "a question of trust and faith." "Yeah," I muttered to myself, "trust, faith, and blind stupidity." What had possessed me? I mean, who takes a surfboard out into the ocean currents at night because an old woman writes him a note?

"This can't be happening," I said, startled by the sound of my own voice. My words sounded muffled, drowned by the vast spaces above and below. I could already feel the heat of the morning sun on my back.

The clouds dissipated, leaving a burning azure sky. I had time to consider my situation—nothing but time. Except for the occasional call of an albatross or the faint drone of an airplane far above, silence was my only companion.

Once in a while, I splashed my feet in the salty water, or hummed a tune to reassure my ears. But soon enough, the tunes died. A sense of dread crept slowly up my spine.

As the day wore on, I grew thirsty, and my fear intensified with the heat of the sun. It wasn't the sudden fear of a gun in my ribs or a car weaving head-on into my lane—just a quiet kind of knowingness, a stark inevitability that unless someone rescued me soon, I would burn to death on the cool green sea.

The hours passed with agonizing slowness, and my skin started turning pink. By the late afternoon, my thirst became an obsession. I tried everything I could think of to protect myself: I paddled the board around to face different directions; I slipped into the cooling water many times, under the shelter of the board, careful to maintain my hold on its cracked surface. The water was my only protection from the sun and carried me into the blessed dark.

All night, my body burned with fever, then shook with chills. Even the slightest movement felt painful. I shivered as I hugged myself, overcome with remorse. Why had I done such a foolish thing? How could I have trusted that old woman, and why would she have done this to me? Was she cruel, or merely mistaken? Either way, the outcome was the same: I would die without ever knowing why. *Why?* I asked myself again and again as my mind clouded over.

When morning came, I lay still, my skin blistered and my lips cracked. I think I would have died, but for a gift from the sky: Dark clouds appeared with the dawn, and a rainstorm swept over, giving me a few hours of shade, and of life. Raindrops, mixed with tears of gratitude, stung my blistered face.

I had nothing to hold the water save my open mouth. I lay back with my jaws wide, trying to catch every drop, until my muscles began to spasm. I removed my trunks so they could soak up every possible bit of rainwater.

Too soon, the scorching sun returned, rising higher in the empty blue sky, as if the storm had never happened. My lips cracked into deep fissures. Surrounded by water, I was dying of thirst.

Mahatma Gandhi once said, "To a starving man, God can only appear in the form of bread." Now, water had become my god, my goddess, my one thought and one passion—not enlightenment, not understanding—I would have traded them in an instant for one glass of pure, cool, quenching water.

I stayed in the ocean, clinging to the board, for most of the morning. But it did nothing for the horrible thirst. Later, in the afternoon, I thought I saw a dorsal fin circling nearby, and I quickly scrambled back onto the board. But as my skin continued to blister and I grew more parched, the thought entered my mind that a shark's jaws might be my only deliverance from slow death. Like a deer that bares its throat to the lion, a small but growing part of me wanted to give in, to just slip into the sea and disappear.

When night came again, I again burned with fever. In my delirium, I dreamed of swimming in a mountain spring, drinking my fill, lying in a calm pool, and letting the water seep into my pores. Then the smiling face of Ruth Johnson appeared, with her silver hair, her deep eyes mocking my foolishness.

Drifting in and out of consciousness with the rise and fall of the sea, my rational mind faded in, then out, like a ghost presence. In a lucid moment, I knew that if I didn't find land by the next day, it would be over.

Pictures flashed by: home in Ohio, in my backyard, sitting back in my lounge chair in the shade of a birch tree sipping a lemonade, reading a novel, playing with my daughter, eating a snack just because I was a little hungry—the comforts and safety of home. Now, all that seemed a far-off dream, and this, a nightmarish reality. If I slept at all, I don't remember.

Morning came much too soon.

That day I learned about hell: pain and burning, fear and waiting. I was ready to slip off the board and swim away in the cool water, to let Death take me—anything to stop the pain. I cursed the body, this mortal body. It was a burden now, a source of suffering. But another part of me hung on, determined to fight to my last breath.

The sun moved with agonizing slowness across the sky. I learned to hate the clear blue, and gave silent thanks for every cloud that covered the sun as I clung to the board, submerged in the water I could not drink.

I lay exhausted through the next night—neither awake nor asleep—floating in purgatory. Squinting through swollen lids, I saw a vision of cliffs in the distance, and imagined I heard the faint pounding of surf against the rocks. Then, suddenly alert, I realized it was no vision. It was real! Hope lay ahead, and life. I was going to survive. I started to cry, but found I had no tears left.

A surge of energy coursed through me; my mind, now crystal clear, snapped into focus. I couldn't die now—I was too close! With all my remaining strength, I started paddling toward shore. I was going to *live.*

The cliffs now towered above me like gigantic skyscrapers, dropping straight down to the sea. With increasing speed, driven by the surf, I moved toward the rocks. Abruptly, the surf turned angry. I remember grabbing for my board as it snapped into the air and came crashing down. Then I must have passed out.

5

New Beginnings

Healing is a matter of time,
but it is sometimes also
a matter of opportunity.
Hippocrates, *Precepts,* Ch. 1

On the island of Molokai, in Pelekunu Valley, set deep among moss-covered crags, lay a small cabin. Inside that cabin, a woman's screams pierced the air. "Mama Chia!* Mama Chia!" she cried out in pain and fear as she struggled in the throes of a difficult childbirth.

Molokai—where, in the 1800s, the lepers had been exiled, left to die, isolated from the rest of the world by fear and ignorance.

Molokai—home of native Hawaiians, Japanese, Chinese, and Filipinos, with a small American and European population; a retreat for counterculture and alternative life-styles; home of hardy, independent folk who avoid development and the tourist trade of the other islands, who work hard and live simply, who teach their children basic values and love of nature.

Molokai—island of nature spirits and legend, secret burial place of the *kahuna kupuas,* the shamans, magicians, and healers, the spiritual warriors attuned to the energies of the earth.

Molokai was ready to welcome another soul to the earth.

Mitsu Fujimoto, a small Japanese-American in her early

*Chia is pronounced "Chee-ah."

forties, tossed her head from side to side, soaked in sweat. She prayed and moaned and cried for her child, calling weakly, "Mama Chia!" Pushing on, panting with each contraction, she fought for her baby's life.

Hours or minutes later—I couldn't tell—after drifting, delirious, in and out of consciousness, I awoke, desperately thirsty. If I felt thirsty, I was alive! The logic of that realization shocked me to my senses and, for a few rational moments, I scanned my body, taking stock inside and out. My head throbbed; my skin burned. And I couldn't see; I was blind! I moved my arm, now incredibly weak, and felt my eyes, discovering with great relief that they were covered with gauze.

I had no idea where I was—in a hospital, in a room, in Ohio, or maybe back in California. Maybe I had been ill or in some kind of accident. Or maybe it was all a dream.

Mitsu's long black hair lay tangled and matted across her face and pillow. After her first child had died, nearly ten years before, she had vowed never to have another; she couldn't live through the pain of another such loss.

But when she passed the age of forty, she knew that this would be her last chance. It was now or never. So Mitsu Fujimoto and her husband, Sei, made their decision.

After many months, Mitsu's face grew radiant, and her belly ripe. The Fujimotos were to be blessed with a child.

Sei had run into the valley to find help. Now Mitsu lay contorted on her mattress, panting and resting between the contractions—exhausted, alone, and afraid that something was terribly wrong, that the baby was turned around. As each tidal wave of contractions hardened her uterine wall like stone, Mitsu screamed again for Mama Chia.

When I regained consciousness, the world remained dark, my eyes still covered with gauze. My skin was on fire; all I could do was moan, and bear it.

I heard a sound—what was it?—like someone wringing out a wet cloth over a bowl of water. As if in answer, a cool cloth touched my forehead; then a soothing odor filled my nostrils.

My emotions very close to the surface, I felt a tear run down my cheek. "Thank you," I muttered, my scratchy voice barely audible.

I reached up slowly and clasped the small hand that held the cloth, now cooling my chest and shoulders.

I was surprised by the voice of a girl—a young girl, maybe nine or ten years old. "Rest now" was all she said.

"Thank you," I said again, then asked, "Water . . . please."

The girl's hand, behind my neck, gently lifted my head so I could drink. I grabbed the cup and poured more, until it spilled over my lips and down my chest. She pulled the cup back. "I'm sorry; I'm only supposed to let you sip a little at a time," she apologized, letting my head back down. Then, I must have slept.

Mitsu's pains continued, but she was now too exhausted to push, too weary to call out. Suddenly, the front door opened, and her husband rushed in, panting from the exertion of the steep dirt road. "Mitsu!" he called, "I've brought her!"

"Fuji, I need clean sheets—now," Mama Chia said, going straight to the exhausted mother-to-be and checking her vital signs. Then she quickly scrubbed her hands. "I'll need three clean towels as well—and boil a gallon of water. Then run back down to the truck and bring the oxygen."

Working quickly and efficiently, Mama Chia—midwife, healer, kahuna—again checked Mitsu's vital signs, and prepared to turn the baby. This might be a difficult birthing, but God willing, and with the help of the island spirits, she would save the mother and, together, they would bring a new life into the world.

The burning had subsided from incessant pain to a mild throbbing. I tried, cautiously, to move the muscles of my face.

"What have I done to myself?" I asked in despair, still hoping to awaken from this nightmare—crazy, stupid, unnecessary. But it wasn't a dream. Tears stung my eyes. So weak I could hardly move, my mouth cracked and dry, I could barely mouth the words again, "Water . . . please." But no one heard.

I remembered something Socrates had told me about the search for meaning. "Better never begin—but once begun, better finish."

"Better never begin, better never begin," I muttered, before dropping off to sleep.

The cry of an infant boy resounded through the open windows of that tiny cabin in the rain forest. Mitsu managed a smile as she held the child to her breast. Fuji sat nearby, beaming, touching his wife, then his baby. Tears of joy ran down his cheeks.

Mama Chia cleaned up, as she had done many times in the past. "Mitsu and your son are going to be fine, Fuji. I'll leave them in your care now—and, I'm sure, in very good hands." She smiled.

He cried unabashedly, taking both her hands in his and lapsing from Hawaiian to Japanese to English: "Mama Chia, mahalo! Mahalo! *Arigato gosaimas!* How can we ever thank you?" he asked, his eyes still wet with tears.

"You just did," she answered. But his expression told her that neither his thanks nor his tears would be adequate payment in Fuji's eyes—it was a matter of pride and honor—so she added, "I'd love some vegetables when you harvest. You grow the best yams on the island."

"You'll get the best of the best!" he promised.

With a last look at Mitsu's tired but radiant face as she nursed her baby, Mama Chia gathered her backpack and left for her slow hike down into the valley. She had another patient to see.

I awoke as the small, now familiar hands lifted my head and gently poured some liquid onto my tongue. I sucked it down greedily; it tasted strange, but good. After a few more sips, the hands carefully smoothed some kind of salve over my face, and then over my chest and arms.

"This is a poultice made from the fruit of the noni tree, mixed with aloe," she said in her soft young voice. "It will help your skin heal."

When I next awoke, I felt better. My headache was nearly gone, and my skin, though it felt tight, no longer burned. I opened my eyes; the gauze bandages were gone. Glad to have my sight once again, I turned my head slowly and looked around: I was alone, on a cot, in the corner of a small, but clean, one-room cabin built of logs. Light poured in through makeshift shades. A wooden chest sat at the foot of the bed. A chest of drawers stood against the far wall.

Many questions passed through my mind: Where am I? I asked myself. Who saved me? Who brought me here?

"Hello?" I said. "Hello?" I repeated louder. I heard footsteps, then a young girl entered. She had jet black hair and a beautiful smile.

"Hello," she said. "Are you feeling any better?"

"Yes," I answered. "Who . . . who are you? Where am I?"

"You're *here*!" she answered, amused. "And I'm Sachi, Mama Chia's assistant," she said proudly. "My real name's Sachiko, but Mama Chia calls me Sachi for short—"

"Who is Mama Chia?" I interrupted.

"She's my auntie. She's teaching me about the kahuna ways."

"Kahuna—then I'm still in Hawaii?"

"Of course!" she said, smiling at my silly question. "This is Molokai." She pointed to a faded map of the Hawaiian islands on the wall behind my head.

"Molokai? I drifted to *Molokai?*" I asked with amazement.

Mama Chia made her way slowly down the winding path.

It had been a busy week, and these past few days had left her tired. But her work called forth an energy beyond that of her physical body.

She continued down the path through the forest. No time to rest now; she wanted to check on her new patient. Her flowered dress, still damp from a rain shower, bore spots of mud on its lower border. Her hair clung to her forehead in wet strands. Unconcerned about her appearance, she quickened her pace the best she could on the slippery forest trail on the way to her patient.

She turned a final bend in the path—her body remembered it so well she could walk it on a moonless night—and saw the small clearing and the cabin nestled, almost hidden, against a green wall of trees. "Just where I left it," she joked to herself. She passed the nearby storage shed and vegetable garden, and entered.

I tried sitting up and looking out the open window. The late afternoon sun slanted in and lit the opposite wall. Feeling woozy, I lay back down. "Sachi," I asked weakly, "how did I get here? And—"

Then, with a shock, I sat up again, and nearly passed out as a woman limped into the room and turned toward me.

"*Ruth Johnson*?" I cried out, dumbfounded. How could this be? "Am I dreaming?" I asked.

"Entirely possible," she said. But this was no dream. The woman who had sent me out on the surfboard was standing over me now.

"You almost killed me!" I yelled.

The old woman set her cane against the wall, fluffed up my pillow, and gently pushed me back on the bed. She wasn't smiling, but her face had a tenderness I hadn't seen before. She turned to the young girl. "You've done a good job taking care of him, Sachi; I know your parents will be pleased." Sachi smiled brightly; I had other things on my mind.

"Who *are* you?" I asked the woman. "Why did you do this to me? *What's going on here?*"

She didn't answer right away, but as she massaged another salve into the skin of my face, she said quietly, "I don't understand—you don't seem like a foolish young man—why did you ignore my directions? Why did you go out without any sunscreen, or food, or water?"

I pushed her hand away from my face and sat up again. "*What* directions? Why would I need sunscreen at night? Who takes food and water out on a surfboard? Why didn't you tell me what I would need?"

"But I *did* tell you," she interrupted. "I wrote it down—told you to be sure to take three days' supply of water, food, and sunscreen, and—"

"There was nothing about any of that in your note," I interrupted.

She paused, puzzled and thoughtful. "How can that be?" she asked, staring into space. "On the second page I wrote down everything—"

"What do you mean, 'second page'?" I asked. "All you gave me was the newspaper clipping, and a note. You wrote on the front and the back—"

"But there was another *page!*" she said, cutting me off.

Then it dawned on me: "The note," I said. "It ended with the words, 'Be sure . . . ' I thought you were just telling me to be certain!"

As she realized what must have happened, Mama Chia closed her eyes; a mixture of emotions passed over her face for a moment, then disappeared. Shaking her head sadly, she sighed. "The next page told you everything you'd need and where the currents would take you."

"I—I must have dropped the other page when I was putting the papers in my pocket."

I lay back down against the pillows. I didn't know whether to laugh or cry. "And I assumed, out there on the ocean, that you were just from 'the hard school.'"

"Not *that* hard!" she replied. We laughed, because there was nothing else to do, and because the whole thing was so ludicrous.

Still laughing, she added, "And when you're feeling stronger, to finish the job, we can throw you off a cliff!"

I laughed even louder than she; it made my head hurt again. And, just for a moment, I wasn't sure whether or not she was serious.

"But who are you? I mean—"

"On Oahu, I was Ruth Johnson. Here, my friends, students, patients—and people I've almost killed—call me Mama Chia." She smiled.

"Well, Mama Chia, how *did* I get here?"

She walked over to the island map and pointed: "The currents took you across the Kaiwi Channel, around Ilio Point, and eastward along the north shore of Molokai, past Kahiu Point, toward Kamakou, and you landed—ungracefully, I might add, but right on time—at Pelekunu Valley, just as I knew you would. There is a trail, a stairwell known by few people. Some friends helped carry you here."

"Where are we?"

"In a secluded place—a forest reserve."

I shook my head, then winced as it throbbed. "I don't understand any of this. Why all the mystery?"

"All part of your initiation—I told you. If you had been prepared . . . " Her words trailed off. "I acted carelessly. I'm sorry for what you had to endure, Dan. I intended to give you a test of faith, not get you deep-fried," she apologized again. "But like Socrates, I suppose I have a flair for the dramatic."

"Well," I said, "can I at least consider myself initiated?"

She sighed. "I should hope so."

After a pause, I asked, "How did you know I was coming to Hawaii? Until a few days ago, *I* didn't even know. Did you know who I was when we met, outside the bank? And how did you find me in the first place?"

Mama Chia gazed out the window for a moment before she answered. "There are other forces at work here—that's the only way I can explain it. I don't often read the local papers, and I almost never read the 'Personals' column. But I was staying at my sister's house on Oahu, for Victor's party, when I found the paper on her coffee table. We were going out, and while I was waiting for her to get ready, I picked up the paper and skimmed through it. When my eyes somehow locked onto your message, a surge of electricity passed through me. I felt a sense of *destiny*."

I lay very still, but chills ran up and down my spine.

"When I read that ad," she continued, "I could almost see your face, as clearly as I see you now." She tenderly touched my blistered cheeks. "I was so glad you had finally arrived."

"But why would you be glad? Why would you care?"

"When I read the ad, it all came back to me—what Socrates had written about you."

"What did he write?"

"Never mind that now. It's time you ate something," she said. Reaching into her backpack, she pulled out a mango and a papaya.

"I'm not really hungry," I said. "My stomach has shrunk. And I'd rather hear what Socrates wrote about me."

"You've eaten nothing for seven days," she gently chided.

"I've done that before," I replied. "Besides, I needed to lose weight." I pointed to my waist, now much leaner.

"Perhaps—but this fruit has been blessed, and will help you heal more rapidly."

"You really believe that?"

"I don't believe; I *know*," she answered, cutting open a fresh papaya, scooping out the black seeds, and handing me half.

I looked at the fresh fruit. "Maybe I am a *little* hungry," I said, and nibbled a small piece. I felt its sweetness melt onto my tongue; I inhaled its aroma. "Mmmmmm," I said, nibbling another piece. "Healing, huh?"

"Yes," she replied, handing me a slice of ripe mango. "This, too."

Eating obediently, with growing enthusiasm, I asked between bites, "So how did you find me—on the street?"

"Another twist of fate," she replied. "When I found your ad, I decided to somehow make contact—or perhaps observe you for a while, to see if you could find me."

"I never would have found you—you don't even work at a bank."

"Not for six years."

"I guess we found each other," I said, taking another bite of mango.

Mama Chia smiled. "Yes. And now it's time for me to go, and for you to rest."

"I'm feeling much better, now—really—and I still want to know why you were so glad I arrived."

She paused before speaking. "There's a bigger picture you don't yet see—one day you may reach out to many people; you may find the right leverage and make a real difference. Now close your eyes, and sleep."

"Leverage," I thought as my eyes closed. The word stuck in my mind, and pulled me back to an incident years before, to a time with Socrates. We were walking back toward the Berkeley campus after a breakfast at Joseph's café. As Soc and I neared campus, a student handed me a flyer. I glanced at it. "Soc," I said, "will you look at this. It's about saving the whales and dolphins. Last week," I sighed, "I got one about oppressed peoples; the week before it was about starving children. Sometimes I feel so guilty, doing all this work on myself when there are so many people in need out there."

Socrates looked at me without expression, but kept walking as if I'd said nothing.

"Did you hear me, Socrates?"

In response, he stopped, turned, and said, "I'll give you five bucks if you can slap me on the cheek."

"What? What does that have to do with—"

"Ten bucks," he interrupted, upping the ante. Then he started playfully slapping me, but I refused his ploy.

"I've never hit an old man before, and I don't intend—"

"Believe me, junior, there's no danger of your hitting this old man; you have the reflexes of a snail."

That did it. I took a few trial swings, then really went for it.

I found myself on the ground in a painful wrist lock. As Soc helped me up, he asked, "You notice that a little leverage can be very effective?"

"Yeah, I sure did," I replied, shaking my wrist.

"To really help people, you first need to understand them—but you can't understand someone else until you understand yourself. Know yourself; prepare yourself; develop the clarity, the courage, and the sensitivity to exert the right leverage, in the right place, at the right time. *Then* act."

That was the last thing I remembered before falling into a deep sleep.

The next morning, Sachiko arrived with some fresh fruit and a pitcher of water. Then, with a wave, she said, "Time for school," and ran out the door.

Soon after, Mama Chia entered. She rubbed more of the clean-smelling salve on my face, neck, and chest. "You're healing well—as I expected."

"In a few days, I should be ready to travel." I sat up and stretched, carefully.

"Travel?" she asked. "You think you're ready to go somewhere? And what will you find when you get there—what you found in India?"

"*How did you know about that?*" I asked, dumbfounded.

"When you understand how I knew," she said, "you'll be ready to continue your journey." Mama Chia gave me a piercing stare. "Abe Lincoln once said that if he had six hours to chop down a tree, he'd spend the first five hours sharpening the axe. You have a great task ahead, and you are not yet sharpened. It will take time, and require tremendous energy."

"But I'm feeling better all the time. Soon I'll have enough energy."

"It's not your energy I'm talking about; it's mine."

I lay back down, suddenly feeling like a burden. "I really should go," I said. "You have other people to attend to; I don't want to impose."

"Impose?" she responded. "Does the diamond impose on the gem polisher? Does the steel impose on the swordsmith? Please, Dan. Stay a while. I can think of no better way to use my energy."

Her words encouraged me. "Well," I said, smiling, "it may not be as hard as you think. I've trained as a gymnast; I know how to apply myself. And I did spend a lot of time with Socrates."

"Yes," she said. "Socrates prepared you for me; I'm to prepare you for what follows." She closed the container and put the salve on the bureau.

"Well, what's going to follow? Do you have something planned? What do you do here anyway?"

She laughed. "I play different roles, wear different hats for different people. For you, no hat at all." She paused. "Most of the time, I help my friends. Sometimes I just sit and do nothing at all. Sometimes I practice shape shifting."

"Shape shifting?"

"Yes."

"What's that?"

"Oh, becoming different things—merging with the spirits of animals, or rocks, or water—that sort of thing. Seeing life from another point of view, if you know what I mean."

"But you don't actually—"

"I need to go now," she said, cutting my question in half. "I have people to see." She picked up the backpack she had set down near the bookcase, grabbed her cane, and walked out the door before I could say another word.

I sat up again with some effort. I could barely see her through the open front door as she limped, swinging her cane, up the winding path into the forest.

I leaned back and watched the narrow rays of sunlight passing through holes in the drawn curtains, and wondered if I'd ever feel good about the sun again.

I'd suffered a setback, but I had found her! My body tingled with a rising excitement. The road ahead might be difficult—even dangerous—but at least it was open.

6

Barefoot on a Forest Path

The clearest way into the Universe
is through
a forest wilderness.
John Muir

The next morning found me ravenous, glad for the bowl of fruit on the nightstand. I found a knife and spoon in the drawer and ate two bananas, a passion fruit, and a papaya in quick succession. I reminded myself to slow down and chew, but the food just seemed to disappear.

Feeling better after breakfast, I decided to explore my surroundings. Swinging my legs over the edge of the bed, I grew dizzy for a few moments, waited for it to pass, then stood. Weak and unsteady, I looked down at myself; I'd lost so much weight, my swim trunks nearly fell off. "I'll have to write a diet book," I muttered. "I'll call it 'The Surfboard Diet'—probably make a million dollars."

Still shaky, I tottered toward a pitcher of water on the dresser, took a slow drink, then made my way to some kind of chemical toilet in a curtained-off area. It would do just fine. At least my kidneys were still functioning.

I stared at my face in an old mirror. With its oozing sores and scabs, it seemed like the face of a stranger. Parts of my back were still bandaged. How could that little girl Sachi bear to look at me, let alone touch me?

Making my way outside, resting often, I stayed in the shade of the cabin and trees. The solid ground felt good under me, but my feet were still tender. Without shoes, I couldn't go far. I wondered if my backpack, with all my belongings, had been discovered. If so, they might think I had drowned. Or, I thought darkly, maybe a thief had found my wallet, my air tickets, my credit card! No, I'd hidden the pack too well. It was set in a deep thicket, covered by dried brush. I'd mention it to Mama Chia the next time I saw her, which, as it turned out, wasn't to happen for several more days.

I managed to walk up the trail a little ways until I found a good vantage point. High above me, in the distance, stood the bare lava cliffs jutting skyward in the center of the island, above the thick rain forest. Far below, through the lush trees, I could just make out bits of blue sky. My cabin, I estimated, lay about halfway between the upper cliffs and the sea below.

Tired, and a little depressed by my infirmity, I made my way back down the trail to the cabin, lay down, and slept again.

As the days passed, my hunger returned in a flood. I ate tropical fruit, then sweet yams, potatoes, corn, taro, and—although my diet was normally vegetarian—a small sampling of fresh fish along with some kind of seaweed soup I found on the bureau each morning, delivered, I suspected, by Sachiko. Mama Chia had insisted I eat the soup "to help cure the burns and radiation."

Early mornings and late afternoons, I started walking farther, hiking a few hundred yards into the lush valley, up through the rain forest filled with the smooth-skinned kukui tree, the twisting banyan, towering palm, and the eucalyptus, whose leaves shimmered in the sea breezes. Red and white ginger plants grew everywhere among the delicate *amaumau* ferns, and the red earth was covered with a rich carpet of moss, grasses, and leaves.

Except for the small clearing that surrounded my cabin, everything stood on a slant here. At first I tired quickly, but I soon got my breath back, climbing up into the moist, healing air of the rain forest. Below, a few miles away, sheer cliffs, the *pali*, dropped to the sea. How had they ever carried me up to the cabin?

The next few mornings, traces of dreams lingered in my awareness—images of Mama Chia and the sound of her voice. And each morning I felt unusually refreshed. With amazement, I noticed that my sores had peeled away rapidly, leaving tender new skin, now nearly healed—almost as good as new. My strength was returning and, with it, a renewed sense of urgency. I had found Mama Chia; I was here. Now what? What did I need to learn or do before she would direct me to the next step on my journey?

When I awoke the next day, the sun was already rising toward its zenith. I lay there and listened to the shrill cries of a bird outside, then set out on another short hike. My bare feet were getting used to the earth.

Later, returning from the hike, I saw Mama Chia entering the cabin, probably expecting to find me in bed. I walked quickly down the grade, nearly slipping on wet leaves, slick from an earlier downpour. Thinking I'd have a little fun with her, and proud of my speedy recovery, I hid behind the shed and peered out as she emerged, puzzled, and looked around. I ducked behind the shed again and put my hand over my mouth to stifle a laugh, then took a deep breath and peeked around the corner again. She was no longer there.

Afraid that she had gone away to look for me, I stepped out from concealment and was about to call her when a hand tapped me on the shoulder; I turned to see her smiling at me. "How did you know where I was?" I asked.

"I heard you call to me."

"I didn't call to you!"

"Yes, you did."

"No, I didn't! I was going to, but—"

"Then how did I know you were here?"

"I asked *you* that!"

"Then I guess we've come full circle," she said. "Sit down; I brought lunch."

At the word "lunch," I obeyed promptly, sitting on a thick

carpet of damp leaves in the shade of a tree. My stomach growled as she offered me sumptuous yams—the best I'd ever tasted—specially prepared rice, and an assortment of crisp vegetables. I don't know how she got it all into her backpack.

The conversation died while we concentrated on eating; finally, between bites, I said, "Thanks. You really know how to cook."

"I didn't make it," she said. "Sachi did."

"Sachiko? Who taught her to cook like that?" I asked.

"Her father."

"She's quite a talent. Her parents must be proud of her."

"They are more than proud of her." Mama Chia put down her food and gazed past the clearing into the thick emerald forest. "Let me tell you a true story: Nine years ago, I helped bring Sachi into the world. When she was four, I also welcomed her little brother.

"Soon after her brother was born, little Sachi began to ask her parents to leave her alone with the new baby. They worried that, like most four-year olds, she might feel jealous and want to hit or shake him, so they said no. But she showed no signs of jealousy at all; she treated the baby with kindness—and her pleas to be left alone with him became more urgent. They decided to allow it.

"Elated, she went into the baby's room and shut the door, but it opened a crack—enough for her curious parents to peek in and listen. They saw little Sachi walk quietly up to her baby brother, put her face close to his, and say quietly, 'Baby, tell me what God feels like. I'm starting to forget.'"

"She said that?" I asked, in awe.

"Yes."

After a long pause, I remarked, "I can understand why she's your apprentice."

We sat in silence a while, in the shade of a tree, until Mama Chia said, "Tomorrow we go for a hike."

"Together?" I asked.

"No," she teased. "You'll take the high road, and I'll take the low road."

I still didn't know Mama Chia very well, and it was sometimes hard to tell whether she was joking. Seeing my confusion, Mama Chia laughed, and said, "Yes, we'll hike together."

I had a feeling things were about to pick up. Then I looked down at my worn trunks, and bare feet and chest. I looked up at her and explained, "I don't know if I can hike far without—"

Smiling, she pointed behind me. "Look behind the tree."

"My backpack!" I cried, amazed. As she grinned, I ran over to it and looked inside. My wallet—with a few dollars cash and credit card—my watch, a clean pair of shorts, my sneakers, toothbrush, and razor—everything was there!

"Sachi's father was working on a carpentry job on Oahu," she explained. "I sent him to Makapuu Point to find your things. He said you'd hidden them well."

"When can I meet him and thank him?" I asked.

"He's looking forward to meeting you, too, but he had to go back to Oahu to finish the job; he'll return in a few weeks. I'm glad you have new shorts," she added, holding her nose with one hand and pointing to my ragged trunks with the other, "so you can wash those."

Smiling, I took her hand. "Thank you, Mama Chia. I'm really grateful for all you've done."

"Yes, I've certainly done a lot," she said, brushing off my thanks with a wave of her hand. "Have you heard about the new breed of dog that's a cross between a pit bull and a collie? First it takes your arm off, then it runs for help." She smiled. "I've already done enough damage; this is my way of 'running for help.'"

Packing the remains of our lunch, she stood. I started to stand, too, but I was so weak I could barely get up. "I feel like such a wimp," I said as she walked me back into the cabin.

"Your muscles only feel weak because your body is using the energy to heal the rest of you. You've been through a great deal; most people would have given up and died. Your Basic Self is very strong."

"My basic what?" I asked, puzzled, as I sat down on the bed.

"Your Basic Self," Mama Chia replied. "A part of who you are—an awareness separate from your conscious mind. Didn't Socrates teach you about the three selves?"

"No," I replied, intrigued. "Tell me about the three selves—sounds like an interesting concept."

Mama Chia stood, walked to the window, and gazed outside. "The three selves are much more than a concept, Dan; they are as real to me as the earth, the trees, the sky, and the sea."

Mama Chia sat against the windowsill and said, "A few hundred years ago, before the invention of the microscope, almost no one believed in the existence of bacteria and viruses, and so, humanity remained powerless before these unseen invaders. Those who did believe in their existence were labeled 'crackpots.'

"I, too, work with elements invisible to most people—with nature spirits and subtle energies. But 'invisible' is not the same as imaginary, Dan. Each new generation forgets this, and so the cycle repeats itself—the blind leading the blind," she said without a trace of rancor. "Ignorance, as well as wisdom, is handed down from one generation to the next like a precious heirloom.

"The three selves—the Basic Self, Conscious Self, and Higher Self—are part of a secret teaching. The secrets have never been hidden, really, but few people are interested, and fewer still have the eyes to see."

She paced, in her limping style, across the room to the doorway, and turned back toward me. "When I speak to you of 'invisible things,' know that *they are not invisible to me.* But what is true for me does not have to be true for you; I'm not telling you what to believe—only sharing my experience."

"So how can *I* experience these selves? And when?" I asked.

She poured a glass of water and handed it to me. "When you're strong enough—if Socrates has prepared you well—I'll be able to take you to the edge, and point the way; all you'll have to do is open your eyes and leap." She walked to the door and said, "Now rest."

"Wait!" I said, sitting up. "Before you go, can you tell me a little more about the three selves? I'd like to hear more—"

"And there's more I'd like to tell you," she interrupted. "But first you need to *sleep*."

"I *am* tired," I said, yawning.

"Yes. Tomorrow we'll walk, and tomorrow we'll talk." Through the open doorway, I watched her swinging her cane and limping back into the forest. I yawned again, then my eyes shut and the world went black.

Book Two
Illuminations

The real voyage of discovery consists
not in seeking new landscapes,
but in having new eyes.
Marcel Proust

7

The Three Selves

You cannot transcend
what you do not know.
To go beyond yourself,
you must know yourself.
Sri Nisargadatta Maharaj

The next day, the birds' song seemed sweeter and the world more beautiful. My strength was returning; only a few scabs remained. Running my hand across my two-week growth of beard, I decided I would keep it for now.

After filling up on tropical fruit and home-baked bread that had mysteriously appeared on my chest of drawers—another gift from Sachi, I guessed—I stepped outside, stripped naked, and showered in a warm, drenching downpour. The rain passed as quickly as it had come, leaving clear, sunny skies.

I had just finished combing my wet hair and smoothing on a thick layer of sunscreen when Mama Chia came down the path with her familiar backpack, cane, and a large muumuu dress—her typical hiking outfit, I learned.

After a brief greeting, she led me down a narrow, winding path toward the sea. As she lumbered along the slippery trail, a few feet ahead of me, I could see it wasn't easy for her to get around and was struck by her determination.

She stopped a few times—once, to point out a colorful bird, another time to show me a small waterfall and pond, hidden from the casual eye. After we sat a while, listening to the sounds of water falling into a pond, I offered to carry her backpack for her, but she refused, saying, "Maybe next time."

Conversation was sparse after that. We both had to concentrate on our footing along the perennially muddy trail, criss-crossed by tree roots.

Finally, we made our way down a steep ravine and emerged into a small sandy clearing, one of the few beach areas among the rocky cliffs. On either side of us, lava rock shot straight up into the sky to form the towering cliffs.

Mama Chia took a light blanket out of her pack and spread it on the beach. The tide had just gone out, leaving the sand smooth, hard, and wet. The relaxing sea breeze felt good on my face and chest.

"Mama Chia," I asked, "maybe it's my imagination, but I've only been here about ten days is that right?"

"Yes."

"And didn't I almost die of exposure and thirst?"

"Yes," she answered again.

"Well, aren't I healing awfully fast?"

She nodded. "I've been working with you at night."

"What?"

"When you sleep, your Conscious Self steps back; that's when I can work directly with the Basic Self—your subconscious—which is in charge of healing your body."

"You were going to tell me more about the Basic Self."

Mama Chia stared at me, as if considering something. Then she picked up a nearby twig and drew a circle in the sand. "Better to show than tell," she said, scratching the figure of a human body within the circle, his arms outstretched—a crude rendition of Leonardo da Vinci's famous drawing.

Without further comment, she sat down on a mound of sand, crossed her legs, and said, "I need to do some inner work to recharge my batteries. Unless you've learned to do the same, I suggest you take a nap. Perhaps later we can talk."

"But—"

With one breath, Mama Chia seemed instantly to go into a deep trance. I watched her for a few moments, then my attention turned once again to her drawing in the sand. Feeling suddenly drowsy on this sultry day, glad for the shade of the sheltering cliffs, I stretched out on the blanket and closed my eyes.

My thoughts turned to Holly, and Linda, back in Ohio—light-years away, it seemed, from this hidden cove, where I rested a few feet away from a woman shaman whose full powers were yet to be revealed. A few weeks ago, she had existed for me only in the deepest recesses of my mind. Life is amazing, I thought; then I dropped headlong into a dreamlike vision. I don't always remember my dreams. I'll never forget this vision.

I was asleep, yet wide awake. In fact, I saw with greater clarity than ever before. Mama Chia's smiling face flashed before me, then vanished. In the blackness that followed, a human form appeared: a man's body within a circle, his arms outstretched—not the figure Mama Chia had sketched in the sand, but a vivid image of da Vinci's original.

Then, in the blink of an eye, I saw my own body appear within the circle, and it started spinning, cartwheeling through space.

From my point of awareness, I saw my physical form come to rest, standing upright in a forest, under a starry sky. Illuminated by the pale moon, clothed only in a pair of shorts, the figure stood with arms open wide, as if to embrace life itself, with head tilting slightly up and to the left, gazing up through the trees at the stars sparkling in the black velvet sky. I could see all this in the sharpest detail—every moon shadow on every leaf.

Then, three glowing lights appeared within and around the body, separate and distinct from the body's auras or energy fields. First, my attention rested on an earthy reddish glow illuminating the belly region. I recognized this instantly as the Basic Self.

My attention shifted to the head, where the white light of awareness filled the Conscious Self, shining so brightly that the head disappeared.

Then my awareness rose above the head, where I began to see a swirl of radiant, iridescent colors. . . .

Suddenly, everything tilted crazily, and thunder exploded in the distance. Flashes of lightning ripped the sky. The wind wailed, and trees came crashing down. Then the physical form in front of me split into three separate beings!

The Higher Self, which I had only begun to see in the blaze of radiant color, vanished. The two beings that remained changed into distinct physical forms. The Basic Self now appeared as a child, surrounded by a reddish glow. It quailed and shrank back as the next flash of lightning lit its face, revealing primal fear.

The Conscious Self took the form of a gray robot, whose computerized head glowed with electricity; it whirred and clicked, then looked up stiffly at the sky, expressionless, as if sorting information and weighing the best course of action.

With the next crack of thunder, the child bolted, and ran instinctively for the cover of a hollow tree. I found myself following it, and watched as it huddled there. The child seemed shy, and didn't speak. As I gazed at it, I felt myself drawn deeper into its glow.

In a microsecond, my consciousness had merged with that of the child. I saw life through its eyes, and experienced all its emotions. Confused by myriad images of past storms and associations going back lifetimes, I huddled instinctively as fearful pictures—a patchwork of genetic memories—flashed through my childlike awareness. What I lacked in clear logic, I improvised with primal instinct. I felt a vast storehouse of vital energy; my emotions were wide open, amplified. Motivated by a primitive impulse to survive, to seek pleasure and avoid pain, I felt more inclined to act than contemplate. My inner world was untamed, unrefined by culture, rules, or logic. In my wildness and fleshiness, I was energy in motion—closely tied to the natural world, completely at home in the body, with its feelings and impulses.

I had little means to perceive refined beauty or higher

faith; I knew only good feelings and bad feelings. Right now, I felt a compelling need for guidance, for someone to interpret for me, to reassure and direct me. I needed the Conscious Self.

Just then, having devised its plan, the robot-computer also entered the hollow tree. But it ignored me, the child, almost completely, as if I didn't matter. Resentful and feeling unappreciated, I nudged it to get its attention. Why didn't it listen to me? After all, I'd found shelter first! It still ignored me; I pushed it and slapped it, with no better results. Furious, I ran outside, got a rock, and smashed it into the robot's leg. *That* got its attention.

"What—do—you—want?" it asked in a monotone.

"Listen to me!" I cried.

In the next instant, my consciousness left the child and merged with the robot-computer. I looked through the eyes of this reasoning machine, and saw the world with objectivity and icy calm. The child I had been now appeared as a distraction. I formulated a solution to appease it.

Just then, the storm passed, and the child ran outside to play. I set this problem aside and walked stiffly into the forest. Untroubled by emotions or sentiment, my world was orderly, structured, and terribly limited. I saw the forest in shades of gray. Beauty to me was a definition, a category. I knew nothing of the Higher Self, or faith. I sought what was useful and constructive. The body to me was a necessary burden, a machine that enabled me to move and reproduce—a tool of the mind.

Safe within the computer mind, I was immune to the vagaries of emotion. And yet, without the playful spirit, the emotional energy, and the vitality of the child, I didn't really live; I only existed in a sterile world of problems and solutions.

My awareness awoke, as if from a dream, and feeling a sudden and overwhelming urge to feel the forest once again, to experience the rising energies of life, I broke free of the Conscious Self.

From my new vantage point, I saw both the Conscious Self and the Basic Self with their backs to each other, in their own worlds. If only they were together, how much richer both their lives would be!

I appreciated the childlike innocence and instinctive body wisdom of the Basic Self; I valued the reason, logic, and learning abilities of the robot-computer, the Conscious Self. But without the inspiration of the Higher Self, life felt insipid, shallow, and incomplete.

As I realized this, I heard the Higher Self calling me from somewhere in the forest, and I felt an intense longing to merge with it. I recognized this longing as one I had felt for many years, perhaps my whole life. For the first time, I knew what I had been searching for.

Moments later, I was captured by the Conscious Self again. Trapped within its steel mind, I heard its droning voice, slow at first, then more rapidly playing again and again: "I—am—all—there—is. The—Higher—Self—is—an—illusion."

My awareness snapped back into the childlike Basic Self once again. Now all I wanted to do was play, and feel good, and powerful, and secure.

Again, I snapped back into the Conscious Self and saw one reality—then I rebounded back into the Basic Self and felt another. Faster and faster, I bounced back and forth between Conscious Self and Basic Self, mind and body, robot and child, thinking and feeling, logic and impulse. Faster and faster!

I sat up, staring into space—terrified, sweating, crying out softly. Then, gradually, I became aware of my surroundings: the sheltered ocean cove, the warm beach, a sky turning pink and purple above a calm sea. And nearby sat Mama Chia, unmoving, gazing at me.

Shaking off the remnants of this vision, I tried to slow my breathing and relax. I managed to explain, "I—I had a bad dream."

She spoke slowly and deliberately: "Was it a bad dream, or a mirror of your life?"

"I don't know what you mean," I said. But I was lying; I knew this as soon as the words were out of my mouth. With my newfound awareness of the three selves, I could no longer maintain the pretense of being "together." I was a self divided, wavering between the self-centered, childlike needs of the Basic Self, and the cold detachment of the Conscious Self—out of touch with my Higher Self.

These past years, my mind had constantly smothered my feelings; it had ignored and devalued them. Rather than acknowledge the pain and passion I felt, my Conscious Self had maintained control and swept my feelings, and my relationships, under the rug.

I now understood that the physical symptoms I had experienced back home—the infections, the aches, and the pains—had been my Basic Self, crying for attention like a young child; it wanted me to express all the feelings inside. Suddenly I understood the aphorism "The organs weep the tears the eyes refuse to shed." And something Wilhelm Reich had once said came into my mind: "Unexpressed emotion is stored in the muscles of the body." These troubling revelations depressed and disheartened me. I saw how far I still had to go.

"Are you all right?" Mama Chia asked.

"Sure, I'm okay," I started to answer, then stopped myself. "No, I don't feel all right. I feel drained and depressed."

"Good!" she said, beaming. "You've learned something. Now you're on the right track."

Nodding, I asked, "In the dream, I only experienced two of the selves. My Higher Self vanished. Why did it leave me?"

"It didn't leave you, Dan—it was there all the time—but you were so preoccupied with the your Basic Self and your Conscious Self that you couldn't see it, or feel its love and support."

"Well, how *can* I feel it? Where do I go from here?"

"A good question—a very good question!" she said, laughing to herself as she stood. Then she slipped her pack over her shoulders, and started slowly up the rocky trail. Still full of unanswered questions, I followed.

The sand turned to stones and earth as we climbed up a steep path along the cliff face. I turned and looked back at the cove, slightly below us. The tide was coming in. Twenty yards away, a wave rushed up close to the figure Mama Chia had drawn in the sand. I blinked and looked again. Where the figure and circle had been, I thought I saw three figures—a small body, like that of a child; a square, boxlike figure; and a large oval—just before a wave rushed past, washing the sand clean.

The climb up was more difficult than the hike down. Mama Chia seemed in high spirits, but my mood was glum. Neither of us spoke. An array of images from the vision passed through my mind as I followed her up the path into the darkening forest.

By the time we entered the clearing, the half-moon had neared its zenith. Mama Chia bade me good night and continued up the path.

I stood outside the cabin for a few moments, listening to the crickets' song. The warm night breeze seemed to pass right through me. I didn't realize how fatigued I felt until I entered the cabin. I vaguely remember visiting the bathroom, then falling onto the bed. I heard the crickets a moment more, then silence. That night, in a dream, I searched for my Higher Self, but found only emptiness.

8

Eyes of the Shaman

A great teacher
never strives to explain her vision;
she simply invites you
to stand beside her
and see for yourself.
The Rev. R. Inman

Not yet fully awake—in more ways than one, I concluded—I opened my eyes and saw Mama Chia standing by my bedside. At first I thought I was still dreaming, but came back to earth quickly when she yelled, "Out of bed!" I jumped up so fast I nearly fell over.

"I'll—I'll be ready in a minute," I slurred, still groggy, vowing to get up before she arrived next time. I stumbled into the bathroom, slipped into my shorts, and stepped outside into a rainsquall for my morning shower.

Dripping wet, I stepped back inside and grabbed a towel. "It must be nearly noon."

"Just after eleven," she said.

"Wow, I—"

"On Thursday," she interrupted. "You've been out cold for thirty-six hours."

I nearly dropped the towel. "Almost *two days*?" I sat down heavily on the bed.

"You look upset. Did you miss an appointment?" she asked.

"No, I guess not." I looked up at her. "Did I?"

"Not with me, you didn't; besides, appointments are not native to Hawaii." She explained, "Mainlanders tried to import them, but it's like trying to sell beef to vegetarians. You feeling better?"

"Much better," I answered, toweling off my hair. "But I'm not exactly sure what I'm supposed to be *doing* here or what you're supposed to help me with. Are you going to help me see my Higher Self?"

"That remains to be seen," she answered, smiling at her play on words, and handing me my shirt.

"Mama Chia," I said, putting on the shirt, "those things I saw—that vision on the beach—did you hypnotize me?"

"Not exactly. What you saw came from the Inner Records."

"What are they?"

"That's not easy to describe. You can call it the 'universal unconscious,' or the 'journal of Spirit.' Everything is written there."

"*Everything?*"

"Yes," she replied. "Everything."

"Can you . . . read these records?"

"Sometimes—it depends."

"Well, how did *I* read them?"

"Let's just say I turned the pages for you."

"Like a mother reading to her child?"

"Something like that."

The rain stopped, so she stepped outside. I followed her to a log near the shed and sat down. "Mama Chia," I said, "I need to talk with you about something that's really starting to bother me. It seems like the more I learn, the worse it gets. You see—"

She interrupted me. "Just handle what's in front of you now, and the future will take care of itself. Otherwise, you'll spend most of your life wondering which foot you'll use to step off the curb when you're still only halfway to the corner."

"What about planning ahead, and preparing for the future?"

"Plans are useful, but don't get attached to them; life has

too many surprises. Preparation, on the other hand, has value, even if the future you planned never comes."

"How's that?"

She paused before answering. "An old friend of mine here on the island, Sei Fujimoto—you haven't met him yet—has worked as a gardener and handyman most of his life. But photography was his first love. I never saw a man so passionate about images on paper! Years ago, he would spend most of his days searching for the perfect shot. Fuji especially loved landscapes: the shapes of trees, waves breaking with the sun shining through them, and clouds by the light of the moon, or the morning sun. When he wasn't taking pictures, he was developing them in his own darkroom at home.

"Fuji practiced photography for nearly thirty years, accumulating in that time a treasury of inspired photographs. He kept the negatives in a locked file in his office. He sold some photos, and gave others to friends.

"Then, about six years ago, a fire destroyed all the photographs he had taken over those thirty years, and all the negatives, as well as most of his equipment. He had no fire insurance—all the evidence and fruits of a generation of creative work—a total and irreplaceable loss.

"Fuji mourned this as he might mourn the loss of a child. Three years before, he *had* lost a child, and he understood very well that suffering was a relative thing, and that if he could make it through his child's death, he could make it through anything.

"But more than that, he understood the bigger picture, and came to a growing realization that something of great value remained that was never touched by the fire: *Fuji had learned to see life in a different way.* Every day, when he got up, he saw a world of light and shadow, shapes and textures—a world of beauty and harmony and balance.

"When he shared this insight with me, Dan, he was so happy! His realization mirrors that of the Zen masters who share with their students that all paths, all activities—professions, sports, arts, crafts—serve as a means of internal development, merely a boat to get across the river. Once you get across, you no longer need the boat." Mama Chia took a deep breath and smiled serenely at me.

"I'd like to meet Sei Fujimoto."

"And you will," she assured me.

"I just remembered something Socrates once told me: 'It's not the way *to* the peaceful warrior; it's the way *of* the peaceful warrior; and *the journey itself creates the warrior.*'"

"Socrates always had a way with words," she said. Then she sighed wistfully. "You know, I was once quite taken with him."

"You were? When? How? What happened?"

"Nothing happened," she said. "He kept occupied with his own training and teaching; I was busy, too. And though he respected and liked me, I don't believe he felt the same way. Except for my late husband, Bradford, not many men have."

This seemed so sad and unfair to me. "Mama Chia," I said gallantly, "if I were a few years older, I do believe I'd ask you to go courting."

"That's very kind of you," she said.

"Well, I'm that kinda guy," I responded. "Will you tell me more about when you met Socrates, and about your life?"

She thought for a moment, then said, "Perhaps some other time. Right now, I have things to attend to—and, I think, you need a little more time to consider what you've learned, before—" she stopped herself. "Before we see what happens next."

"I'm ready."

Mama Chia stared at me a moment, but said nothing. She only reached into her pack and tossed me a small pack of macadamia nuts. "See you tomorrow." With that, she left.

I did feel much stronger, but she was right; I was in no condition for anything rigorous. I spent the rest of the morning in a kind of reverie—sitting and gazing at the trees surrounding my home here on Molokai. A troubling feeling was growing inside me, but I didn't have words for it yet. Preoccupied, I hardly tasted the small chunks of bread, the macadamia nuts, or the fruit I consumed.

As the afternoon sun touched the tips of the trees at the edge of the clearing, I realized I was lonely. Strange, I reflected, I used to like being alone. I had chosen solitude for most of my college years. But after floating out on that surfboard—when I thought I might never see a human being again—something changed. And now—

My reverie was interrupted by a bright "Hi!" off to my left. Sachi hopped, skipped, and danced toward me, her jet black hair, cut short like Mama Chia's, bounced and swirled with each movement. Jumping from a stone to a log, she skipped over and set down a small package. "I brought some more bread—made it myself."

"Thank you, Sachi. That was very thoughtful."

"No, it wasn't," she replied. "I didn't *think* much at all. How're you feeling?"

"Much better, now that you've dropped in. I've been alone so much I was starting to talk to myself."

"I do that sometimes," she said.

"Well, then, now that *you're* here, we can sit and both talk to ourselves—no, *wait!*" I teased. "I have a better idea: Why don't we sit here and talk to *each other*?"

She smiled at my corny attempt at humor. "Sounds okay to me. Want to see the frog pond?"

"Sure."

"It's not far. Follow me," she said, scampering into the forest.

Doing my best to keep up, I saw her up ahead, appearing and disappearing about ten yards away, dodging around trees. By the time I caught up with her, she was sitting on a large rock, pointing to a couple of frogs. One graced us with a loud croak.

"You weren't kidding, girl; these are some great frogs."

"That's the queen over there," she said. "And I call this one here 'Grumpy,' because he always hops away when I pet him." Sachi reached slowly down and stroked one of the frogs. "My brother likes to feed 'em, but I don't like squishy bugs—used to, but not anymore." Then, like a little woods sprite, she bounded off, back toward the cabin. I said a silent good-bye to Grumpy, and walked after her. As I left, I heard a loud "Grrrumph." I turned to see the water splash as the frog dove under.

Back in the clearing, Sachi was practicing some dance steps. "Mama Chia showed me this," she said. "She teaches me a lot of things."

"I bet she does," I replied. Then I had an idea. "Maybe I could teach you something, too. Can you do a cartwheel?"

"Sort of," she replied, throwing her arms down and legs up. "I bet I look like one of those frogs," she giggled. "Can you show me one?"

"I guess so—I used to be pretty good at it," I said, doing a one-arm cartwheel over the log.

"Wow!" she said, impressed. "That was smooth!" Inspired, she tried again, but improved only slightly.

"Here, Sachi, let me show you again," I said.

The rest of the afternoon passed like a snap of the fingers, I was so immersed in doing what I loved. And, I'm glad to say, Sachi learned a very graceful cartwheel.

I spotted a bright red flower growing nearby, and on impulse, I picked it and placed it in her hair. "You know, I have a daughter—younger than you—I miss her. I'm glad you came by to visit."

"Me, too," she replied. Touching the flower, Sachi graced me with the sweetest smile. "Well, I gotta go. Thanks for the cartwheel, Dan." She ran up the trail, then turned and called back to me, "Don't forget your bread!"

That smile really made my day.

When Mama Chia arrived the next morning, I was ready and waiting, tossing pebbles at a tree. "Want some fresh bread?" I asked. "I already ate, but if you're hungry—"

"I'm fine," she said. "Let's get moving; we have a few miles to cover by sundown."

"Where are we going?" I asked as we left the cabin and headed up the path.

"That way." She pointed up to the central range of ridges formed of black lava rock, several thousand feet above us. Handing me her backpack, she said, simply, "You're strong enough now to carry this."

We hiked slowly upward along an ever-steepening trail, with many turns and switchbacks. Mama Chia walked steadily upward. The forest was silent, except for the cry of an occasional bird, and my rhythmic tread, beating a countertempo to her swinging cane and limping gait.

She stopped every now and then to admire a colorful bird or to point out an unusual tree or small waterfall.

By late morning, my concerns began rising to the surface, and I called to her. "Mama Chia, Socrates once told me I haven't *really* learned something until I could do it."

She stopped, turned to me, and said in affirmation, "I hear and I forget, I see and I remember, I do and I understand."

"That's just it," I confessed. "I've *heard* about and *seen* a lot of things, but I haven't really *done* anything. I've learned some things about healing, but can I heal? I know about the Higher Self, but I can't *feel* it!"

My words finally spilled out as all the frustration I'd kept bottled up for five years exploded. "I was a world champion gymnast; I graduated from the University of California; I have a beautiful daughter. I take care of myself, eat right, do the right thing. I'm a *college professor*—I've done what I'm *supposed* to do—but even after all that, even after my training with Socrates, my life feels like it's falling apart!

"I used to believe if I learned enough, if I made all the right moves, that life was going to get easier, more under control, but now it only feels worse—like something slipping away and I don't know how to stop it! It's like I've fallen off the path, gotten lost somehow.

"I know there are people a lot worse off than I am; I'm not being victimized by other people; I'm not living in poverty or hunger or oppression. Maybe it sounds like I'm whining or complaining, but I'm not feeling sorry for myself, Mama Chia—I just want it to stop!"

I looked into her eyes and told her, "I once broke my leg pretty badly—my thigh bone was shattered in about forty pieces—so I know what pain feels like. And this feels just as real to me. Do you understand?"

"I understand you very well," she said. "Pain and suffering are a part of everyone's life. It just takes different forms."

"Then can you help me find whatever it is I'm looking for?"

"Perhaps," she said, then turned and continued up the trail.

As we rose up out of the forest, the trees thinned out; the moss and leaves beneath our feet gave way to reddish brown earth, which turned to mud as a torrential rain came and passed quickly. I slipped now and then. Mama Chia, though slow paced, was surefooted. Finally, just when I thought she had forgotten my plea, she spoke.

"Dan, have you ever considered that no *one* person could ever create a building? No matter how smart, how strong, a single individual may be, he can't make a building without the combined efforts of architects, contractors, laborers, accountants, manufacturers, truckers, chemists, and hundreds more. No one is smarter than all of us."

"But what does that have to do with—"

"For example, take Socrates," she continued. "He has many talents, but also the wisdom not to apply them all at the same time; he understood that he couldn't do everything for you—at least not all at once. He knew that he could not force-feed your psyche. He could only teach you what you had ears to hear, or eyes to see.

"When Socrates wrote to me, he warned me that you would be hard on yourself—that you got excitable—and that now and then I might have to calm you down." She turned back and grinned at me as we continued our slow climb. "He also told me of seeds he has sown within your mind and heart that will sprout later. I'm here to nourish them, to help them grow.

"Your training hasn't made you perfect, Dan, but it has served you well. Nothing is lost or wasted; Socrates accomplished a great deal, and so did you. He helped you clear away the worst illusions, helped you see the bigger picture. He gave you a foundation; and, now, even if you can't always hear, you're at least willing to *listen*. If he hadn't prepared you, I don't believe you would ever have found me."

"But I didn't find you; you found me."

"No matter how strange the circumstances of our meeting, I don't believe it would have happened had you not been ready. That's how these things work. I might not have chosen to work with you; you might not have come to the party. Who can say?"

We stopped briefly to survey the view as we entered the highlands, not far from the base of the rocky peak. Green treetops stretched almost as far as I could see. The moist, humid air dampened my arms and forehead. Wiping it from my brow, I heard Mama Chia say, "I once knew a man who climbed up to a mountaintop and reached up to God. He stretched his arms to heaven and cried, 'Fill me full of light! I'm ready. I'm waiting!' The voice of God answered him, and said, 'I'm *always* filling you with light—but you keep leaking!'"

She put her arm on my shoulder, and added, "We all have 'leaks,' Dan. You, me, Socrates. They're not cause for alarm. Just remember that you are a 'human in training.' You're still going to stumble; we all do. I can only help you turn your experience into lessons, and your lessons into wisdom. For now, I can only encourage you to trust the process of your life."

She stopped, and knelt down next to a yellow flower, growing up through a small crack in a large stone. "Our lives are like this flower. We appear so fragile, and yet, when we meet obstacles, we push through them, always growing toward the Light."

I touched the yellow petals. "But flowers grow so slowly! I don't feel I have that much time. I feel like I should do something *now.*"

Her cool smile calmed my frustration. "Flowers grow in their own good time. It's not easy, seeing the path twist and disappear ahead, knowing it's a long climb. You want to go into action because that's what you have been trained to do. But first you need to understand."

"Understanding without action seems useless!"

"And acting without understanding can be dangerous. If you act before you understand, you won't even know what you're doing! So relax," she advised, taking a deep breath, practicing what she preached. "There's no need to rush, and nowhere to rush to. You have plenty of time to accomplish anything."

"This life?"

"Or the next."

"Well, I want to start a little sooner than that!" I said. "And I feel an *ache* inside, a message from my Basic Self. And it's not saying, 'Kick back and relax, go to the beach'—it's telling me there's something I have to do, something about my Higher Self."

"Why all this concern about your Higher Self? Aren't you having enough fun now?"

Ignoring her attempts to cheer me up, I sank deeper into self-criticism. How could I dream of contacting my Higher Self when I couldn't even stand in line without getting fidgety, or drive under the speed limit, or relax in a traffic jam? Or keep my marriage together?

Mama Chia jarred me out of my dark reverie. "You *are* hard on yourself, Dan Millman—I can see it all over your face. You assume you have a serious problem to solve, but do you really?

"In my life, I've learned that at precisely those times when life seems to get worse that you may actually be getting ready to make a leap. When you feel like you're getting nowhere—stagnating, even slipping backward—what you're actually doing is backing up to get a running start."

"You really think so?"

"What *I* think isn't the point. Look at your life right now. Check it out with your Basic Self; *it* knows—it has already told me. You're about to make the leap—maybe not today, or tomorrow, but soon enough. And just as Socrates prepared you for me, I'll do my part to get you ready for the next step."

"You make it sound simple."

"Not simple, or easy, but inevitable—sooner or later. You're still stuck in the drama, and can't yet see beyond it. Like a gnat on a TV screen," she said, "all you see is a bunch of dots, but there is a bigger picture, Dan. Each of us has our role to play. When the time is right, you'll find your purpose. Maybe it's waiting for you in the desert." Before I could ask what she meant, she continued. "The way of the peaceful warrior begins by embracing all three selves—having your head in the clouds and your feet on the ground.

"We have some work to do together, you and I," she concluded. "And we're going to prepare you the same way we're climbing this mountain—one step at a time." At that, she turned and continued pushing upward. I felt encouraged by her words, but my body, feeling the exertion, was growing weary. Yet Mama Chia limped on and on.

"Where exactly are we going, anyway?" I asked, panting.

"To the top."

"What are we going to do when we get there?"

"You'll find out when we arrive," she answered, heading up the rocky trail.

The hike soon became much steeper, like an endless stairway. The air grew thinner and our breathing more labored with each step, as we climbed toward the peak of Kamakau, almost five thousand feet high.

Two hours later, just before dusk, we reached the peak and stepped at last onto level ground. With a wave of her hand, Mama Chia directed my eyes to an incredible panorama of the island of Molokai. Turning slowly around, I gazed out over the expanse of lush green forest at the sea. The edge of the sky was ablaze with color as the setting sun painted the clouds red, purple, orange, and pink.

"Well, here we are," I said with a sigh.

"Yes, here we are," she echoed, still gazing at the setting sun.

"Now that we're here, what are we going to do?"

"Gather some wood. We'll camp nearby tonight. I know a spot. Tomorrow, we reach our destination." She pointed toward the eastern tip of the island.

She led me to a small waterfall, where we drank deeply of the sparkling water, rich with minerals. Nearby stood a rock overhang that would shelter us in case of sudden rain. Glad for a rest, I swung Mama Chia's pack off my shoulders, and felt lighter than air. My legs wobbled, and I knew they would be stiff tomorrow.

I had no idea how this elderly woman, smaller than I but much heavier, could sustain this kind of effort. If she had intended us to hike all night, it wouldn't have surprised me.

We made a fire big enough to heat some rocks and bury them with foil-wrapped yams. Served with some raw vegetables, the yams tasted as delectable as any meal I'd ever eaten.

We made our beds of a thick moss, and put some small branches in the fire—not for warmth, but for the glow, and the comforting crackle.

As we lay down for the night, I asked quietly, "Mama Chia, being out there on that surfboard must have frightened me more than I'd thought, because ever since then, I've been thinking a lot about life, and death. A few days ago, as I was going to sleep I saw the face of a friend at Oberlin who died some time ago," I told her. "He was young, and full of life; then he came down with an illness the doctors said was terminal. I remember he prayed a lot. But he died just the same."

Mama Chia sighed. "Our prayers are always answered. It's just that, sometimes, God says no."

"Why would God say no?"

"Why does a loving parent say no? Sometimes children's wants run counter to their needs. People turn to God when their foundations are shaking, only to discover it is God who's shaking them. The conscious mind cannot always foresee what is for our highest good. Faith involves a basic trust in the universe—that *everything* is for our highest good. This is what I believe."

"Do you think that's really true?"

"I don't know for certain, but I *choose* to believe it because when I do, and when I act accordingly, my life flows better. I never feel like a victim of circumstance. My attitude stays strong and positive. And I see difficulty as a kind of 'spiritual weight lifting,' a challenge to strengthen the spirit.

"My physical problems, painful as they have been, have always brought a gift, though I didn't always appreciate it at the time," she said. "For me, the gift was deeper compassion; for someone else, the gift might be greater sensitivity to the body, or a stronger motivation to exercise more, to express feelings instead of hiding them, or maybe to eat better, relax more, or play more.

"Pain or discomfort is often a way of shaking us up, of getting our attention."

"It sure works for me," I said, gazing into the fire.

"Yes, but I don't recommend it as a method," she added with a wry smile. "Although pain makes us take a closer look at ourselves, it's usually the Basic Self's last resort. It only sends harsh messages when the gentler ones—your intuitions and dreams—have been ignored."

"Basic Selves," she continued, "like children, take a lot of abuse. Loyal by nature, they are not easily alienated. But when they've had enough, they have had *enough*."

Reminded of another question, I asked, "If the Basic Self is in charge of the body, it can cure any disease, right?"

"Under the right circumstances, if it's permitted within the destiny of that individual, yes."

"Then medicines don't really matter."

"Everything matters. Medicines are one way to assist the Basic Self—they're a gift from the natural world," she said, reaching up and plucking a seedpod from a nearby bush. Opening the pod, she showed me the small seeds, and said, "Basic Selves, as you've experienced, have a close connection to the natural world; each plant and herb carries specific messages and energies that the Basic Self understands. So does each color, or aroma, or sound. Or dance for that matter.

"Healing is a great mystery, even for today's physicians; we are still discovering nature's laws of balance. But as we get in closer touch with our Basic Selves and the subtle forces at work, we will see more 'miracles.'"

"Most physicians tend to rely on their Conscious Selves, on their minds rather than on their intuitions, don't they?"

"It's not a matter of trusting the Basic Self *or* the Conscious Self," she replied. "It's a matter of trusting *both*—each at the appropriate time. The Arabs have a saying: 'Trust in God, but tie your camel.' It's important to trust the Basic Self to heal a cut, for example, but the Conscious Self reminds us to use a Band-Aid.

"If you overeat junk food, smoke cigarettes, drink too much alcohol, or use other drugs—if you exhaust yourself, or hold in your emotions—you make it harder for the Basic Self to do its job and maintain a strong immune system; it can't always heal without the cooperation of the Conscious Self; it can only send painful body messages to get your attention. Prayer alone may not be enough; also do what you can to assist. Francis Cardinal Spellman once said, 'Pray as if everything depended on God, and work as if everything depended on man.'"

I watched Mama Chia with growing admiration and wonder. "Mama Chia, how do you know so much? Where did you learn all these things?"

She said nothing at first. I glanced over at her in the firelight, thinking she had fallen asleep. But her eyes were wide open, as if staring into another world. Finally, she answered, "I'll think on it tonight. Perhaps I'll tell you some of my story tomorrow. We still have a long hike ahead." With that, she turned on her side and went quickly to sleep. I lay awake for a while before joining her, staring at the dying embers of the fire.

9

A Well-Rounded Woman

God comforts the disturbed
and disturbs
the comfortable.
Unknown

In the morning, a refreshing shower under the waterfall helped clear the stiffness from my legs, back, and shoulders. Though I hadn't regained my full strength, the simple diet and outdoor exercise had given me more vitality than I had felt in several years.

After a small breakfast of papaya, banana, and water from the falls, we continued along the range of volcanic rock that burst from the sea a million years before, breathing to the rhythm of our footsteps. Mama Chia must have known this range intimately; she seemed instinctively to know the correct path at every turn.

As we walked, I once again asked Mama Chia to tell me about her life.

"I don't usually talk much about my life," she began. "But I feel it's important for you to know a little."

"Why is that?"

"I'm not certain, but I believe you'll write about your own journey someday, for the benefit of others—and you might want to mention me."

"Maybe you'll even get famous—do beer commercials," I teased.

Smiling, she said, "You know better than that; I prefer to remain unknown. It's just that—one life may inspire another."

"Well, you have my attention," I said, walking closely behind her on the narrowing trail.

She began: "I was born here, on Molokai, in 1910. My father was part Hawaiian and part Japanese, the same as my mother. Like this island, I have a rich heritage, but not a strong body," she said, holding up her cane.

"Strong enough," I countered. "I have trouble keeping up with you."

She smiled, and nodded. "Jack London once wrote, 'Life is not always a matter of holding good cards, but sometimes, playing a poor hand well.' I suppose I've played my hand as well as I could. As a child, I felt fatigued most of the time. I had many allergies and often fell ill. I was confined to bed much of the time, and couldn't attend school regularly.

"My father used to tell me how Teddy Roosevelt was also a sickly, delicate child, but he grew up to be a 'rough rider,' and president of the United States. My father's stories gave me hope, but my body only grew weaker."

Mama Chia took some macadamia nuts out of her pack and shared them with me as she continued. "Then, when I was seven, my parents heard about a kahuna kupua—a shaman—named Papa Kahili. A powerful healer, he was revered by those who knew him, and his reputation grew among those who understood the ancient ways.

"As devout Christians, my parents mistrusted those who spoke of nature spirits. But finally, because I was growing weaker and no one else had been able to help me, their love overcame their fears and they asked Papa Kahili to see me.

"The first time we met, he offered no medicines—nor any of the ceremonial magic that my parents had expected. He just spoke with me quietly. I felt that he really cared about me. That day, though I didn't know it, my healing had begun.

"Later, he brought herbal medicines, and spoke of many things—of the healing power inside me. He told me inspiring stories, painting beautiful pictures in my mind. Papa Kahili took me on many journeys, and each time I returned, I was stronger."

"Did your parents ever accept him?" I asked.

"Months later, yes. They would call him a 'priest of God,' and they liked how he never took credit for my improvement, but said it was the Holy Spirit that guided and worked through him.

"During this time, World War One raged on in Europe. The great events of history were recorded in the daily newspapers. But Papa Kahili would never appear in the papers; he would never be listed in the history books. He was part of the secret history, like the underground spring that gives life to fields of flowers. And yet, in our smaller world, he was one of the greatest of men.

"When the war ended, I was eight years old, and strong enough to attend school. Though I was overweight, shy, and not very pretty, I made a few friends. For the next seven years, I immersed myself in what I had missed, what I had yearned for as a young girl: I traveled to Oahu and the other islands. I went to parties; I went shopping with my girlfriends; I even dated boys.

"Eventually, I grew weary of the parties and travel and shopping. I had always felt—different from other people, like a stranger in a strange land. I had always believed it was because of my illnesses. But now I felt like a stranger even with my friends. They enjoyed noisy social gatherings and parties, and buying the latest fashions. I preferred reading and sitting out in the moonlight among the trees," she said, gesturing with her walking stick up toward the towering kukui trees above and around us.

"Maybe all those years confined to bed, in solitude, and all my reading, had made me thoughtful about other things, bigger issues. I began to spend more time alone."

"Mama Chia," I said, "I don't want to interrupt, but I know what you mean about feeling different from other people."

She stopped, looked back at me, and nodded.

"Please," I said, "go on."

"Well," she said, as we continued up the trail, "I knew I had disappointed my parents, and I wanted very much to make them proud of me. My father had worked hard in the sugarcane business, and had saved his money so I could attend college. So I studied hard, and read many more books than my schoolmates—vowing to meet my parents' expectations. In 1928, I was admitted to Stanford University."

"You went to *Stanford?*" I asked, incredulous.

"Yes," she said. "Does that surprise you?"

"Well, yes—I don't know why."

"Lying in bed all those years, I read and read. My parents went to great expense and energy getting me books on every subject. I thought I had fallen behind in school, but I was far ahead. I did very well in the entrance examinations—"

"That's where we differ!" I grinned.

She smiled back at me and went on. "My parents believed I was there to find a good husband, but for me, college was the greatest adventure; there was so much to learn, and libraries *full* of books. I wasn't going to waste a moment. Fascinated with the human body—maybe because of my own physical problems—I entered the premedical program.

"In my senior year, however, I came across a small article about the Hawaiian kahuna tradition. I found it totally absorbing. I also read about other systems of spiritual or holistic healing, including hypnosis and psychoanalysis—working with beliefs and the mind. I realized that *healing* was my calling, not conventional medicine."

"You don't believe in conventional medicine?"

"I appreciate the place of Western medicine and its technologies," she said. "But I believe that most physicians, like their patients, have become enamored with the quick relief of symptoms through drugs and remedial surgery, rather than educating and inspiring people to transform their habits and life-styles, working in harmony with the principles of nature.

Medicine will someday change," she predicted, "as soon as people are ready."

"Well, did you leave Stanford? What happened?"

"When least expected, as these things can happen, I met my future husband. One day, as I was leaving the library, a book slipped from my arms. Before I could even reach down, a handsome young man appeared from nowhere, scooped up the book, and handed it to me with a smile. We began to talk, and never stopped. His name was Bradford Johnson. We were married right after graduation. I never understood how he—a handsome, athletic man—could ever love someone like me. I used to tell him I must have saved his life in a previous incarnation, and that he owed me one!

"Anyway, in 1932, when we graduated, Bradford got a teaching job in California and I got pregnant. We were so happy!" Mama Chia's voice changed, growing softer so I could barely hear her as she said, "I lost the baby." She fell silent for a few moments. "I learned that I couldn't have babies. Not ever. I felt betrayed once again by my body.

"Bradford was a very understanding man; he said we could always adopt, but somehow we were so busy—and, after all, I had a nephew, and two nieces." She smiled, but her smile soon faded.

"One month later, my father died quite suddenly. My mother was losing her eyesight, and needed me. Bradford found a teaching position on Oahu so I could spend the weekdays home on Molokai, with my mother, and weekends on Oahu with him. We settled into this routine until Bradford's school closed during the Great Depression. He came to live with me here on Molokai. Those were lean times, but we had shelter, and our garden.

"Then came 1941 and the bombing of Pearl Harbor. That, and the events that followed, one after the next, were among the most painful of my life."

Mama Chia stopped, and turned to take in a panoramic view of the rain forest far below and the sea beyond. "I'm not used to going on like this," she said. "Few people know these things about me, and I have no personal need to reveal this; do you understand? Perhaps we should stop—"

I touched her arm to interrupt her. "Mama Chia, I care about you; I'm *interested* in your life, and your experiences. So many older people are living treasures—a part of history. But they never tell their story because they think it's ordinary."

Shaking my head sadly, I added, "I cared about Socrates, too, and asked him many times to tell me about his past, but he never would. It was like he didn't trust me, or something—I don't know. That hurt me, but I never told him. Maybe I'll never know where he came from—and it's like a part of *my* life is missing. And you wonder if I'm interested in your life?"

She nodded in silence, her face revealing nothing—until I saw tears forming in her eyes as she gazed over the blue sea. Clouds passed overhead, touching the peaks above us. Mama Chia picked up her walking stick and led the way up a switchback trail. As I followed, she returned to her story.

"Like many people in Honolulu, Bradford saw the destruction of Pearl Harbor, and, like a good Stanford man, he joined the Navy to help defend our country. And like countless other women, I said a prayer for my husband each night and morning.

"Ugly rumors started that Japanese-Americans were being sent to detention camps on the mainland for fear of sabotage. I didn't believe such a thing; I couldn't. But the rumors were true. Though only part Japanese by descent, I moved to this isolated part of the rain forest and lived quietly with my mother, now in her sixties and suffering from a number of ills beyond my powers to alleviate.

"Papa Kahili, who had spent nearly a decade studying with an African shaman on that continent, returned to Molokai. I asked him to help my mother. By this time he was very old, and his service work in Africa—racing against starvation, dysentery, and a host of other afflictions—had taken its toll. He told me that Spirit was calling my mother, and that she would soon be happily free of her painful body—and that he would soon follow.

"He spoke with my mother and counseled her and, one week after his return, she died quietly in her sleep. After that, I was alone, and spent every day helping Papa Kahili. Gathering my courage, I asked him if he would teach me the kahuna ways; I told him I felt this was my destiny.

"He began to cry the tears of an old man because he had always known that—all these years—but he had to wait for me to ask. So, he adopted me into his family, and into the kahuna tradition.

"Papa Kahili is in the spirit world now, but I feel his presence with me always. It is like that when you have found a teacher. He gave me the tools to help others in need.

"I began helping people he had served, here on Molokai; I took special training as a midwife as well. After seeing enough people die during my days as a premedical student," she said, "I wanted to balance things out by seeing more babies come into the world. In this way, I could participate in the miracle of birth, even if the babies weren't mine.

"One day, I received a letter from the Department of the Navy. Before I opened it, I knew its contents—every word. When I had finished crying, I opened the envelope with trembling hands; the letter only confirmed what I had dreamed for several days. Bradford, my husband, was lost at sea.

"The war ended, and I became restless. Too many ghosts, too many memories. I had saved enough money, and so, in 1952—"

"When I was six years old," I interjected.

"When you were six years old, I began a twelve-year journey around the world. Following no map except my intuition, I spent the first two years traveling across the United States mainland, by bus, train, and on foot, visiting people and places my Higher Self directed me to."

I asked her, "Did you ever visit Berkeley, California?"

"Yes," she said. "I passed through Berkeley, but, if you're

wondering, I wasn't to meet Socrates for another eight years. First I made pilgrimages to Northern Europe to study the folk traditions and Viking lore, then down through Spain and across Central Europe, then south to several villages in Africa, then to the Middle East and Arabic cultures, and to India, Nepal, Tibet, and the great Pamir—"

"I visited there," I interjected. "But I didn't find what I was looking for—"

"I'm glad I waited until I was older; if I had traveled when I was young, before I had been prepared, I would have passed right by the school."

"What school?" I asked, remembering Socrates' words.

"After an entry into China, arranged by friends, I visited Thailand and parts of Indonesia—"

"*What school?*" I repeated.

"A hidden school—in Japan."

"How was it hidden?" I asked.

"No advertising—low profile." She smiled, then added, more seriously, "Few people had the eyes to see it. By this time, I understood many disciplines of healing body and mind; I wanted to learn more about the spiritual path, but I wanted to confront physical challenges as well, and see if I could actually change this body of mine. The master showed me what I was capable of. And that's where I met one of his most unusual students—the man you call Socrates."

"*Really?*" I said, almost tripping over a large stone. "Tell me more about Socrates—about this school! What was it like? What was he doing there?"

Mama Chia paused. "If Socrates didn't tell you, he must have had his reasons." She saw my disappointment and added, "You can trust that whatever Socrates told you or didn't tell you was for your own good. And I don't think this is the time to speak of such things."

"Where is this school? Who is the master? And what about the other places I'm to go?"

"Now is not the time," she repeated. "You have to learn

some things from your own intuition and insight, your own experience."

Disappointed, I looked up and saw we were nearly at the highest point for miles around.

"I need to finish this story," she said, "to help establish where we are now, and what we are to do together. I trained in that school for two years and three months. For the first time in my life, my body, if not lean and sinewy, was at least cut down to size. I could *run*! I could *leap*, and spin, and kick high in the air. Believe it or not," she said with delight, "I became a pretty fair acrobat and martial artist." She whirled her cane in an impressive, if rusty, display of movements. "And I learned much about my power and my spirit.

"I learned even more about healing. As soon as I returned home, to Molokai, in 1964, filled with new enthusiasm and energy, ready to call forth miracles and heal even the lepers, I was called upon by Sei Fujimoto. Distraught, he told me his infant son had suddenly taken ill, and begged me to come with him. As we hurried to the road and his pickup truck, Sei explained that his child had gone into convulsions, then passed out. Sei was numb with panic; his wife, Mitsu, was no better—completely beside herself when I arrived.

"They were poor, and isolated, so no helicoper would be on its way. By that time it might be too late; the child was in a bad way." Mama Chia stopped, sat down, and gestured for me to do the same. We sat on an outcropping of rock that covered the central mountains, and she related sadly, "I did everything within my knowledge and power to help that child; I exerted every last ounce of my will and energy. I prayed, I whispered to him, I called to him. But he died, just the same." As she remembered this, her eyes filled with tears.

She looked at me. "There are few things in this world more painful than the loss of a child," she said. "Neither faith nor philosophy can heal the heart. Only time has the power to help us forget. And the Fujimotos mourned their child a very long time.

"The child had died in my arms. And something died in me, too. I saw him in my dreams after that. First I believed I might have saved him, if only I had studied harder, known more. Then I obsessed over the idea that I wasn't meant to heal others. This thought possessed me and—over the protest of those people I had helped, and in spite of the Fujimotos' compassionate thanks for my efforts on behalf of their child—I vowed never to practice healing again. It seemed a sham; I felt like a charlatan. I had lost faith in myself and in Spirit.

"That's when I moved to Oahu, in 1965, and started working at the bank. I began to gain weight again."

"Did it bother you?" I asked. "I mean, after what you had learned, and felt like, in that school. Didn't you want to get back in shape?"

"Everyone has both strengths and weaknesses," she reminded me. "My emotions have sometimes gotten the best of me, as they did during my banking years. I just didn't care enough, or have reason enough, to change. I sank into a sad but secure routine, going through the motions, wearing a smile like a two-piece suit. Looking back, for me it was like hell. But that's where I chose to be, what I chose to do. This went on for almost two years, until I received a letter from Socrates, six years ago."

"That would be 1967," I said.

"Yes. I don't know how he found me, or why he chose to write to me just then. We had been out of touch for years. But his letter was wonderful. What he wrote reminded me of things I had forgotten; his words strengthened me, inspired me, and gave me a purpose once again."

"Yeah, he's good at that." I smiled.

"Yeah," she echoed, smiling back at me. "He's *very* good at that. And that's when he told me about you—that you might one day seek me out. I returned to Molokai, and have been doing the work I was born to do since that time. I kept my inner eyes peeled for you."

"And the rest, as they say, is history." I smiled.

"Not quite," Mama Chia said. "About three weeks ago," she beamed, "I helped welcome Mitsu and Sei Fujimoto's new son into the world!"

"Hey, that's great!" I said. "I love happy endings!"

Mama Chia stopped, and rested, leaning against the trunk of a lone tree. Then, her smile faded as she said, "I hope, when your ending comes, you will be as happy."

10

Down the Razor's Edge

Forget about likes and dislikes.
They are of no consequence.
Just do what must be done.
This may not be happiness,
but it is greatness.
George Bernard Shaw

By the early afternoon, the steep descent gave way to a gentle grade. Following the crest as we were, the rocky trail had shrunk to the size of a balance beam, with no margin for error.

Conversation was out of the question as we stepped carefully along the precarious ridge. It must look like a razor's edge from the air, I thought, looking down hundreds of feet on either side. Fighting vertigo, I forced myself to concentrate on Mama Chia, ten feet in front of me, balancing like a mountain goat. With loose rocks, strewn along the razorback ridge, footing was treacherous, and a misstep would be disastrous. We continued in this manner, single file, gradually descending to the east, until the path widened, and Mama Chia gestured for us to sit down and rest.

I breathed deeply, and relaxed. Mama Chia, perfectly calm, reached into her pack, which I had gratefully set down, and handed me a sandwich. "*Kaukau,*" she said, pointing to the sandwich. "Food."

"Yes, I recognize it," I replied dryly, biting into the thick slices of bread. "Ummmm, delicious," I said with my mouth full.

While we ate, I told Mama Chia how impressed I was

by her fearlessness along a ridge that gave me, an ex-gymnast, knots in my stomach.

"So you think I'm courageous?" she said.

"Yes, I do."

"Perhaps I am. But that's because I've had some inspiring teachers. I'll tell you about one of them: Many years ago, when I worked as a volunteer at Stanford Hospital, I'd gotten to know a little girl named Liza who was suffering from a rare and serious disease. Her only chance of recovery appeared to be a blood transfusion from her five-year-old brother, who had miraculously survived the same disease, and had developed the antibodies needed to combat the illness. The doctor explained the situation to her little brother, and asked the boy if he would be willing to give his blood to his sister. I saw him hesitate for only a moment before taking a deep breath and saying, 'Yes, I'll do it if it will save Liza.'

"As the transfusion progressed, he lay in a bed next to his sister, and smiled, as we all did, seeing the color returning to her cheeks. Then his face grew pale and his smile faded. He looked up at the doctor and asked, with a trembling voice, 'Will I start to die right away?'"

Mama Chia looked over at me. "Being young, the boy had misunderstood the doctor; he thought he was going to have to give her *all* his blood.

"Yes, I've learned courage," she added, "because I've had inspiring teachers."

After that, we ate in silence. Then, I lay down for a brief nap. Just as I was drifting into a restful state, Mama Chia's voice jarred me to wakefulness. "Time to get going; we have to arrive before nightfall."

"Are we visiting someone?"

She paused before answering. "In a manner of speaking."

Dark clouds moved overhead, obscuring the sun, now sinking behind the trees, falling toward the horizon. We turned down off the ridge, back into the forest.

"Hurry!" she urged, quickening her pace. "It's getting late."

We pushed across the uneven terrain. Another hour passed, and we pushed on through tangled branches. The hike had taken the better part of a day, and I was ready to drop. I called ahead to Mama Chia as we descended farther. "We must have walked five or six miles today. Can we take a rest?"

"Closer to nine miles," she said, "and no, we can't rest yet."

A light drizzle started, but the cover of trees over our heads kept us dry.

"I can hardly believe how fast you can move for someone who's so—well, substantial," I said, nearly running to catch up.

"I can access a lot of energy," she explained.

"How do you do it? Is there some kind of secret?"

"Let me put it this way," she answered. "You know how a mother, even though she's very tired, will get up again and again during the night, responding to the calls of a sick child?"

"Yes, I know."

"That's how I keep going with you," she said. I couldn't see if she was smiling, but I felt that she was.

She continued to set the pace; I followed, slipping occasionally on some moss-covered rocks—up and down ridges, past many small waterfalls fed from the constant runoff on this part of the island, then on through the forest for several more miles.

As we headed up over another rise, and then down, into Halawa Valley, I felt unaccountably refreshed. This feeling of vigor increased as we descended further. Finally, we came to a small clearing, protected on every side by the thick cover of trees.

Rays of sun, low on the horizon, cut through the thick foliage, creating ribbons of light through the greenery. "Make yourself comfortable," she said.

Grateful, I sat down heavily on a soft bed of leaves, only slightly damp, and dropped her backpack on the forest floor. She remained standing, next to the branch of a kukui tree, staring into space.

I was just lying back on a bed of leaves and looking up through the branches when I heard Mama Chia's voice. "Dan," she said slowly, "do you recall what I said before about shape shifting?"

"Uh, you didn't really say that much—" Startled by the loud chirping of a bird, I turned quickly toward Mama Chia. She had vanished, and in her place, right where she had been sitting, on the low branch of a tree, sat a bird, staring into space.

The bird stood perfectly still, as if waiting for something. "It can't be!" I said aloud. "You're not . . . "

The bird fixed me with an unblinking gaze; I stared back, waiting for a sign, when Mama Chia's grinning face peeked out from behind the tree trunk. The moment she saw me gaping, her smile turned to laughter. "Dan, I wish I'd had a camera; your expression was priceless!"

She stepped forward and winked at the bird; it flew to her shoulder. "So, you thought I'd become a bird," she said. "Well, I think you've been reading too much Carlos Castaneda."

"I've seen stranger things," I said defensively.

Quoting William Shakespeare, she pronounced, "'There are more things in heaven and earth . . . than are dreamt of in your philosophies.' Yes, Dan, and many everyday miracles go unnoticed by everyday people. *But people don't physically turn into little birds.* Shape shifting involves the transference of consciousness, a form of deep empathy. Nothing more, and nothing less."

She stroked the little bird, smoothing his blood red chest and white feathers, as he chirped. "This is an apapane bird. He's sort of a pet, and follows me occasionally," she said, touching his curved beak. I call him 'Redbird.'"

"Is he tame?" I asked, recovering from my embarrassment. "Can I hold him?"

"I don't know. You'll have to ask him."

"What am I supposed to do—whistle in bird language?"

She shared a look with the bird, who appeared to roll

his eyes in his head as if to say, "Who *is* this guy?"

I reached out slowly, and the semiwild apapane allowed me to stroke his belly.

"I have to admit, that was a nice trick. You had me fooled."

Her expression darkened, like the sky overhead, and she stood. "What we are about to do tonight is not about 'tricks,'" she declared, taking the small bird into her hand. "It's about life and *death*." Suddenly, she closed her hand tightly on the bird, squeezing him until he lay still and limp in her hand.

In shock, I stammered, unbelieving, "How *could* you?"

"It's also about death and *life*," she interrupted, tossing the little bird up into the air, where he spread his wings, flew up into a tree, and started to sing beautifully, undisturbed by a sudden drizzle, and apparently no worse for wear.

The rain would soon pass, but would this eerie feeling? I wondered as Mama Chia lay down and curled up like a mother bear, a creature of the forest.

I rested for about fifteen minutes, but couldn't sleep; I was too full of anticipation about whatever was coming next. "I guess we're going to be gone for a couple of days, huh?" I asked.

"Looks that way," she said, without stirring.

"Aren't I keeping you from—the other people you help out?"

She shifted gracefully, and looked me in the eye. "Let's say I'm on an extended emergency leave."

"What's the emergency?"

"You," she said, a faint smile appearing on her face, which then turned sober as she sat up. "Which brings us to where we are, right now."

"And where is that?"

"Inside the boundaries of Kalanikaula, a sacred kukui grove."

"Sacred?" I said, sitting up and looking around.

"Yes. Can you feel it?"

I looked up into the gray bark, light green leaves, and white flowers of the beautiful trees, then closed my eyes and realized that the beauty wasn't so much the look, but the *feel,* of the place. "Yes," I answered. "I can feel it. But why did we come all this way?"

"You go to a sacred place for a sacred teaching." Abruptly, she stood. "Come. It will soon be dark." Erasing any signs of herself, she turned and walked into the forest. I stood quickly, and followed her example.

"You want to tell me what this is about?" I asked, walking swiftly through the trees, trying to keep her in sight.

"When we get there," she called back.

"Get where?"

Though muffled by the trees, the sound of her voice carried clearly enough. "The burial ground," she said.

"Burial ground? Tonight? Now?" The hairs on the back of my neck were standing up—a clear message from my Basic Self that something was coming. What was that old saying? "The light at the end of the tunnel just might be an oncoming train."

11

The Tower of Life

Symbolically, then,
a tower was originally conceived
as a vehicle for connecting
spirit and matter. . . .
The gods must find a way to enter–
by force, if necessary.
Sallie Nichols, *Jung and Tarot*

By the time I looked up, Mama Chia was already twenty yards ahead. I ran to stay close to her. As we climbed out of the kukui grove, over the narrow ridge on the way to the burial ground, the forest changed. As far as the eye could see, in the silver sheen of a half-moon overhead, lay miles of withered forest —trees that were once the proud *ohi'a* and beautiful *koa*—now gaunt skeletons, scarring the ridges above Wailau Valley. "Deer were introduced here to satisfy the hunters who kill for sport," Mama Chia explained. "The deer eat the seedlings, so young trees never grow. Most of the older trees are dying of dry rot and choked with sticky grass and vines even the deer won't touch."

We walked upward, over the ridge, and downward, passing these gnarled patriarchs, the last remains of the dying trees. In the moonlit forest, Mama Chia began to speak, and her words, like a powerful magnet, drew me into a new vision of reality. "The human body is like a tower of seven stories," she said. "This has been known for centuries by inner explorers who have mapped the subtle bodies and energy centers. The Indian mystics called these seven levels *chakras*. Here, let me show you." She stopped and reached behind me into her backpack for a pen and notepad. Squatting down, she drew a diagram on the notepad:

The Tower of Seven Floors

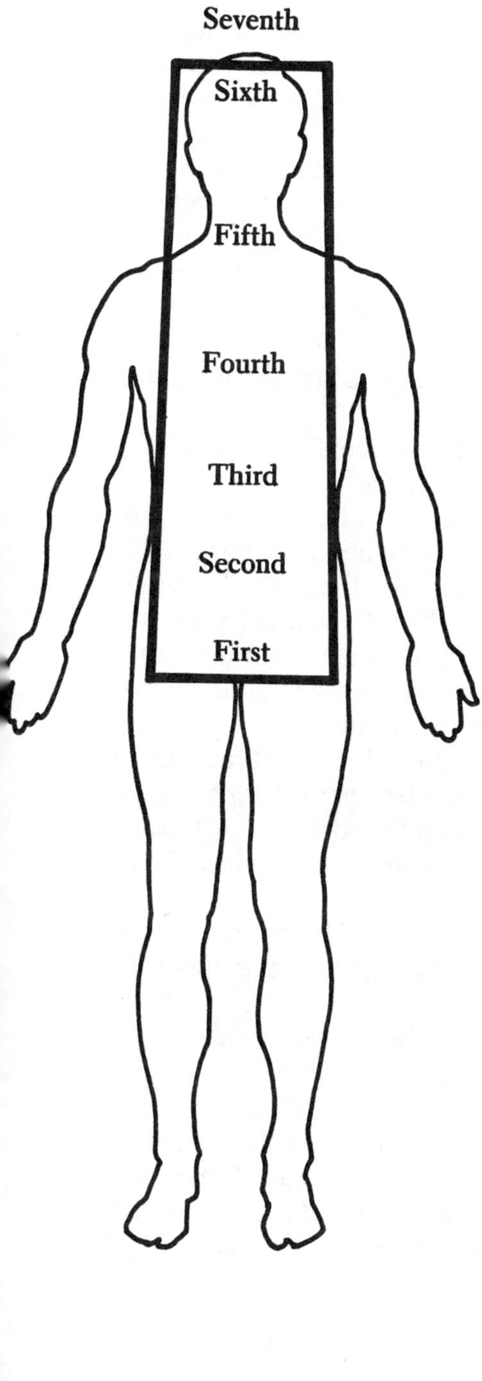

7: PURE BEING AND BLISS
Pure Spirit; no self remains.

6: UNITY
Pure Light; communion with Spirit.

5: MYSTICAL REVELATION
Pure Inspiration; eyes turned toward Spirit.

4: TRANSPERSONAL LOVE
Pure Compassion; open heart; ego no longer center.
Emotions: Love; happiness.
Issue: How best to serve.

THE GREAT LEAP

3: PERSONAL POWER
Emotions: Anger; tension.
Issues: Discipline; commitment; will.

2: SEXUALITY/CREATIVITY
Emotions: Sorrow; weakness.
Issues: Reaching out; embracing life; energy and relationship.

1: PERSONAL SURVIVAL
Emotions: Fear; paralysis.
Issue: Taking care of self.

As Mama Chia finished, she tapped the diagram with her pencil. "This conveys the essence of what you need to know for now," she said. "The tower of life is within you. And each floor has distinct qualities, and each, from the lowest to the highest, represents a more expanded state of awareness.

"The lowest three floors, survival, creativity, and power, are the domain of the Basic Self; it is neither interested in, nor responsible for, the higher floors. Clearing the lowest three floors and dealing with the issues there strengthens the Basic Self.

"On the fourth floor, the realm of the heart, you first make contact with the Higher Self."

"What about the upper three floors?" I asked.

"They are not yet your concern."

"But they are!" I said, excited. "This map, or whatever it is—that's what my search has been about. I know that now! I'm tired of constantly struggling with the lower floors. *That,*" I said, pointing to the seventh floor, "is where I want to go."

Mama Chia looked up from the diagram, and pointed to a nearby kukui tree, its smooth bark glowing in the moonlight. "Like that tree," she said, "or like a tower, the human being is here to connect heaven and earth, to embrace all three selves. But unless the roots of a tree are deep, it can't blossom; unless the tower has a strong foundation, it will crumble. Clean up the basement, Dan, before you move into the penthouse!"

I considered this for a moment. The truth is, I had always imagined myself to be living on one of the upper floors. But now, I wasn't so sure.

"What do these words mean, here in the middle?" I asked, pointing to the diagram. "The Great Leap?"

"It refers to the most difficult and wonderful leap for any human being," she answered, "up out of the personal concerns of the lower three floors, into the heart. Once you get to the fourth floor," she promised, "the rest is an elevator ride.

"And Dan," she continued, growing more passionate, "*all*

your external goals and adventures reflect this inner quest, and every person on earth will eventually ascend these seven steps to the soul."

She started to say something else, but stopped and came around behind me. "Sit down—that's right, get comfortable." She started to rub my shoulders.

"You're giving me a back rub—here, now?" I asked, just before my legs began to twitch as she pressed her fingers into a point on my neck. I saw flashes of light.

"Relax as much as you can," she urged, as she pressed her knuckles into my temples—harder, harder. Her voice began to fade as I heard her say, "There are archetypes within the deepest recesses of every human mind . . ." I felt my eyes closing, then heard the sound of a faraway wind.

I opened my eyes and blinked as clouds of dust blew across a gray plateau, stark as a crater on the moon, stretching for miles in every direction. The wind gusted again, moaning, howling, across the vast expanse. Then my attention focused on a distant object, still too far to distinguish clearly. Was it a tower? Yes, a white tower. And I knew I must go there. By an act of will, and without effort, I felt myself drawing closer. The tower grew larger, until it loomed above me.

Overwhelmed by a wonderful and terrible sense of awe, I found myself outside a window at the base of the tower—the first floor—and I sensed that this floor and those above it were each cluttered with the debris of lifetimes: unexamined issues, symbols, and fears—hidden artifacts in a dusty basement.

As my awareness penetrated the dim light inside, I saw a desolate, empty world, a dust-blown plateau populated only with opponents and enemies.

I soon discovered that each window of each floor offered a different perspective on the world, because inside the second-floor window I viewed a brighter realm of trees and streams and grasses, where couples were engaging in every kind of pleasure, and I was filled with desire.

The third window revealed a world of order, architectural balance, and beauty, where structure rose in a creative crescendo, and people stood straight and tall. On this floor, I spied the gray robot, the Conscious Self, looking out through the window of the senses. And somehow I knew that the Conscious Self had its tiny office here, because this was the highest level it could maintain, in my case.

My awareness then rose to the fourth window, through which I saw all the people of the world, of every color and culture and belief, clasping arms, loving and helping one another and singing in harmony. Feelings of compassion washed over me, and I heard the voices of angels.

My awareness rose swiftly, then, through the upper three floors and, in a wave of rising bliss, I felt, saw, heard, tasted, and smelled far beyond the range of everyday senses, beyond the veils, as I tuned in to subtle energies, to other dimensions and realities, and then—ah, the Light!

In the next jarring instant, like an elevator falling, my awareness dropped down, distracted by alarms from the lower three floors—and I knew that my Conscious Self would be drawn down, again and again, to the issues of fear, sexual energy, and power, until those issues had been cleared.

I remembered, then, with intense longing, that in peaceful, expansive moments of my childhood, I had been invited to the higher floors by angelic energies. I wanted so much to return, because part of me had always known that above the tower, in the place of Light, lay home.

This was my soul's task, my sacred journey: As a Conscious Self, beginning on the ground floor, I needed to find the lights on each rising floor, and turn them on, seeing the issues and artifacts there—dealing with them, clearing them. But this would only be possible if I were first willing to see and accept what *is*, rather than cling to dreamlike illusions.

Returning to a vantage point out on the dusty plain, I once again saw the tower standing before me, stretching up to the heavens, a swirling mist of violet, pink, and gold, and a light shone so brightly above the tower that I couldn't fix my attention there for long.

The next thing I remember, I was sitting, leaning against a tree. My eyes were wide open, but I still saw the tower; then it dissolved as I came back to normal consciousness, and saw only the leaves of the kukui tree, blowing in a warm breeze.

I sat, unmoving. Even after what Socrates had put me through, I was filled with wonder. Taking a breath, I turned slowly, and saw Mama Chia sitting quietly, not far away. Her eyes were closed.

Finally, I could speak. "Whatever you did, I—I understand now, about the tower."

"No, you don't—not yet," she replied, opening her eyes. "But you will." Slapping the notebook shut, she stood, and started down the path. I jumped to my feet, grabbed her backpack, and followed.

"What do you mean, 'not yet'?" I called out.

Her reply was almost lost in the wind. "Before you can see the Light, you have to deal with the darkness."

12

Into the Jaws of Fear

Imminent hanging
sharpens a man's wits.
Samuel Johnson

"Slow down, will you? What's the hurry?" I called out as I trailed behind on the moonlit trail. "*Will you wait up?*" I yelled again. "Where are we going? What are we doing here?"

"You'll know when we get there," she said. Her tone was dark, and her answer gave me no comfort. Dodging vines and bushes, I followed as best I could.

Years before, when I practiced gymnastics, fear had been my friendly adversary. Nearly every day, I attempted risky movements—performing twisting somersaults, soaring from the high bar or trampoline. I could handle that fear because I knew exactly what I was afraid of, and I was in control. But now, a formless terror spread like a chill inside my chest and belly, and I didn't know how to deal with it. Like my first roller coaster ride as a young boy, I remembered being pulled clickety-clack up the steep ascent, where there could be no turning back, where giggles turned to screams, as we rounded the top. Then the bottom dropped out, and my nerves shredded into terror.

Mama Chia spoke with an urgency I hadn't heard before. "Follow me—this way!" she commanded, turning at a sharp angle. As we headed down, nearer to the burial ground, my mind raced. What could a graveyard have to do with the tower? Filled with foreboding, I fought the urge to run away.

"Walk exactly where I do," she said, her voice muffled by the thick air. "Do not stray from this path; do you understand?"

We broke into a clearing. I saw gravestones ahead, and my stomach started knotting up.

"Why are we doing this?" I asked. "I—I thought you were teaching me about the three selves."

Mama Chia took a deep breath, turned to face me, and gestured for me to follow. Her expression was somber, and another wave of fear passed up through my abdomen and chest. This increased my confusion, because I had been in cemeteries before, but didn't remember when I had ever been this frightened. My Basic Self was petrified, my body numb, as we walked through the ancient burial site. I wanted to tell her, "I don't think I can do this," but I couldn't even speak. I didn't consciously know what was frightening me. But my Basic Self knew; that much was obvious.

Though the night was warm, my teeth were chattering as I followed Mama Chia on a narrow path through the graveyard. Some of the grave markers stood upright; others were tilted slightly askew. I tiptoed carefully over the graves, until she stopped by a vacant space, and turned to me.

"We are here to confront the darkness of the first floor," she said—"the realm of survival, isolation, and fear. This is a sacred site, protected from the eyes of outsiders. Only kahunas are buried here. Can you feel the power of the place?"

"Y-yes," I stuttered.

"Lanikaula, the guardian, is here, with us now—behind you," she pointed.

I whirled around, but saw nothing, at first. Just an overpowering presence, a force that made me take a step backward. My body turned to ice. It wasn't evil that I felt, but something that could turn me into ashes in a moment without batting an eye—an energy of great compassion, but no mercy.

"He was, and is, a powerful kahuna, and has been here, watching over Molokai, since his death, four centuries ago. We need to ask for permission to be here," she said with great reverence.

"How?"

"Have you ever asked permission to enter someone's home?"

"Yes—"

"Then I advise you to do it, *now*," she hissed.

She closed her eyes; I did the same. As soon as I closed them, I saw him—right in front of me, in my mind's eye. I snapped my eyes open, and saw only the trees in the distance and the gravestones in this small clearing. I closed them again, and there he was, staring at me with a fierce but somehow loving expression—a large man, wearing some kind of ceremonial Hawaiian headdress. He looked as if he could embrace me or wipe me off the face of the earth. I was reminded of Shiva, the Hindu God—the changer, the transformer, the destroyer.

Silently, respectfully, I asked for his permission to be there, explaining my search. All this happened in a few seconds. He smiled, nodded, and faded out of my vision.

"So be it," I heard Mama Chia say.

Almost immediately, the atmosphere changed. I was bathed in a warm breeze, where before the wind had blown cold on the back of my neck. I opened my eyes.

Mama Chia nodded. "He said you are welcome here," she said. "I think he actually likes you. That is a very good sign." She reached behind one of the gravestones.

I relaxed. "I'm glad to hear th—" I stopped abruptly as she slapped a shovel into my hand and led me to a bare spot in the earth.

"Time to dig."

"What?" I did a double take so fast I nearly pulled a neck muscle.

"Dig here," she said, ignoring my reaction.

"Dig? Here? A hole? Are we looking for something?"

"A grave."

"Look," I said. "I'm a grown man; I make responsible choices. Before I start, I'd really like to know what this is about."

"And I'd really like you to stop talking and start digging," she responded.

"What you are about to do is necessary—based on a Tibetan ritual that involves facing all your fears. If someone who chooses this way is unprepared, it can result in permanent psychosis. I feel you're ready, but there is no way to be certain of it. Are you willing to go ahead?"

There it was: Do or die. Or maybe: Do *and* die. Socrates once told me I could "get off the bus" anytime I wished—if I was willing to let it pull away without me.

"I have to know now, Dan."

I jerked my head toward her as if I'd been slapped. "Oh, uh, well—" I paused to take a breath, and decided to follow the course I'd always set for myself: When a challenge was there, I went for it. "Y-yes," I stammered, "R-ready as I'll ever b-be."

This was about facing fear, so I started to dig. The earth was soft, and the work went faster than I'd expected. As Mama Chia watched, her arms folded, I started with a two-foot-wide channel and lengthened it to about six feet. The hole deepened to three feet, then four. I was sweating profusely now. The deeper I dug, and the more it got to looking like a grave, the less I liked this. And I wasn't enthusiastic to start with.

My fear expanded, then turned to anger. "No," I said, climbing out of the grave. "I don't have to do this, and I don't want to play mysterious games in graveyards without knowing what it's about. I'm not some puppet! Who is this grave for? Why am I doing this?" I demanded.

Mama Chia stared at me for what seemed like a minute, then said, "Come here." She led me to a nearby gravestone and pointed to the epitaph written there. I peered at it.

The writing was old and faded; I could just make it out:

Remember, friend, as you pass by,
As you are now, so once was I.
As I am now, so you must be.
Prepare yourself to follow me.

I looked over at her face, dead serious. "I think you know who this grave is for," she responded.

I stood and faced her. "I have a choice here," I said.

"You always have a choice," she agreed. "You can start digging, or catch the next surfboard out of here."

I didn't think she meant it—about the surfboard—but it was clear that if I wanted to continue as her student, I was going to have to see this through. I had come this far. I had to see where it led. Managing a wan smile, I said, "Well, since you put it so nicely." I climbed back down into the grave, and continued digging until she said, "That's deep enough. Hand me the shovel and come on out."

"You mean I'm done?"

"Yes."

"Whoa, I have to admit—that was pretty frightening, all right," I said, climbing up out of the damp grave and laying the shovel nearby. "But all in all, it wasn't too bad." I stretched my weary muscles.

"Lie down here," she said, pointing to a sheet she had placed on the ground next to the open grave.

"Another massage? Doesn't this strike you as a little strange?" I asked.

She wasn't smiling, just pointing. I lay down on my stomach.

"On your back," she said.

I turned over and stared up at her, standing above me. "Now do I play dead, or what?"

She gave me a fierce look. "Sorry," I said. "I guess I'm just a little nervous."

"This is no game; if you offend the spirits here, you'll have a lot more to be nervous about!"

Trying to relax, I said, "Well, I could use a rest."

"A long rest," Mama Chia said, picking up the shovel, and bringing its blade down. I threw my arms up protectively, thinking for an instant that she was about to stab me with it, but she planted it firmly into the earth beside the grave.

Then she knelt down behind my head, on the edge of the grave, and closed her eyes.

Lying there, I gazed up at her face, upside-down in my vision, and pale in the moonlight. For a terrible moment of paranoia, I felt I didn't really know this woman at all. Maybe she wasn't the one Socrates sent me to; maybe she was the Enemy.

She began to speak in a voice that resounded through the burial ground. She spoke an invocation, and I knew this was definitely no game.

"Great Spirit, called by many names," she intoned, "we ask to be placed in the Light. We ask for your protection for this soul. In the name of the One, and with that authority, we ask that any and all evil be cut off and removed from him, sealed in its own light, and returned to its source. We ask that whatever may come be for his highest good. May thy will be done."

The metallic taste of fear rose in my throat. Then Mama Chia slowly began pressing, with her knuckles, along my collarbone, chest, and arms—gently at first, then with increasing pressure. I saw flashes of light again, then heard popping sounds. Then she grabbed my head as Socrates had done, years before. My teeth started to chatter; then the curtain of darkness descended.

I heard the wind, felt the dust blow in my face, and saw the tower directly in front of me. This didn't feel like a disembodied vision, with my awareness merely an observer. I looked down and saw my body. I was *here*.

Then I was standing in the doorway. The huge door swung open, like a gaping mouth, and I entered, stepping into thin air. I fell, somersaulted, and landed in a heap. I quickly stood and looked around, but barely made out anything in the darkness. "This must be the first floor—the basement," I said. My voice sounded muffled. My clothing clung to my skin, and the dank air and fetid smell of decay was somehow familiar. Find the lights, I said to myself. Be willing to *see*.

Before, I had only looked through the windows of the tower. Did I really want to see what lay inside me, in this, the lowest realm?

"Yes," I answered out loud. "Yes, I want to see!" I proceeded forward slowly, reaching out in the darkness. My hand felt something—a large handle, a switch! I pulled it, heard a humming sound that changed to a soft whoosh, and squinted as dim lights slowly began to illuminate the scene in front of me.

Why was it still so dark? As my eyes adapted, the answer came. I had entered the tower and fallen to the first floor, but it somehow contained the night itself and the same burial ground—the graveyard of the kahunas. But this time, I didn't feel welcome at all. And this time, I was alone. I saw the gaping hole of the open grave nearby. My body began to shiver; my mind crossed the border of nervousness, over the raw edge of fear as I was pulled by an unseen force toward the open grave. I turned and twisted, levitating in the air. Then my body became as stiff as a corpse in rigor mortis, as I floated down on the sheet next to the grave.

I tried to get up, but couldn't move. My lungs started pumping, breathing deeper, faster, deeper, faster. Then I heard Mama Chia's voice, from far away: "Your Higher Self is your guardian angel; whatever happens, remember that it will always be with you . . . "

"*Then why can't I feel it?*" I cried out.

Then, as if in answer, I heard Mama Chia's words echo back to me: "Before you can see the Light, you have to deal with the darkness."

Something pushed me. Paralyzed, I had no control; I couldn't resist. I fell, tumbling down in slow motion, landing on my back with a soundless thud in the open grave. A sheet was wrapped around me like a shroud. Then, in a moment of absolute terror, I felt shovelfuls of dirt rain down onto me. My heart began to pound wildly in my chest.

I heard the sound of distant thunder. Flashes of lightning exploded in the darkness. Then, as the dirt covered me, I heard the voice of Jesus. He wasn't speaking to me; he wasn't full of comfort. He cried out, filled with agony, screaming from the cross at Golgotha as the lightning flashed: "*Why hast thou forsaken me?*" All at once, I realized that it was my voice screaming those words. But it didn't matter; no one could hear me. The shower of earth had covered my face completely, muffling the sound of my screams.

Wait! I cried out in my mind. I'm not ready for this! I can't! Stop! I'm not dead. *I'm not dead!* my mind screamed again and again.

The earth fall ceased. I felt a stillness and silence more complete than any I'd ever known. All I could hear was my labored breathing and pounding heart, like a kettle drum. Alone in the cold earth. Absolute blackness. Isolation. Frozen, gut-ripping fear. I was buried.

An instant of rational reflection: Why did I let this happen? Then that, too, was smothered, and I fell over the edge of madness. My hands, clawlike, desperate, pushed upward against the impossible weight. Soundless screams. Just as the earth began to crush the air out of my lungs, the ground beneath me suddenly caved in, and I fell into an underground tunnel. Clawing wildly, gagging and choking, spitting dirt out of my mouth and nose, I fought my way free of the moist earth.

I began crawling, slithering like a snake, on my belly, up or down—I couldn't tell which—through a long tunnel. I had to get out. Out! Out, out, out, out . . . repeated itself in a rhythmic babble of dread. I could only squeeze forward; there was no way to turn around. Soon, terrified, I noticed the tunnel was getting narrower, tighter, until I could scarcely move.

Once, as a child, bullies had stuffed me into a burlap sack and threatened to bury me. Instead, they stuck me in an old storage trunk. Trapped in the blackness, I went absolutely berserk—drooling, wetting myself, hysterical. It scared them, so they let me out.

Ever since then, I'd had recurring dreams about being trapped in small dark places. Now my worst nightmares had been realized; I felt sheer, unendurable terror. I was so afraid, I just wanted to go unconscious, to die.

My eyes stinging with sweat and dirt, I fought on, narrowing my shoulders, but it was no use. I could go no farther. Noises of desperation, fright mixed with cries of anguish, were quickly extinguished. I was stuck, suffocating; I started to scream again, to whimper.

But—was my imagination playing tricks?—I thought I saw a dim light somewhere ahead. I managed to squeeze a few inches more and saw around a slight curve in the tunnel. The tunnel opened slightly, just enough. I inched my way, sweating and streaked with dirt falling in my eyes, toward the light.

Now it was imprinted deep in my body's memory: Whenever I could go no farther, I would remember—just a few more inches, just a few more minutes, just a few more seconds . . .

I looked up through clouded vision, and thought I saw an opening ahead. Yes, I was sure of it! I reached it and tried to squeeze my head through. I was stuck! Too tight! My head felt crushed by a thousand hands. Desperately, I pushed. The opening started to give, then, suddenly, I burst through. Space! Freedom! Like being born.

Blindly, I pulled the rest of my body out, then fell into an abyss. Below me, impossibly, I saw the gaping mouth and fangs of a gigantic serpent, and I plummeted, screaming.

The next thing I remember, I was sitting in a room I'd never seen before, huddled in the corner, gripped by paranoia. Outside, the Enemy was waiting for me. All of them. No one understood. I was alone, but I would survive. They wanted what I had—a nearby storage freezer with food. I'd kill the bastards first! On a small table next to me lay cases of ammunition. Surrounded by a variety of carbines and semiautomatics, I wore a shoulder holster with a Glock nine millimeter, its clip holding nineteen rounds, inserted, the safety off. Cradling an AK-47 in my arms, I stared fixedly at the door, waiting for them. They would not take what was mine. I'd kill them first. I'd kill them all!

A cannister exploded through the window, and suddenly the room was aflame. In an instant, I was engulfed by searing heat. The air was sucked from my lungs and my skin started to melt. That moment, I remembered a past life as a young girl, hiding in a trunk, hiding from the Huns, burning to death in a room full of flames rather than being raped and enslaved.

The flames shot up and I saw the beginnings of the earth: volcanoes exploding everywhere, burning lava searing everything in its path.

And in the heat, the burning heat, I relived every nightmare of my childhood, every fear that had ever been visited or forced upon me.

I opened my eyes. I was lying on my back at the bottom of my grave, on a sweat-soaked sheet. But I wasn't covered with dirt. Realizing where I was—and that I was holding my breath—I let it out with one huge gasp and began to calm down. Exhausted and disoriented, I was glad to be alive. It was a dream. It was over. I would sit up and climb out. But my legs wouldn't work; neither would my arms.

I heard something above me. "Mama Chia?" I called weakly. "Is that you?" There was no answer—only a soft, padding noise. Someone, or something, was approaching from above.

I heard a soft growl, then the face of a tiger appeared above me. There are no tigers in the rain forests of Hawaii; still, this was a tiger, looking down at me. I stared back; I couldn't take my eyes off it. I'd seen tigers in the zoo—so beautiful, like big pussy cats. This one was so close I could smell its breath. Oh, please, I said to myself. Let this be a dream.

Completely helpless, I played dead, until it reached down

and prodded me, giving me four deep test gashes. I gasped and uttered a brief, stifled cry.

The tiger reached down, clamped its jaws on my arm, and dragged my limp form up out of the grave, then began ripping me apart. I'd felt pain before—searing pain—but now I understood agony.

I tried to go unconscious, to leave my body, to dissociate. But I was attached enough to experience fully the beast tearing open my chest and abdomen, and chewing on my organs.

Shock-borne adrenaline poured through my body. I fell screaming into a cauldron of terror as the huge cat ripped my chest asunder. Then, clamping his jaws around my face and head, the beast tore away part of my face in a seesawing motion, and began to pull my head from my shoulders. Fear is the ultimate pain. It filled my universe, then exploded.

Instantly, the fear, the pain, the tiger, and the universe all vanished. What remained was the deepest peace I had ever known.

13

In the Realm of the Senses

God gave us memories
so that we might have roses
in December.
James Barrie

I lay curled on my side, next to the grave, my head in Mama Chia's lap. The sheet, soaked with sweat, twisted beneath me. I sat up, unable to speak. My eyes wide, staring at nothing, I rocked back and forth, hugging myself and shivering. Mama Chia embraced me protectively, stroking my matted hair. "There, there," she said. "It's over now. It's really over."

A few more moments passed. Slowly, I realized I still had eyes, and a face, and a body. I was safe, here in Mama Chia's arms. I relaxed; then my chest heaved, my breathing came out in gasps, and I started to cry.

Panting, I gripped her hand and stammered, "It—it f-felt like a tour of hell."

"Only your hell, Dan—we each create our own. You just toured the first floor, the realm of isolation and fear, of mindless instinct to survive at any price.

"Warriors confront their demons head on, and by confronting yours, you've dissolved them," she said gently.

My crying finally ceased. My breathing grew calm and rhythmic. Exhausted, I slept.

When I awoke, the sky was growing light. "Is it dawn?" I asked weakly.

Mama Chia stood, pointed around us, and said, "Look, Dan, what do you notice?"

I stood slowly, drained of all tension, and looked around. A bird landed on a gravestone and began to warble; its song carried up into the blue sky. Lime green lichen and moss decorated the stones; a feeling of peace and reverence pervaded the scene.

"It's different," I said.

"No," she replied. "You are."

"You mean I've cleared away all my fears?" I asked.

"No—you'll still face fears," she assured me. "Perhaps the fear of expressing your feelings, showing your emotions—or maybe the fear of speaking before groups of people, or the fear of failing, or looking foolish, or standing up to those you consider somehow superior or more powerful. Fear will arise as long as the ego remains—but you've changed your relationship to it. Fear will never again overpower you; when it comes, you'll know how to deal with it."

"If I weren't afraid of anything, wouldn't that be dangerous?"

Mama Chia paused, then explained, "Fear can paralyze you just when you need to act. *That* is dangerous. It contracts the body's energies, and that contraction attracts the very thing most feared. The absence of fear is not bravado; it's courage. Courage opens the space to act. You will still know caution when it's called for."

Still incredulous, I said, "I can imagine situations, or people, that might still frighten me."

"Neither people nor situations contain the fear; they can only stir it within you, if you haven't yet mastered it.

"Fear is a wonderful servant, but a terrible master. It pervades the daily lives of most people, moment to moment. You won't miss it, I assure you. When you've conquered your fears by acting courageous in spite of them, life blossoms; you look out at a different world through the windows of the second floor.

"But the first floor isn't just fear and survival; it's about 'self against the universe,' about the self-protective hoarding of energy for oneself. Now, open and vulnerable, you're ready to bring that energy fully into life, to share it in relationship."

"You mean I'm ready to find door number two?" I asked, smiling.

"You already found it." She smiled back. "Here, in my arms, when you cried." As she said this, she began to shimmer, and Mama Chia dissolved into thin air, right in front of my startled eyes. Then, everything around me vanished. I saw a fleeting image of the tower, and found myself standing in a sylvan glade, on the second floor. I was certain of it.

But what does it mean? I asked myself as I surveyed the rich meadow, bathed in soft sunlight and cool breezes. This could have been an idyllic forest in lusty old England. "Strange," I caught myself saying out loud. "Why did I think of the word 'lusty'?"

Then, gradually, I became increasingly aware of energy, building up in my whole body—more energy than I had felt in years. I felt so awake and alive! I had to move, to let the energy fly! Sprinting through the forest, I felt as if I could run miles and miles. I leaped, I turned handsprings, and then I ran some more.

Finally, I rested in the warm sunshine. Somehow, the seasons had changed. Spring was, as they say, in the air, when a young man's fancy turns to . . .

The energy started building up again as a familiar, uncomfortable pressure in my loins. Mama Chia had said the second floor dealt with "energy in relationship." That meant creative energy, sexual energy. But what was I going to do with it?

Out of nowhere, I could hear the words of Socrates, from years before. "Every human capacity," he said, "is amplified by energy. The mind becomes brighter, healing accelerates, strength magnifies, imagination intensifies, emotional power and charisma expand. So energy can be a blessing . . . "

Yes, I said to myself. I felt all those things.

"But life energy must flow somewhere," his voice continued. "Where internal obstructions lie, the energy burns, and if it builds up beyond what an individual body/mind can tolerate, it explodes. Anger grows into rage, sorrow turns to despair, concern becomes obsession, and physical aches become agony. So energy can also be a curse. Like a river, it can bring life, but untamed it can unleash a raging flood of destruction."

"What can I do now?" I asked, talking to the air.

Memories of Socrates' wisdom echoed in my mind: "The body will do whatever it has to in order to bleed off excess energy. If it isn't spent consciously, in creative endeavors, physical activity, or sexual relations, then the subconscious will blow off this energy, in fits of anger or cruelty, or nightmares, or crime, or illnesses, or through abuse of alcohol, tobacco, other drugs, or food, or sex. Untamed energy, meeting internal obstacles, is the source of all addictions. Don't try to manage the addictions—clear the obstructions!"

I was so distracted by the building pressure in my body that I could barely concentrate. The energy continued to grow, demanding release. I could run some more, or I could make something—yes, something creative. That's it, I decided. I'll make up a song. But all I could come up with was "There once was a beaut from Killervy, whose body was nubile and curvy; a man found her there, in her lace underwear, and . . . "

I couldn't think of a damn ending; I couldn't think at all. I just wanted a woman. Any woman!

Should I find release by myself? No big deal, simple and efficient. But then I remembered that this level was about bringing energy into life, into *relationship*. Damn! How was I going to manage that?

The next instant, I found myself in a cave—not a gloomy, foreboding cave, but what appeared to be a luxurious bedroom. Thick rugs overlapped on the floor; rays of sunlight bathed the room through a natural skylight. The entrance, concealed by a thick growth of small trees and bushes, rendered the place completely private to outsiders.

In the center of the cave stood a sleeping platform, covered by a thick bed of soft leaves, a few feet off the cave floor. I heard the comforting trickle of a lovely waterfall pouring into a miniature pond and smelled the sweet fragrance of wildflowers.

Then I gasped with surprise and excitement as a soft breeze blew over my entire body; a sensual wind, a beautiful ghost, caressed me with invisible hands. I felt a oneness with the earth and with all my physical senses, now amplified. I was so happy to have this body, to feel the body, to be the body completely.

All I needed was a loaf of bread, a jug of wine, and—I could forgo the bread and wine, but . . .

What was that? Was that voices I heard? Female voices?

I peered out through the leafy door and saw a picture out of an artist's dream. The picture would be titled "Maidens of Spring." Three young women, all voluptuous, were laughing, running under some apple trees, their rosy cheeks reflecting the reddish glow of the fruit above. They wore dark, flowing skirts and low-cut, frilly blouses that clearly differentiated the sexes. I felt like a near-crazed teenager as I spied on these women.

Two of them waved good-bye, and the third, a flaxen-haired angel whose green eyes flashed in the sunlight, stopped, looked left and right, then, smiling, ran straight for my hiding place! "Oh, shit!" I said to myself, half afraid she was going to find me here, half afraid she wasn't.

She slipped into the cave and saw me standing there like a love-starved lunatic. Her eyes met mine, and grew larger. She was going to cry out!

"I—" I began to speak but her cry cut me off.

"Dan!" she uttered, and, breathless, she ran into my arms.

My mind was empty, except for three words: Thank you, God.

Passion overtook me completely. We laughed, we cried, we were lost in each another. I don't know what happened to our clothing; whatever got in the way of our union was cast aside. Time passed; I don't know how long. We lay there, cradling each other, completely spent, asleep in each other's arms. But not for long.

When I awoke, she stood over me, draped in a robe made of flowers. Her angelic face, surrounded by silken hair, shone in the soft light. She let the robe slip off her shoulders; her luminous skin shone like a baby's.

For a moment, questions arose: Who was she? Should I be doing this?

She knelt down and kissed me on the forehead, on my cheeks and chest and lips. Sexual energy coursed through me, arousing me to a fever pitch. Images floated through my mind—earthy, sensual, fertility rites—and it almost seemed as if I could hear, deep inside me, the pulsating beat of drums. She kissed every part of me until my body hummed and pulsated to the beat of the drums, and my questions fell away like dry leaves on a windy autumn day.

I drew her to me, we cradled each other, and I returned, in kind, what she had given. Soon, there was no her, and no me—just us, and the feeling.

It was a feeling I'd had before in moments I remembered—during completely uninhibited sexual play—when my mind was free and my heart open. But now it intensified manyfold—not just because she was a desirable woman, but because I was so . . . open. Having just faced the blackest death, I was now fully capable of celebrating life and all that it entailed. The monk inside had succumbed to Zorba the Greek. Nothing stood between me and life!

The feeling intensified many times over, as waves of pleasure pulsated, not just in my loins, but in every cell in my body. But I was taken slightly aback, just for a moment, when I noticed that I was making love with a man. And the man was me—Dan Millman!

I sat up with a shock. I looked down at my hands, my legs, my breasts: I was a woman! I was her! I felt her insides, her emotions, her energy—soft, but strong. The energy flow was different than I was accustomed to, and in my state I could sense a larger, more sensitive emotional aura. It felt so good—like a completion.

Then we embraced again, and I lost all sense of separation. I was her, I was him, I was her and him.

I stayed with the body. I trusted it. I became like a naked baby, completely free, without rules or inhibitions. I was skin, nerves, and blood—throbbing, tingling, delighting in the realm of the senses. Shapes, touching, moistness, sucking, stroking, feeling, throbbing, smooth, warm, I entered the moment completely.

We were locked in a passionate embrace, completely mindless, building like a tidal wave, toward the shore, when she vanished. No! my body cried out, wanting her. Overcome by both desire and sorrow, I felt the snares of the second floor.

I sat up, panting, ready to explode, the energy swirling inside me like a caged animal, pacing madly, looking for an escape. Would I touch myself to find release? I had no moral dilemma in this regard; I had experienced a place beyond the long-faced dogma of lifeless morality.

But something stopped me, this time—an intuition. Maybe it was my past training with Socrates, the discipline I'd found. There was nothing wrong with pleasure, but now was not the time.

I would *use* the energy, circulate it. I didn't fight my body; I didn't deny it—instead, I breathed, deeply and slowly, until the force of desire spread from my genitals upward, up my spine, up my torso, to the tips of my fingers and toes and the center of my brain.

My mind became light. A gateway had opened; energy rose up from the earth itself, through my spine. Energy that had been trapped below now flowed upward. I tasted the purity of being, the body electric, singing.

But I wasn't fully prepared for this, or practiced, and despite the good intentions of my Conscious Self, my Basic Self apparently had other ideas. The waves continued, growing stronger, until I could stop it no longer. Images passed through my mind like nocturnal fantasies, body parts, moaning sweetness, and suddenly, inevitably, though not of my own accord, the tidal wave, the pulsing wave, crashed into the shore, and subsided.

After a time, I stood up. I felt a gentle, unaccountable sorrow, a sense of loss—not in my mind, but in my body. Perhaps it mourned the loss of that brightness, that energy. She was gone; the object of my desire had vanished, as all objects do. Now, there was only the wind blowing through the trees. Until Mama Chia appeared, snapping me back to whatever reality I could hold onto in my present state.

I stood naked before her; she could see my body and my mind. She knew everything about me, and all that I had just experienced. And she accepted me completely, as I was. Any traces of embarrassment dissolved. I stood before her, naked and unconcerned, like an infant. There was no shame in being seen, no disgrace in being human.

On the first floor, I had broken the thread of fear; now, I broke the thread of shame. For the remainder of my days, however long that might be, I would allow life energy to flow freely through me. I would learn how to use it wisely, choosing where to channel it, celebrating life, but not exploiting it. I was not a master of energy, by any means, but I was a willing apprentice.

Two things happened in quick succession: I saw that I was now fully clothed, and then my surroundings, the cave and glade beyond, flickered and vanished. Neither of these things surprised me.

My next moment of awareness found me standing somewhere high in the mountains. The wind whistled loudly past rocky crags and granite crevices, almost drowning out Mama Chia's voice behind me.

"Come," she said. "Time to move on."

"I was alone before; why are you with me now?" I asked, my voice echoing strangely from the cliffs facing over a deep gorge.

"You had to be alone before; now you're in relationship with the world. Besides, we're in dream time, and I wasn't doing anything. Welcome to the third floor!"

As we hiked upward, I gathered strength from the ground beneath me, from the stones, the trees, the wind—flesh of my flesh. No longer at war with my body, accepting my physical imperfections, trusting my own human nature, I felt a closer connection to the earth.

We found a small lake, and swam through the cool waters, then lay on warm rocks to dry. My body opened to the natural world; I felt the lake's serenity, the river's power, the stability of the mountain and the lightness of the breeze.

Mama Chia looked over at me. "In this place, I feel what you feel, I am what you are," she said. "You just shape shifted—at least the beginning stages."

"I did?"

"You did. Shape shifting begins with a gesture of the imagination—a sense of curiosity and wonder: What would it feel like to be a mountain, a lake, a bird, a stone? Later, you actually resonate with the frequencies of these elements or beings. We have the power to do this because, after all, we're made of the same stuff," she concluded.

"And speaking of shape shifting, I think you know I was attuned to you in that cave on the second floor. Quite an adventure!" she said. "Made me feel young again!"

"I think you'll always be young, Mama Chia."

She smiled. "You're right about that—until the day I die—"

Interrupting her, I said lightly, "You'll probably outlive me at this rate."

She looked deep into my eyes, and she smiled. But this smile was different; it made me sad, though I didn't know why. I saw the love in her eyes, but also something else. I felt a sense of concern—an intuition—but I couldn't fathom what it was about.

Mama Chia quelled my preoccupations as she led me forward, reminding me of the lessons of the second floor: "You created your own experience, Dan, just as you did on the first floor; you experienced exactly what you needed. The energies are the same for everyone; the experience is different. Each of us chooses how to respond to and channel our energy. Some hoard it; others squander it. The warrior channels the flow of life energy like a farmer irrigating his crops.

"On the first floor, alone and fighting for survival, you fearfully hoard the energies of life like a lonely miser with his money; because the energies are blocked, they cause pain.

"On the second floor, you are in a relationship with life, with other people; both the male and female principles are active and in balance.

"The second floor is not just about sex; it's about celebrating the energy of life. Energy is Spirit; energy is sacred. Those unschooled in its use tend to treat energy like coin of the realm, and life becomes a shopping mall or amusement park.

"You have chosen another way—that of a peaceful warrior—to become truly human, by mastering energy.

"The myth of Pandora's box is not about letting mischievous imps and demons out of a container; it is about ways of dealing with life energy. When energy is squandered randomly, you feel a loss of life, and a deep sense of sorrow.

"Fear is the shadow side of the first level; sorrow is the shadow side of the second."

"And the third?" I said. "What do you have planned for me now?"

14

Flying on Wings of Stone

Nothing real can be threatened.
Nothing unreal exists.
Therein lies the peace of God.
A Course in Miracles

"It's not what I have planned; it's what you have planned. I just follow your lead," she said.

"Like a dancer."

"Yes," she said with a curtsy.

"So, what's next?"

"Not much—a token experience, really. Socrates already helped prepare you for the lower floors, so it shouldn't require a great deal." She led me through a rocky canyon, through a short tunnel of stone, then up onto a narrow trail along the spine of a razorback ridge. "First, let's sit here a while."

She closed her eyes. Not wanting to disturb her with questions, I did likewise. There wasn't much else to do up here, or so I thought.

When I opened my eyes again, I could see the sun setting over the far western edge of wherever-we-were. Then Mama Chia opened her eyes and handed me some corn and nuts from her never-empty backpack. "Eat this; you'll need it."

"Why do I have to eat? This is a dream, isn't it? Come to think of it," I noticed, "this floor feels more real than the others. This *is* some kind of vision, isn't it?"

Ignoring me, she said, "The third level is about power—not power over others—that is the negative side—but personal power over the impulses of the Basic Self and the desires of the ego. Here you find the challenges of self-discipline, clear intention, duty, integrity, responsibility, focus, commitment, will—those things that most apprentice humans find so difficult.

"Now that you've cleared the second level and have a sense of connection to others, your attention is freed for higher impulses. It will be easier for you to take others' needs into account as well, though true altruism doesn't exist on the third floor. Your Basic Self is still in control, but better disciplined. What you do for others, you do out of duty and responsibility. Love still eludes you."

"Are you saying I can't really love?" I asked, disturbed by her statement.

"There are many kinds of love," she said. "Just as there are many kinds of music or films or food or drink. There is first-floor love, limited to the most primitive, even abusive, sexual encounters. Second-floor love is vital and pleasure oriented, and the partner is also taken into account. Third-floor love is an artful, conscientious practice."

"I asked you about love, and you keep talking about sex."

"Until you are settled on the fourth floor, that's about it."

"Go on."

"No need to; you get the idea."

"What about love on the higher floors?"

"Let's deal with that when you're ready," she said. "The main thing I want to emphasize now is that the world mirrors your level of awareness. Like attracts like—and people whose home base is the first floor are attracted to first-floor kinds of music, books, movies, drink, food, sports, and so forth. The same is true of the second and third floors. Until your awareness rests stably on the fourth floor, in the heart, your motives are ultimately self-serving."

"Maybe that's why Socrates never had a self-service station!" I suggested.

Mama Chia chuckled through my next question.

"Are you saying that when I'm coming from the fourth floor, I won't be so self-centered?"

"Short of the seventh floor, when the self dissolves, we're

all 'self-centered,' Dan. The question is: Which 'self' are you centered *on*? You are in the process of consciously shifting from the childish neediness of the Basic Self to higher motives as you rise from the third to the fourth floor."

"What does all that have to do with where we are now?" I asked, gesturing toward the mountain peak on which we stood.

"I'm glad you asked me that," she said. "Because you are to do this one thing to pass beyond the third floor," she said, as we stepped around an outcropping of rock and pointed to a narrow, level but rocky path about fifty yards long.

"So, what is it I'm supposed to do?" I asked.

"For starters, walk along this path as far as you can; see what there is to see."

"Door number four?"

"Perhaps," she answered.

I walked carefully down the narrow ridge but stopped short as I came to the edge of a precipice—a chasm that dropped to nothingness as far as I could see—maybe two thousand feet—straight down. I took a step back from the dizzying height and looked across the gaping abyss at the opposite cliff wall about thirty feet away. It looked as if the mountain peak had been sliced in half by a gigantic knife.

Suddenly behind me, Mama Chia said, "You've learned a degree of self-control with Socrates, and through your athletic training. You already have a strong will, and much of the debris has been cleared. The door is there," she said, pointing across the abyss to a small ledge, little more than an indentation on the opposite cliff wall. But, sure enough, there did appear to be a doorway there. "All you have to do is leap across."

I gauged the distance again—obviously too far to jump. I looked to Mama Chia to see if she was joking. Her face showed no sign that she was.

"That's not possible," I argued. "First of all, it's twenty-five or thirty feet away, and I'm no long jumper. And even if I made the jump, if I miss that narrow ledge I'll slam into the cliff face and slide down to oblivion."

"You're not afraid, are you?" she asked.

"No, not really—but I'm not stupid, either. It's suicidal."

She just looked at me, with a know-it-all smile.

"I said no."

She waited.

"This isn't a dream now," I bellowed. "And I'm no bird!"

"It can be done," she said, pointing across the chasm.

I started to walk with her back up the trail, shaking my head. "This isn't about fear, Mama Chia—you know that. It would just be foolish. I don't mind testing my limits, but if I overreach myself here, I'm dead."

I felt her hand even before it touched me. The hairs shot up on my neck and goose bumps raised; then I saw a flash of light. Something changed. Or had it? Everything *looked* the same, but felt different. I was still standing there, talking to her. "Is this a dream?"

"Everything is," she replied.

"No, but I mean right now—"

"There is always the chance," she added, "that you may fail."

"If I fail, will I really die?"

"Your physical body will be undamaged, but the pain will feel very real, and, yes, a part of you will most certainly die."

"But if this is some kind of vision, I can do anything I want."

"It's not that simple," she replied. "You'll only be able to accomplish what you believe you can; it will still take a leap of faith to make it across. This isn't really a test of your body, but of your mind—your focus, discipline, intention, and, in a way, your integrity, or integration.

"You've already accomplished much—a lifetime's worth for many. Only accept this challenge if you truly wish to go on. Ask yourself: Can you *will* yourself across? This is your test of personal power. And there," she pointed again across the chasm, "lies the path to the fourth door."

I stared once more out over the chasm. I jumped up off the ground, and came down with a physical sensation of landing, having gone no higher than I normally would. I tried again; the results were the same.

This is crazy, I thought. Maybe it was a trick, a test of my judgment. She had said that "a part of me would die" only if I jumped and failed to make it across. Maybe I wasn't supposed to accept a foolish challenge. What if I declined to jump at all? "Yes, that must be it!" I said aloud, turning to Mama Chia. She was gone.

Then I heard someone calling for me. "Dan! Help me, please! Help!" I looked across the chasm, where the voice echoed from, and saw—Sachi. It was impossible! A trick. She cried out again as she clung to the ledge on which I was to land. She was slipping, struggling to climb back to the ledge.

"This isn't fair, Mama Chia!" I said. "This isn't real!"

"Daaaaannnn!" Sachi yelled desperately. She got a foothold, then lost it.

Then I saw the tiger. It padded along a narrow ledge on the cliff face, toward Sachi. She didn't see it.

"Please!" she called again. I had no choice. I had to try. I ran quickly back along the narrow path for about thirty yards, turned, and took off.

As I picked up speed, doubts assailed me: What am I doing? I don't think I can make this. Then a kind of cold anger overwhelmed me. Not anger *at* anything or anyone—just a forceful energy, like a giant wave that washed away everything in its path. Nothing was going to stop me!

Accelerating, focused completely on my goal, I raced toward the precipice. With a surge of power, my mind forgot past and future, tigers or chasms, as I locked onto one thing: the landing spot. I leaped.

For a moment, floating through space, I felt that I might not make it. Still aloft, I soared through space and time, as if in slow motion. I felt the heavy pull of gravity taking control. I felt myself dropping. Then, something happened. Maybe it was my imagination, but drawing on everything within me, I *willed* myself across. I felt like I was flying.

An instant later, I landed with a very real thud, and, rolling into the shallow cave, I hit the wall. The tiger was running toward us. Dazed, I stumbled to the edge, reached down, and pulled Sachi up. Then, just as the tiger leaped, I pulled her through the doorway.

I must have hit the wall pretty hard. As soon as I was through the door, I passed out.

I awoke, moments later, in the dim light. My arms were bruised, and my head hurt. I hurt all over. I looked at my wrist; it was crooked—broken. Then, as I watched it, the wrist straightened itself out, the bruises disappeared, and the pain subsided. I closed my eyes for a few moments.

When I opened them, I was sitting up, on an old sheet, beside an open grave at the sacred burial site of the kahunas.

The morning sun struck Mama Chia's face, bathing it in a rosy glow. But she looked pale and drawn, in spite of it. Noticing me staring, she smiled wanly, and said, "The last few days have been challenging for both of us. If you think *I* look bad, you should see yourself."

She handed me a plastic bottle with water. "Drink this."

"Thanks." I was parched, and gratefully I took the water. Since my episode out at sea, I had little tolerance for going thirsty. That fear, at least, seemed to remain in the depths of my Basic Self.

When I finished drinking, Mama Chia stood. "Come on. We have a long walk back." We said a respectful good-bye to Lanikaula, and though he didn't appear to us in the daylight, I could feel his presence and blessing.

On the way back, it struck me: Although I'd cleared the third floor and shown sufficient discipline, focus, and self-mastery to find and pass through the door to the fourth floor, my vision had ended then; I had not made it to the fourth floor. I had some sense of what had happened, but I asked Mama Chia for her view.

She gave a simple, straightforward response: "You aren't ready yet. Your psyche rejected it. You came back."

"So I blew it," I said.

"That's oversimplifying, but it comes out to about the same thing."

"So what do I do now?"

"Well, Dan, your training with Socrates helped you with the first three floors, as I've said. You are prepared to enter the fourth level. It may happen at any time. But, you see, the Great Leap requires that the Conscious Self, the ego, loosen its grip. That may be what's holding you back."

It soon turned dark. We camped in the rain forest. Tomorrow, I thought, we would have an easy walk—a couple of hours, then home.

Soon after starting out in the morning, however, we came to the foot of a dramatic waterfall, thundering down from a shelf forty feet above.

"You know," I said, gazing at the pounding falls, "Socrates once cautioned me about getting too fascinated with inner stuff, with visions and such. He said it can lead some people, who aren't too grounded to start with, into all kinds of illusions. He used to tell me, even after sending me on an inner journey, to keep the lesson and throw away the experience.

"So I've been thinking—maybe all these visions don't prove anything conclusive. It's a lot easier to be courageous or uninhibited or disciplined in a dream than in real life. I don't really feel that different. How do I know anything's really changed?"

"What you've gone through was much more than a dream, Dan. And keep an open mind about what you call 'real life.' "

"But I still want to prove something to myself."

Mama Chia smiled and shook her head, amused. She gazed intently at me for a few moments, then looked at the falls, then back at me. "Okay," she said. "You need to prove something? Go meditate under that waterfall for a while."

I took a fresh look at the falls, and considered it. That was a lot of water crashing down; it wouldn't be like taking a shower. "Yeah, I can do that," I answered casually. I had once seen something like this in a martial arts movie. "Okay. I accept. I'll do it for twenty minutes."

"Five hours would prove a lot more," she said quickly.

"*Five hours?* I'd drown in five hours! I'd probably have brain damage!"

"You might already have brain damage," she suggested with a smile.

"Okay—one hour, but that's tops. I don't even know if *that's* possible without drowning." I removed my shirt and started to take off my sneakers, then decided against that and left them on. I stepped carefully on the slippery, moss-covered rocks, and climbed out under the falls.

I was almost knocked flat by the force of the water. Fighting my way in, almost slipping twice, I found a place to perch on a flat rock and sat, pushing my spine straight up under the force of the deluge. The water was cold, but in this climate bearable. I'm glad the weather's warm, I thought, before the liquid avalanche drowned out all thoughts.

Through sheer determination and a growing tension headache, I stuck it out for what felt like an hour, so I figured it was at least twenty minutes. I was preparing to "call this game on account of rain," when something stopped me. Maybe it was courage, or determination, or discipline. Or maybe it was pigheaded stubbornness.

Years before, when the coach would ask for fifteen handstand push-ups, I would always do twenty. I'd always been like that, as long as I could remember. So, while I kept wanting to get up, get out, quit—something kept stopping me. Somewhere in the back of my mind (the front of my mind had already drowned) was Mama Chia's challenge, playing again and again like a mantra: five hours, five hours, five hours . . .

In my years of gymnastics, my Basic Self had been trained to respond to the word "challenge" by pulling out all the stops. I felt a surge of energy rising up through my abdomen and chest as I realized *I was actually going for it*—five hours—I was committed. Then the world disappeared in the deluge, and my mind was no more.

Somewhere in the pounding, in the noise that grew fainter and fainter and farther away, I heard the wind, and I saw a white tower flying toward me in my mind's eye.

I found myself in a tiny room. Acrid smells filled the air, odors of sewage and decay, partly masked by strong incense. I recognized the dress—colorful saris even in this terrible poverty. There was no mistaking this place. I was somewhere in India.

Across the room, a woman, wearing the garb of a nun, was caring for a bedridden leper, his face a mass of sores. He had a deep, oozing fissure in his cheek, I noted with disgust, and he was missing an ear. He was dying. Recoiling from the sight, revolted by the smells, and the sickness, I stepped back, in shock, and withdrew.

The wind gusted; I leaned against a worn brick wall in an alleyway in France, just off the narrow Rue de Pigalle. A gendarme was picking up a drunk, covered with vomit, smelling of the gutter, to help him into the police van. Disgusted, I stepped back, and this scene, too, receded in the distance.

The wind blew again; I sat like a ghost, unseen, on the bed of a teenage boy, in an upper-class suburban house in Los Angeles. He was sniffing powder up his nose. Stupid kid, I thought. Get me out of here.

The next instant, I stood outside a hut in Africa, gazing through the doorway at a very old man, moving painfully, trying to get some water into the cracked mouth of a young baby, its belly swollen, its ribs almost breaking through the skin.

"What is this?" I cried out loud, feeling like I was back in hell. "What do these people have to do with me? Take me away from here! I can't take this; I don't want anymore!"

My eyes closed, I shook my head back and forth to shut out these people and their suffering. I heard a voice calling me, growing louder. "Dan! Dan!"

I became vaguely aware of Mama Chia, under the waterfall with me, pulling my arm, yelling, "Dan! Come on, champ. You proved what you needed to."

Completely waterlogged, looking like a drowned cat, I staggered and crawled out from under the falls, muttering, "A nice place to visit, but I wouldn't want to live there. Look"—I pointed to my neck—"I think I grew gills."

"Brrrrrrrr!" I shook my head, trying to clear it. Feeling like a soppy sponge, I stumbled and fell. Getting up, pointing to the falls, I mimicked a stuntman and spoke into an imaginary camera. "Don't try this at home, kids; I'm an expert." Then my eyes rolled back in my head; I tipped over backward and passed out.

When I came to after drying in the sun's heat, I sat up. "I'm not taking a shower for a year," I swore.

I turned to Mama Chia, sitting not far away, finishing a juicy mango, watching me.

"Well, that proves something, doesn't it?" I asked.

"Yes," she replied, smiling. "While you were sitting like a jackass getting beaten half to death and drowned under a waterfall, I hiked to my house, took a nap, visited with a friend, walked back, and enjoyed this mango." She tossed the seed into the bushes. "It proves something all right—that one of us is a fool." Then she laughed so sweetly that her voice was like music, and I had to laugh, too.

"You have good spirit, Dan. I knew that from the start. Socrates really helped you clean up your act—to turn on the lights of the third floor. So now, when your Conscious Self resolves to do something, your Basic Self knows your level of commitment and gives you the energy to accomplish it.

I'll grant you that much," she said with solemnity. "You have become a human being."

"I've become a human being? That's all?"

"Quite an accomplishment—it means you've done a pretty good housecleaning on the first three floors. You've gotten in touch with your body, with the world, with your humanity."

"But, something happened under the waterfall," I told her. "I saw all these poor people—the sick, the dying. Somehow, I think I visited the—"

"Fourth floor," she finished for me. "Yes, I sensed that—down at the cabin, in my sleep." She nodded, but her eyes looked a little sad.

"Well, what did it mean? Did I pass?"

"The waterfall, yes. The fourth floor, no."

"What do you mean? What happened?"

"Let's go. We'll walk, then we'll talk."

15

In the Service of Spirit

I slept, and I dreamt that life was all joy.
I woke, and saw that life was but service.
I served, and discovered
that service was joy.
Rabindranath Tagore

As we slowly wound our way down into the forest, I asked, "What exactly happened to me back there—leaping that chasm, and then under the falls?"

Limping upward, Mama Chia answered with compassion and understanding. "Dan, for you, as well as for many others, the third floor remains an arena of battle. Cluttered with issues of discipline, commitment, will, and self-restraint, it is finishing school for the Basic Self.

"Until we clear these issues and master ourselves, our lives reflect a constant struggle to bridge the chasm between knowing what to do and actually doing it. The warrior has mastered the Basic Self—trained it—so that what it wants and what it needs are the same, no longer in opposition.

"In leaping the chasm, you showed a strong will; otherwise, you would have fallen into the abyss."

"What would have happened then?"

"A long climb back!" she said, laughing.

"Was Sachi really there?"

"In your mind, yes—she was really there," she answered, adding, "Perhaps she represents the daughter you left hanging back in Ohio."

I felt pangs of regret, responsibility, and love as Holly's little face appeared in my mind. "I should be getting home to see her."

"Yes, of course," she agreed. "But will you bring her a whole father—or a man with a lot of unfinished business?"

Again Soc's words resounded inside me: "Once begun, better finish."

"Have you finished here yet?" Mama Chia asked, as if reading my thoughts.

"I don't know; I still don't understand what happened to me under that waterfall—"

She cut me off. "You made a tremendous jump across that chasm. But an even greater leap awaits you."

"To the fourth floor?"

"Yes—into the heart."

"Into the heart," I repeated. "Sounds kind of sentimental."

"Sentiment has nothing to do with it," she said. "It's a matter of physics—*meta*physics. And you *can* make this leap, Dan. But it will take great courage, and great love. These qualities remain latent—or partially developed—in most people; they are coming alive in you. It begins with a longing, as you've described." Mama Chia paused, then revealed, "I know you better than you know yourself, Dan. All your adventures are nothing more, and nothing less, than Spirit searching for Itself. Your Higher Self is waiting for you, filled with love. That meeting is so close. I only hope I live to see—" she caught herself and stopped in midsentence.

"What do you mean, you hope you'll live to see it?" I asked. "Is it going to take me that long—or is there something I don't know?"

Mama Chia stopped walking for a moment, and looked as if she were about to respond to my question. Instead, she resumed her limping gait, and continued talking where she had left off. "You'll meet your Higher Self the moment your awareness rises out of the sea of personal concerns, into the heart. You don't have to climb the mountains of Tibet, you see, for the kingdom of heaven is *within*," she reminded me. "In and up—the heart and above—it's all there."

"What about the floors above?"

"I've told you—one step at a time! Find the heart, first; then the higher floors will take care of themselves, but you'll be too busy loving and serving to care."

"I don't know if I'm cut out to play 'Saint Dan.'" I grinned at her. "For one thing, I like cookies too much."

"Well," Mama Chia replied, smiling. "When you leap into the heart, you'll truly *love* cookies. I know *I* do!" She laughed, but said nothing more for a while, as if to let all she had said sink in, the way a gardener lets water seep down deep, toward the roots.

I looked up and around; clouds passed over the midday sun. Mama Chia's words had reached in and touched someplace deep inside me. We continued walking, in silence, until more questions arose in my mind.

"Mama Chia, I've seen people who have unusual powers or abilities. Does that mean they are on the higher floors?"

"People sometimes manifest gifts through work in past embodiments. But most often—unless they've cleared all the debris below—they only have a 'temporary pass' to the upper floors to contact those points of energy and see through those windows."

"How about spiritual masters?"

"The awareness of a genuine master is present at birth, but may remain latent—even through periods of inner turmoil and confusion—until it blossoms rapidly, catalyzed by an event or teacher. Great masters can access the higher floors—indeed, they manifest great love, energy, clarity, wisdom, charisma, compassion, sensitivity, and power—but if they haven't also mastered the lower floors, they end up absconding with the money or sleeping with their students."

"I'd sure like to experience those upper floors."

"Certain mystical techniques and substances have been known for centuries to provide glimpses of the upper floors. These are best treated as sacred, rather than recreational, activities; they can be useful as a 'previews of coming attractions.'

"Many well-intentioned, lonely, bored, or desperate people generate spiritual experiences through a variety of tech niques," she continued. "But then what? What have they got: They return to their normal states more depressed than ever

"Spirit is always here, always with us, around us, inside us. But there are no shortcuts to this realization. Mystical practices generate heightened awareness, but if experiences aren't grounded in a responsible life in *this* dimension, they lead nowhere," she said, following a turn in the path.

"Those who seek to escape the world through spiritual experiences are barking up the wrong tree, because their search only intensifies the sense of dilemma that motivated the search in the first place.

"The desire to rise above the boredom, fleshiness, and mortality of this world is natural and understandable. But those who practice self-involved techniques to distract themselves from the dilemmas of daily life are going to ascend the ladder only to find out it's leaning against the wrong wall.

"You meet the Higher Self not by imagining colored lights or doing lovely visualizations, but by accepting its will—by *becoming* the Higher Self. This process cannot be forced; it happens of its own accord.

"Daily life is the training arena of the peaceful warrior," she continued. "Spirit gives you everything you need, here and now. You evolve not by seeking to go elsewhere, but by paying attention to, and embracing, what's right in front of you. Only then can you take the next step on whatever floor you are working.

"And then," she said, stopping and facing me, "when the lower floors are clear, something very subtle and exciting occurs: Your motives make a rare and dramatic shift from *seeking* happiness to *creating* it.

"Ultimately, it comes down to service. Jesus said, 'Whoever would be the greatest among you is the servant of all.' This, Dan, is the way to the heart, the path up the inner mountain. And mark my words: One day you will serve others not out of self-interest or guilt or social conscience, but *be-*

cause there's nothing else you'd rather do. It will feel as simple and pleasurable as seeing a wonderful film that makes you feel happy and wanting to share it with others."

"I don't know if I'm capable of making service the center of my life. It still sounds like a burden."

"Of *course* it does," she replied, "because you are still seeing it from the third floor. But from the fourth-floor window, from the eyes of the heart, convenience, personal comfort, and satisfaction are no longer the center of your existence. You will look forward to getting up each day just to help another soul, another part of your Self."

Mama Chia stopped talking as a rainsquall made our footing treacherous. Stepping over twisted roots, it was hard to walk and talk at the same time. I concentrated on my mud-caked sneakers, beating a squishy cadence on the wet earth, and thought about what she had told me. We sloshed down through the rain that saturated the forest, leaving several small but scenic waterfalls along this narrow, slippery path.

Later, when the path widened, Mama Chia glanced back at my concerned expression and said, "Don't be too hard on yourself, Dan. Accept where you are. Trust your Higher Self. It has been calling to you since you were a child. It brought you to Socrates, and to me. Accept yourself and just serve. Serve out of duty until you can serve out of love—without attachment to the results.

"And when you'd be content to spend a hundred lifetimes—or an eternity—serving others, you no longer need to practice a way, because you've *become* the Way. Through service, 'you,' the Conscious Self, evolve into a Higher Self, even while in human form."

"How will I know when this happens?" I asked her.

"You won't. You'll be too ecstatic to notice!" she replied, her face radiant. "As the ego dissolves into the arms of God; the mind dissolves into the will of God. No longer trying to control your life or make it work out in a particular way, you stop living, and start *being lived.* You merge with a larger purpose, the 'bigger picture.' You become the Way," she added, "by getting out of the way!"

"I don't know," I sighed. "It sounds impossible."

"When has that stopped you before?" she asked.

"You've got a point," I said, smiling.

"When Joseph de Veuster was a boy," she added, "if someone had told him he would spend his adult life ministering to lepers on the island of Molokai, he might have thought that impossible, too. But Joseph became Father Damien, and when the lepers were abandoned here to languish and die, he found his calling, and served them for the rest of his life. And look at Mother Teresa, and Mahatma Gandhi, and—"

"And look at you," I interjected.

We passed down into the rain forest, down toward my cabin, and a needed rest. The tree roots and rocks gave way to grass, leaves, and damp red earth. We were both weary, and traveled in silence. I concentrated on breathing slowly and deeply, keeping my tongue on the roof of my mouth, allowing my Basic Self to circulate and balance the energies that flowed through me. I inhaled not only air, but light and energy and spirit.

I became aware of birdsong, and the everpresent trickle and rushing of streams and waterfalls—runoff from the rain showers—drew me once again into the beauty and mystery of Molokai. But the nagging issue of service, certainly a weak link in the chain of my life, kept rising to the surface of my mind, pressing me.

"Mama Chia," I said, breaking our silence, "when you mention Father Damien or Mother Teresa, I realize how far I am from anything like that. The idea of working with lepers and serving the poor just doesn't appeal to me at this point in my life, though I know it would be a good thing to do."

Without turning around, she answered. "Most of humanity joins in your sentiments. Good deeds are done for many motives: On the first floor, you only find self-service; on the second floor, service always has strings attached; on the third floor, it is motivated by duty and responsibility. I say again: True service begins at the fourth level, when awareness resides in the heart."

We walked on into the afternoon, stopping once to pick some mangoes. My hunger only slightly appeased, I felt glad for the remaining nuts from Mama Chia's pack. She just nibbled, content with her meager fare.

"Keep eating like this," I said, "and you'll soon be slim as a model."

"A model *what?*" she asked, smiling.

"A model saint."

"I'm no saint," she said. "You should see me at parties."

"I already have, remember? On Oahu." My thoughts flew back there—could it have been only a few weeks ago? It seemed like years had passed since I had arrived; I felt much older, and maybe a little wiser.

As we resumed the final leg of our downward hike, I asked Mama Chia, "How am I ever going to make that leap you talk about? After all, I have a job, a family to support, and other commitments. I can't just go around giving things away, spending all my time volunteering."

"Whoever suggested you should? And where have you gotten all these ideas?" she asked. Then Mama Chia smiled. "Perhaps you got them from the same place I did," she said, and, slowing her pace, she told me, "When I entered the university, ideals didn't come any higher. I was going for the Holy Grail, and that was that. Not a day passed that I didn't feel guilty about attending such a fine university—reading books and studying and attending films—while children were starving in other parts of the world. I vowed that my studies would enable me to help those less fortunate than I.

"That summer, I was sent to India on a study grant, and my ideals suffered a rude jolt. I had saved some money to give to the poor and, as soon as I got off the train, a child approached me. She was beautiful—neat and clean, with shining white teeth in spite of her poverty. She begged politely, and I was happy to give her a coin. Her eyes lit up! And I felt so good.

"Then three more children ran up and, smiling graciously, I gave each of them a coin as well. Then I was surrounded by fifteen children, and that was just the start. Everywhere, there were children begging. I soon ran out of coins. I gave away my carrying bag and an umbrella; I gave away nearly everything but the clothes I was wearing and my air tickets. Soon, if this kept up, *I* would be begging, too. It had to stop somewhere; I had to learn how to say no without hardening my heart. It was painful for me, but necessary. I had not taken vows of poverty—and neither have you.

"Yes, this world needs more compassion. But we all have different callings. Some people work in the stock market, others in the prisons. Some live in luxury, while others are homeless. Some people deliberate on what type of imported marble to place in their indoor pools, while others starve on the streets. Does this make villains of the rich or saints of the poor? I think not. Complex karmas are at work. Each of us plays our role. Each of us is born into life circumstances to challenge us and allow us to evolve. A beggar in this life may have been wealthy in another life. Inequity has always existed, and until the awareness of humanity rises *at least* to the third floor, it will continue.

"Over time, I have come to accept my guilt about being comfortable and having enough to eat. Otherwise, how can we take a bite of food while others starve?"

"How do you deal with these feelings?" I asked.

"The question itself reveals your awakening heart," she said. "The way I deal with such feelings is I act with kindness to the people in my immediate surroundings. I accept the role I have been given, and I suggest you do the same. It is all right for a peaceful warrior to make good money, doing what he or she loves, serving other people. All three elements are important. It is *all right* to hurt, to love, to be happy, in spite of the difficulties of this world.

"Find your own balance. Do what you can, but take time to laugh and enjoy life. Yet, at the same time, know that as your consciousness rises up into the tower of life, your lifestyle naturally changes. Your needs simplify; your priorities—how you spend your time and money and energy—all change."

"I have high ideals, too, Mama Chia. I want to get closer to them. I *want* to change."

"The first step to change," she said, "is accepting where you are right now. *Completely* accept your process. Negative judgments about yourself only hold the patterns in place, because the Basic Self can get very stubborn and defensive. Accepting yourself gives the subconscious child in you the space it needs to grow. When it happens is completely in God's hands, not yours."

16

Dark Clouds on a Sunny Day

Here are the tears of things;
mortality touches the heart.
Virgil, *The Aeneid*

I had absorbed all I could; Mama Chia clearly sensed that. I spent the last few miles resting my mind and heart, but alas, not my feet. I was running on empty, carried more by downhill momentum than by any reserves of energy. Once again, it struck me as incredible that this elderly woman could have traveled all these miles, limping every step of the way.

When we were within a mile of my cabin, Mama Chia turned off onto another trail than the one I'd remembered. A few minutes later, we came to a small cabin next to a cascading stream. As we approached from above, I could see a Japenese rock garden with one large rock—an island in a sea of raked gravel—with a bonsai tree arching up in perfect balance with the whole. Above it lay another terraced garden with vegetables and flowers.

The cabin itself stood up off the ground on stilts. "We sometimes get a lot of water," she explained without my asking, as we went up three log steps and inside. The decor was perfect Mama Chia: a long, low futon couch, green carpeting like the forest leaves, a few paintings on the walls, and some zafus—meditation cushions—and assorted pillows.

"Can I make you some iced tea?" she asked.

"Sure," I said. "Need any help?"

She smiled. "While this is tea for two, it doesn't take two to make tea. The bathroom's over there." She pointed to my left as she headed into a kitchen area. "Make yourself at home.

Spin a record on the turntable if you want."

Coming out of the bathroom, I looked for the record player and found an old windup model, an antique.

When she brought out the tea, and some fresh papaya slices, Mama Chia seemed so peaceful—at home in her environment—as if she'd been here all the time instead of taking me on a grueling cross-country hike.

When we finished our tea, I cleared our plates and washed them. She said, "We're only about a mile from your cabin. You could use a rest, I imagine."

"Yes," I said. "You, too."

Mama Chia knelt, Japanese style, on a cushion in front of me, and gazed directly into my eyes. "I feel I've come to know you well, these past few days."

"The feeling's mutual," I replied. "You amaze me! Socrates sure knows how to pick friends!" I smiled.

"Yes, he does," she added. I guessed she was referring to me.

"You know, it's strange—we've only known each other for a few weeks, but it feels like so much longer."

"Like a time warp," she said.

"Yes, exactly—and it's going to take me some time for me to take in all that I've learned," I told her.

She paused for a moment, then said, "Perhaps that's what life is for—giving us time to take in what we learn."

We sat quietly for a while, enjoying the serenity of her house and the pleasure of each other's company. I was suddenly moved to tell her, "I feel so grateful to you, Mama Chia."

"Grateful to *me*?" She laughed, apparently thinking this humorous, or even absurd. "I'm happy for you; gratitude is a good, wholesome feeling. But when you're thirsty and someone gives you water, are you grateful to the glass, or to the person who gave you the water?"

"Well, to the person," I answered.

"I am only the glass," she said. "Send your gratitude to the Source."

"I will, Mama Chia, but I also appreciate the glass!"

We shared a laugh, and then her smile faded slightly.

"There's something I feel I should tell you, Dan, just in case. . . ." She hesitated for a moment. "I have trouble with blood clots—a high risk of strokes. The last one gave me this limp, this shaky hand, and some sight loss in one eye. The next one, if it happens, will be fatal."

She said all this matter-of-factly. I felt a shock wave pass through my whole body. "The doctor who originally diagnosed it," she continued, "and the specialist who offered the same diagnosis, said I could function normally—except for the usual cautions—but that my life expectancy at this point is very tenuous. There's not much they can do—they give me some medicine, but . . . "

She sat still, as I absorbed this. I stared into her eyes, to the floor, and into her eyes again. "Did those 'usual cautions' the doctors told you include not pushing yourself to your limits on endurance hikes?"

Mama Chia smiled at me with compassion. "You understand why I didn't tell you before."

"Yes—because I would never have gone!" Feelings of anger, concern, sorrow, fear, tenderness, betrayal, and guilt washed over me.

A heavy silence settled on the room. "You said the next stroke would be fatal. Don't you mean *might* be fatal?"

She hesitated, then said, "I sense I'll be dying soon. I can feel it. I just don't know exactly when."

"Is there anything I can do?" I finally asked.

"I'll let you know," she said with a comforting smile.

"With everything you know—all your rapport with your Basic Self—can't you heal yourself?"

"I've asked myself that question many times, Dan. I do what I can; the rest is up to Spirit. There are some things one must accept. All the positive thinking in the world will not grow back a missing leg; my problem is like that."

"That friend I told you about—the one who died," I

reminded her. "When he first found out he was ill, he felt all those things people feel in his situation—the shock, the denial, the anger, and, finally, the acceptance. Well, it seemed to me that he had an opportunity either to conquer the illness—to commit all his time, energy, and will to healing—or, to accept on the deepest level that he was going to die, surrender, make peace with the world, take care of business, and somehow use it for his evolution.

"But he never did," I said sadly. "He did what I imagine most people do. He wobbled with halfhearted efforts, never really fighting death *or* accepting it, until the end. I was . . . disappointed in him." It was the first time I had ever shared that feeling with anyone.

Mama Chia's eyes were bright. "Socrates would be proud of you, Dan. That was very wise of you to see that. I've seen people completely surrender to death, and in that surrender, they were healed.

"In my own case, I'm both fighting for my life *and* accepting my death at the same time. And I'm going to live, really live, until I die—whether it's today, tomorrow, next month, or next year. That's all anyone can do."

She looked at me, and I think she could sense my frustration, and how much I wanted to help her.

"There are no guarantees in this life," she said. "We all live the best way we know how. I listen to, and trust, the messages from my Basic Self. But sometimes, in spite of everything—" She finished her sentence with a shrug.

"How do you deal with that—with knowing that at any time . . . "

"I don't fear death; I understand it far too well. But I do love life! And the more laughter and fun I have, the more energy my Basic Self gives me to keep right on dancing." She squeezed both my hands. "You've given me some fun *and* some laughs, these last few days!" she said. My eyes started to sting. As tears spilled over, we embraced.

"Come on," she offered, "I'll walk you home."

"No!" I said quickly. "I mean—I can find my way. You get some rest."

"That sounds appealing," she said, stretching and yawning.

As I turned to go, she called to me and said, "Now that you mention it, there is something you can do for me."

"Name it."

"I have some errands to run, people to see. You can assist me, if you like—carry my extra pack, that sort of thing. You doing anything tomorrow?"

"I'll check my appointment book," I said, happy for the invitation.

"Okay!" she responded. "See you then. And, Dan, please, don't be troubled by this." Then, with a little wave, she turned away. I walked slowly down her front steps to find the path back to my cabin. As I headed down through the trees, I wondered if I would ever feel the way she did—helping others just for the love of it, with no thought of myself. Then something else occurred to me. Was it possible that Socrates sent me here not only to receive her help but to somehow help her as well? It struck me once again: He worked at a service station—a *service* station.

By the time I got back to the cabin, two things felt clear: first, that Socrates had indeed sent me here to learn how to serve; second, that I had a lot of paying back to do.

The next morning, bright and early, I heard the loud chirp of a bird right in my ear, and felt a tiny weight on my chest. I opened my eyes cautiously, and saw Redbird, Mama Chia's friend, the apapane bird. "Hello, Redbird," I said quietly, not moving. He just tilted his head, gave another chirp, and flew out the window.

"I see the early bird got here before me," Mama Chia said as she entered, gesturing toward a tree just outside, where he was singing.

"I'm ready to go," I said, tying my shoes, remembering

that I'd promised myself not to act gloomy and maudlin around her. "What's first?"

"Breakfast." She handed me some fresh bread, still warm.

"Thanks!" I said, sitting on the bed and munching. "By the way, I've been meaning to ask you, does this cabin belong to you?"

"It was a gift; Sachi's father built it a few years ago."

"Pretty nice gift," I said with my mouth full.

"He's a pretty nice guy."

"So when do I meet him?"

"He's away, working on a building job. There's not much construction on Molokai these days, so when an opportunity comes up . . . " She shrugged.

"Where's Sachi been?"

"She ought to be along any minute now; I said she could come along."

"Good; I really like that young lady."

Sachi walked in, blushing as she heard this.

Mama Chia picked up one backpack, and pointed to the one I was to carry. I reached down. "Whoa, this is heavy," I said. "Is it full of rocks, or what?"

"As a matter of fact, it is," she said. "I wanted to bring Fuji and Mitsu some choice stones—for their rock garden. And the exercise will do you good."

"If it gets too heavy for you, I can carry it," Sachi volunteered with a dimpled smile.

"If it gets too heavy, you can carry *me*." I grinned back, and turned to Mama Chia. "Isn't Fuji the photographer you told me about? Didn't he and his wife just have a baby?"

"Yes. Now he does landscape gardening—works at Molokai Ranch. Very handy with tools."

Fuji and Mitsu greeted us with warmth and courtesy, and introduced us to their infant son, Toby, who was unimpressed, and sound asleep. "He arrived only a few weeks ago, with Mama Chia's help," Fuji announced.

"The same is true of me. I hope his trip here was easier than mine," I said, grinning at Mama Chia and slipping the rock-filled pack off my back. I placed it on the porch with a thud.

"Rocks for your garden," Mama Chia explained to Fuji while I stretched my arms and shoulders. Then she offered, mostly for my benefit, "If they aren't exactly what you want, we'll be glad to take them back."

One look at my expression, and they all laughed.

Their cabin was filled with bric-a-brac and memorabilia, neatly arranged on many shelves. I also noticed beautiful photos of the surf and trees and sky—probably taken by Fuji. Surrounded by trees on every side, with hanging plants decorating the walls, it was a beautiful house, a happy house. We heard the squalls of the baby, waking up hungry.

While Mama Chia attended to Mitsu and her newborn son, Fuji offered to give us a tour of the garden. "Mitsu and Fuji have a beautiful garden!" Sachi said enthusiastically.

And so they did: cabbages, cornstalks, rows of beans, and squash. I saw taro root greens sticking up through the soil. Bordering the garden on one side was an avocado tree, and, standing sentry on the other, a fig tree. "We have good potatoes, too!" Fuji said proudly.

I could feel nature spirits all over the place; my Basic Self, I noted, was speaking to me more clearly lately—or maybe I was just listening better.

After our tour, we sat on the porch and talked about landscaping, photography, and other things, until Mama Chia emerged.

When we said good-bye, Fuji made a big point of shaking my hand. "If there's ever anything I can do for you, Dan, please ask."

"Thank you," I said, genuinely liking this man, but not expecting to see him again. "My best to your family."

Mitsu waved from the house, her baby at her breast, and we turned down toward the road.

"We're going to town," Mama Chia told me. "I borrow Fuji's pickup when he doesn't need it."

She squeezed herself behind the wheel of his little truck and moved the seat back so she could breathe. I slid into the passenger side; Sachi hippity-hopped onto the back of the truck. "Hold on for dear life!" Mama Chia yelled out to Sachi, who squealed with delight as we bumped down the dirt and gravel road, to the two-lane main highway.

"Going to town," I thought. "What a phrase." I hadn't seen much of civilization since I walked down that beach toward Makapuu Point, weeks ago. I felt a little silly, but I was actually excited.

The town of Kaunakakai, on the southern side of the island, reminded me of a false-front Hollywood set—a three-block long commercial section, with buildings of wood, brick, and faded paint. A sign at the outskirts read "Pop. 2,200." A wharf stretched about a mile out into the harbor of this seaside town.

Mama Chia went into a store to shop. I waited outside with Sachi, now entranced by a gift shop window display next door. As we stood there, I glanced over at four Hawaiian boys in their late teens as they approached and stopped next to us. Ignoring my Basic Self's "something is wrong here" feeling, I didn't pay much attention to the youths, until one of them suddenly turned and snatched the flower out of Sachi's hair.

She turned to them and said indignantly, "Give me that!"

Ignoring her, he started to pull off the petals, one by one. "She do love me, she don't love me, she do, she don't . . . "

One of the other boys said, "Who cares—she ain' big enough to do nothin' but—"

"Come on, give me the flower," I said, in a show of bravado. Or stupidity. They turned and glared at me; now I'd done it.

"You want dis flowa?" said the biggest of the boys, six inches taller and about a hundred pounds heavier than I, with a beer belly and, I suspected, some muscle under his flabby bulk. "Why don' you take it?" he challenged, grinning at his friends.

As the other young toughs surrounded me, Beer Belly suggested, "Maybe you wanna wear it?"

"Nah," said another punk. "He ain' no queer; I think she his girlfren'," he said, jerking his head toward Sachi, now embarrassed, and a little afraid.

"Just give me the flower!" I commanded—a big mistake.

Beer Belly stepped up and shoved me backward. "Why don' you take it from me, *haole*," he spit.

I grabbed his wrist with one hand, and tried to get the flower. He threw it away and took a swing at me.

The blow glanced off my scalp as I hurried to avoid it. I didn't want to hit this guy; I just wanted to get Sachi out of there. But it had gone too far. I shoved him with all my might. He stepped backward, tripped on a beer can, and fell awkwardly. One of his friends laughed. He came up furious, mad enough to kill, and fully capable of it. But just then, the storekeeper ran out in time to save my skin.

"Hey! You boys!" he yelled as if he knew them. "No fighting around here if you want to come back, you hear?"

Beer Belly stopped, looked at the storekeeper, then glared and pointed at me. With his finger jabbing the air like a knife, he said, "Next time, bro', you dead meat!"

They sauntered off. "You just made a bad enemy," the storekeeper said to me. "What were you fighting over?"

"This," I answered, picking up the flower and blowing it off. "Thanks for chasing them off."

Shaking his head, the storekeeper went back inside, muttering, "Crazy tourists."

As Sachi came over and touched my arm, I realized I was shaking.

"Are you all right?" she said.

"I'm fine," I answered, but I knew that was only partly true. My Conscious Self had stayed cool, but my Basic Self was shaken up. Ever since I was a little boy, I'd been told, "Never fight! Never fight!" by an idealistic mother in a not-so-idealistic world. I had no brothers, and I just didn't know how to cope with physical confrontations. I wished Socrates had taught me some of his martial arts.

"I'll be okay," I repeated. "How are you doing?"

"Okay, I guess," she said.

I handed her the flower. "Here—nearly as good as new."

"Thanks." She smiled, then her smile faded as she watched the rowdy gang walking away. "I've seen them before; they're just bullies. Let's go inside. I think Mama Chia's done."

As I carried the groceries to the truck, I looked around for those boys, and resolved to learn how to defend myself, and protect others, if necessary. The world could be a dangerous place, and people weren't always nice. If it wasn't a street punk, it might be someone else; I couldn't ignore this area of my life. If that storekeeper hadn't come out . . . I vowed never to let something like this happen again.

"You two have a good time?" Mama Chia asked as we got into the truck.

"Sure," I said, giving Sachi a look. "I even got to make some new friends."

"That's good," she said, smiling. "After we put away these groceries, I'm going to introduce you to some special people."

"That's nice," I said automatically, not having the faintest notion about who they might be.

By late afternoon, our errands complete, we returned Fuji's truck. Sachi hopped out of the back and, with a "See you later!" took off with a running start, up the dirt road.

"The keys are in the truck!" Mama Chia called to Fuji with a wave of her hand, and we started up the path to her cabin. I insisted on carrying most of the groceries—three large bags—but left Mama Chia with one small bag. "I don't see why I have to carry this bag," she whined loudly. "After all,

I am an important kahuna shaman and your elder—and you could easily have carried this in your teeth, or between your legs."

"I am a lazy person," I confessed, "but I know you'll free me from my slothful ways."

"The slothful warrior," she said. "I like it; it has a certain ring."

I helped her put the groceries away, then headed out the door. I heard Mama Chia call after me, "I'll meet you at your cabin in about an hour."

17

Courage of the Outcast

If I am not for myself,
Who will be for me?
And if I am only for myself,
What am I?
And if not now, when?
Hillel, *Sayings of the Fathers*

As it turned out, this hike was nearly as far as the previous one, but in the opposite direction. But this time we hitched a ride part way with a Molokai rancher up a long dirt road, nearly to the ridge, and from there stayed on the trail until it dropped steeply, then climbed again.

Every time Mama Chia started breathing hard, I asked her how she was doing. When I did this the fourth or fifth time, she turned to me and, as close to angry as I'd seen her, said, "If you ask me how I'm doing one more time, I'm sending you back home with a swift kick! You understand?"

In the late afternoon, as we cleared a final rise, Mama Chia stopped quickly and put her arm out to halt me, too. If she hadn't, the next moment I might have had a short-lived career as a bird. We stood at the edge of a cliff, dropping a thousand feet down to a dramatic view: clouds floated past a blue-green sea, and an albatross glided across the surf far below. My eyes followed the soaring bird until I noticed some kind of settlement, surrounded by tall palms. "Kalaupapa," she pointed.

"What's down there?" I asked.

"A key to the elevator."

I only had a moment to consider this before Mama Chia

turned and stepped down into a hole in the earth. As I caught up with her, I found my footing on some kind of hidden stairwell in the cliff face. It was steep and dark. We didn't talk at all; it was all I could do to stay on my feet.

As she led me down the stairwell, we were treated to a dancing play of light and shadow as beams of sunlight penetrated the holes in this winding staircase. Finally, we emerged from the cliff wall into the sunlight and descended farther, relying on handholds to avert a fatal plunge to the rocks below.

"Only a few people use this trail," she said.

"I can understand why; are you sure you're okay—"

Shooting me a fierce glance, she interrupted. "There's a mule trail, but it has twenty-six switchbacks. This is quicker."

We said nothing more until we rounded a steep bend and walked down into a broad valley between the higher ridges, the cliffs, and the sea. Lush foliage and rows of trees bordered a small settlement ahead, and, beyond that, sand and water. Orderly rows of barracklike apartments, simple and sparse, and some small cottages stood by the sea amidst the palm trees. Even in this sheltered cove, the settlement was more spartan than luxurious—more like an army outpost than a vacation getaway.

As we drew closer, I saw a few people outside. Some older women were working in what looked like a garden area; a lone man, also older, was working with some kind of grinding machine—I couldn't quite make it out from this distance.

As we drew near and walked through the settlement, people looked up at us, with friendly, but often scarred, faces. Most turned toward us and nodded, smiling at Mama Chia—apparently a familiar face here—while others remained intent on their work. "These are the lepers of Molokai," Mama Chia whispered softly as a warm drizzle passed over us. "First abandoned here, out of fear and ignorance—quarantined and left to die—in 1866. In 1873, Father Damien came here and served this community until he contracted the disease and died sixteen years later," she said.

"He died of the disease? It's catching?"

"Yes, but it's not easy to catch; I wouldn't worry about it."

Despite her assurance, I *was* worried about it. Lepers! I had only seen them portrayed in biblical movies, when Jesus performed healing miracles. *He* wasn't worried about catching anything, but then, he was *Jesus—and I* was *worried.*

"There are conventional doctors who serve these people," she said quietly as we walked into the village. "Though the lepers are, for the most part, full-blooded Hawaiians, many are Christian, and don't believe in *huna* medicine. But there are a few I counsel. These are the people who have had unusual dreams or experiences—things their doctors don't understand."

Trying not to stare, I saw a few people with obvious disfigurements: One woman sat in a chair, reading; she had only a tiny stump for a leg. A man was missing both hands, but that didn't stop him from grinding something with an electric tool. "He makes fine jewelry—silver dolphins," Mama Chia said.

More people emerged from their bungalows as word of our arrival spread. The youngest person I saw was in his forties. His head was bandaged. An older woman with scraggly hair came up to us and smiled; there were sores on her face, and she was missing a few teeth.

"Aloha," she said to Mama Chia, then to me. Her smile was bright, friendly, and curious. To Mama Chia, she gestured with her head toward me. "Who dis *kane* [man]?"

"He's come make *kokua* [help]," Mama Chia replied in her best pidgin English. "My packhorse," she added proudly, pointing to me and generating a beaming, if fragmented, smile from the crone. "Maybe he stay a few days, help out—only way I get these good-looking boys out of my hair," she added for good measure. The old woman laughed and said something in Hawaiian. Mama Chia raised her eyebrows and laughed heartily at this.

Puzzled, I turned to Mama Chia. "Did you say we're staying a few days?" That was the first I'd heard of it.

"*We're* not staying; *you* are."

"You want me to stay here a few days? Is this really necessary?"

Mama Chia looked at me a little sadly, but said nothing. I felt ashamed, but I had absolutely no desire to stay here.

"Look, I know you mean well, and it might be good for me and all that, but there are people who like to do this kind of thing—like that Father Damien—but, the truth is, I've never been the type to hang around hospitals or soup kitchens. I respect people who do those things, but it's just not my calling, you know?"

She gave me that look again, and the silent treatment.

"Mama Chia," I tried to explain, "I jump backward if someone *sneezes* in my direction. I don't like to hang around illnesses. And you're suggesting I stay here and mingle with lepers?"

"Absolutely," she said, and turned toward a cottage down on the beach. I followed her to some kind of central building, a dining hall.

Just before we stepped inside, she said to me: "Except for the doctors and priests, visitors here are not common. Your eyes will be a mirror for these people; they are sensitive to you. If you look at them with fear or revulsion, that is how they will see themselves. Do you understand?"

Before I could answer, we were surrounded by several men and women who rose from their food, obviously glad to see Mama Chia, who took her backpack from me and brought out a package of nuts and what looked like some kind of fruitcake she had baked. "This is for Tia," she said. "Where's Tia?"

People were coming up to me, too. "Aloha," said one woman, touching me lightly on the shoulder. I tried not to shrink back, and noticed both her hands looked normal. "Aloha," I answered, smiling on the outside.

Just then, I noticed people making way for a woman, the youngest I had seen here—in her late thirties, I guessed. She looked about six months pregnant. It was a sight to watch her and Mama Chia attempt to hug. Smiling, they approached each other warily, smiling and leaning sideways, like two blimps trying to dock.

Tia actually looked very pretty, even with a crippled hand and a bandaged arm. Mama Chia then gave her the cake. "This is for you—and the baby," she said.

"Mahalo!" Tia said, laughing, then turned to me. "This is your new boyfriend?" she asked Mama Chia.

"No!" she declared. "You know my boyfriends are better looking—and younger." They laughed again.

"He insisted on coming here to help out in the garden for a few days; he's a strong boy and was glad to hear the rule that volunteers work until dark." Mama Chia turned toward me, and with a flourish said, "Tia, this fella named Dan."

Tia hugged me warmly. Then she turned back to Mama Chia: "I'm so glad to see you!" With another hug—they had it down now—she walked off to show Mama Chia's cake to the others.

We sat down to eat. A woman offered me a tray of fresh fruit; she was very gracious, but I couldn't help noticing that she had only one eye on a scarred face. I wasn't very hungry, and was about to tell her so, when I looked up into her one eye. And we made some kind of contact; her eye was so clear, and bright—for a moment, I think I saw her soul in there, and it looked just like mine. I accepted what she offered. "Mahalo," I said.

Later, while Mama Chia and I sat alone on two old wooden chairs, I asked her, "Why was that woman Tia so grateful for a cake?"

She laughed, "That wasn't about the cake—though I do make wonderful cakes! She was grateful because I've found a home for her baby."

"You what?"

She looked at me as if I were very dense, and she was

going to have to move her lips very slowly. "Did you notice that there are no children here? None are allowed, because of the disease. Children born of lepers do not usually have the disease, but they are more susceptible, so they cannot live here. That's perhaps the saddest thing of all, because these people have a special affection for children. Two months before the birth of a child, the woman must leave, have it elsewhere, and say good-bye."

"You mean Tia won't see her child—she has to give it up?"

"Yes, but I found a family not too far away. She'll be able to visit her child; that's what she's so happy about." Mama Chia stood abruptly. "I have people to see, and things to do, so I'll see you around."

"Wait a minute! I didn't say I was staying."

"Well, are you?"

I didn't answer right away. We walked in silence, down toward some bungalows, and the beach area a few hundred yards farther. Then I asked, "Do you come here to teach them?"

"No, to learn from them." She paused, searching for words. "These are ordinary people, Dan. Were it not for their disease, they would have been working in the cane fields, selling insurance, practicing medicine, working in banks—whatever other people do. I don't want to idealize them; they have the typical problems and same fears as anyone else.

"But courage is like a muscle; it gets stronger with practice. People don't test their spirit until they're faced with adversity. These people have faced some of the hardest emotional as well as physical battles: Ostracized by fearful people, they live in a village without the laughter of children. The word 'leper' has become synonymous for 'one who is turned away from,' avoided—a pariah—abandoned by the world. Few have faced as much, and few have shown such spirit.

"I'm attracted anywhere there's a lot of spirit. That's why I've taken a special interest in these people—not as a healer—as a friend."

"Aren't they the same thing?"

"Yes," she smiled. "I suppose they are."

"Well, I guess I can be a friend, too. I'll stay—but just for a few days."

"If you grit your teeth and just put in your time, you'll have wasted it. This week is about opening your heart—as much as you can."

"A week? I thought you said a few days!"

"Aloha," she said, tossing me a bottle of sunscreen and heading off to visit a nearby settlement. Shaking my head, I turned and walked back down toward the row of cottages, thinking about adversity, and about spirit.

I found my way to the main hall, and entered. It turned out to be the infirmary, full of strange smells and people in beds, and behind curtains. A very lean, emaciated man about Mama Chia's age took me by the arm. "Come," he said, releasing my arm as we left the infirmary, indicating I should follow him.

Then he pointed to another larger, barrack-style building. "Where you eat. Later," he said. Then, pointing to himself, he added, "My name—Manoa."

"Aloha," I said. "Glad to meet you, Manoa." Not sure he understood me, I pointed to myself: "Dan."

He extended a stump with three fingers to shake hands; I hesitated only a moment. He smiled warmly, nodding as if he understood, then gestured for me to follow.

We walked to a large plot of earth, now being cleared. Someone else greeted me, handed me a hoe, and pointed to a section of earth. That was that.

I spent the rest of that day, until nightfall, working in the garden. Disorienting as it was, I felt glad to have a clear task to do—to be helping out—giving something for a change.

Manoa showed me where I'd sleep; at least I had my own room. I slept well and woke up hungry.

In the main dining hall, I sat across from some people

who smiled at me, but spoke mostly to one another in Hawaiian with a bit of pidgin English. Everyone at my table was friendly, handing me food again and again, while I tried to ignore their lesions.

That day, we—the gardening crew and I—made good progress, turning and breaking the soil, as rainsqualls passed over and were gone. I was careful to wear the sunscreen, and someone had loaned me a wide-brimmed hat.

The first few days were the hardest—the strangeness of being alone in this different world. The residents seemed to understand this. Another day passed in that garden. I was getting used to the routine.

Though nothing changed outwardly, something shifted inside me. As the people of this colony had come to accept their lives, I came to accept them, too, not as "lepers," but as people. I stopped being an observer, and started to feel a sense of community.

After this, I was able to tune in to a special camaraderie here, born of isolation; from their own suffering came a deeper compassion for the pain of the world.

The next morning, returning from the latrine area, I saw an old man with twisted, deformed feet, making his way across the compound, trembling as he leaned on a pair of crutches. Just then, one of the crutches broke and he fell. I ran over to help him up. He waved me off, muttering something and smiling a toothless smile, then stood by himself. Holding the broken crutch in one hand, he hobbled, on the other one, off toward the infirmary.

There was no more work to be done in the garden until the seed arrived, but I was able to find plenty to do—in fact, I was busy morning till night—carrying water, helping change bandages. Someone even asked me to cut his hair, which I botched, but he didn't seem to mind at all.

All the while we chattered and laughed, half understanding each other. Tears come to my eyes as I write this, but strange as it seems, these were among the most satisfying days I'd ever spent. It was all very ordinary, and very human. Just helping. For those few days, I was simply one of them.

So it was that on the fifth day I felt a compassion I had not experienced before. Ever. And I understood Mama Chia's purpose. On that day I stopped worrying about getting "tainted" by the disease, and started wanting, really *wanting,* to be of service, any way I could.

My heart was opening. I searched for something more I could contribute. I couldn't teach gymnastics; most of them were too old. I didn't have any other special skills that I knew of.

Then, as I walked past a peaceful area just off the central compound, it came to me: I'd help make a pond. That was it! Something of beauty I could leave behind.

I'd worked for a landscape gardener one summer, and had learned the basics. I found out that the community had some bags of concrete stored in a shed, and all the tools we needed. A picture formed in my mind: the vision of a beautiful, serene pond, a place to sit and meditate, or just take a brief rest. The ocean was just a few hundred yards away, but this pond would be special.

I showed a sketch to Manoa; he showed it to some of the others. They agreed it was a good idea, and a few men and I began digging.

The next day, just when we were ready to mix the concrete, Mama Chia showed up: "Well, Dan, the week is up; I hope you've stayed out of mischief."

"No! It hasn't been a week!" I said.

She smiled. "It's been a week all right."

"Well, you see—look, we're right in the middle of a project. Can you come back in a few days?"

"I don't know," she said, shaking her head. "We have other things to do—your training . . . "

"Yes I know, but I'd really like to finish this."

Mama Chia sighed and shrugged her shoulders. "Then

we may not have time for a special technique to get in touch with—"

"Just a few more days!"

"Have it your way," she said, turning toward one of the bungalows. I caught a glimpse of her face. She looked positively smug. I only gave it a moment's reflection before lifting another bag of concrete.

Mama Chia returned just in time to see us complete the stonework. And the moment it was done, I knew it was time to leave. Several men came up to shake my hand. We'd formed a bond based on working on a common goal, sweating together—a bond men must have experienced for thousands of years. It felt good.

I was going to miss them all. I felt even closer to these outcasts from society than to my professional colleagues back in Ohio. Maybe because I had always felt like an outcast, too. Or maybe it was because of our shared task, or their openness, directness, and honesty. These men had nothing left to hide. They weren't trying to look good or save face. They had dropped their social masks, allowing me to drop mine, too.

I was turning to leave with Mama Chia, when Tia came over and hugged both of us. I hugged her tenderly, feeling her sorrow and courage, knowing that she would soon have to give up her baby.

As Mama Chia led me down toward the beach, other feelings surfaced, too: All the gratitude, sorrow, and love for Mama Chia I had set aside these past ten days flooded back in. Facing her, I placed my hands on her shoulders and looked into her eyes.

"You've been so good to me," I told her. "I wish there were something more I could do for you . . . " I had to take a slow, deep breath to hold off my sorrow. "Mama Chia, you're such a kind person—it just doesn't seem fair! And I don't feel I deserve all this—the time, the energy, the life you've given me. How can I possibly thank you—how can I ever repay you?"

In answer, Mama Chia hugged me for a long time. I embraced this old woman in a way I'd never been able to hold Socrates, and I cried.

Then, stepping back from our embrace, she flashed me a bright smile: "I *love* what I do—someday you will understand this. And what I do is not for you, not even for Socrates, so thanks are neither necessary nor appropriate. I act for a larger cause, a bigger mission. By assisting you, I'll be assisting many others through you. Come," she said. "Let's go for a walk on the beach."

I surveyed the village, now back to its normal routine, and I felt inspired by the aloha spirit of these people. I saw them with different eyes than those I had come with. Even though other memories might fade, this would remain one of the most vivid—more real, and lasting, than any vision.

18

Illuminations in the Dead of Night

The seed of God is in us:
Pear seeds grow into pear trees;
Hazel seeds into hazel trees;
and God seeds into God.
Meister Eckehart

Neither of us said much as we walked along the stretch of white sand; we just listened to the rush of waves, and the shrill cries of the albatross, patrolling the coast. Mama Chia scanned the horizon, watching the long shadows cast by the late afternoon sun like a cat, seeing things not visible to most of us. I examined the driftwood, pushed far up onto the beach by an unusually high tide, generated by a storm the night before. I combed the beach, looking for shells. Sachi wouldn't be impressed by shells, but Holly would like them. My little daughter, I thought, picturing Holly's sweet face, and missing her. I thought of Linda, too, and wondered if perhaps our lives were meant to go separate ways.

Glancing back, I saw the shadows cut across our meandering trail of footprints in the wet sand. I gazed down, searching for souvenirs from the sea, and Mama Chia continued to scan the horizon, and the stretch of beach ahead.

We sloshed out into knee-deep surf to go around a rocky point. She took a deep breath and I thought she was going to tell me something. But Mama Chia was reacting to one of the saddest and strangest sights I'd ever beheld: *Thousands* of starfish, washed up by the recent storm, littered the beach. Beautiful five-pointed stars, pink and tan, lay in the hot sand, drying out and dying.

I stopped in my tracks, awestruck by this massive marine graveyard. I'd read about grounded whales and dolphins, but I had never actually seen one. Now, confronted by thousands of dying creatures, I felt numb and helpless.

Mama Chia, however, without missing a single limping step, walked over to a nearby starfish, bent over, picked it up, walked to the water's edge, and placed it in the water. She then walked back and picked up another little star, and returned the creature to the sea.

Completely overwhelmed by the sheer numbers of starfish, I said, "Mama Chia, there are so many—how can what you're doing make any difference?"

She looked up at me for a moment as she lowered another starfish into the sea. "It makes a difference to this one," she replied.

Of course she was right. I picked up a starfish in each hand, and followed her example. Then I delivered another two into the sea. We continued through the afternoon and into the evening, under the light of the moon. Many starfish died, anyway. But we did our best.

Mama Chia kept bending down, again and again and again. But there was nothing I could say to dissuade her. She would live until she died. And as long as I was here, on the island, I would help her. We worked long into the night. Finally, bone weary but feeling good, we lay in the soft sand, and slept.

I awoke and sat up abruptly, thinking it was dawn. But the light that flickered in my eyes was a crackling fire, with Mama Chia sitting nearby, her back to me.

"Couldn't sleep?" I said as I approached, so as not to startle her.

"Had enough sleep," she said, never taking her eyes from the fire.

I stood behind her and massaged her shoulders and back. "What do you see in the fire?" I asked, without expecting a reply.

"What if I told you I wasn't from this planet?" she asked.

"*What?*"

"Suppose I told you that neither was Socrates? Or you?"

I didn't know what to say—whether to take her seriously. "Is that what you saw in the fire?" was all I could think to ask.

"Sit down," she said. "See for yourself."

I sat, and gazed into the dancing flames.

Mama Chia rose slowly, and began to knead the muscles of my back with her strong hands. "You asked me why I've been here for you. It's because we're family," she revealed. "Part of the same spiritual family."

"What do you mean—" I never got to finish my sentence. Mama Chia gave me a solid whack at the back of my neck. I saw stars, then only the fire . . . deeper . . . deeper . . .

I saw the beginnings of time and space, when Spirit became the "ten thousand things": the star forms, the planets, and the mountains, the seas, and the creatures great and small that spawned there.

But there were no humans. Before history, in a time of magic, when Mind allowed it, the legends were born. The animals evolved on earth, growing from all that preceded them. But no human souls existed on the planet.

I saw a vision of the ancient universe, where, within the curves of space, angelic souls played in realms of freedom and bliss. This memory, stored within the most ancient records of the psyche, became the archetype for that place we call heaven.

A wave of these souls came down to earth because they were curious about the material realm—about the animal forms, and about sexual-creative energy—about what it would be like in a body.

And so, they overshadowed the primitive forms of animals that roamed the earth; they entered them, saw through their eyes, felt through their skin, and experienced the material realm and life on earth.

I saw them, I felt them, as they grew ready to leave their animal hosts, and return to their Source. But these souls misjudged the magnetic attraction of the material realm; they became trapped, identified with the animal consciousness. Thus began a great adventure on this planet.

These soul energies, and their humanlike higher consciousness within the animals, impacted the DNA structure, causing immediate and radical evolutionary leaps. This was revealed to me in visions within the genetic spirals themselves.

The next generation of creatures provided the basis for the Greek myths—centaurs, mermaids, satyrs, and nymphs; half animal, half human, they were the source of legends, the Olympian gods cohabiting with animals and humans.

The first wave had forgotten that they were of Spirit, not of flesh; they had become identified with their hosts. So a wave of missionary souls came down to rescue the first wave, to pull them out. But they, too, were trapped.

Time flashed by, centuries in an instant. A second rescue mission was sent; this time, only the most powerful souls made the attempt—and very few escaped. They, too, remained, trapped by their own desire for power. They became the kings, the queens, the pharaohs, and the chiefs—the rulers of the lands of earth. Some were like King Arthur; others, like Attila the Hun.

A third and final rescue mission was sent. These very special souls were the most courageous of all—the peaceful warrior souls—because they knew they weren't coming back; they knew they would be destined to live within a mortal body for aeons—suffering, losing loved ones, in mortal pain and fear, until all souls were free.

They were a volunteer mission. And they came to remind all others who they are. They include carpenters, students, doctors, artists, athletes, musicians, and ne'er-do-wells—geniuses and madmen, criminals and saints. Most have forgotten their mission, but an ember still glows within the hearts and memories of those who are destined to awaken to their heritage as the servants of humanity, and to awaken others.

These rescuers are not "better" souls, unless love makes them so. They may be lost, or found. But they are awakening, now. Hundreds of thousands of souls on the planet—becoming a spiritual family.

Suddenly I was shocked back into normal consciousness. I pulled my eyes from the flames and turned to Mama Chia, still sitting next to me.

Still gazing into the fire, she said, "My soul is one of the final rescue mission. So is Socrates', and so is yours. So are the souls of hundreds of thousands of others—all those who feel a call to serve. Think of it! Hundreds of thousands, more coming in all the time, in our children—awakening to who they are and what they are here to do.

"What we all have in common is an almost lifelong feeling of being somehow *different*, of being oddballs, of being strangers in a strange land, never quite fitting in. We feel at times a longing to 'go home,' but we're not exactly sure where that is. We often have giving, but rather insecure, natures.

"Well, we are not here to 'fit in,' as much as we might like to. We are here to teach, to lead, to heal, to remind others, if only by our example.

"The earth has been the school for most human souls, but our souls are not yet completely of this earth. We have been schooled elsewhere; there are things we just know without knowing how we know—things we recognize, as if this is a refresher course, and we are most definitely here on a service mission.

"Your search, Dan, will be for ways to make a difference—first to awaken yourself, then to find the right leverage, the best means to prepare to find the calling most natural and effective in reaching out to others. It is like this for all the peaceful warriors who share this mission. One of us might become a haircutter; another, a teacher; a third, a stockbroker or pet groomer or counselor. Some of us become famous;

others remain anonymous. Each of us plays a part."

We sat there, staring out to sea for a while—I don't know how long—before she spoke again. "So here you are, one of many like-minded souls in very different 'wrapping,' treading water in the ocean of karma, but there's a rowboat nearby—much closer to you than to many others. Before you can help others into the boat, you have to get in yourself.

"And that is what your preparation is about. That is why you met Socrates, and why I am here working with you. Not because you are somehow special or more deserving, but because you have within you that unstoppable impulse to share yourself with others." She paused. "Someday, you will write, teach, and other things, too, to reach out to your spiritual family, to remind them of their mission, to give the clarion call."

The weight of responsibility hit me like a falling safe. "Teach these things? I can't even remember half of what you say. And I've no talent for writing," I protested. "My grades in English weren't so good."

She smiled. "I see what I see."

In another few hours, it would be dawn; the fire had died down to embers when I spoke again. "You say there are many souls like me—"

"Yes, but you combine a particular set of talents and qualities that make you a good transmitter. So you and Socrates found each other, and he sent you to me."

Mama Chia then lay down, curled up, and slept. I stared out to sea until the first hint of the sun lit the sky at the western tip of the island, and sleep finally came.

Morning. Strange, waking up on a beach, the warm tropical air my only blanket. Here the air felt comfortable even at dawn, like a summer morning in the Midwest.

Sleeping in the open air whetted my appetite, and breakfast, courtesy of Mama Chia's bottomless backpack, was both simple and memorable: a handful of figs, a few macadamia nuts, an orange, and a banana. An illuminating night had passed; I wondered what the new day would bring.

As it turned out, the day was uneventful. We spent most of it hiking home, and the evening having tea and listening to music on her old phonograph. Mama Chia retired early; I slept on her living room floor.

The following day, I would meet a ghost. I would also set in motion a series of events that was to change the course of my life.

19

Revelation and the Warrior's Way

Take time to deliberate;
but when the time for action arrives,
stop thinking and go in.
Andrew Jackson

It came out of nowhere, on an ordinary day, as surprises do. It came from seeds planted in the past. "I thought you might like to meet Sachi's family," Mama Chia said as we walked along an unfamiliar path into the forest. Why was she smiling like the Cheshire cat?

Half a mile later, we entered a clearing where a lovely house stood, larger than Mama Chia's but similar in design, with a garden to the side.

A little boy, about five years old, emerged, jumped down the two steps, and ran straight at me, down the path. With a "Hi, Dan!" he jumped up into my arms, laughing, as if he'd known me all my life.

"Well, hi . . . "

"My name's Socrates," he said proudly.

"Really?" I said, surprised. "Well, that's a very important name." I looked up to see a small, slim woman, very lovely, wrapped in a deep blue, flowered sarong, following her son. But she had no intention, it turned out, of jumping into my arms.

Smiling graciously, she held out her hand. "Hello, Dan, I'm Sarah."

"Hello, Sarah. I'm glad to meet you." I glanced at Mama Chia, quizzically. "Does everyone around here know me?" I asked.

Mama Chia, Sarah, Sachi, and little Socrates all laughed

with delight; I didn't understand what was so funny, but they were certainly enjoying something.

"Sachi and Soc's father has told them a lot about you," Mama Chia said, pointing behind me.

I turned, "Well, who is he?"

"Hello, Dan," a voice interrupted me.

I turned and stared, then gaped, my jaw open wide. I had never seen a ghost before. But there he was—tall and slim, with a soft blond beard, deep-set eyes, and a warm smile. "Joseph, is that really you?"

He just grabbed me and gave me the biggest bear hug I'd had in years. Then I stepped back. "But—but, Socrates told me you died—of leukemia!"

"I did not!" his little boy yelled.

We all laughed again. "Not you, Socrates—an older man, years ago," I said.

"Dead?" he said, still smiling. "Well, I *am* a little tired, and you know how Socrates can exaggerate!"

"What happened?" I asked. "How . . . "

"Why don't you two go for a walk?" Sarah suggested. "You have some catching up to do!"

"Good idea," Joseph answered.

As we walked slowly into the forest, Joseph cleared up the mystery of his apparent death.

"I did have leukemia," he confirmed. "I still do, but with Mama Chia's help, my body is handling it okay.

"But in a way, Socrates was right. I did die to the world. For several months. I became a renunciate, a hermit. I told him I was going to disappear into the forest, fast, and pray, until I healed, or died. Come to think of it," he said, "I'd better go back a few years to fill you in.

"I was raised in the Midwest by a family of strangers. I'll always be grateful to them for getting me through my childhood diseases—all those nights I kept them up—and for giving me food and shelter. But I never felt I belonged; I felt somehow different, you know?"

"Yes," I said. "I know."

"So the first chance I got, I hit the road—worked my way across the country, headed out toward the West Coast, doing odd jobs, mostly. And when I got to L.A., I just kept going. I ended up here, on Molokai. I had a friend who lived here. He encouraged me to settle. So I became a young 'agricultural entrepreneur,' and cultivated cannabis—"

"You grew marijuana?"

"Yes. That was 1960, and it just seemed like the thing to do. I don't do that anymore, because—well, now it just doesn't seem like the thing to do.

"Now I build cabinets, bureaus—some carpentry—that sort of thing. Pays the bills and keeps me out of mischief." He smiled. "Anyway, back then, I made a lot of money, and about that time, I married Sarah. In 1964, Sachi was born, and"—Joseph paused here—I think it pained him to recall it—"I just split. I . . . " Joseph searched for the right words. "Dan, you understand about the three selves, right?"

I nodded. "I'm acquainted with my Basic Self, but I sort of lost touch with my Higher Self," I answered.

"Just the opposite with me," said Joseph. "I rejected my Basic Self. All I wanted was to be up and out of here. I couldn't cope with the hassles of daily life here on planet earth. I told myself I was a 'spiritual being,' a 'creative artist' who didn't have to deal with 'reality.' I spent most of my time meditating, communing with nature, reading—all the time hoping to go 'somewhere else'—anywhere I wouldn't have to deal with the drudgery, the details, the *physicality* of the material realm.

"Then, when Sachi came along—I wasn't ready to have children, to work on a relationship or responsibilities; I didn't know how to deal with it. So I took half our funds and split. I didn't know where to go, but I ended up in Berkeley, California, and after a few weeks, I ran into this old guy—"

"At a gas station," I laughed, completing Joseph's sentence for him.

"You can imagine the rest. Socrates insisted I get responsible work before he'd teach me, so I started the café. We made a deal," he said. "I fed him some good food, and he turned my life upside down."

"Sounds fair to me." I grinned.

"More than fair," Joseph agreed. "I got my money's worth; he really kicked my ass. I haven't seen him for about five years, though. Went back to visit two years ago, but he'd gone. He once said something about going to the mountains, maybe somewhere in the Sierras—I don't know. I doubt we'll see him for a while."

"Well, how did you turn it around? I mean, you came back here, made a go of your relationship—you build cabinets, maintain a business . . . "

Joseph smiled at me as I counted all the responsible things he did on my fingers. "It still isn't easy," he said. "But do you remember what Soc used to remind us? You know, about a chain breaking at its weakest link—and so do we? Well, I just decided I'd better work on my weak links."

"I still have my work cut out for me," I said. "But I'm really not sure how to 'work on' getting into my heart. Mama Chia said it had to come of its own accord."

Joseph paused, thoughtful, and said, "I think it's just a matter of becoming more and more aware. That awareness alone can set in motion any kind of healing—physical or mental or emotional—quite naturally."

We sat quietly for a while, then I reminded him, "You said you were ill."

Startled out of reverie, Joseph replied, "Yes—and I had intended to go to the mountains to fast and pray, as I told you. But then I remembered something Socrates had told me about life being hard either way, whether you space out and give up, or whether you go for it. Well, it sank in. I realized that the mountain hermit thing would just be another way to get out of the body, to escape. I probably would have died.

"But I decided to return to Molokai, come what may, to take up where I'd left off—but do it right—with as much time as I had left to do it in, if Sarah would have me back.

"She welcomed me with open arms," he said. "Everything worked out so incredibly," he said. "As soon as I *committed* to coming back and digging in and going for it, it all fell into place."

"What do you mean?"

"That's when I started working with Mama Chia. She taught me, and helped me to heal."

"It sure worked," I said. "I've seen your family."

Joseph gave me a look of complete contentment—a look I envied. And I reflected sadly about the shambles in which I'd left my own marriage and family. But that was going to change, I told myself.

Joseph stood slowly. "I'm glad to see you again, Dan."

"Best thing that's happened to me in a long time," I replied. "And a lot of very good things have happened."

"I believe *that*," he said with a smile.

"Life is amazing, isn't it?" I said, walking him back toward his house. "How we both found our way to Mama Chia."

"It sure is amazing," he echoed. "And so is she."

"Hey, and speaking of amazing, that daughter of yours is a wonder." Then I remembered what had happened in town. "She did get a bit of a scare, though."

"I know; she told me about it. And from what I hear," he said with a wry grin, "*she* wasn't the one who was in trouble."

"You got that right," I declared. "But the incident taught me something; I need to learn some martial arts."

"I'm surprised Socrates never taught you. He was pretty good at it, you know."

"Yes," I smiled. "I know. But I was focused on gymnastics—you remember."

"Oh, that's right." Joseph looked thoughtful, then said, "Well, Fuji used to study some kind of karate. He's a good man. Maybe he can help you, but, Dan, for this situation, I don't think learning to fight is really the answer. I know those boys. They're not really bad kids. Once they helped me push my car half a mile to a gas station. They're just bored, and frustrated. There aren't many jobs; they probably don't feel terribly good about themselves—same old story." He sighed.

"Yeah, I know," I replied. I looked at Joseph. "I'm glad you're alive."

"Me, too," he answered.

As we emerged from the forest and approached Joseph's front steps, little Socrates came running, jumped up into Joseph's arms, then turned his dad's face so they were nose to nose. It was clear he wanted his father's undivided attention.

Joseph kissed Soc on the nose and turned to me. "I'm going back to Oahu tomorrow to complete a job, and, well—I need to spend some time with my family."

"Oh—sure," I said. "Maybe I'll see you when you get back."

"Count on it," he smiled. Sarah came out, too, and put her arm around her husband. They waved as I turned back down the path. I heard Sachiko's voice from their cabin as she called to her family, "Food's ready!"

Walking back to my cabin, I felt a stab of regret as I thought of Linda and Holly. I wondered if I'd ever have a happy family of my own.

That afternoon, wandering through the forest paths, I found my way to Sei Fujimoto's house. Mitsu answered the door. "I just put the baby down," she whispered. "Fuji's not here, but he should be back any time. You want to wait inside?"

"Thanks, Mrs. Fujimoto—"

"Call me Mitsu!"

"Thanks, Mitsu, but I'd like to wait in the garden for a while, if that's okay."

"Play with the garden spirits, eh?" she said, smiling.

"Something like that," I replied.

I had always had a special feeling about gardens, about sitting in the dirt, surrounded by plants. So I lay on my side, feeling the warm, rich earth radiate pleasant heat on my chest and stomach, and I gazed up close at a squash blossom, its yellow flower so delicate, with the most subtle fragrance, waving in the gentle breeze.

And I did feel the garden spirits—a distinctive energy so different from the cold, functional concrete of the cities and sidewalks, expanses of stark gray blocks, with their stiffness and rigidity. Here, I felt at peace . . .

The honk of Fuji's truck brought me back to the business at hand. I walked over to him, waved, and helped him unload some bags of fertilizer to complement his compost pile. "Nice to see you, Dan—glad to have some help."

"Actually, Fuji, I came to ask for *your* help," I said.

He stopped and looked over at me, curious. "How can I help you?"

"Joseph said you used to know some karate."

A smile of recognition passed over his face. "Oh, I see. Yes, I've studied a little of this, a little of that. I'm not as quick now—have to hit the bad guys with bags of fertilizer, or with my car," he joked. "What do you want with karate—somebody you want me to beat up?" His smile broadened as he struck a pose, puffing out his chest in mock bravado.

"No," I laughed. "Nothing like that. It's just that I think I should learn how to defend myself."

"Not a bad idea; you never know when you'll need it," he said. "There's a pretty good school in town—I've stopped by and watched a few times."

"Oh, I don't think I'd be able to take lessons in town right now; I don't have the time."

"What you want to do, take a self-defense pill?" he asked.

"No," I answered, laughing again.

"I was wondering if you could teach me something."

"Me?" He shook his head. "It's been too many years, Dan. I've forgotten more than I know." He took a stance, kicked the air, then held his back, comically. "See what I mean?"

"Fuji, I'm serious. This is important to me."

He hesitated. "I'd like to help you, Dan, but you better study with a real teacher. Besides, I've got to run up to the ranch and mend some fence."

"Well, I've got nothing else to do; how about if I help you with the fence?"

"Okay. Then at least I can teach you the fine art of fencing," he punned. "I'll tell Mitsu we're going."

"And think about the other lessons, too, okay?"

He called back to me: "I don't like to think too much about anything."

We spent the rest of the day mending fences. It was hard work—digging post holes, pounding the uprights, sawing and chopping. Fuji loaned me a pair of his gloves or my hands would have blistered; it reminded me of the old gymnastic days. Mitsu invited me for a vegetarian dinner of steaming rice, vegetables, and tofu. Then the baby's cry was Mitsu's signal to say good night.

"You did a good job, today, Dan," Fuji said, handing me a ten-dollar bill—the first money I'd earned in a while.

"I can't take your money, Fuji."

"Not my money—yours. I don't work for free; neither do you," he insisted, pressing it into my hand.

"Well, then, maybe I can use it to pay you for a martial arts lesson."

Fuji knit his brows in thought before answering. "I could give you one painting lesson, but that wouldn't make you a painter."

"Sure it would!" I smiled. "Just not a very good one!"

Scratching his head as if the idea pained him, Fuji said, "Let me think about it."

"Good enough, and good night."

The next morning, Fuji woke me. "Okay," he said. "I can show you one or two things." I opened my eyes to see him standing over me. "I'll wait outside," he said.

Jumping out of bed, I made a quick pit stop, then emerged from the cabin with shorts on and shirt in hand.

I followed him to a spot of level ground about twenty feet from the cabin, where he turned, and said, "Stand here. Face me."

"Uh, shouldn't we warm up or something?" I asked, accustomed to my old gymnastic habits.

"Don't need a warm-up in Hawaii," he said. "Hawaii *is* a warm-up. Besides, no warm-up required for what we do; we get warmer as we go. Okay?

"Okay; now I'm gonna show you very good martial arts movement." Taking a comfortable stance, he said, "Copy me." He let both arms drop to his sides, then began to bend his right arm at the elbow, raising his hand. I did the same. Then he extended his hand forward, toward me. I mirrored each movement as precisely as I could. As I did this, he reached out with that hand and started shaking mine! "How do you do," he said, grinning, "nice to meet you, let's be friends, okay?"

"*Fuji,*" I said, letting go of his hand. "Quit playing around; I'm serious!"

"Me, too," he assured me. "This is one of my favorite techniques. It's called 'making friends.' I always teach it first."

"Then there's more?" I asked, hopeful.

"Sure, but if the first technique works, you don't need any others. I also have a move called 'handing wallet to thief.' Sometimes avoids pain."

"Fuji, if those bully boys in town ever run into me again, I may not be able to shake hands, and they don't want my wallet; they want my head."

"Okay," he said, serious this time. "I better show you a few things."

"Kicks and punches?"

"No—they hurt people."

Getting frustrated, I asked, "What kind of martial artist are you, anyway?"

"Pacifist kind," he replied. "You hurt other people enough

times, you get tired of seeing blood. Anyway, I can help you with self-*defense,* not offense."

For the next several hours, he proceeded to show me a series of evasive maneuvers, twists, and turns, and ways to shield myself with circular movements of my arms—simple, and elegant. "I like to keep it simple," he said. "Easier to practice."

He told me to visualize actual attackers, larger and meaner than I would ever be likely to meet. Soon, the defensive elements took on a life of their own.

I reached into my pocket and offered him back his ten dollars.

"No," he waved me off. "This wasn't a lesson—this was play. Brought back some good memories. Keep your money—may come in handy."

"Thank you, Fuji."

"Thank you, too, Dan."

We shook hands. "Still my favorite move, that one," he said.

"Fuji," I asked as I walked with him back to his cabin, "did a spry old man with white hair, a friend of Mama Chia's, ever visit around here? His name is Socrates."

Fuji knit his brows, then a smile came to his face. "Yes, I think so—once, some years ago—short white hair, wearing the brightest Hawaiian shirt I ever saw. Must have come from California," he added with a grin. "Very interesting man."

I could just imagine Socrates in a Hawaiian shirt. I wondered if I would ever see my old teacher and friend again.

Book Three
The Great Leap

Anything can be achieved
in small, deliberate steps.
But there are times you need the courage
to take a great leap;
you can't cross a chasm
in two small jumps.

David Lloyd George

20

Odyssey

The secret
of success in life:
Prepare for opportunity
when it comes.
Benjamin Disraeli

As we neared Fuji's house, the stars were just coming out, and the moon was nearly full. Except for the crickets, and a soft wind, the silent forest was asleep.

"You sure you won't stay for dinner?" he asked. "Mitsu is always happy to set out one more plate."

"No, really, I have some things to do," I said, but the truth was, with the baby and all, I didn't want to impose.

Smiling, Fuji started to turn down the path, then stopped, and stared into space. He wasn't smiling anymore.

Just then, I had a kind of premonition—not bad, exactly, but unsettling.

"What is it, Fuji? Do you feel something, too?"

"Yes," he said.

"What could it—" My thoughts naturally drifted to Mama Chia. "Mama Chia?" I said. "Do you think—"

Fuji looked at me. "I'll drop by—just in case."

"I'll go with you," I said.

"No," he replied. "It may be nothing."

"I want to go."

Fuji hesitated, then said, "Okay." We walked quickly up the path toward her house.

The feeling of foreboding grew stronger for both of us

as we drew near her house. "It's probably nothing," I said, trying to convince myself that everything was all right.

We were about to go inside when Fuji spotted her, slumped against a tree, adjacent to the garden. She looked so peaceful there, so still, with the moonlight shining on her closed eyes. Fuji rushed to her side and started to check her pulse.

In shock, I knelt slowly down next to him, and stroked her silver hair. My eyes filled with tears. "I wanted to thank you, Mama Chia," I said. "I wanted to say good—"

We jumped back in surprise as Mama Chia sat up quickly and yelled, "Can't a woman take a nap under the stars anymore?"

Fuji and I looked at each other, delighted. "We thought you—you—" I stammered.

"I was checking your pulse—" Fuji fared no better.

Then she realized what we had assumed. "You thought I'd kicked the bucket, did you? Well, don't worry, I was just practicing. I want to get it right. We may have to rehearse every day until you two can stop acting like bumbling fools!" she laughed.

A very happy Fuji excused himself; dinner was waiting. But before he left, he stopped to give me some good advice. "Dan, about those boys in town—"

"Yes?" I asked.

"Sometimes, the best way to win a fight is to lose it."

"What do you mean?"

"Think about it," he said, then turned and headed home for Mitsu's vegetarian stew.

That night, in Mama Chia's living room, she and I toasted each other's health with several glasses of saki. My system was so clean from the exercise and simple diet that the saki's effect was devastating—which is to say I got even more maudlin than usual. With moist eyes, I swore everlasting devotion to Mama Chia, and said good-bye to her "forever, just in case."

She patted my hand indulgently, smiled, and remained silent.

At some point, I must have fallen asleep on the floor, because that's where I found myself the next morning, my ears ringing like the bells of Notre Dame. I wanted desperately to distance myself from my throbbing head, but there was nowhere to run.

Mama Chia got up looking obnoxiously chipper, and made me one of her "special remedies—worse than death itself."

"Speaking of death," I said, each word sending stabbing pains through me, "I don't think you're the one who's going to die soon—it's me, I can tell—and I hope it's real soon," I added, rolling my eyes. "Oh, I feel sick."

"Stop rolling your eyes," she suggested. "That will help."

"Thanks. I didn't know I was rolling them."

An hour later, I felt much better, much clearer, and with that clarity came a new wave of concern.

"You know, you really scared me last night. I just stood there. I felt helpless—like there was nothing I could do."

Mama Chia sat on a cushion on the floor and looked at me. "Let's get this straight once and for all, Dan. There is nothing you're supposed to do. If you want peace of mind, I suggest you resign as general manager of the universe.

"I'm telling you, Dan, it's homestretch for me—whatever you do or don't do. Maybe tomorrow, maybe a few months—but soon. I'm packed and ready to go," she said, putting her feet on the edge of the couch, and gazing up at the ceiling.

"Mama Chia," I confessed, "when I first came here, I believed I needed you only to tell me where to go next."

She smiled at this.

"But now, I don't know what I could learn that you and Socrates haven't already taught me."

She looked at me. "There's always more to learn; one thing prepares you for the next."

"That school in Japan—where you met Socrates—is that where I'm to go next?"

She offered no response.

"What is it—don't you trust me enough to tell me?"

"These are all fair questions, Dan, and I understand how you feel. But I can't simply hand you a name and an address."

"Why not?"

Mama Chia took a breath as she considered how to respond. "Call it the House Rules," she said. "Or call it a safety device, an initiation. Only those sensitive enough, open enough, are meant to find it."

"Socrates was about as helpful as you in terms of specifics. He told me that if I couldn't find my way to you, I wasn't ready."

"So you understand."

"Yes, but that doesn't mean I like it."

"Like it or not, there's a bigger picture here," she reminded me. "And more people are involved than just you and me and Socrates. We are only a few interwoven threads in a larger quilt. And there are mysteries I don't even try to fathom; I just enjoy them."

"Socrates once gave me a business card," I told her. "It's at home for safekeeping. Below his name, it says, 'Paradox, Humor, and Change.' "

Smiling, Mama Chia said, "That's life, all right. Socrates always did have a way of cutting to the heart of things." Then she touched my arm, and said, "So you see, it's not a matter of whether or not I trust you, Dan. It's more a matter of you trusting yourself."

"I'm not sure what you mean."

"Then trust that, too!"

"But I remember Socrates saying you would show me the way."

"Yes, *show* you the way—not send you a telegram. To find the hidden schools, you have to discover the *Inner* Records. The House Rules don't permit me to tell you directly; I can only train you to see, to help prepare you. The map is inside."

"Inside? Where?"

"The hidden schools are often in the middle of a city, or in a small village—maybe right next door to where you live—not invisible at all. But most people walk right past—too busy visiting the caves in Nepal and Tibet, searching where they expect to find holiness. Until we warriors explore the caves and shadow places within our own minds, we see only our own reflections—and the masters sound like fools, because only fools are listening.

"Now," she continued, "is the time when the invisible becomes visible again, and angels take wing. You are one of these. It has been my duty, my happy duty, to help you along. Like Socrates, I'm a cheerleader to the soul," she said. "We're here to support you, not to make it easy for you.

"*You* have to find the path ahead, as you found me. All I can do is point in the right direction, push you onward, and wish you Godspeed."

She saw my expression. "Relax your brows, Dan. And stop trying to figure everything out. You don't have to know everything about the ocean to swim in it."

"Do you think I'm ready to move on?"

"No, not yet. If you left now—" She left the sentence unfinished, and changed course. "You're almost there—maybe an hour from now, or a few years. I hope to remain here long enough to see you—"

"Make the leap," I finished for her.

"Yes. Because, as I've said, after the fourth floor, it's an express elevator."

"I'd make the leap today, right now, if I knew how," I said, frustrated. "I'd do anything for you, Mama Chia; just tell me what to do!"

"I wish it were that simple, Dan. But it has to come from inside you—like a flower from its seed—you can't rush it. We don't control the timetable.

"In the meantime, just do what feels right; deal with whatever stands in front of you. Use everything to grow, to uplift. Take care of any unfinished business on the lower floors. Face your fears; do whatever you have to do to maximize your health and energy. Channel and discipline that energy; you have to master yourself before you can go beyond that self."

She paused, and took another deep breath before saying, "I've shown you what you need to know. It will help you, or not, depending on what you do with it."

Heavyhearted, I stared at the floor, and said in a hushed tone, almost to myself, "I keep losing teachers. First Socrates sends me away, and now you tell me you'll be leaving soon."

"You don't ever want to get too attached to any one teacher," she said. "Don't mistake the wrapping for the gift. Do you understand?"

"I think I do," I replied. "It means I have another wild goose chase in store—looking for someone without a face in a place with no name."

She smiled. "When the student is ready, the teacher appears."

"I've heard that one before," I said.

"But do you really understand? That statement really means 'When the student is ready, the teacher appears—*everywhere*': in the sky, in the trees, in taxicabs and banks, in therapists' offices and service stations, in your friends and in your enemies. We're all teachers for one another. There are teachers in every neighborhood, in every city, state, and country—teachers for every level of consciousness. As in every field, some are more skilled or aware than others. *But it doesn't matter.* Because *everything* is an oracle; it's all connected; every piece mirrors the Whole, when you have eyes to see, and ears to hear. This may sound abstract to you now, but one day—and that day may not be too far away—you will absolutely understand it. And when you do," she said, picking up a shiny stone, "you'll be able to gaze into this stone, or examine the veins on this leaf, or watch a paper cup blowing in the wind, and you'll understand the hidden principles of the universe."

After pondering this, I asked, "Is there something wrong with human teachers?"

"Of course there is! Because every teacher in a human body is going to have some kind of frailty, eccentricity, or weakness. Maybe the problems are big, and maybe little. Maybe it's sex or food or power—or worse, the teacher may go and die on you." She paused here, for effect.

"But for most people," she continued, "a human teacher is the best game in town—a living example, a mirror. It's easier to understand a human's writing or speaking than the language of clouds or cats or a shaft of lightning in a purple sky.

"Humans, too, have their wisdom to share, but human teachers come and go; once you open the Inner Records, you see it all *directly*, from the inside, and the Universal Teacher appears everywhere."

"What can I do now to prepare myself?" I asked.

Mama Chia paused, grew very quiet, and stared at nothing. Then she turned to me. "I've done what I can to help you prepare."

"Prepare for what?" I asked.

"For what's to come."

"I've never liked riddles."

"Maybe that's why life has given you so many." She smiled.

"How do I know I'm ready?"

"You could know by faith," she said. "But your faith in yourself isn't strong enough. So you need a challenge—a test—to mirror and prove what you have, or haven't, yet learned."

Mama Chia stood, and began pacing across the room, then gazing out the window, then pacing some more. Finally, she stopped, and said to me, "There is a treasure on this island—well hidden from unprepared eyes. I want you to find it. If you do, then you're ready to leave, and go on with my blessings. If not—" She didn't complete the sentence except to say, "Meet me at sunset, tonight, in the forest; I'll explain everything to you then."

Redbird landed on the windowsill outside. Watching him, I said, "I'll be there. Where exactly shall we meet?" When I looked up, she was gone. "Mama Chia?" I called. "*Mama Chia?*" No answer. I searched the house and out in back, but I knew I wouldn't find her, until sunset. But where? And how? That, I sensed, was to be my first task.

I rested most of the afternoon—no telling what I'd have to do after the sun went down. I lay on my bed, too excited to sleep. A part of me kept sorting through the files of everything I'd learned about the three selves and the seven floors of the tower of life; images and feelings kept floating by.

I couldn't even remember how the world looked before I met Mama Chia. I wondered how I saw anything at all. But visions were one thing; real-world tests were another. What did she have in store?

I thought of all the likely, and unlikely, places she would wait, but soon concluded that trying to figure it out would be fruitless.

Then I thought, Basic Selves are in contact, so my Basic Self should know where hers is. I only had to pay attention to its messages through my intuitive sense, my gut feelings. I could home in on her like a Geiger counter! Now I knew how—but could I actually do it?

I knew I'd have to relax my body and clear my Conscious Self in order to sense the messages from my Basic Self. So, in the late afternoon, I found a mound of dirt at the edge of the forest and sat in meditation. Letting my breath rise and fall of its own accord, I let my thoughts, sensations, and emotions rise and fall like waves on the sea. Unperturbed by the currents of the mind, I watched them come, and let them go, without clinging or attachment.

Just before sunset, I rose, stretched, took a few deep breaths, breathing out any tension, concern, or anxiety that might interfere—and strode to the center of the clearing. Stay confident, I reminded myself. Trust the Basic Self; it knows.

First I tried to visualize where she was. I relaxed, and waited for an image. Her face appeared, but it felt like a picture I had constructed from memory, and I couldn't really see her surroundings. Then I listened with my inner ears for some kind of clue, maybe even her voice. But that didn't work either.

As a trained athlete, I had developed a refined kinesthetic sense, acutely aware of my body. So I used this sense, turning slowly in a circle, feeling for a direction. Then my mind intervened: She'll probably be sitting right on her front porch. No, she'll be at the frog pond. Maybe she's in the forest near Joseph and Sarah's, or Fuji and Mitsu's. Or she'll sneak into my cabin and wait for me to give up. Suddenly aware of what I was doing, I threw all that away. This was no time for logic or reason.

Feel it! I told myself. I silently asked my Basic Self to tell me. I waited, still turning slowly. Nothing, and then, "Yes!" In my excitement, I had shouted out loud. I pointed my arm, or it pointed itself—I don't know for certain—and felt an inner confirmation, like gut feelings I'd had in the past, only stronger. My Conscious Self jumped in with all kinds of doubts: This is silly—just your imagination. You can't know this, you're making it up.

Ignoring my thoughts, I followed my arm, up at an angle, to the left of the path toward the ridge. I started walking, and the feeling remained strong. I headed deeper into the forest, off the path, and stopped. I turned, feeling like a blind man, relying on new inner senses. She felt closer; then doubts assaulted me once again.

But the feeling was stronger than my doubts, and it told me she was near. I turned once again in a circle, stopped, and walked forward. Right into a tree. As I touched the tree, it said in a loud voice, "That was too easy; next time, I'll make you wear a blindfold."

"Mama Chia!" I cried, thrilled, stepping around the tree to see her sitting there. "I did it! It worked!" I was jumping up and down. "I didn't *know* where you were; I couldn't have known. But I found you!"

This proved to me that there is more to this world, more to human beings, and more to me, than meets the eye. Actually trusting my Basic Self, and seeing how the Conscious Self could get in the way, brought all the concepts I had learned into focus, and into reality. "This is incredible!" I said. "What a magical world!"

With a considerable but gallant effort, I helped her to her feet and reached around her in a bear hug. "Thank you! That was really fun."

"The Basic Self likes fun," she said. "That's why you feel so much energy."

I soon calmed, however, and told her, "I'll find this treasure, whatever it is, if that's the challenge you have for me. But I don't really have to look anywhere else; you're the treasure. I want to stay here, with you, as long as I can."

"Dan," she said, taking me gently by the shoulders, "this tells me you're close to making the leap, so very close. But I'm not the one you're here to serve. I'm just a *way* station. Remember me with gratitude, if you will. But not for me—for you—because gratitude opens the heart." In the last pink light of the sunset, her face looked beatific as she smiled at me, mirroring back all the love I felt for her.

"And now," she said, "the time has come for you to begin." She sat down once again, took her notepad and a pen out of her pack, and closed her eyes. As I watched her, she just sat and breathed, waiting. Then she began to write in her trembling hand—slowly at first, then faster. When she finished, she handed the note to me. It read:

Over water, under sea,
in the forest high you'll be.
Trust your instinct, in the sea;
bring the treasure home to me.
If you find it, as you might,

you will travel, day and night.
As you see it, you will know,
as above, then so below.
Once you grasp it, you will be
ready then to cross the sea.

I read the note a second time. "What does it mean?" I asked, looking up. She had disappeared again. "*Damn it!* How do you *do* that?" I yelled into the forest. Then, with a sigh, I sat down and wondered what to do next.

So, I was to go on a treasure hunt—some kind of odyssey. Well, I could start in the morning—that made sense. But the riddle said I would travel "day and night." On the other hand, there was no use starting until I knew where I was going. I looked at the riddle again. Clearly, I was to go a number of places: over water, under sea—that part had me baffled—and in the forests, too. Most puzzling was the last part: "As you see it, you will know, as above, then so below."

On an impulse, perhaps hoping for a sign or clue, I decided to hike up into the forest to get a better perspective. A full moon was rising to the east, low on the horizon, but enough to light my way.

"Walking alone in a forest at night playing hide-and-seek with the moon," I sang aloud, in time with my footsteps as I hiked rhythmically up the damp, moonlit path. I felt fresh, alert, and alive. The forest didn't really change much at night, but I did. Mysterious and unaccustomed activity brought my Basic Self to the surface. I enjoyed the excitement.

A warm glow began in my abdomen and, like an expanding energy, bubbled up through my chest so that I had to let out a cry like a bird. "Eeeaaahh," I screeched in a high-pitched tone. I felt like a bird, then like a mountain lion, padding silently through the night. I'd never had a challenge quite like this one.

As I climbed higher, a light sheen of sweat formed on my face and chest in the warm night. And I wondered about the mystery of this life. This magical night seemed unreal, or rather, as real as a dream. Maybe I *was* dreaming. Maybe I fell off that surfboard into the sea; perhaps I was in a delirium in another body, another lifetime, or in my bed in Ohio.

I stopped and surveyed the forest below; the dark trees were highlighted by silver brush strokes of moonlight. No, this wasn't a dream; this was real sweat, and that was a real moon, and I was really tired. Soon, it would be dawn. The ridge was just above—another half hour, maybe. So I pushed on, racing the dawn to the top.

When I made it, breathing hard, I found a sheltered spot and slept until the sun peeked over the rocks and touched my face. I looked out over Molokai. Now what?

Soc's voice came to me then, in my memory. He had been speaking about the koan, an insolvable riddle designed to frustrate the conscious mind. The "solution" or answer was not the right words, but the insight behind them.

I wondered if Mama Chia's riddle was a koan, as well. A part of my mind began to contemplate this question, and would continue contemplating it many hours, whether I was awake or asleep.

Then I thought about shape shifting. Mama Chia had called it a "deep form of empathy." When I was a child, I had played "what-if" games: What if I were a tiger—what would that be like? What if I were a gorilla? And in my own childlike way, I would mimic these beasts, not skillfully, but with real feeling. Maybe that would help me now.

As that idea came to me, I saw an albatross, flying quite low, soaring on a thermal, sitting almost stationary in the air above me. With a shock, I realized that for a single instant I had become the albatross, seeing through its eyes, looking down at me. With a loud caw, the bird flew, in a straight line, as if coasting down an endless slide, toward the town. And I knew the next place I would go—yes—the town of Kaunakakai. What a miraculous night!

Before I started my descent, I surveyed the entire island,

bathed in moonlight. It's perfect that I came here, first, to get an overview, I thought. I was about to leave when I noticed a feather of the albatross at my feet. I picked it up, then felt an ancient urge rising inside me. I was beginning a quest—why not start with a ceremony?

I raised the feather over my head with my left arm, and pointed my right arm to the ground—connecting heaven and earth. I felt, and looked, like the magician card of a tarot deck I remembered. Then, I saluted the North, the South, the East, and the West, and asked the island spirits for assistance.

My Basic Self gave me renewed strength as I headed down, as quickly as my legs could carry me. I stopped only once for a brief rest, in the late morning, picking some papayas on the way, tearing them open, eating them sloppily, with no regard for manners, and tossing the skins to enrich the soil. I walked with a vengeance, with a purpose, although I had no idea yet what it was. Ah, yes, I told myself. Going to town.

A helpful rainsquall washed the papaya juice from my face and hands and chest; then the sun dried me, and the wind blow-dried my hair and beard.

I hitched a ride part way in the back of a pickup truck with "Molokai Ranch" stenciled on the side, and walked the rest of the way to Kaunakakai. I felt quite the rugged mountain man when I sauntered into town—straight into the arms, so to speak, of my recent acquaintance and old nemesis, Beer Belly, along with his companions.

By this time, I wasn't totally grounded, to say the least. Up most of the night, fueled by a few papayas, I felt past tired—approaching slaphappy. As the glow of recognition slowly filled Beer Belly's round face and his fists started clenching, I heard myself say, in my best Gene Autry–Marshall Dillon–John Wayne–Walter Brennan–Gaby Hayes–Gary Cooper voice, "I hear you bin' lookin' fer me, varmits."

This stopped their advance for the moment. "Varmit," mused Beer Belly. "Dis guy called us 'varmits.'"

"I don' think dat's good," one of his larger friends volunteered.

"I don' pay you to think!" their fearless leader announced.

"You don' pay me at all!" Big Fella retorted in a stroke of genius. I noticed that the smallest of these young gentlemen outmatched me by six inches and maybe fifty pounds.

As their discussion continued, Beer Belly recalled his original intent and inspiration: to turn me into poi. Usually you mash up taro root into a white paste, but I would do fine, I believe he surmised, as he stepped forward to clean my chops.

Beer Belly swung and I managed to draw upon enough of my recent training to dodge the blow, rolling with that punch, and the next, and the next. He threw punches like a major-league pitcher—speedballs, curves, and baseline screamers. My Basic Self must have learned its lessons well. Force comes in, get out of the way, I thought, evading each punch.

I was no martial arts master after one lesson. But it had been a very good lesson. And if the truth be known, Beer Belly may have already had a few too many, and was not really at his best.

I had to hand it to this kid; he was persistent. Turning red in the face, huffing and puffing, he tried to swat this hippie *haole* boy, probably from California. And he was failing. In front of his friends.

I continued slipping and bobbing and weaving, starting to feel like Bruce Lee. I even had time to send a silent thanks to Fuji.

Then I remembered something else Fuji had taught me: Sometimes, the best way to win a fight is to lose it.

Instantly, I tuned in to this young fellow, I felt what he was feeling, and I grew sad. This was his domain I had invaded—and fighting was one of the few things he prided himself in, and he was falling apart in front of the only friends he had. As usual, I'd only been thinking about me. Fuji was right. An important part of self-defense is knowing when not to defend the self.

I let down my guard and rolled with the punch as Beer Belly, with one last heroic effort, let loose a right hook that glanced off my cheekbone. It was like getting hit with a flying ham. I heard a loud sound as my head snapped to the side; I saw stars and found myself lying on a pile of scattered trash.

Half sitting up, rubbing my head, I said, “That was one hell of a punch. You have brass knuckles, or what?”

He had saved face. I was the vanquished enemy. I saw his expression change as he held up his fist.

“Deez knuckles are made of *iron*,” he said.

“Help me up, will you?” I said, reaching up. “Let me buy you guys a beer.”

21

Sunlight Under the Sea

In the sea caves,
there's a thirst, there's a love,
there's an ecstasy, all hard like shells,
you can hold them in your palm.
George Seferis, *From the Book of Exercises*

He hesitated, then reached down and pulled me up. "I can drink a lot of beer." He smiled, revealing two missing teeth. As we walked toward the store—the sign over the door said "Spirits"—I rubbed my bruised cheekbone, glad for the ten-spot Fuji had given me since I had almost no other cash. I thought to myself, This is one hell of a way to make new friends.

But make new friends I did. Especially with Beer Belly, whose real name was Kimo. He seemed to take a liking to me, too. The other guys drifted off after my money ran out, but Kimo stayed around. He even offered to buy me one.

"Oh, thanks, Kimo, but I'm full up—hey," I said on impulse, "do you know where I can get hold of a sailboat?" I really don't know where that idea came from, but I was going, as they say, with the flow.

To my surprise, Kimo, who had been staring at the bar and sipping his beer, came alive. His cheeks got more colorful, and he turned to me, excited as a young school kid. "You wanna sail? *I* got a boat! I'm the best sailor in dis town."

To put it mildly, we were out of there. And half an hour later, we were cruising out to sea on a stiff breeze, bouncing over the slight chop. "I know dis good spot for fishin'. You like fishin'?" This question was, of course, purely rhetorical, as if he'd said, "You like breathin'?"—leaving little room for a negative response.

"I haven't been fishing in years," I said diplomatically. As it turned out, there was one rod, so Kimo fished, lost in his own world, and I, glad for the company, leaned over the side and gazed beneath the surface.

The chop had calmed to a glassy surface; the water was clear as crystal. I saw schools of fish swimming below, and wondered what it would be like . . .

Without any conscious effort on my part—maybe that was the key—I found my awareness flying with the fish. That's what it was—flying. To the fish, the sea is air. I felt an unaccustomed sense of aquatic mastery; with a flick of intent, I was a rocket, a shooting star, and the next moment, I was totally relaxed and motionless.

Relaxed, but always, always alert. Death came from any direction here, and suddenly. I saw a larger fish snap and a smaller one was gone. The sea was a living machine of movement and reproduction, eating and death, but in spite of it all, great beauty, and peace.

I snapped back as Kimo said, "You know, Dan, dis boat—and dis ocean—it feels like my life."

Sensing that he was sharing something personal, I listened intently.

"Seem like sometime it's peaceful—like now. Udder times dere's a storm—can't control da storm—but can trim da sail, tie things down, get tru dat storm and you're a lot stronger—you know?"

"Yeah, I know what you mean, Kimo. My life's a lot like that, too."

"Yeah?"

"Yeah. I guess we've all got our storms," I said.

He grinned at me. "You're all right, you know? I didn't think so, before. But I do, now."

I grinned back at him. "I think you're all right, too." I really meant it; Kimo seemed like a different person, now that I had looked beneath the surface.

Kimo was about to say something else, I could tell. He hesitated, maybe working up the nerve, then confided, "Someday, I'm gonna finish high school, an' get a good job. Learn to speak betta, like you." He waited. Somehow, my opinion meant something to him.

"Well," I said, "anyone who understands the sea as well as you do—I think he can do any damn thing he sets his mind to."

I saw a glow spread across his face. "You really think so?"

"I really think so."

Thoughtful, he didn't say anything for a while, so I just sat and gazed into the clear water below. Then, abruptly, he pulled in his fishing rod and set sail. "Dere's someplace I wanna show you." Tacking, we headed south, until we came to a reef, just visible beneath the water's surface.

Kimo trimmed the sail, kicked off his thongs, and dove into the water like a seal. His head quickly reappeared. Clearly in his element, he reached inside the boat, grabbed a diving mask, threw me a pair of goggles, and said, "Come on in!"

"You bet!" I said enthusiastically. Sweaty and dirty, I could use a swim. I slipped off my shirt, rid myself of my sneakers and socks, adjusted and slipped on the goggles, and followed him as he glided smoothly through the water, directly over the beautiful, razor-edged coral reef, about ten feet below the surface.

Kimo swam about twenty yards more, then stopped, treading water, and waited for me. Not being a very strong swimmer, I felt the exertion; by the time I reached him and started treading water like a landlubber, I was already tired. So I had my doubts when he said, "Follow me down!"

"Wait a minute!" I said, panting, wishing I'd spent more time doing laps at the college pool. "What's down there?"

So at home in the water himself, Kimo didn't really appreciate that I might not be entirely comfortable. But he saw my doubtful expression and, floating on his back, otterlike, he explained, “Dere's a cave. Nobody knows about it but me. I'm gonna show it to you.”

“But, it's underwater. How're we going to breathe?”

“At first you gotta hold your breath. But once we get tru da tunnel, we come up in dis cave, an' dere's *air*,” he said, sharing his discovery with growing excitement.

Considerably less enthusiastic, I asked, “How long do we have to hold our br—?” He suddenly turned bottom up and dove straight down beneath the shimmering surface. “Kimo!” I yelled after him. “How long is the tunnel?”

I had a few seconds to make my decision. Would I follow him, or just swim back to the boat? That was safer, and probably wiser. But that little voice I'd heard many times before, said, Go for it!

“Oh, shut up!” I said aloud, as I took some deep, rapid breaths, and dove, following Kimo.

The goggles fit okay, and I was actually more relaxed underwater than trying to hold myself above. And all the breathing exercises I'd done in the past, and the few I did daily, helped. I could take a deep breath and hold it longer than most people, but not necessarily while swimming fifteen feet down, then through a tunnel that went who knows how far.

My ears started hurting from the pressure. I held my nose and blew, then stroked madly to catch up with Kimo, focusing all the while on that cave, with air. I saw him go into a large hole in the side of the reef, and followed him into the dim light.

To my dismay, the tunnel narrowed as we swam; I carefully avoided the sharp coral. A mental image of an eel made me look right and left into the many dark spaces that could hold a sea creature. My lungs told me it was time to breathe—*now*—but the tunnel continued as far as I could see. Then, it began to narrow even more. In a moment of panic, I realized I couldn't turn around. My lungs were pumping madly, but I clamped my lips together and fought on.

I saw Kimo's feet disappear, and just as my mouth was about to burst open to feel the choking water rush in, I angled upward, then gasped like a newborn infant as my head emerged into the air of an underwater cavern.

My mood much improved, I lay panting, half submerged, on a rock ledge.

"Some kinda place, huh?" he asked.

"Uh huh," I managed to say. Recovering, I looked up and around at purple, green, and blue coral, dramatically colored as if it had been decorated by a movie set designer. Then I noticed something odd: A single beam of sunlight shone through the roof of the cave. But the whole reef was underwater! How could there be an opening?

"You noticed da light, huh?" Kimo said. "Up dere, in da ceiling—see dat piece of glass? It covers an opening, so da water don't come in."

"How—?"

"*Ama*—Japanese divers from a long time ago, I think. Maybe dey explore dis cave—put da glass dere," he pointed.

I nodded, still puzzled. "But how did the air get in here?"

"Comes in a few times a year when da tide's low. Sometimes it leaks. I first foun' dis place when I saw some tiny bubbles coming up to da surface."

Feeling better, I sat up, and felt the excitement of being in this hidden alcove, safe from the world. We grinned at each other like two boys in their secret clubhouse. "Do you think anyone else has ever been here?" I asked.

Kimo shrugged. "Jus' dose *ama* divers an' me."

We were silent after that, gazing in awe, feeling the energy of this underwater cave where the sunlight streamed in.

Kimo lay back and stared at the ceiling. I explored, crawling carefully over the sharp coral. In this subsea tidepool, algae and seaweed grew thick, clinging to the coral, giving the cave an eerie greenish hue.

I was turning to crawl back, when my arm slipped. It

plunged down into a crevice in the coral, right up to my shoulder. I was starting to extract my arm when my hand closed around something—maybe a chunk of rock. I pulled it out, opened my hand, and was amazed to see what appeared to be a small statue, so encrusted with tiny barnacles and algae it was hard to be sure. "Look at this!" I called to Kimo.

He came over and looked at it, as awestruck as I. "Looks like a statue or something," he said.

"Here," I said, handing it to him. I didn't want to give it away, but it seemed the right thing to do.

He looked at it, and clearly would have liked it, but he had his standards, too. "No. You found it. You keep it. To remember."

"Thanks for showing me this cave, Kimo."

"You keep it a secret, okay?"

"I'll never tell anyone where it is," I promised, tucking the statue into my pants.

The swim out was challenging, but not as difficult as the way in, because now I knew how far it was, and had time to rest and take many deep breaths to prepare.

By the time we got back to shore, it was getting dark. Kimo insisted that I could stay at his place. So I got to meet his three sisters and four brothers, two of whom I'd already met with him on the street. They all nodded, curious or oblivious, as they passed quickly through the room in which we sat and talked. He offered me a beer, which I accepted, and sipped slowly, and some pungent weed he called "Maui Mindblow," which I declined.

We talked late into the night, and I got to understand the soul of another human being very different from me, yet the same.

Before Kimo flopped onto his unmade sleeper bed, and I stretched out on some blankets on the floor, he shared something else with me: He told me how he'd felt different from other people his whole life, "like I was from another place or something," he added. "And I got a feeling dere's something I'm supposed to do wit' my life, only I don't know what . . . " he trailed off.

"Maybe finish high school first," I said. "Or sail the seven seas."

"Yeah," he said, closing his eyes. "Sail the seven seas."

As I drifted off to sleep, I thought back on this incredible day: starting out on a mountaintop, ending with Kimo and the underwater cave. And finding that barnacle-encrusted statue, now safe in my pack. I'd have to examine it more closely the next chance I got.

In the morning, I said good-bye to Kimo and I set out alone, back into the rain forests of Molokai, toward Pelekunu Valley. I had the feeling that the "treasure" Mama Chia had spoken of might be absorbed in little bits and pieces, not all at once, but that they might add up to something. And if I just stayed alert and open, and traveled where my heart led, I would find the rest of the treasure, whatever it was.

As I walked along the backroads, getting short rides with a rancher or town person, and then entered the forest, I thought about Kimo, and the other people I'd met, from all walks of life. Remembering my vision in the fire, I wondered about their purpose, and how we all fit into the bigger picture. Someday I'd find the tools to help them understand, and to find that purpose. I knew this, if I knew anything.

Walking after dark in a strange part of the rain forest, I felt disoriented, and suddenly weary. Not wanting to travel in circles, I decided to sleep where I was until the first light of dawn, then continue. I lay down and fell quickly asleep, with a vague feeling of ill ease, as if maybe I shouldn't be there, but it was only a very subtle feeling, and it was probably just my fatigue.

In the night, I had a strange and dark but compelling sexual dream. A succubus—a female seductress—both darkly dangerous and terribly erotic, came to love me . . . to death. She wore a filmy blue gown that revealed creamy skin.

I half woke up, and realized where I was, but an icy feeling of horror gripped me as I felt her presence, and saw a woman's shape, blue and gauze covered, floating, moving toward me through the trees. I quickly looked left and right, and saw that I had stumbled into a place of unmarked burials, and restless souls.

The hairs stood up on the back of my neck as my Basic Self told me to get out of there. *Now.*

As the spirit's cold, shapely form floated closer, I could sense that fear and seduction were her only powers, but I had been prepared for this; I had returned from hell, and neither fear nor seduction had the same power over me. "*You'll not have me,*" I said with authority. "I'm not here for you."

I forced myself to wake up fully, and walked slowly out of that place, not looking back, knowing all the time that she was following me, close behind.

At some point, I felt her give up and fall away, but I kept walking through the rest of the night, just the same. Something else was troubling me—a vague feeling again, like I was missing something important. But this time the feeling clarified, like a word on the tip of my tongue.

A phrase from Mama Chia's riddle came to mind: "As above, then so below." Now what could that mean?

I was "above" in the highlands. I was "below" in the town. I had been "beneath the sea." It was all the same. As above, so below. Different, yet the same. Because wherever I went, I was there! The treasure wasn't in any one of these places; it was in *all* of them. Mama Chia had already told me the answer; *it was inside me*—as close as my own heart.

This was more than an intellectual understanding. It hit me with an overwhelming force, an ecstatic realization. For a moment, I lost all awareness of my body. I collapsed on the wet leaves. I had found the treasure, the most important secret of all. Energy welled up inside me. I wanted to cry, to dance!

But in the next moment, ecstasy gave way to another feeling: a sudden sense of loss. And I knew, without knowing how, that Mama Chia was dying. "No!" I cried into the trees. "No. Not yet. Please, wait for me!"

I got to my feet and started to run.

22

Living Until We Die

True teachers
use themselves as bridges
over which they invite their students to cross;
then, having facilitated their crossing,
joyfully collapse, encouraging them
to create bridges
of their own.
Nikos Kazantzakis

I don't know how long I ran, climbed, scrambled, and ran again. Covered with mud, exhausted, cut and bruised, then cleansed by a heavy rain, I finally stumbled and fell at the foot of Mama Chia's stairs about two hours after sunrise.

Fuji, Mitsu, Joseph, and Sarah came out, and Joseph helped me inside. Mama Chia was lying peacefully on the futon bed, surrounded by flowers.

My friends, supporting me at first, stepped back as I went to her and knelt by the bed, my head bowed and tears streaming down my cheeks. I rested my forehead on her arm, so cool, so cool.

I couldn't speak at first; stroking her face, I said farewell, and offered a silent prayer. Mitsu sat nearby, stroking Sachi, comforting her. Socrates, in the blissful ignorance of childhood, slept next to his sister.

Joseph looked like a sad Don Quixote, his eyes dark, one hand on Sarah's shoulder as she rocked in grief.

A stillness pervaded the valley, a sadness, unbroken by

the cries of Redbird, the apapane. Here had passed a very special woman. Even the birds were in mourning.

Just then, the apapane landed on the windowsill, tilted his head to one side, and looked at Mama Chia. Birds have a cry of sadness, and we heard it that morning—an unaccustomed sound—as Redbird flew to her side, made the call again, and flew away, like her soul.

I walked into the moist warm air toward the east, the rising sun just now lighting the sky, silhouetting the hills. Joseph walked with me. "She must have died quietly, in the night," he told me. "Fuji found her only an hour ago. Dan, we heard you were away; how did you know?"

I gazed up at him, and my eyes told him what he needed to know.

Nodding in understanding, Joseph told me, "Some time ago, she left me instructions," he said, "about where to take Tia's baby, and other business matters. She asked to be cremated, in the burial ground of the kahunas. I'll be making the arrangements."

"I want to help with anything I can—with everything," I told him.

"Yes, of course—if you wish. Oh, and there was this," he revealed, holding up a piece of paper. "I think she wrote this last night."

We looked at the note; in Mama Chia's scrawled handwriting were six words: "Among friends, there are no goodbyes."

We looked at each other and smiled, our eyes wet with tears.

I went back inside, sat near her, and just looked at her. When I was young, death was a stranger to me—a phone call, a letter, a piece of information, a solemn announcement about people I rarely saw. Death was a visitor in other homes, other places. People just faded into memory.

But this was real, and it hurt like a razor cut. Sitting there, with the body of Mama Chia, Death whispered into my ears with cold breath, bringing intimations of my own mortality.

I stroked Mama Chia's cheek, feeling an ache in my heart that no metaphysical philosophy could remedy. I missed her already; I felt the void she left, as if a piece of my life had been taken away. And I reflected that, ultimately, we have no control in this life—no ability to stop the waves that come crashing down. We can only learn to surf those waves, embracing whatever comes and using it to grow. Accepting ourselves, our strengths and weaknesses, our foolishness and our love. Accepting everything. Doing what we can, and flowing with the rest.

It may seem strange to some people that I would be so attached to a woman I'd only met a short time before, but my admiration for Mama Chia—for her goodness and courage and wisdom—made up for the brief time of our acquaintance, and made her passing all the more painful. Perhaps I'd known her for lifetimes. She was one of my most beloved teachers who had somehow been waiting for me since my birth.

Joseph contacted Mama Chia's sister, who informed her other relatives. We let the body rest for two days, as Mama Chia had requested. Then, on the third morning, we prepared for the trek up Pelekunu Valley to the sacred kukui grove and the burial site beyond. The old pickup truck became her hearse, decorated with leis and garlands of flowers. We drove carefully over the makeshift roads as far east as the roads would carry us—Fuji and I, followed by Joseph, Sarah, Mitsu, with her little boy, and Joseph's family, as well as Victor, her nieces, other relatives, and a long procession of the many local people Mama Chia had known and helped over the years.

When the road ended, we carried her on the pallet, constructed by her friends from the leper colony, on slippery, winding paths, past waterfalls and through the kukui forest she had loved so well, into the burial site of the kahunas. The lepers were still restricted to their compound, and so couldn't accompany us, but they sent many flowers.

We entered the burial ground in the late afternoon. I felt the ancient kahuna spirit, Lanikaula, welcome Mama Chia, welcome us all, as I knew he would. Now they would both stand eternal watch over the island they loved.

By dusk, we had built her funeral pyre as she had instructed, setting her on a bed of leaves and flower petals, atop many logs, crisscrossed beneath her, gathered from a dry part of the island.

As the pyre was prepared, some of those closest to her said a few words in memorial, or recited quotations that reminded them of Mama Chia.

Fuji was overcome, and couldn't speak; his wife, Mitsu, said, "This is what Mama Chia taught me: We cannot always do great things in life, but we can do small things with great love."

Joseph, quoting Buddha, said "Gifts are great; meditations and religious exercises pacify the mind; comprehension of the great truth leads to nirvana; but greater"—here, he began to cry—"but greater than all is loving kindness."

Never taking her sad eyes off the pyre, Sachi said, simply, "I love you, Mama Chia."

Another woman, a stranger to me, said, "Mama Chia taught me that kind words can be short and easy to speak, but their echoes are endless." Then she sank to her knees and bowed her head in prayer.

When my turn came, my mind went completely blank. I had prepared something to say, but it was gone. I stared another long moment, in silence, at the pyre, as images flashed through my mind—meeting Ruth Johnson on the street, then at the party, then as she nursed me back to health—and then a long-forgotten quotation from Matthew came to me: "I was hungry and you fed me; I was thirsty and you gave me water; I was a stranger and you welcomed me; naked and you clothed me; ill and you comforted me." I spoke these words not just for me, but for all the people gathered there.

Fuji came up to me, and to my surprise, handed me the torch. "She asked in her instructions that you light the pyre,

Dan, if you were still here on Molokai. She said you'd know how to give her a good send-off." He smiled sadly.

I lifted the torch. And I understood that everything she had shown me came to this: Live until you die.

"Good-bye, Mama Chia," I said aloud. I touched the torch to the dry grass and sticks, and the flames began to crackle and dance. And the body of Mama Chia, covered with a thousand petals of red and white and pink and purple, was embraced by the flames, and engulfed.

As the smoke rose to the sky, I stepped back from the blazing heat. Then, in the dying light of day, as this small group of people gazed into the flames, I recalled how Mama Chia enjoyed quoting sources of wisdom, and from out of nowhere, the words of George Bernard Shaw came to me—words she herself might have said—and I found myself calling them out loudly above the crackle of the roaring fire for all to hear: "I want to be thoroughly used up when I die, for the harder I work, the more I live. I rejoice in life for its own sake. Life is no 'brief candle' to me; it is a sort of splendid torch which I have got hold of for the moment, and I want to make it burn as brightly as possible—" My voice quivered then, and I could speak no more.

Others spoke, as Spirit moved them, but I heard none of it. I cried, and I laughed, as Mama Chia would have laughed; then I fell to my knees and bowed my head. My heart was open, my mind silent.

I looked up suddenly because I heard Mama Chia's voice, as loud and clear as if she were standing in front of me. All the others still had their heads bowed, or were staring at the fire, and I realized that the words resounded only in the quiet halls of my mind. In her soft, sometimes lilting voice, Mama Chia spoke to me, and said:

Do not stand at my grave and weep.
I am not there; I do not sleep.

I am a thousand winds that blow.
I am the diamond glints on snow.
I am the sunlight on ripened grain.
I am the gentle autumn rain.
Do not stand at my grave and cry.
I am not there. I did not die.

When I heard these words, my heart broke open; my consciousness leaped to a place I had never been before. I felt the nature of mortality and death within the great circle of life. Overwhelmed, I swooned with a searing compassion for all living things. I fell at once into the depths of despair and soared to the heights of bliss—these two feelings alternated within me at the speed of light.

Then, I was no longer on Molokai, but standing in the tiny room I had seen in my vision under the waterfall. Acrid, pungent smells of sewage and decay filled the air, partly masked by burning incense. I saw a nun caring for a bedridden leper. In the blink of an eye, I became the nun, wearing heavy robes in the sweltering heat. I reached out to smooth an ointment on this poor man's face, my heart completely opened to the love, to the pain, to everything. And in the leper's disfigured face, I saw the faces of all those I had ever loved.

The next moment I stood on the Rue de Pigalle, watching a gendarme help a sick, drunken man into a police ambulance. Then I became that police officer, I smelled the drunkard's putrid breath. A light flashed, and I saw the drunkard as a child, huddled in a corner, quaking as his own father, in a drunken rage, lashed out at him. I felt his pain, his fear—all of it. Looking through the gendarme's eyes, I carried the drunkard gently to the waiting van.

The next moment, I found myself gazing, as if through a mirror, at a teenage boy in his bedroom in a wealthy suburb of Los Angeles. He was sniffing powder up his nose. I knew his guilt, and regret, and self-hatred. Then I felt only compassion.

Next, I was in Africa, gazing at an old man, moving painfully, trying to give a dying baby water. I cried out, and my voice echoed in this timeless place where I stood. I cried for that baby, for the old African, for the teenage boy, for the drunken man, for the nun, for the leper. That baby was my child, and these were my people.

I wanted so much to help, to make things better for every suffering soul, but I knew that from where I stood I could only love, understand, trust in the wisdom of the universe, do what I could, then let go.

As I saw all this, I felt an explosive surge of energy, and was catapulted up, through my heart, in a state of perfect empathy with existence itself.

My body had become transparent, radiating shifting colors of the spectrum. Below, I felt red, rising through orange, and yellow, and green, changing into gold. Then, surrounded by a radiant blue, my inner eyes were drawn up to the center of my forehead, rising into indigo, then violet . . .

Beyond the confines of personal identity, no longer concerned with a physical body, I floated in the place where spirit meets flesh, from a vantage point high above the planet we call earth. Then the earth receded in the vastness, then the solar system became a disappearing speck, and the galaxy, too, until I was beyond the illusions of space and matter and time, seeing It All: paradox, humor, and change.

What followed goes far beyond words. I can write that "I was One with the Light," but such words fall like dust on the page, because there was no "I" to be "One" with anything, and no one left to experience It. Trying to describe this experience has challenged and frustrated the mystic poets for centuries. How do you draw the likeness of a Van Gogh painting with a stick in the mud?

The universe had burned me to cinders, consuming me. Not a trace remained. Only Bliss. Reality. Mystery.

Now I understood the Taoist saying "He who says does not know; he who knows does not say"—not because the wise don't speak, but because It cannot be spoken. Words fall as short of It as a rock thrown at the stars. And if these words sound nonsensical, so be it. But one day, and that day may not be far away, you, too, will know.

I reentered time and space—whirling, disoriented—as if I'd fallen out of an airplane in the night sky, still kneeling before Mama Chia's funeral pyre, set against the clouds that floated past the moon. The ground glistened from a fresh rain; I was soaking. The rain had doused the last embers of the pyre that had consumed her. An hour had passed in a few moments.

The others had gone; only Joseph remained with me. He knelt down next to me and asked, "How are you doing, Dan?"

I couldn't speak, but I nodded. He gently squeezed the back of my neck; I could feel the love and understanding through his fingers. He knew I would be staying a while, so, with a last look at the charred pyre, he left.

I took a deep breath, smelling the wet forest, mixed with the lingering odor of smoke. None of it seemed completely real anymore, as if I were merely playing my role in an eternal drama, and this dimension was but one small practice hall in the infinite theater of God.

Slowly at first, questions trickled back into my mind, then came in a rush, as I fell from grace, back into the mind, into the body, into the world. What had it all meant?

Maybe this had been "the place beyond space and time" Mama Chia had told me about. At the time, her words had sounded abstract, empty, because they had been beyond my experience. Now they were a living reality. She had told me, "In that place, you can meet with anyone you wish." I wanted so much to go to that place again, just to see her one more time.

I stood, shaky and stiff, staring into space until darkness covered the forest.

Then I turned and started to follow the path taken by

the others, back through the rain forest. High above, I could just make out the flow of the torch-lit procession.

But something wouldn't let me leave. The feeling was clear, so I sat down, and waited. I sat through the night, occasionally nodding out, then stirring again. Sometimes my eyes closed, as if in meditation; other times they just opened and stared.

When the first rays of sunlight cut through the forest and shone upon the remains of the pyre, Mama Chia appeared, tangible but translucent, standing in front of me. I don't know if any of the others would have seen her, or whether her image only appeared in my mind.

But there she stood. She raised her arm and pointed to the hillside on my right, gesturing toward a thick glade of trees.

"You want me to go up there?" I asked her aloud. She only smiled, serenely. I closed my eyes for a moment against the bright sun. When I opened them, she was gone.

From my altered—or perhaps refined—perception of reality, all this seemed entirely normal to me. I got up slowly, and went where she had directed.

Still disoriented from the recent events and revelations, I wound my way through the thick bushes—caught once or twice by sticky vines—before the foliage thinned out and a narrow path appeared before me.

23

Lessons of Solitude

We must pass
through solitude and
difficulty, isolation and silence
to find that enchanted place where
we can dance our clumsy dance and sing our
sorrowful song. But in that dance, and in
that song, the most ancient rites of our
conscience fulfill themselves
in the awareness of
being human.

Pablo Neruda, *Toward the Splendid City*

The path led to a tiny hut, about eight feet on each side. I entered and surveyed the darkened interior. Only a few rays of sunshine penetrated the thatched roof and log walls. As my eyes adjusted to the dim light, I saw, coming down through the ceiling, a long, hollow piece of bamboo that carried rain-water, gathered on the roof, into a large wooden tub sitting in one corner. In the opposite corner of this spartan room, I could make out a hole in the ground that served as a toilet and a nearby bucket for flushing. The earthen floor had a bed of thick leaves to one side for sleeping.

From the design of the hut, I assumed that it served as a place of isolation and retreat. I decided to stay here until I received a clear sign about what to do next.

I shut the thatched door behind me. Weary, I lay down and closed my eyes.

Almost immediately, I sensed a nearby presence, and sat up. Mama Chia sat in front of me, her legs crossed, as if in meditation—but her eyes were open, and bright. I sensed that she wanted to communicate something, so I waited in silence, not wanting to disturb this tenuous apparition.

She gestured with a sweep of her arm, and I heard her say as her image began to flicker and fade, "Everything is a dream within a dream."

"I don't understand, Mama Chia. What does it mean?"

"We make our own meanings," she said as her image dissolved.

"Wait! Don't go!" I cried out. I wanted to touch her face, to embrace her; but I knew that this was neither appropriate nor possible.

In the darkness, I heard her final words, echoing from far away. "It's all right, Dan. Everything will be all right . . . " Then silence.

She was gone—I could feel it in my bones. What would I do now? As soon as I asked the question, the answer appeared: There was nothing to do, except stay put and wait for clarity.

Surveying the narrow confines of my quarters, I took stock of my situation: I had no food, but I had dealt with that before. My Basic Self was no longer afraid of not eating, and the wooden tub contained plenty of water.

After a few limbering stretches, I sat and closed my eyes. Soon, bits and pieces of memories, sights, and sounds replayed themselves in my mind, as I relived my entire adventure here in a random montage of fleeting images and emotions.

I recalled that Mama Chia had once told me, "Outer travel at best only reflects the inner journey, and at worst substitutes for it. The world you perceive only provides symbols for what you seek. The sacred journey is inside you; before you can find what you're looking for in the world, you have to find it within. Otherwise, a master may greet you, but you'll walk right past without hearing.

"When you learn inner travel through the psychic spaces of the world, your consciousness will never again be limited by space, or time, or the confines of the physical body."

Although I had heard this before, only now did I understand it. Before I could continue my journey in the world, I had to journey within my psyche. Would I be able to accomplish this? Could my awareness go so deep within that it contacted the gateway beyond my physical senses?

I considered this intensely, that night and the following day. I had found Mama Chia in the forest. I knew that I had hidden capacities, as we all do. But where were they? What did they look like, and feel like?

Socrates had once hinted that there was "more to imagination than meets the eye." He said it was the "bridge to clairvoyant sight—a first step. As it expands," he added, "it becomes something else. Saplings grow into trees, but imagination is like the caterpillar—once set free of the cocoon, it flies."

I would begin there. I closed my eyes and let images float by: kukui trees and Kimo's underwater cave, the palm outside Mama Chia's house, and the thick, twisting trunk of the banyan. Then my daughter, Holly, appeared sitting in her room on the floor, playing quietly. I felt a bittersweet sadness at the karmas of this life, and I sent a message of love from my heart to hers, hoping that, in some way, she would receive it. I sent Linda my blessings, as well, and let go.

I spent the entire night in vivid dreams—not surprising, considering recent events. I visited other places, worlds, and dimensions of color, clarity, and feeling that filled me with awe. But, of course—or so I thought—it was just a dream . . .

As one day followed the next, day and night ceased to have much distinction for me; the dim light of day only gave way to the darkness of night.

The morning of the fifth day, as well as I could track time, brought a deep sense of lightness and peace. My hunger pangs had vanished. As I did a few yoga postures, the walls of the hut caught my eye as specks of sunlight penetrated the darkness like stars in a night sky. I used the specks of light on the wall as a meditation. As I breathed slowly, deeply, the stars began to fade, until I saw only my mind, projected against the darkness like a magic lantern show, a carousel of imagery and sound that played on and on. I spent the entire day gazing at the wall. Boredom ceased to exist as my awareness tuned in to finer, subtler energies. When you don't have TV, I reflected at one point, you find other things to do.

The days passed one like the next, yet never the same. I stretched, breathed, and watched the show. Rays of sunshine, then moonlight, swept slowly across the dirt floor like a pendulum of light. Time passed softly, with infinite slowness as I adjusted to the subtle rhythms and floated on an ocean of silence, disturbed only occasionally by the flotsam and jetsam of my mind.

At one point, something shifted; it was as if, in the face of my persistent awareness, a barrier fell away and a door opened. I understood how the Basic Self and Conscious Self, working together, provided the keys to motivation, discipline, healing, visualization, intuition, learning, courage, and power. In a few moments, I felt as if I'd digested an encyclopedia of metaphysics.

However, like the sorcerer's apprentice, I didn't know how to turn it off. Images flooded my mind until it went into overload. My lungs began pumping like bellows, deeper, faster—the energy building until I thought I would burst.

My face started to tighten; I felt my lips curl back and, to my surprise, I growled like a wolf. Then my hands spontaneously moved into *mudras,* or postures, like those I had seen in India.

In the next moment, my mind stopped, and I found myself in the forest, face to face with the three selves: the childlike Basic Self, the robotlike Conscious Self, and the Higher

Self, a being of radiant colors—swirling pink, indigo, deep violet hues. This being of light reached out with open arms to the other two.

Then the three selves merged.

I saw before me my own body—naked, except for a pair of shorts, illuminated by the pale moon, standing with arms spread wide. A reddish glow shone from the belly region, the head was a ball of light, and above the head iridescent colors swirled—reminding me of my vision on the beach so many weeks before.

This time, I entered the physical body that stood before me. I entered it fully, feeling the unity of its form. I felt the power of my navel, the purity of awareness illuminating the mind, and the inspiring call to ascend up into Spirit.

My long preparation had brought completion; the three selves had become one. There were no inner battles, no resistance within or without, so that my attention rested naturally and spontaneously in the heart. Whatever thoughts or images arose were dissolved there, in feeling and surrender. I became a point of awareness within the domain of the heart, rising up toward the crown of my head, to a point above and behind the brows.

I felt the healing, loving light of the Higher Self surround me, embrace me, pervading every cell and tissue down to the atomic structure. I heard its call, and felt a bridge of light stretching from that point of awareness that I am, and the Higher Self, standing above and behind me. I felt its strength, its wisdom, its tenderness, its courage, its compassion, its mercy. I became aware of its connection to past and future, in the eternal present.

It called again, and I felt myself as that point of light, moving up the bridge, into the consciousness of my Higher Self. I moved within that form of light, watching over my physical form, below. My awareness and that of my Higher Self began to interpenetrate one another. I took in all of its qualities of serenity, strength, wisdom, and compassion.

I now knew what it knew, felt what it felt, as ecstatic waves of unbounded love flooded through me. I saw how angelic energies had crafted the body, and I understood the full opportunity that physical embodiment represents.

Just then, I became aware of other beings of light around my physical form. Waves of happiness washed through me as I realized I had known these beings since childhood, but had somehow ignored their presence. Some were fellow students, others were familiar images from forgotten dreams—angelic energies, healers, guides, and teachers—my spiritual family. I felt their love, and knew I would never again feel alone.

An angel of destiny stepped forward then, and raised its hands to offer symbols to guide me. I couldn't see its gifts until the hands of light came forward, into my vision, and opened. First I saw a bolt of lightning, then a heart. Then a golden eagle appeared, holding a laurel wreath in its talons. I recognized these as symbols of courage and love, the sign of the peaceful warrior.

Then, as its final gift, the angel revealed the shining image of a samurai warrior, his sword at his side—not standing, but kneeling in a meditative posture. Though I couldn't see his eyes, I felt they were open, and shining. Then the image faded. I thanked the angel of destiny for these gifts, and it, too, stepped back and dissolved.

From this place within the Higher Self consciousness, I knew that angels of wisdom, healing, and clarity are always available. I could look to the future, or the past, and send love to anyone in the universe. And from this place, I could extend my vision effortlessly, beyond the physical body, and soar like an eagle.

With this revelation, I felt a pull back to my physical form; I felt my awareness ride down the bridge of light into the center of my forehead, and once again I became aware of the sounds of my nervous system, and of the beating of my heart.

Refreshed and at peace, I opened my physical eyes, feeling a rising wave of energy and bliss. In this state of deep reverie, I scratched a message on the floor:

There is no way to peace;
Peace is the Way.
There is no way to happiness;
Happiness is the Way.
There is no way to love;
Love is the Way.

This was no idle poetry, but a tacit realization.

In the days that followed, even in relatively normal consciousness, I started seeing clear images of places outside the hut, and in the world. My "imagination" could now take me farther than I'd ever dreamed—to any world, any reality; the physical realm was only home base, the grounding place.

The universe had become my playground—filled with an infinite number of dimensions, times, spaces. I could be a knight in medieval Europe or a space adventurer in the fifty-eighth dimension; I could visit other worlds, or spend time within the molecules of a copper penny, because the awareness that we are can never be limited by time or space.

After this, I traveled every day—flying through the forest, or around the world. I visited my little daughter every day and saw her playing with new toys, or reading, or sleeping. No longer limited to the physical body, I now perceived it as only one of my domains. I could never again feel imprisoned by any walls, or by flesh and bones.

And I remembered what Mama Chia had told me: "You can speak of 'my body,' because you are not the body. You can also refer to 'my mind,' 'my selves,' 'my soul,' because you are not these things. You manifest as pure Awareness that shines through the human body, yet itself remains untouched and eternal.

"Awareness diffracts through the prism of the soul to become three forms of light—the three selves—each with a different kind of awareness uniquely suited to its purpose, function, and responsibilities.

"The Basic Self cares for and protects the physical body in cooperation with the other selves, providing support and balance. A foundation and vehicle for the soul's journey in the world, it connects the Conscious and Higher Selves to the earth like the roots of a tree.

"The Conscious Self guides, informs, interprets for, and sometimes reassures the Basic Self, as a parent would a child, educating it to best serve this embodiment. But this parent must cultivate loving ears to hear that child, respecting that child's individual spirit and growing awareness. Parenthood is a sacred training ground.

"The Higher Self radiates love, reminding, inspiring, and rekindling the spark of light within the Conscious Self, drawing it up into Spirit. It accepts the process of the Conscious Self, and waits, eternally patient and understanding.

"Each of the three selves is here to assist the others, integrating, forming a whole, greater than the sum of its parts."

Then a mystical vision played itself out like a movie in my mind, shedding light on her words: I saw a monk hiking through the foothills of a mountain range in late autumn. Multicolored leaves—red, orange, yellow, green—showered down from the branches, waving in the chill wind. Shivering, the monk found a cave and went inside, seeking shelter from the elements.

Inside the cave, the monk found a large bear. They looked each other over; for a few tense moments, the monk didn't know whether he would leave the cave alive. As the bear slowly approached him, the monk spoke. "Let us help each other, Brother Bear. If you let me live in this cave with you, and if you gather wood for the fire, I will bake bread for you every day." The bear agreed, and they became friends—the man always warm, the bear always fed.

The bear represented the Basic Self, and the monk, the Conscious Self. The fire, the bread, and the sheltering cave itself were all blessings of the Higher Self. Each aspect served the others.

After many days of inner travel, returning from far journeys, I came back to earth and into my human form. I was content.

Then I remembered the final gift given to me by the angel of destiny. Before going to sleep, I asked my Basic Self to reveal to me what this gift might mean, and to show me in a way I might understand.

In the morning, I had my answer: I was told to examine the object I'd found in the underwater cave. All the loose ends came together, and I knew it was time to leave the hut.

I stepped outside and squinted as a flood of sunlight stung my eyes and poured through me. I smelled the forest after a fresh rain. I had been in solitude for twenty-one days.

Weak from lack of food, I walked slowly through the hills, feeling as if I weren't quite made of flesh and bones—like a newborn, fresh out of my thatched womb. With a deep breath, I surveyed the sights and sounds of a new world.

I knew that the intensity, the peace, and the bliss I was now experiencing would pass. Once I returned to the everyday world, thoughts would return, but that was all right. I accepted my human condition. I would, like Mama Chia, live until I died. But for now, I bathed happily in the ecstasy of conscious rebirth.

I passed a papaya tree just as one of the fruits fell. I caught it, smiled, and thanked Spirit for all of its blessings, large and small. Chewing slowly, I inhaled the sweet aroma.

Then I noticed a tiny sprout nearby, rising through the red earth, pushing upward, toward the sun. Within the seed of this tiny sprout lay the mature land tree, all the laws of nature. As that seed evolved, so would we all: Basic Selves evolving into Conscious Selves, expanding and refining their awareness; Conscious Selves rising through the heart to become Higher Selves by surrendering to the laws of Spirit; and Higher Selves evolving back into the very Light of Spirit.

And each lifts and guides that which is below; each supports that which is above.

If a tiny sprout could reveal this to me, would the sky someday reveal its own secrets? And what could the stones tell me, or the trees whisper? Would I learn the way of the flowing stream, the ancient wisdom of the mountains? That was still to be discovered.

What did it all add up to? I remembered a story about Aldous Huxley. In his later years, a friend once asked him, "Professor Huxley, after all your spiritual studies and practice, what have you learned?"

With a twinkle in his eye, Aldous answered, "Perhaps . . . to be a little kinder."

Little things make a big difference, I thought. And I breathed a sigh of compassion for those people, stuck in the details of life, who had, like me, lost sight of the bigger picture, the liberating truth at the core of our lives.

Then I remembered Mama Chia's final words: "It's all right, Dan. Everything will be all right."

My heart opened, and tears of happiness flowed, but also tears of sorrow for those who still feel alone, cut off, in their own huts of solitude. Then, in a rising wave, I laughed with joy, because I knew with absolute certainty that they, too, would be able to feel the love and support of Spirit—if only they would open the eyes of their heart.

Epilogue

There Are No Good-byes

There are no maps;
no more creeds or philosophies.
From here on in, the directions come
straight from the Universe.
Akshara Noor

As soon as I returned to my cabin, I reached into my pack and took out the encrusted object from Kimo's cave. I spent several hours cleaning it, carefully scraping with my Swiss army knife. After numerous washings and scrubbings, I began to make out, with growing understanding and awe, the shape of a samurai warrior, kneeling in meditation—revealing the next step on my journey—to Japan, where I would find the master of the hidden school.

That night, I dreamed of an elderly man, an Asian, his face sad and wise. Something weighed heavily on his heart. Behind him, acrobats somersaulted through the air. And I knew I would find him—not only to receive, but to serve.

I said quiet farewells, without ceremony, to each of the friends who had become so dear to me—to Joseph and Sarah, to Sachi and little Socrates, to Fuji and Mitsu with their baby, and to Manoa, Tia, and the others I'd come to know and care about deeply.

Joseph had told me the location of a small boat Mama Chia had left for me, anchored in a shallow cove hidden by trees at Kalaupapa, the leper colony. This time, I brought sufficient provisions to take me home. On a warm morning in November, with the sun rising out of the sea, I tossed my pack under the seat, and slid the boat down the sand, out into the shallow surf, and climbed in. A breeze caught the sail.

Out past the surf, on the gentle rise and fall of the sea, I looked back to see rain streaking the cliffs with myriad cascades, some exploding into wind-whipped mist and rainbows before they reached the sea.

A larger rainbow, glorious in its colors, formed and stretched the length of the island as it arched across the sky. Then, gazing once more toward shore, just for a moment, I saw the limping figure of a large, rounded woman emerging from the curtain of trees through the mist. Her hand raised in farewell, then she was gone.

I turned forward, into the wind, tacking across the channel toward Oahu.

On that little island of Molokai, guided by an unexpected teacher, I had seen the invisible world, the larger view of life, with eyes that see no duality—no "me" and "others," no separate self, no light or shadow, nothing within or without not made of Spirit—and that vision would illuminate all the days of my life.

I knew the visions and experiences would fade, and the restless feeling would continue, because my journey wasn't over—not yet. I would return home to see my daughter, clear up unfinished business, and put my affairs in order, just in case. Then I would find the school in Japan, and discover another part of Socrates' and Mama Chia's past—and my own future. Throwing my life to the winds, I would follow, once again, where Spirit leads.

The island began to fade, then disappear under the cover of clouds. A gust of wind filled the sail, and a sweet fragrance perfumed the air. I looked up, gazing with wonder, as flower petals of every color rained down from the sky. Awestruck, I shut my eyes. When I opened them again, the petals had vanished. Had this shower really happened? Did it matter?

Smiling, I gazed out to sea. About a hundred yards away, a great humpback whale, rarely seen this time of year, breached the surface and slapped the water with its magnificent tail, sending a wave to greet me, pushing me onward, sending me surfing, like the ancient Hawaiian kings, toward home. And I knew that, like this small boat, Spirit would carry me, as it carries us all, inexorably, toward the Light.

For information about Dan Millman's
lecture and training schedule, books, and tapes,
as well as answers to frequently asked questions
—or if you would like to be on our mailing list—
we invite you to visit the Peaceful Warrior Web Site:
http://www.danmillman.com

Peaceful Warrior
P.O. Box 6148
San Rafael, CA 94903
Phone: (415) 491-0301
Fax: (415) 491-0856